How to access your on-line resources

Kaplan Financial students will have a MyKaplan account and these extra resources will be available to you online. You do not need to register again, as this process was completed when you enrolled. If you are having problems accessing online materials, please ask your course administrator.

If you are not studying with Kaplan and did not purchase your book via a Kaplan website, to unlock your extra online resources please go to **www.en-gage.co.uk** (even if you have set up an account and registered books previously). You will then need to enter the ISBN number (on the title page and back cover) and the unique pass key number contained in the scratch panel below to gain access.

You will also be required to enter additional information during this process to set up or confirm your account details.

If you purchased through the Kaplan Publishing website you will automatically receive an e-mail invitation to register your details and gain access to your content. If you do not receive the e-mail or book content, please contact Kaplan Publishing.

This code can only be used once for the registration of this book online. This registration and your online content will expire when the examinations covered by this book have taken place. Please allow one hour from the time you submit your book details for us to process your request.

Please scratch the film to access your unique code.

Please be aware that this code is case-sensitive and you will need to include the dashes within the passcode, but not when entering the ISBN.

CIMA

Subject E2

Managing Performance

Study Text

KAPLAN PUBLISHING'S STATEMENT OF PRINCIPLES

LINGUISTIC DIVERSITY, EQUALITY AND INCLUSION

We are committed to diversity, equality and inclusion and strive to deliver content that all users can relate to.

We are here to make a difference to the success of every learner.

Clarity, accessibility and ease of use for our learners are key to our approach.

We will use contemporary examples that are rich, engaging and representative of a diverse workplace.

We will include a representative mix of race and gender at the various levels of seniority within the businesses in our examples to support all our learners in aspiring to achieve their potential within their chosen careers.

Roles played by characters in our examples will demonstrate richness and diversity by the use of different names, backgrounds, ethnicity and gender, with a mix of sexuality, relationships and beliefs where these are relevant to the syllabus.

It must always be obvious who is being referred to in each stage of any example so that we do not detract from clarity and ease of use for each of our learners.

We will actively seek feedback from our learners on our approach and keep our policy under continuous review. If you would like to provide any feedback on our linguistic approach, please use this form (you will need to enter the link below into your browser).

https://docs.google.com/forms/d/1YNo3A16mtXGTDIFJzgJhcu377QA4Q4ihUgfYvVKclF8/edit

We will seek to devise simple measures that can be used by independent assessors to randomly check our success in the implementation of our Linguistic Equality, Diversity and Inclusion Policy.

Published by: Kaplan Publishing UK

Unit 2 The Business Centre, Molly Millars Lane, Wokingham, Berkshire RG41 2QZ

Acknowledgements

We are grateful to the AICPA® & CIMA® for permission to reproduce past examination questions. The answers to CIMA Exams have been prepared by Kaplan Publishing, except in the case of the CIMA November 2010 and subsequent CIMA Exam answers where the official CIMA answers have been reproduced.

Notice

The text in this material and any others made available by any Kaplan Group company does not amount to advice on a particular matter and should not be taken as such. No reliance should be placed on the content as the basis for any investment or other decision or in connection with any advice given to third parties. Please consult your appropriate professional adviser as necessary. Kaplan Publishing Limited and all other Kaplan group companies expressly disclaim all liability to any person in respect of any losses or other claims, whether direct, indirect, incidental, consequential or otherwise arising in relation to the use of such materials.

Kaplan is not responsible for the content of external websites. The inclusion of a link to a third party website in this text should not be taken as an endorsement.

Kaplan Publishing's learning materials are designed to help students succeed in their examinations. In certain circumstances, CIMA can make post-exam adjustment to a student's mark or grade to reflect adverse circumstances which may have disadvantaged a student's ability to take an exam or demonstrate their normal level of attainment (see CIMA's Special Consideration policy). However, it should be noted that students will not be eligible for special consideration by CIMA if preparation for or performance in a CIMA exam is affected by any failure by their tuition provider to prepare them properly for the exam for any reason including, but not limited to, staff shortages, building work or a lack of facilities etc.

Similarly, CIMA will not accept applications for special consideration on any of the following grounds:

- failure by a tuition provider to cover the whole syllabus
- failure by the student to cover the whole syllabus, for instance as a result of joining a course part way through
- failure by the student to prepare adequately for the exam, or to use the correct pre-seen material
- errors in the Kaplan Official Study Text, including sample (practice) questions or any other Kaplan content or
- errors in any other study materials (from any other tuition provider or publisher).

British Library Cataloguing in Publication Data

A catalogue record for this book is available from the British Library.

ISBN: 978-1-83996-461-9

Printed and bound in Great Britain.

Contents

Introduction

How to use the Materials

These official CIMA® learning materials have been carefully designed to make your learning experience as easy as possible and to give you the best chances of success in your Objective Tests.

The product range contains a number of features to help you in the study process. They include:

- a detailed explanation of all syllabus areas
- extensive 'practical' materials
- generous question practice, together with full solutions.

This Study Text has been designed with the needs of home study and distance learning candidates in mind. Such students require very full coverage of the syllabus topics, and also the facility to undertake extensive question practice. However, the Study Text is also ideal for fully taught courses.

The main body of the text is divided into a number of chapters, each of which is organised on the following pattern:

- **Detailed learning outcomes.** These describe the knowledge expected after your studies of the chapter are complete. You should assimilate these before beginning detailed work on the chapter, so that you can appreciate where your studies are leading.
- **Step-by-step topic coverage.** This is the heart of each chapter, containing detailed explanatory text supported where appropriate by worked examples and exercises. You should work carefully through this section, ensuring that you understand the material being explained and can tackle the examples and exercises successfully. Remember that in many cases knowledge is cumulative: if you fail to digest earlier material thoroughly, you may struggle to understand later chapters.
- **Activities.** Some chapters are illustrated by more practical elements, such as comments and questions designed to stimulate discussion.
- **Question practice.** The text contains three styles of question:
  - Exam-style objective test questions (OTQs).
  - 'Integration' questions – these test your ability to understand topics within a wider context. This is particularly important with calculations where OTQs may focus on just one element but an integration question tackles the full calculation, just as you would be expected to do in the workplace.
  - 'Case' style questions – these test your ability to analyse and discuss issues in greater depth, particularly focusing on scenarios that are less clear cut than in the objective tests, and thus provide excellent practice for developing the skills needed for success in the Management Level Case Study Examination.

- **Solutions.** Avoid the temptation merely to 'audit' the solutions provided. It is an illusion to think that this provides the same benefits as you would gain from a serious attempt of your own. However, if you are struggling to get started on a question you should read the introductory guidance provided at the beginning of the solution, where provided, and then make your own attempt before referring back to the full solution.

If you work conscientiously through this official CIMA Study Text according to the guidelines above you will be giving yourself an excellent chance of success in your objective tests. Good luck with your studies!

Quality and accuracy are of the utmost importance to us so if you spot an error in any of our products, please send an email to mykaplanreporting@kaplan.com with full details, or follow the link to the feedback form in MyKaplan.

Our Quality Co-ordinator will work with our technical team to verify the error and take action to ensure it is corrected in future editions.

Icon explanations

Definition – These sections explain important areas of knowledge which must be understood and reproduced in an assessment environment.

Key point – Identifies topics which are key to success and are often examined.

Supplementary reading – These sections will help to provide a deeper understanding of core areas. The supplementary reading is **NOT** optional reading. It is vital to provide you with the breadth of knowledge you will need to address the wide range of topics within your syllabus that could feature in an assessment question. **Reference to this text is vital when self-studying.**

Test your understanding – Following key points and definitions are exercises which give the opportunity to assess the understanding of these core areas.

Illustration – To help develop an understanding of particular topics. The illustrative examples are useful in preparing for the Test your understanding exercises.

Study technique

Passing exams is partly a matter of intellectual ability, but however accomplished you are in that respect you can improve your chances significantly by the use of appropriate study and revision techniques. In this section we briefly outline some tips for effective study during the earlier stages of your approach to the Objective Tests. We also mention some techniques that you will find useful at the revision stage.

Planning

To begin with, formal planning is essential to get the best return from the time you spend studying. Estimate how much time in total you are going to need for each subject you are studying. Remember that you need to allow time for revision as well as for initial study of the material.

With your study material before you, decide which chapters you are going to study in each week, and which weeks you will devote to revision and final question practice.

Prepare a written schedule summarising the above and stick to it!

It is essential to know your syllabus. As your studies progress you will become more familiar with how long it takes to cover topics in sufficient depth. Your timetable may need to be adapted to allocate enough time for the whole syllabus.

Students are advised to refer to the examination blueprints (see page P.13 for further information) and the AICPA® & CIMA website, www.aicpa-cima.com, to ensure they are up-to-date.

The amount of space allocated to a topic in the Study Text is not a very good guide as to how long it will take you. The syllabus weighting is the better guide as to how long you should spend on a syllabus topic.

Tips for effective studying

(1) Aim to find a quiet and undisturbed location for your study, and plan as far as possible to use the same period of time each day. Getting into a routine helps to avoid wasting time. Make sure that you have all the materials you need before you begin so as to minimise interruptions.

(2) Store all your materials in one place, so that you do not waste time searching for items every time you want to begin studying. If you have to pack everything away after each study period, keep your study materials in a box, or even a suitcase, which will not be disturbed until the next time.

(3) Limit distractions. To make the most effective use of your study periods you should be able to apply total concentration, so turn off all entertainment equipment, set your phones to message mode, and put up your 'do not disturb' sign.

(4) Your timetable will tell you which topic to study. However, before diving in and becoming engrossed in the finer points, make sure you have an overall picture of all the areas that need to be covered by the end of that session. After an hour, allow yourself a short break and move away from your Study Text. With experience, you will learn to assess the pace you need to work at. Each study session should focus on component learning outcomes – the basis for all questions.

(5) Work carefully through a chapter, making notes as you go. When you have covered a suitable amount of material, vary the pattern by attempting a practice question. When you have finished your attempt, make notes of any mistakes you made, or any areas that you failed to cover or covered more briefly. Be aware that all component learning outcomes will be tested in each examination.

(6) Make notes as you study, and discover the techniques that work best for you. Your notes may be in the form of lists, bullet points, diagrams, summaries, 'mind maps', or the written word, but remember that you will need to refer back to them at a later date, so they must be intelligible. If you are on a taught course, make sure you highlight any issues you would like to follow up with your lecturer.

(7) Organise your notes. Make sure that all your notes, calculations etc. can be effectively filed and easily retrieved later.

Progression

There are two elements of progression that we can measure: how quickly students move through individual topics within a subject; and how quickly they move from one course to the next. We know that there is an optimum for both, but it can vary from subject to subject and from student to student. However, using data and our experience of student performance over many years, we can make some generalisations.

A fixed period of study set out at the start of a course with key milestones is important. This can be within a subject, for example 'I will finish this topic by 30 June', or for overall achievement, such as 'I want to be qualified by the end of next year'.

Your qualification is cumulative, as earlier papers provide a foundation for your subsequent studies, so do not allow there to be too big a gap between one subject and another. For example, E2 *Managing Performance* builds on your knowledge of data use from E1 *Managing Finance in a digital world* and lays the foundations for E3 *Strategic Management*.

We know that exams encourage techniques that lead to some degree of short term retention, the result being that you will simply forget much of what you have already learned unless it is refreshed (look up Ebbinghaus Forgetting Curve for more details on this). This makes it more difficult as you move from one subject to another: not only will you have to learn the new subject, you will also have to relearn all the underpinning knowledge as well. This is very inefficient and slows down your overall progression which makes it more likely you may not succeed at all.

Also, it is important to realise that CIMA's CGMA® Management Case Study (MCS) Exam tests knowledge of all subjects within the Management Level. Please note that candidates will need to return to this E2 material when studying for MCS as it forms a significant part of the MCS syllabus content.

In addition, delaying your studies slows your path to qualification which can have negative impacts on your career, postponing the opportunity to apply for higher level positions and therefore higher pay.

You can use the following diagram showing the whole structure of your qualification to help you keep track of your progress. Make sure you seek appropriate advice if you are unsure about your progression through the qualification.

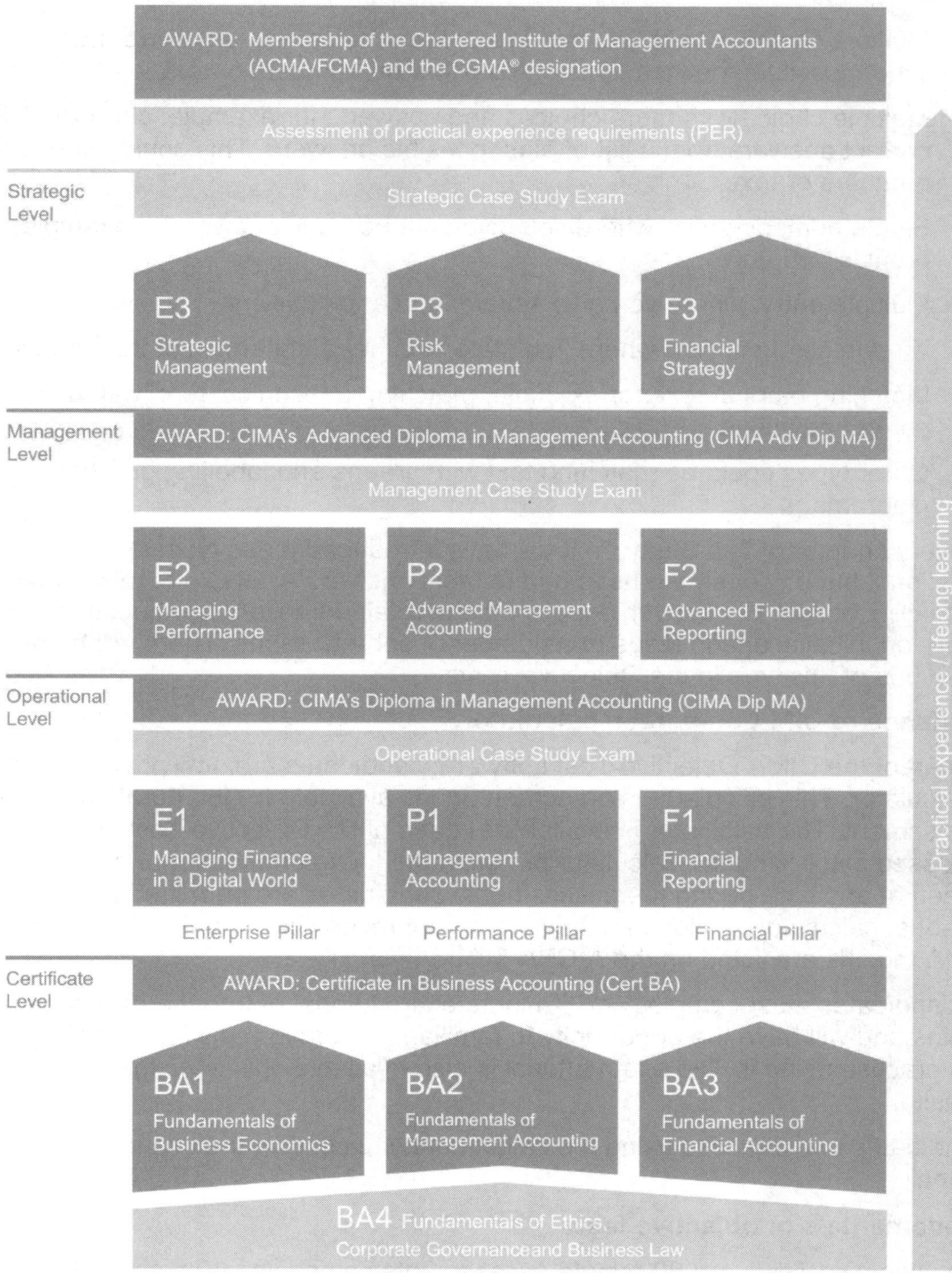

Reproduced with CIMA's permission

Objective Test

Objective test questions require you to choose or provide a response to a question whose correct answer is predetermined.

The most common types of Objective Test question you will see are:

- Multiple choice, where you have to choose the correct answer(s) from a list of possible answers. This could either be numbers or text.
- Multiple choice with more choices and answers, for example, choosing two correct answers from a list of eight possible answers. This could either be numbers or text.
- Single numeric entry, where you give your numeric answer, for example, profit is $10,000.
- Multiple entry, where you give several numeric answers.
- True/false questions, where you state whether a statement is true or false.
- Matching pairs of text, for example, matching a technical term with the correct definition.
- Other types could be matching text with graphs and labelling graphs/ diagrams.

In every chapter of this Study Text we have introduced these types of questions, but obviously we have had to label answers A, B, C etc. rather than using click boxes. For convenience, we have retained quite a few questions where an initial scenario leads to a number of sub-questions. There will be no questions of this type in the Objective Tests.

Guidance re CIMA on-screen calculator

As part of the CIMA Objective Test software, candidates are now provided with a calculator. This calculator is on-screen and is available for the duration of the assessment. The calculator is available in each of the Objective Tests and is accessed by clicking the calculator button in the top left hand corner of the screen at any time during the assessment. Candidates are permitted to utilise personal calculators as long as they are an approved CIMA model. Authorised CIMA models are listed on the AICPA & CIMA website.

All candidates must complete a 15-minute exam tutorial before the assessment begins and will have the opportunity to familiarise themselves with the calculator and practise using it. The exam tutorial is also available online via the CIMA website.

Candidates may practise using the calculator by accessing the online exam tutorial.

Fundamentals of objective tests

The Objective Tests are 90-minute assessments comprising 60 compulsory questions, with one or more parts. There will be no choice and all questions should be attempted. All elements of a question must be answered correctly for the question to be marked correctly. All questions are equally weighted.

CIMA's CGMA® 2019 syllabus– Structure of subjects and learning outcomes

Details regarding the content of CIMA's new CGMA syllabus can be located within CIMA's CGMA 2019 professional syllabus document.

Each subject within the CGMA syllabus is divided into a number of broad syllabus topics. The topics contain one or more lead learning outcomes, related component learning outcomes and indicative knowledge content.

A learning outcome has two main purposes:

(a) To define the skill or ability that a well prepared candidate should be able to exhibit in the examination.

(b) To demonstrate the approach likely to be taken in examination questions.

The learning outcomes are part of a hierarchy of learning objectives. The verbs used at the beginning of each learning outcome relate to a specific learning objective, e.g.

Calculate the break-even point, profit target, margin of safety and profit/volume ratio for a single product or service.

The verb '**calculate**' indicates a level three learning objective. The following tables list the verbs that appear in the syllabus learning outcomes and examination questions.

The examination blueprints and representative task statements

CIMA have also published the CGMA® Exam Blueprints, giving learners clear expectations regarding what is expected of them.

The blueprint is structured as follows:

- Exam content sections (reflecting the syllabus document)
- Lead and component outcomes (reflecting the syllabus document)
- Representative task statements.

A representative task statement is a plain English description of what a CGMA® finance professional should know and be able to do.

The content and skill level determine the language and verbs used in the representative task.

CIMA will test up to the level of the task statement in the Objective Tests (an Objective Test question on a particular topic could be set at a lower level than the task statement in the blueprint).

The format of the Objective Test blueprints follows that of the published syllabus for the 2019 Professional Qualification.

Weightings for content sections are also included in the individual subject blueprints.

CIMA VERB HIERARCHY

CIMA® place great importance on the definition of verbs in structuring Objective Tests. It is therefore crucial that you understand the verbs in order to appreciate the depth and breadth of a topic and the level of skill required. The Objective Tests will focus on levels one, two and three of the CIMA hierarchy of verbs. However, they will also test levels four and five, especially at the Management and Strategic levels.

Skill level	Verbs used	Definition
Level 5 Evaluation How you are expected to use your learning to evaluate, make decisions or recommendations	Advise	Counsel, inform or notify
	Assess	Evaluate or estimate the nature, ability or quality of
	Evaluate	Appraise or assess the value of
	Recommend	Propose a course of action
	Review	Assess and evaluate in order, to change if necessary
Level 4 Analysis How you are expected to analyse the detail of what you have learned	Align	Arrange in an orderly way
	Analyse	Examine in detail the structure of
	Communicate	Share or exchange information
	Compare and contrast	Show the similarities and/or differences between
	Develop	Grow and expand a concept
	Discuss	Examine in detail by argument
	Examine	Inspect thoroughly
	Interpret	Translate into intelligible or familiar terms
	Monitor	Observe and check the progress of
	Prioritise	Place in order of priority or sequence for action
	Produce	Create or bring into existence
Level 3 Application How you are expected to apply your knowledge	Apply	Put to practical use
	Calculate	Ascertain or reckon mathematically
	Conduct	Organise and carry out
	Demonstrate	Prove with certainty or exhibit by practical means
	Prepare	Make or get ready for use
	Reconcile	Make or prove consistent/compatible

Skill level	Verbs used	Definition
Level 2 **Comprehension** What you are expected to understand	Describe	Communicate the key features of
	Distinguish	Highlight the differences between
	Explain	Make clear or intelligible/state the meaning or purpose of
	Identify	Recognise, establish or select after consideration
	Illustrate	Use an example to describe or explain something
Level 1 **Knowledge** What you are expected to know	List	Make a list of
	State	Express, fully or clearly, the details/facts of
	Define	Give the exact meaning of
	Outline	Give a summary of

SYLLABUS GRIDS

E2: Managing Performance

Mechanisms to implement decisions and manage people performance

Content weighting

Content area		Weighting
A	Business models and value creation	30%
B	Managing people performance	40%
C	Managing projects	30%
		100%

E2A: Business models and value creation

The digital world is characterised by disruptions to business models by new entrants and incumbents who seek superior performance and competitive advantage. This section covers the fundamentals of business models and how new business and operating models can be developed to improve the performance of organisations.

Lead outcome	Component outcome	Topics to be covered	Explanatory notes	Study Test Chapter
1. Explain the ecosystems of organisations.	Explain: a. Markets and competition b. Society and regulation	• Definition of ecosystems • Participants and roles • Interactions and dynamics • Rules and governance • Technology • Risks and opportunities	What is the nature of the ecosystem? What are its critical elements and how do they interact with each other? How do they impact the organisation?	1
2. Explain the elements of business models.	Explain the following a. Concept of value and the business model b. Defining value c. Creating value d. Delivering value e. Capturing and sharing value	• Stakeholders and relevant value • Stakeholder analysis • Resources, process, activities and people in creating value • Products, services, customer segments, channels and platforms to deliver value • Distribution of value to key stakeholders	This section covers the concept of value from different stakeholder perspectives. It examines the various elements of the business model, their interaction with each other and their implication for costs and revenue. The section also covers the connectivity and alignment between the ecosystem and the elements of the business model.	2
3. Analyse new business models in digital ecosystems.	a. Analyse digital business models and their related operating models	• Disruption • Ways to build disruptive and resilient business models • Creating digital operating models • Types of digital operating models	New business models have evolved to disrupt industries and their ecosystems. What are they? How have they redefined their industries?	3

E2B: Managing people performance

Human capital is one of the key intangible assets of organisations in an age where intangible assets are the dominant means by which organisations create and preserve value. Leadership is a crucial means for managing individual performance and the relationships between people. This section examines how different styles of leadership can be used to improve the performance of individuals so they can achieve organisational goals.

Lead outcome	Component outcome	Topics to be covered	Explanatory notes	Study Test Chapter
1. Compare and contrast different types of leadership and management styles.	Compare and contrast: a. Different leadership concepts b. Types of leadership c. Leadership in different contexts	• Power, authority, delegation and empowerment • Contingent and situational leadership • Transactional and transformational leadership • Leadership of virtual teams • Leadership and ethics	Leadership is key to performance management. In a digital world it is an area that is least susceptible to automation. What constitutes leadership? What are the different types of leadership? How does one choose a style of leadership that is appropriate for the particular context?	4
2. Analyse individual and team performance.	Analyse the following: a. Employee performance objective setting b. Employee appraisals c. Coaching and mentoring d. Managing workplace environment	• Target setting and employee alignment • Employee empowerment and engagement • Performance reporting and review • Rewards and sanctions in managing performance • Different approaches to coaching and mentoring to improve performance • Diversity and equity practices • Health and safety • Organisational culture	Individual performance is achieved through structured processes and approaches. These include objective setting and regular review of performance against objectives. How should these processes be developed to ensure employee engagement, empowerment and alignment? How should the work environment be configured to enhance performance? What is the role of the leader in coaching and mentoring for high performance?	5, 6

3. Explain how to manage relationships.	Explain the following in the context of managing relationships: a. Building and leading teams b. Communications c. Negotiations d. Managing conflicts	• Characteristics of high-performing teams • Motivating team members • Communication process • Digital tools for communication • Negotiation process • Strategies for negotiation • Sources and types of conflicts • Strategies for managing conflicts • Leadership and ethics	Individuals work in teams and their performance contributes to the team performance. How should teams be built and led to improve performance? How is collaboration enhanced using technology? How can conflicts be managed?	7, 8

E2C: Managing projects

Projects have become pervasive means by which organisations execute their strategies. This section shows candidates how to use project management concepts and techniques to implement strategies effectively and efficiently. It is linked to capital investment decision-making that is covered in other areas of the Management Level.

Lead outcome	Component outcome	Topics to be covered	Explanatory notes	
1. Describe the concepts and phases of projects.	Describe the following: a. Project objectives b. Key stages of the project life cycle c. Project control	• Overall project objectives • Objectives relating to time, cost and quality • Purpose and activities associated with key stages of the project life cycle	Projects are the primary means by which many organisations implement strategic decisions. It is also how organisations ensure cross-functional collaboration. This section covers the key elements of project management. It seeks to provide both awareness and understanding of the project management process and the ability to apply tools and techniques to participate in projects and to identify, evaluate and manage project risks. The objective is not to train project managers but to equip finance people to work within projects and to lead some parts of projects.	9
2. Apply tools and techniques to manage projects.	Apply the following to manage projects: a. Project management tools and techniques b. Project risk management tools	• Workstreams • Work breakdown schedule, Gantt charts, network analysis • PERT charts • Sources and types of project risks • Scenario planning • Managing project risks • Project management software		10
3. Explain the concepts of project leadership.	Explain a. Project structure b. Roles of key project personnel c. How to manage project stakeholders	• Project structures and their impact on project performance • Role of project manager • Role of key members of project team • Life cycle of project teams • Managing key stakeholders of projects • Leading and motivating project team		11

Information concerning formulae and tables will be provided via the AICPA & CIMA website, www.aicpa-cima.com.

Chapter

1

The concept of business ecosystems

Chapter learning objectives

Lead	Component
A1: Explain the ecosystems of organisations	(a) Markets and competition (b) Society and regulation

Topics to be covered

- Definition of ecosystems
- Participants and roles
- Interactions and dynamics
- Rules and governance
- Technology
- Risks and opportunities.

1 Session content diagram

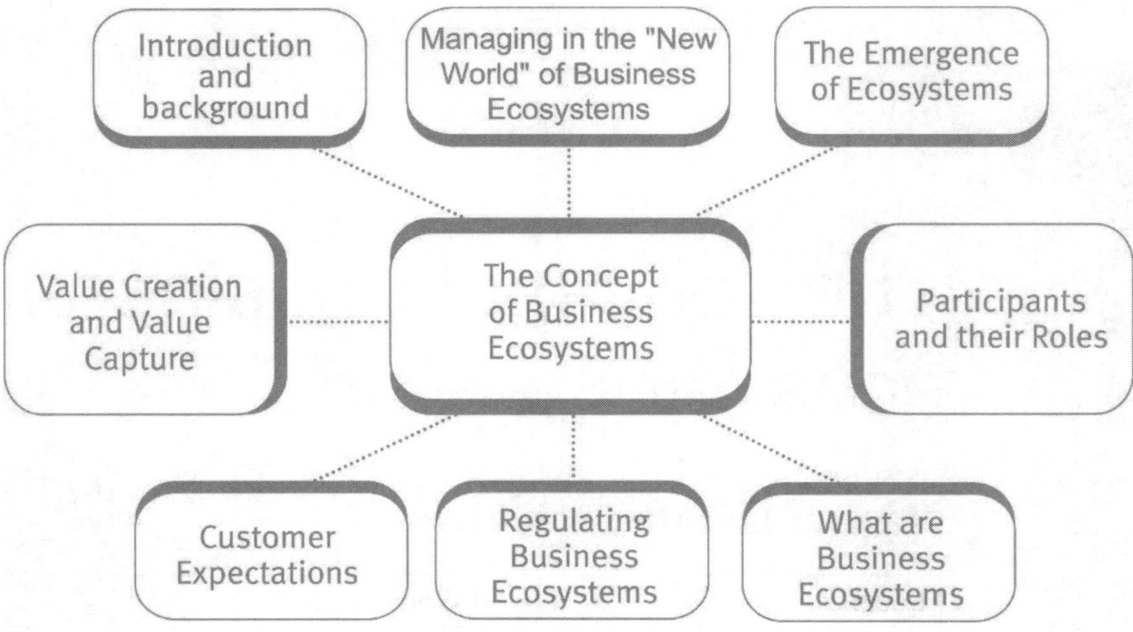

2 Introduction and background

2.1 Key terms

To understand the nature of ecosystems, why ecosystems are beginning to emerge and how they differ from traditional markets, it is important to provide some foundational explanation of some key concepts i.e. markets, competition, society and regulation.

The term **'market'** has various meanings. As used by economists in a business context market has a different meaning from ordinary usage. It does not mean (literally) the physical place in which commodities are sold or purchased (as in 'village market'), nor does it mean the stages that a commodity passes through between the producer and the consumer (as in marketing channels). It refers in an abstract way to the purchase and sale transactions of a commodity and the formation of its price. Used in this way, the term refers to the countless decisions made by producers of a commodity (the supply side of the market) and consumers of a commodity (the demand side of the market), which taken together determine the price level of the commodity. In this way, the term is detached from any particular geographical coverage.

Markets are a type of 'institution' or mechanism that exists to facilitate exchange, co-ordination and allocation of resources, goods and services between buyers and sellers, between producers, intermediaries and consumers. Competitive markets can provide 'efficient' co-ordination by reducing the cost and risk of carrying out transactions, can encourage business development and also help to achieve broader economic objectives.

In business the term 'market' is used to describe the groups of individuals or organisations that make up the pool of actual and potential customers for their goods and services.

Competition arises whenever at least two parties strive for a goal which cannot be shared: where one's gain is the other's loss. Competition is a major tenet of market economies and business, often associated with business competition as companies are usually in competition with at least one other firm over the same group of customers. Competition is often considered to be the opposite of cooperation, however in the real world mixtures of cooperation and competition are often the norm.

A society is a group of individuals involved in persistent social interaction, or a large social group sharing the same spatial or social territory, typically subject to the same political authority and dominant cultural expectations. Societies are characterised by patterns of relationships between individuals who share a distinctive culture and institutions; a given society may be described as the sum total of such relationships among its constituent of members. In the social sciences, a larger society often exhibits stratification or dominance patterns in subgroups.

Societies construct patterns of behaviour by deeming certain actions or speech as acceptable or unacceptable. These patterns of behaviour within a given society are known as societal norms.

Regulation is the management of complex systems according to a set of rules and trends. In systems theory, these types of rules exist in various fields of biology and society, but the term has slightly different meanings according to context.

For example: in biology, gene regulation and metabolic regulation allow living organisms to adapt to their environment; in government, typically regulation means stipulations of the delegated legislation which is drafted by subject-matter experts to enforce primary legislation; in business, industry self-regulation occurs through self-regulatory organisations and trade associations which allow industries to set and enforce rules with less government involvement; and, in psychology, self-regulation theory is the study of how individuals regulate their thoughts and behaviours to reach goals.

2.2 The traditional approach to understanding markets

A “market” is a place where two parties can gather to facilitate the exchange of goods and services. The parties involved are usually buyers and sellers.

The market may be physical e.g. a retail outlet, where people meet face-to-face, or virtual e.g. online, where there is no direct physical contact between buyers and sellers.

Markets are therefore comprised of individuals or organisations who exchange products or services within an environment governed by the laws of supply and demand.

Business is however changing and the growth of technologies, such as social, mobile, analytics, cloud, 3D printing, bio- and nanotechnology and most recently Artificial Intelligence (AI) are rapidly altering the competitive landscape.

Traditional methods of analysing these markets and competitive landscape may still apply but will need to be updated to reflect the disruption that these rapidly advancing technologies provide.

The changing business environments associated with these developments provide organisations with new and uncharted opportunities and threats. If they do not adapt and reflect these changes in their chosen strategies, organisations will miss what threatens to be a seismic shift in the way business is conducted. This will provide competitors who adapt quicker with the opportunity to leave the more traditional market players behind by creating new experiences for the consumer.

To create these experiences, businesses must embrace the concept, mechanics and implications of ecosystems and revise and review the methods used to analyse the competitive landscape.

The analysis of traditional markets

Traditionally the business environment has been analysed by the use of, for example, business models and tools such as PESTLE, Porter's Five Forces and Porter's Generic Strategies. They are often used to analyse and understand the operating environments of firms and the changing business environments associated with new developments such as technology. They are therefore included for reference purposes and will be revisited again at the Strategic Level.

NB – These models are not explicitly mentioned in the E2 syllabus blueprint but the language and terms used are widely referred to in the literature on ecosystems, new business models and by CIMA in the report "Rethinking the Business Model".

PESTLE is an acronym used to help organise the analysis of the business environment into broad categories. PESTLE analysis divides the business environment into political, economic, social (and cultural), technical, legal and ecological/environmental factors. Analysing these factors can help organisations understand the opportunities and threats within their environment and this understanding is crucial in shaping the organisation's current and future strategic decisions, for example:

- **political influences and events** – legislation, government policies, changes to competition policy or import duties, etc.
- **economic influences** – a multinational company will be concerned about the international situation, while an organisation trading exclusively in one country might be more concerned with the level and timing of domestic development. Items of information relevant to marketing plans might include changes in the gross domestic product, changes in consumers' income and expenditure, and population growth.

- **social influences** – includes social, cultural or demographic factors (i.e. population shifts, age profiles, etc.) and refers to attitudes, value and beliefs held by people; also changes in lifestyles, education and health and so on.
- **technological influences** – changes in material supply, processing methods and new product development.
- **legal influences** – changes in laws and regulations affecting, for example, competition, patents, sale of goods, pollution, working regulations and industrial standards.
- **ecological/environmental influences** – includes the impact the organisation has on its external environment in terms of pollution etc.

Porter's five forces analysis

Just because a market is growing, it does not follow that it is possible to make money in it. Porter's five forces approach looks in detail at the company's competitive environment by analysing five forces. Companies must identify these forces and assess the strength of each force. The relative strength of each of these forces (high, moderate or low) will determine the **profit potential of the industry**.

1. **New entrants** – new entrants into a market will bring extra capacity and intensify competition and any barriers to entry which may exist.
2. **Rivalry amongst competitors** – existing competition and its intensity.
3. **Substitutes** – this threat is across industries (e.g. rail travel or bus travel or private car).
4. **Power of buyers** – powerful buyers can force price cuts and/or quality improvements.
5. **Power of suppliers** – powerful suppliers can charge higher prices, forcing down profit margins.

Porter's three generic strategies

According to Porter, there are three generic strategies' through which an organisation can generate superior competitive performance (known as generic because they are widely applicable to firms of all sizes and in all industries):

1. **Cost leadership** – offering products and services of the same quality as competitors but at lower prices.
2. **Differentiation** – charging higher prices by offering more innovative products, or products with a higher perceived quality.
3. **Focus** – concentrating only on a small part of the market.

The adoption of one or other of these strategies by a business unit is made on the basis of:

- an analysis of the threats and opportunities posed by forces operating in the specific industry of which the business is a part
- the general environment in which the business operates
- an assessment of the organisation's strengths and weaknesses relative to competitors.

The general idea is that the strategy to be adopted by the organisation is one which best positions the company relative to its rivals and other threats from suppliers, buyers, new entrants, substitutes and the macro environment, and to take opportunities offered by the market and general environment.

Decisions on the above questions will determine the generic strategy options for achieving competitive advantage.

Example of traditional analysis

Charlton Inc. is a major manufacturer of ground-source heat-pumps. These devices allow users to extract geothermal energy from the earth, and to use that energy to heat their premises. In order to develop new products and services, Charlton has already developed mutually-beneficial relationships with its supply chain.

Charlton Inc. is currently analysing its business environment, and has realised that there might be competitive advantage to be gained by treating its environment as an 'ecosystem'. This is not something that has ever been done in Charlton's industry.

Using the traditional approach outlined above for assessing the profit potential and attractiveness of an industry align each of the following 'competitive forces' to match the likely effect of Charlton's new approach. You may use each effect more than once.

Force	Effect
Bargaining power of suppliers	Increase
Bargaining power of customers	Decrease
Rivalry	Remain stable
Threat of new entrants	

2.3 The impact and effect of technology on traditional markets

Organisations will always have to evolve to keep up with changing environments e.g. expectations of customers, advances in technology, environmental change etc.

Technology impacts markets through its effect on productivity, efficiency and the production and delivery of new types of goods and services. As a result it has been the source of competitive advantage for organisations and strongly influences how value is created and delivered.

Advances in technology and increasing globalisation have changed ideas about the best ways to do business. The idea of a business ecosystem is thought to help companies understand how to thrive in this rapidly changing environment.

In recent years, the rapid increase in the development of new technologies, greater openness and escalating customer expectations are converging into a fundamental business change.

Customers have begun to experience individualised and integrated experiences in areas such as telephony and are now expecting similar experiences across all their interactions, regardless of whether they are in a business-to-consumer, business-to-business or consumer-to-government context.

Most organisations are not set up to deliver these types of experiences and, as a result, are often faced with customer frustration and, at times, anger. At the same time, customers know that technology is already available to make such experiences possible—cloud, analytics, mobile and social media.

Organisations therefore face increased risk for the future success if they do respond and increased costs (at least in the short term) to ensure that they understand the changes within key stakeholder groups and respond appropriately.

Illustration 1 – The music industry

In the music industry the accepted offering for listening to music was, for many years, vinyl and cassette format. This then changed in the 1980s to CD, before the advent of the internet enabled consumers to purchase online and download to mobile devices such as MP3 players. This then progressed further to streaming instead of outright purchase. Each successive development lead to a decline in demand for the previous format (although interestingly there has been a recent resurgence in demand for how it all started, as sales of vinyl have started to grow again!).

However, since the start of the new millennium, the rate of change has grown considerably, driven by 2 principal factors: organisations are adopting technologies that enable them to transform the experience that customers can enjoy; and the expectations of the customers themselves are changing at a much faster rate. This latter point is only likely to continue, as present and future consumers, who have been born and raised in such a digital world, embrace new technologies more quickly and expect that they will be able to benefit from improvements to their lives as a result, meaning that organisations will find it much more difficult to surprise them.

Organisations will therefore need to constantly reinvent what they offer to customers if they are to satisfy their rapidly changing expectations.

Drivers of the digital revolution

If organisations are to meet these ever-changing needs, it is important that they understand the key drivers behind such change. The following are identified as key factors:

- **Mobile and internet penetration** – the increasing rate of mobile phone ownership, combined with access to the internet (with mobile beginning to exceed broadband). It is estimated that by 2025 the number of smartphone subscriptions will reach 4 billion, with much of the growth coming from emerging economies.
- **Connected devices** – the number of connected devices are expected to grow from 2.5 billion in 2009 to 27.1 billion by 2025. This will help enable real-time customisation of products and services.
- **Data analytics and the cloud** – the increasing use of e-commerce platforms, social networks, apps etc. will result in increased need for automated data analytics.
- **User interfaces** – advances in how human beings interact with machines (e.g. through voice recognition or motion-tracking systems) means that carrying out tasks becomes quicker and more efficient for humans.
- **Global accessibility** – rising living standards in developing economies means that more and more people are gaining access to the internet and so increased connectivity.
- **Increasing urbanisation** – the growing percentage of people who live in urban as opposed to rural areas. The United Nations estimates that, from approximately 54% of the global population in 2014, this will grow to almost 60% by 2050.
- **Artificial Intelligence** – a machine's ability to perform the cognitive functions we associate with human minds, such as perceiving, reasoning, learning, interacting with an environment, problem solving, and even exercising creativity.

In essence, more and more people are becoming connected to technology, enjoying the benefits that it delivers, and demanding that such benefits increase, not just within 1 industry but across industries – there is no reason to believe that advances in 1 area of business cannot be transferred to other areas.

Illustration 2 – Pager

Based in New York, Pager is a company that provides on-demand health care from local medical professionals via mobile-based services. Users can request services such as check-ups, arranging prescriptions and diagnosis of illnesses from the doctor of their choice within their local area. House calls are made within 2 hours of the service being requested.

In many respects, this is an example of how benefits can be transferred from 1 industry (such as Uber and transport requirements) to another (healthcare). It is therefore little surprise that Pager was founded by Oscar Salazar, a former Uber engineer.

3 The emergence of "business ecosystems"

As noted earlier, technologies mature and grow e.g. social, mobile, analytics, cloud, 3D printing, bio- and nanotechnology. The external competitive environment for industry and business is similarly changing rapidly as these emerging technologies create an environment that is connected and open, simple and intelligent, fast and scalable:

- **Connected and open** – the proliferation of mobile devices and Internet access, necessitating new levels of trust and accountability with partners and consumers.
- **Simple and intelligent** – advances in technology continue to reduce and mask complexity and organisations gain more information and use data analytics and insights to drive decision-making.
- **Fast and scalable** – transactions increase both in number and frequency but the cost of collaboration inside and outside the organisation continues to decline.

The conundrum that market players face is that despite the technology driving this transparency by becoming more sophisticated, intelligent and predictive, it is also becoming easier to use by focussing on ease and "usability". This allows organisations to tap into structured and unstructured data, motivating intelligent and predictive decision-making.

This rapid development of new technologies, greater openness and escalating customer expectations are converging to create a fundamental business change from traditional markets to the new concept of "business ecosystems".

It is these experiences with these new technologies and resulting change to traditional business models (see Chapter 2) that is increasing the expectations and the empowerment of the consumer stakeholder group.

Organisations must react to these changes and adapt their business models or risk being left in the wilderness. The increasing technological sophistication is leading to:

- More information to consumers, allowing more choices and enabling greater opportunity to influence organisations
- Higher expectations of integrated and sophisticated experiences that are simple to use and access
- Decreasing brand loyalty, as consumers have less patience and are more willing to switch interchangeably among brands.

In response, organisations face increasing pressure to play catch-up and meet the next generation of consumer demands by providing integrated, customised, consumer centric experiences.

Consumers expect personalisation across all of their business dealings experiences. Whether it be buying cars or purchasing airline tickets, they expect integration across channels and touch points, and they are quick to change loyalties to organisations that can better meet their needs.

For example, in a recent survey by IBM in which one of the questions was "To want extent should organisations change to meet customer expectations":

- 81 percent of millennial consumers demand improved response time
- 76 percent expect organisations to understand individual needs
- 68 percent anticipate organisations to harmonise consumer experiences.

Illustration 3 – Xiaomi

Chinese smartphone manufacturer Xiaomi is seeking to engage connected consumers. Xiaomi uses customer segmentation as a brand differentiator. It sells high-end phones for prices close to cost, less than half the price of some rivals. The company leverages consumer feedback captured via Weibo (i.e. Twitter-like social media application) to release new versions of its operating system, which it does on a weekly schedule.

The Xiaomi illustration demonstrates that, to create an opportunity to provide a differentiated experience in line with consumer expectations, organisations must embrace data and analytics to underpin experience and pursue social media to promote collaboration.

Conclusion

As the business world rapidly develops beyond traditional markets, organisations will need to rethink how their business environment operates, how they partner and how they interact with customers.

They must embrace the concept of **mutuality** (see later discussion) a level of formal or informal collaboration among organisations around shared ideals, standards, or goals.

More detail on ecosystems

Ecosystems exist in the natural world

The word "ecosystem" was coined in the 1930s by British botanist Arthur Tansley to refer to a localised community of living organisms interacting with each other and their particular environment of air, water, mineral soil, and other elements. These organisms influence each other, and their terrain; they compete and collaborate, share and create resources, and coevolve; and they are inevitably subject to external disruptions, to which they adapt together to be able to grow and thrive in ever changing conditions.

In the 1993 Harvard Business Review article "Predators and Prey: A New Ecology of Competition" business strategist James Moore adopted this biological concept to the world of commerce.

He suggested that a company be viewed not as a single firm in an industry, but as a member of a business ecosystem with participants spanning across multiple industries.

From a business perspective therefore an ecosystem can be thought of as a complex web of interdependent enterprises and relationships that creates and allocates business value.

In the 1993 Harvard Business Review, business strategist James Moore adapted the concept to the business world –

"Successful businesses are those that evolve rapidly and effectively. Yet innovative businesses can't evolve in a vacuum.

They must attract resources of all sorts, drawing in capital, partners, suppliers, and customers to create cooperative networks. I suggest that a company be viewed not as a member of a single industry but as part of a business ecosystem that crosses a variety of industries.

In a business ecosystem, companies co-evolve capabilities around a new innovation: They work cooperatively and competitively to support new products, satisfy customer needs, and eventually incorporate the next round of innovations"

e.g

Illustration 4 – Digital Marketing Ecosystem

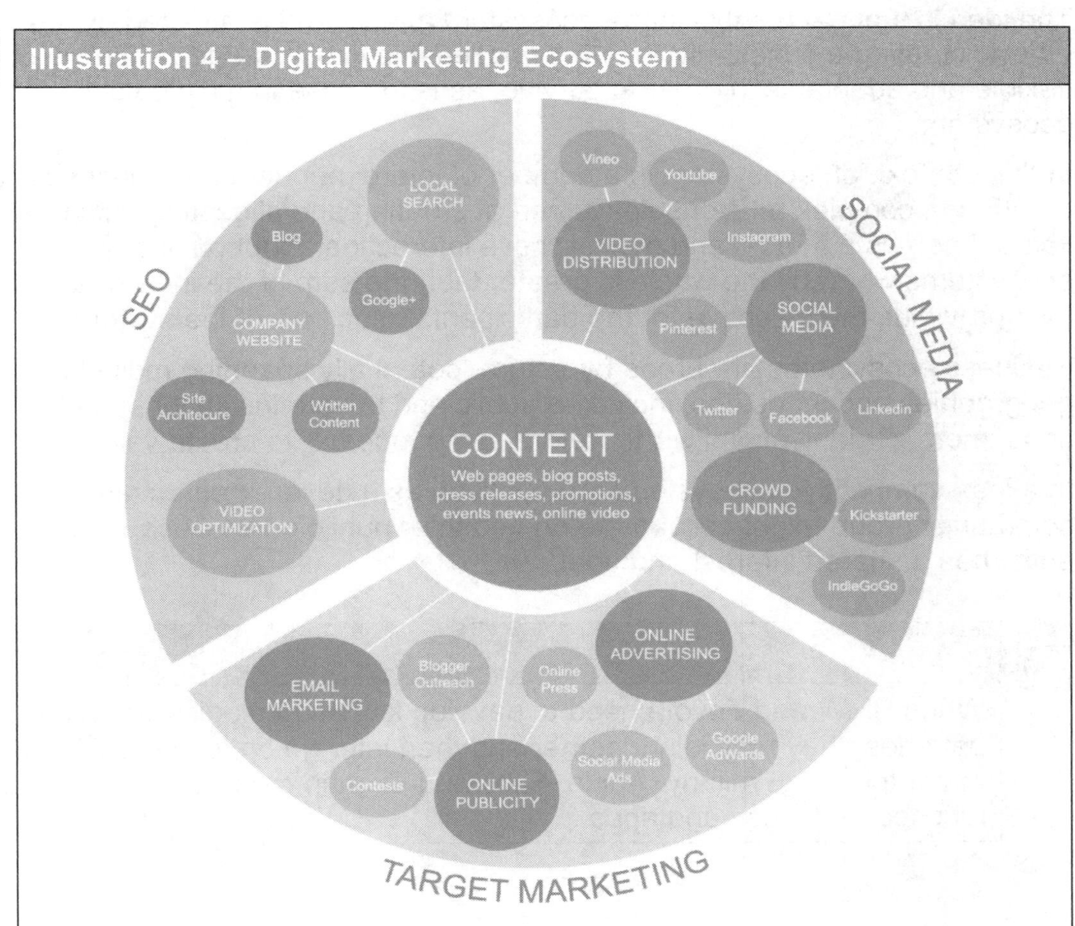

Consider online marketing to be an ecosystem – a system of interconnecting and interacting parts – formed by three distinct areas of content creation: search engine optimisation, social media, and target marketing.

Sustainable success in digital marketing is achieved using strategies that leverage the interrelationship of these ecosystem elements.

The specific strategies and individual tools included in a marketing ecosystem (and used to execute digital marketing campaigns) are dependent on many factors including the goals for the campaign as well as the company's industry and their customer's buying habits.

It is therefore key for organisations to maintain a keen eye on new developments, monitor trends, and test new tools as they emerge.

4 What are Business Ecosystems?

A business ecosystem can be defined as a network of organisations (suppliers, distributors, customers, competitors, government agencies, etc.), who are involved in the delivery of a specific product or service through both competition and cooperation. This network of organisations and individuals will collaborate and evolve roles and capabilities to build value and increase efficiency.

The idea is that each entity in the ecosystem affects and is affected by the others, creating a constantly evolving relationship in which each entity must be flexible and adaptable in order to survive, as is the case in a biological ecosystem.

In this context, an ecosystem is a number of interdependent enterprises drawn together in complex relationships aimed at creating and allocating business value. There is a mutual and multiplicative interaction about business ecosystems whereby the whole is greater than the sum of the individual part, thus providing the incentive for the participants to be part of the system.

Business ecosystems are broad by nature, potentially spanning multiple geographies and industries, including public and private institutions, and consumers. Organisations will therefore come together to create value.

In a less-competitive ecosystem, groups such as a government, charity and a community group might collaborate on health or public policy because each entity has a shared interest and goal.

Illustration 5 – Business Ecosystems

When BMW and Toyota need to develop key technologies, such as batteries, they may join together and then later go on to compete in the marketplace. Similarly, Apple, Fitbit and Garmin created an ecosystem focused on fitness and apps.

Ecosystems and traditional markets are not unlike however being composed of participants and interactions. These are:

- **Participants** – the individual players or organisations within the environment defined by:
  - Participants function (or part played in a given environment)
  - Participants ability to extend activity or interactions through the environment
  - Range of activities that participants are able to pursue or undertake within the environment (key value proposition).
- **Interactions** – the products or services exchanged among participants defined by:
  - Set of explicit or implicit principles governing conduct within the environment
  - Linkages across the environment connecting elements such as data, knowledge, or products
  - Speed and direction at which content or value is exchanged among participants.

4.1 Fundamental characteristics of a business ecosystem

As we noted earlier, within a market individuals or organisations who exchange products or services within an environment which is governed by the laws of supply and demand.

A business ecosystem comprises individual and organisations that operate out of mutual self-interest and who formally or informally operate together to produce something of greater value for the mutual benefit of the organisation and the ecosystem as a whole. Organisations may therefore

- Be a part of one or many ecosystems
- Play different roles in different ecosystems
- Evolve their roles in the ecosystem, as ecosystems evolve.

Ecosystems exist because participants can deliver more value within the ecosystem acting together and have two defining characteristics.

These are orchestration and mutuality and are based on the premise that ecosystems exist because participants acting together can deliver more value.

- **Orchestration** refers to the formal or informal coordination of interactions or collaborations among participants within the ecosystem i.e. the coordination, arrangement and management of these complex environments.

Orchestration can be informal, for example via the culture of an organisation, or it may be formal through explicit rules or the presence of an actual "orchestrator" – i.e. an explicit entity that facilitates orchestration processes.

For example, according to PwC, firms need to orchestrate the interactions of both the different players in their operating environment and the customers to maximise the value delivered, make money out of that for all players and give the firms a fair share of that value.

Illustration 6 – Orchestration (Kaiser Permanente

Kaiser Permanente is a U.S.-based integrated managed care consortium that orchestrates insurance, hospitals, and physicians to provide integrated healthcare services. The company coordinates and orchestrates a membership base of 9 million members, along with physicians, doctors and medical centres. Kaiser Permanente's "My Health Manager" program facilitates the delivery of preventative care by connecting care providers, pharmacies and physicians.

- **Mutuality** reflects an enhanced level of coordination with formally or informally shared ideals, standards, or goals.

Illustration 7 – Mutuality (Doorman)

Doorman, a San Francisco-based logistics service, orchestrates storage and delivery to solve the "last mile" problem of package delivery. The service facilitates carriers such as FedEx and UPS by receiving packages and delivering them at the customer's convenience after traditional carrier delivery hours, up until midnight. This enables consumers to control logistics in a manner previously unavailable.

4.2 The goals of business ecosystems

As we have established already, a business ecosystem consists of a network of interlinked companies that dynamically interact with each other through competition and cooperation to grow sales and survive. It includes many different stakeholder groups e.g. suppliers, distributors, consumers, government, processes, products and competitors.

When an ecosystem thrives, it means that the participants have developed patterns of behaviour that streamline the flow of ideas, talent and capital throughout the system.

Ecosystems will also create strong barriers to entry for new competition, as potential entrants not only have to duplicate or better the core product, but they also must compete against the entire system of independent complementing businesses and suppliers that form the network.

Being a part of a business ecosystem provides mechanisms to leverage technology achieve excellence in research and business competence and compete effectively against other companies.

Some other goals of a business ecosystem may include:

- driving new collaborations to address rising social and environmental challenges
- harnessing creativity and innovation to lower the cost of production or allow members to reach new customers
- accelerating the learning process to effectively collaborate and share insights, skills, expertise and knowledge
- creating new ways to address fundamental human needs and desires.

Test your understanding 1

Dragon Breath is a consultancy firm, specialising in the provision of advice on the use of disruptive technologies in FMCG production, logistics and retail. It has previously used traditional 'environment analysis' to identify opportunities and threats in its environment.

Jane Li, the Chief Strategy Officer of Dragon Breath, is considering changing the approach taken to environment analysis. She feels that the environment of Dragon Breath resembles an 'ecosystem', rather than a traditional linear supply chain.

Required:

Identify which TWO of the following characteristics distinguish an ecosystem from a traditional supply chain.

- Interaction
- Orchestration
- Mutuality
- Communication
- Conflict

5 Value creation and value capture in a business ecosystem

The way organisations create and capture value in an ecosystem differs from traditional markets.

Two fundamental questions need to be addressed.

- Firstly, what can organisations do to create value in ecosystems?
- Secondly, how do organisations capture the value they help to create within an ecosystem?

How is value created?

Value creation refers to the act of bringing something of value into existence. Participants can therefore create value by products enhancements, product development, and the creation of new services or customer experience.

In an ecosystem partners must collaborate to create and deliver something of a mutually beneficial value to all of the participants.

How is value captured?

Value capture is the act or process of appropriating or allocating value. Participants can capture value directly through transactions or indirectly from an orchestrator.

Ecosystem complexity and the extent or intensity of orchestration impact the potential and govern the nature of value capture.

As a result, ecosystems can produce more value as a whole than the sum of the individual participants acting independently.

5.1 The difference between traditional markets and ecosystems

Value creation in traditional markets tends to be linear; value creation in ecosystems tends to be networked and mutual.

To create value, organisations need to identify opportunities, develop competencies and leverage synergies. Organisations must understand how value is created in the ecosystem and, as a result, identify and exploit opportunities for value creation. To facilitate this, organisations must maintain flexibility in the role they adopt within the ecosystem and interactions they may have with other ecosystem participants.

Organisations must also leverage common synergies and complementary strengths within ecosystems to drive value creation. To do so, they will need to apply their capabilities across the ecosystem, identifying and pursuing compatibility gaps and needs, and develop contracting and connectivity arrangement to insinuate themselves to fill gaps and exploit other opportunities. The more essential and unique the activity organisations can fulfil within an ecosystem, the more sustainable will be their position and role.

In identifying opportunities, organisations must understand how value is created in the ecosystem. They will need to identify and exploit pockets of potential value creation. However, given the extent and speed of the change, they must maintain flexibility in the role they adopt within the ecosystem, as well as the type of interactions they have with other ecosystem participants.

Illustration 8 – Value Creation (Google)

Recently, Google initiated and coordinated the Open Automotive Alliance to innovate in-car operating systems with GM, Honda, Audi, Hyundai, along with organizations such as Nvidia. Google aims to become the centre of personal operating systems through partnerships. Google seeks to capitalize on the 80 million new cars and light trucks sold each year – a major opportunity for Internet-based services.

Illustration 9 – Partnerships (Amazon)

One opportunity being pursued by Amazon, for example, is to use existing partnerships to target the next frontier of online sales. The online retailer has established a physical presence in the warehouses and distribution centres of existing suppliers (e.g. Procter & Gamble) through its "Vendor Flex" initiative. As a result, Amazon is expanding its selling efforts into new and different markets through partnering arrangements. It reduces fulfilment costs and delivery time and allows Amazon to compete even more aggressively with other retailers.

The participants in an ecosystem can capture value directly through transactions or indirectly from the orchestrator.

Direct value capture

Organisations can capture value directly through transactions that occur within the ecosystem. Participants facilitate an exchange of value for goods or services rendered, for example, when they buy a ticket on public transport. Value capture is instantaneous and corresponds with the transaction.

Indirect value capture

Alternatively, organisations may capture value indirectly by transfer from an orchestrator (which captures value directly from consumers) for goods or services.

Consumers will pay an orchestrator for goods and services (pay to play), and the orchestrator will then allocate payment to participants within the ecosystem thereby incentivising them to continue participating in the ecosystem e.g. buying a pass for all public transport in a city for unlimited trips on trains, trams, buses or subways within a defined time.

A third option is a combination of direct and indirect, with some pay-to-play component and some direct component. For example, in the transportation ecosystem of the future, organisations will most likely capture value both directly and indirectly.

Illustration 10 – Direct and indirect value capture

The mobility (transportation) ecosystem of the future in which consumers pay to have access to services that transport them from one location to another, irrespective where they are, when they want to travel and where they want to travel to.

Organisations will most likely capture value both directly and indirectly. Mobility providers will operate in an orchestrated environment, but with specific usage-based transactions co-existing with overall pay-to-play.

Orchestrators will facilitate overarching ecosystems that are composed of numerous implicit services and will allocate value to participants based on the role they play in the ecosystem.

Consumers may be able to choose to pay directly for specific distance-related or transportation type-related services. Direct transactions for usage-based services and infrastructure access could therefore co-exist with an orchestrated, indirect-payment pay-to-play environment.

5.2 Strategies to capture value

Each organisation will need to pursue different actions to capture value, depending on the underlying nature of the ecosystems in which they operate.

Each organisation will face differences within their own ecosystem and therefore a strategy developed and pursued in one environment may differ drastically from strategies pursued in other environments.

Key drivers of these differences are firstly the level of complexity in the activities undertaken, and secondly the extent and formality of the orchestration in and around the ecosystem.

Complexity:

Complexity is a function of the number and diversity of participants, the sophistication of activities within the ecosystem and the range and nature of relationships that exist within that ecosystem.

- High complexity – an environment in which barriers to entry are high and the threat of new entrants is low. It suggests that a participant's role in the ecosystem is relatively secure as their particular capabilities are typically difficult to replicate e.g. nuclear power, or oil exploration.
- Low complexity – an environment in which barriers to entry are low and the threat of new entrants is high. In this environment, a participant's position in the ecosystem is vulnerable, as their capabilities are typically easy to copy e.g. production of consumables (bakeries), retailing (individual boutiques), fitness instruction etc.

Orchestration

Orchestration depicts the extent of an organisation's influence over others within an ecosystem, the formality of ecosystem interactions and the degree of enforceability and compliance.

- Tight orchestration reflects an environment in which orchestrators have an ability to influence behaviour or actions across the entire ecosystem. For example, financial services, in which transactions are governed by stringent and regulated rules of privacy, security and compliance. Interactions will by necessity be rules-based, with orchestrators able to enforce their will over others.
- Loose orchestration refers to an environment in which no individual participant has significant influence across the ecosystem. There is often an absence of strong regulation with limited ability for any particular participant to enforce its will over others. For example, the Internet in regimes that have freedom of speech laws. While some content and behaviour is specifically outlawed on criminal grounds in the most part, individuals and organizations are free to express themselves and behave any way they want.

Based on this premise that Ecosystems are not all alike and as they differ in specific fundamental ways there will be a number of approaches necessary to depict appropriate strategies to deal with these differences.

Complexity and orchestration characterize a spectrum of ecosystem archetypes.

In the IBM Report "The new age of ecosystems: Redefining partnership in an ecosystem environment" The following matrix depicts how some of these different combinations may be characterised in a "spectrum of ecosystem archetypes"

Ecosystem Archetypes

	Orchestration		
		Loose	**Tight**
Complexity	**High**	**Hornet's Nest** Where high complexity and loose orchestration promotes fragmented competition	**Lion's Pride** Where high complexity and tight orchestration motivate a winner-take-all mentality
	Low	**Shark Tank** Where low complexity and loose orchestration creates a turbulent environment	**Wolf Pack** Low complexity and tight orchestration promotes collaboration

These are referred to as the Shark Tank, the Hornet's Nest, the Wolf Pack and the Lion's Pride

- **Shark Tank** – low orchestration and low complexity. Each participant will fend for themselves, identifying opportunities, aligning capabilities and making connections. An example of Shark Tank is the retail ecosystem of the future where new technologies will make entry costs into retail ever lower and competition will become even more intense. Consumers will have low switching costs, changing between products at will, while the potential competitive threat will increase as new entrants or existing players watch on ready to take advantage of opportunities. Search costs will become ever lower, with multiple organisations seeking to attract and connect with consumers.
- **Lion's Pride** – threats of new entrants are low due to the relative complexity of the activities in which participants are engaged. In the Lion's Pride orchestration tends to be formal. The orchestrator will enable and monitor activities within the ecosystem and remunerate individuals or organisations for their participation. An example of Lions Pride will be the future healthcare industry where an orchestrator will facilitate and manage the interaction between patients, providers and physicians into a fully integrated health, wellness and medical experience.
- **Hornet's Nest** – complexity is high, but orchestration is low. Ecosystems of this type tend to be simpler, with most of the value being transferred directly by means of payment for specific activities. An example will be the future of Media and Entertainment business where will likely become the Hornet's Nest ecosystem where consumers will likely be unwilling to be tied to a single system to view content. They will demand whatever content they want, on whatever platform or device they want, whenever they want it, anywhere in the world.
- **Wolf Pack** – low complexity and high levels of orchestration. Barriers to entry are low, indicating that entry into the ecosystem is relatively easy. Orchestration is however high, suggesting that while individual activities within the ecosystem are simple, the overall environment created is potentially highly sophisticated. An example of Wolf Pack maybe the future Energy and Utilities industry. In the future, every home, building, facility or appliance may be both a consumer and producer of energy. The presence of a strong orchestrator will ensure that energy flows are measured, reserve energy is stored and networks remain in good working order.

Test your understanding 2

Geronimo is a consumer electronics manufacturer. It produces hardware communications devices (tablets, laptops, PCs and phones) and also supplies a range of software to operate on those devices (operating systems, tools and apps).

Geronimo has developed a close working relationship, for mutual benefit, with a network of other organisations and individuals. These include software developers, suppliers, retailers and consumers. As a result of these arrangements, Geronimo and its partners create and capture value added, which is shared between the partners.

Required:

Identify which of the following approaches is being taken by Geronimo

- Franchising
- Ecosystem development
- Upstream supply chain management
- Customer relationship management

6 Participants and their roles

We have seen above that the business ecosystem is "an economic community supported by a foundation of interacting organisations and individuals – the organisms of the business world."

The interacting organisations and individuals are the participants. For example, the economic community produces goods and services of value to customers, who are themselves members of the ecosystem.

Other participants include suppliers, lead producers, competitors and other stakeholders. These participants will, over time, co-evolve their capabilities and roles and tend to align themselves with the directions set by one or more central companies.

Illustration 11 – The Apple ecosystem

Apple exists in a highly complex business ecosystem, made up of many participants. Examples would include:

Software developers – both those employed by the company and those who are not e.g. developers of apps which are then marketed via the App Store.

Suppliers – of components, organisations that assemble the product, of accessories (e.g. Belkin is an approved manufacturer of Apple accessories).

Retailers – not just employees in Apple Stores, but also approved 3rd party retailers.

Competitors – organisations such as Microsoft and Samsung, which are constantly innovating and therefore forcing Apple to do the same.

Customers – both individuals and also corporate customers.

Learning institutions – such as universities, that develop potential employees with the necessary skills.

Governments – e.g. much of Apple's product is sourced from China. Any trade wars between the US and China will inevitably impact Apple.

Legislators – those who formulate the law, which impacts not just on Apple but also other organisations e.g. privacy laws and Facebook.

NB This list is not exhaustive; there are many other elements of Apple's ecosystem!

An ecosystem therefore reflects interaction and collaboration between participants to create an opportunity to provide a differentiated experience in line with consumer expectations.

It is important for organisations to embrace data and analytics to underpin these customer experiences and pursue social media to promote collaboration. They will also need to reduce or minimise any barriers to engagement and partnering with other participants.

3 key questions need to be asked with regards to each participant that makes up the ecosystem, and thus how it might impact on any one organisation's strategy:

- **The precise role of the participant within the environment** – what is that participant bringing to the party? It may be cloud computing capacity, distribution capability, unique software skills or access to certain markets due to owning a particular licence to operate. It makes sense that, for the ecosystem to create the value that is possible, all necessary participants are present.
- **Each participant's reach through the environment** – this relates to the participant's ability to extend activity or interactions through the environment. For example, can the participant operate on a global or just a local level and deal with both consumer (B2C) and industrial (B2B) markets?
- **The capability or key value proposition** – this is the range of activities that participants are able to pursue or undertake in the environment. What is the key value that each participant is able to deliver?

Illustration 12 – Nest

Nest is a US-based provider of home automation products, from thermostats that control the central heating system to surveillance cameras and smoke alarms. It has created a new technology platform that offers homeowners a unique experience because it has correctly brought in other companies such as Mercedes Benz and LG to bring capabilities that Nest itself does not possess.

Illustration 13 – Burberry

Luxury fashion house Burberry, a traditionally conservative brand, digitized its organization to create a seamless consumer experience.

Burberry removed organizational boundaries between digital and physical; for example, it equipped employees with iPads to enable online access to leverage consumer data to improve the in-store experience.

Through digital-physical integration, Burberry has transformed into a modern, relevant, and hip luxury brand.

Ecosystems provide a new frame and mind-set that captures a profound shift in the economy and the business landscape.

The importance of relationships, partnerships, networks, alliances, and collaborations is not new but it is of increased significance in the ecosystem discussion. It is becoming increasingly possible for firms to deploy and activate assets they neither own nor control, to engage and mobilise larger and larger numbers of participants.

- ecosystems enable and encourage the participation of a diverse range of organisations, and often individuals, who together can create, scale, and serve markets beyond the capabilities of any single organisation.
- participants interact and co-create in increasingly sophisticated ways that would historically have been hard to formally coordinate in a "top-down" manner, by deploying a proliferation of technologies, tools of connectivity and collaboration. There is dynamism and substantial potential for increasingly productive ecosystem development in the years ahead.
- participants including customers—are bonded by some combination of shared interests, purpose, and values which incentivises them to collectively nurture, sustain, and protect the ecosystem as a shared common ground. Everyone contributes, everyone benefits enhancing the longevity and durability of ecosystems.

The rise of business ecosystems is fundamentally altering the key success factors for organisations, forcing them to think and act very differently regarding their strategies, business models, leadership, core capabilities, value creation and capture systems, and organisational models.

7 Regulating ecosystems

As was noted above, the economy is fast becoming characterised by ecosystems—dynamic and co-evolving communities of diverse participants who create and capture new value through both collaboration and competition.

In that context, these new markets will need to be regulated. Regulation is always contentious to some degree but in relatively slow-moving industries the historical intent and enforcement of the rules can be understood well enough by all involved. This understanding become less clear however when the boundaries of traditional industries becomes less defined, when products blend with services to create customer-centric solutions, and when knowledge assets take on as much importance as physical assets in the creation of value. Constant, high-impact innovation is a prominent new feature in businesses that used to advance only incrementally.

Examples of reasons for regulation

Some of today's most popular products, like the smartphone and tablet, didn't even exist eight years ago. Apple Inc. estimated in 2011 that over 60 percent of its revenue came from products that were less than three years old. Business models are being reinvented to take advantage of technological change, for example enabling peer-to peer transactions, asset sharing, and social collaboration.

The nature of work itself is in flux. Sites like Task Rabbit allow anyone to outsource small jobs to people with extra time, and the "creative economy" continues to expand. By one reckoning, half of today's jobs are in occupations that didn't exist 25 years ago.

In a recent study researchers at Oxford University estimate that up to 45 percent of American jobs are at a high risk of disappearing within the next two decades. In fast-changing environments like this, as the US Office of Management and Budget has observed, regulations "have enormous potential for both good and harm."

The challenge is to exercise due caution on behalf of the public while minimizing any "adverse effects on flexibility and innovation."

The case of Uber shows how tricky this balance is to achieve. As of January 2015, the company was engaged in no fewer than 40 concurrent regulatory conflicts around the world. Ordinary citizens may love having an alternative to taxis, but their governments are not giving the service a free ride.

One of the longest running issues had been the classification of Uber drivers as independent contractors rather than employees, which has led to legal battles over workers' rights and protections. There have also been concerns raised about passenger safety and security, as well as the impact of Uber on the traditional taxi industry.

In the United Kingdom, the government released a proposal for regulating the use of **AI technologies** in June 2022. This focuses on a "light touch" sectoral approach where guidance, voluntary measures, and sandbox environments (isolated virtual machine in which potentially unsafe software code can execute without affecting network resources or local applications) are encouraged as a means to assess and test AI technologies before they are marketed.

Regulatory frameworks are being challenged on several fronts – for example

- **Speed of change** – effective regulation depends upon the regulators' understanding of the solutions being offered by businesses, their efficacy, and their possible unintended consequences. Constant innovation makes that very difficult e.g. regulators are confronted with the exponential expansion of digital information assets "big data". This flood of data combined with ever-sharper analytics allows the discovery of previously unseen patterns and behaviours. Businesses can personalise marketing to better engage consumers, challenging privacy. Traditional means of protecting privacy were not designed for an automated, digital world where much is seen and monitored without explicit consent.
- **Innovators find "back doors"** e.g. Uber has attempted to find legitimate ways around regulatory hurdles which have governed taxis and liveries for ages, including stringent controls over taxi medallions and the licensing fees dictating their ownership and transfer. Uber is a system that helps people access transportation, affordably, fast, and reliably. It is about making life easier for potentially millions of people, and regulation has to be rethought to ensure that it is consumer-safe and socially beneficial, rather than stifle innovation.
- **Ecosystems evolve** and new and clever business models proliferate, the sheer diversity of competitors and competitive modes is yet another complicating factor for regulators. In a market-based economy, a major objective of regulation is preserving an even playing field for competitive businesses. Regulators must set the terms of engagement that will keep these non-comparable entities working in ways that benefit society.
- **Innovations cross lines of jurisdiction** and in business ecosystems, product definitions, market boundaries, the traditional distinction between digital and physical goods blur. These blurring lines complicate the decision as to which agency or authority has jurisdiction?

Test your understanding 3

The Competition and Markets Regulator (CMR) of Newlandia is tasked with regulating the activities of firms within that country. The regulators are finding it increasingly difficult to regulate the activities of organisations who choose to participate in a 'business ecosystem'.

Required:

Identify which THREE of the following are major challenges to the CMR as a result of firms taking an ecosystem approach.

- New legislation is expensive to develop
- Speed of change
- Date protection is a major issue
- Ecosystems evolve
- Innovations cross lines of jurisdiction

8 What does the digital customer want?

In the context of the syllabus component outcomes, it is vital that organisations understand the changes in the way that markets and competition will be affected by the development of the concept of business ecosystems.

Organisations need to understand the critical elements of these changes, how key stakeholders interact with each other and how they will impact the organisation.

According to the World Economic Forum/Accenture analysis, there are a number of factors that drive customer demands in the digital era. These include the following:

- **Contextualised interactions** – this is a rather complicated way of saying that customers expect a product or service that is tailored to their own specific needs. The video streaming service Netflix helps meets this demand by making recommendations on programmes that are likely to be of interest to the viewer based on historic patterns.
- **Seamless experience across channels** – from being made aware that a product or service exists, to doing the research about the product or service, to then taking the decision to purchase, customers expect a seamless service throughout the process. This can also be extended to how the customer pays and takes delivery of the goods.
- **Anytime, anywhere** – there is an expectation of being able to access real time information about a product or service. This does not just mean characteristics of the product; it also relates to inventory levels, how soon delivery will occur, the ability to track progress etc.

- **Great service** (it doesn't matter who provides it) – there is less instance these days of customers remaining loyal to a provider following an example of poor service. Customers are prepared to shop around for products or services if they have had a bad experience.
- **Self-service** – customers are prepared to invest more time and energy into getting exactly what they want. This doesn't simply mean customising the features of an existing product; it may mean developing new models that correspond exactly to their needs. Innovations such as 3D printing are an example of just how this is becoming possible.
- **Transparency** – the digital customer expects to have full transparency of information about a product or service before they commit to a purchase. This includes details such as precise features of the product, but also extends to how personal information is to be collected and used. Customers are protective of their personal data and want choice in deciding whether or not it is shared.
- **Peer review and advocacy** – there is greater instance these days of customers attaching more importance to independent reviews of products or services than to marketing information provided by the business or reviews from other organisations (such as trade journals). The purchase decision will be influenced by what fellow customers have said, meaning that a poor review can have a disastrous effect on future sales potential.

  For example, many customers on Amazon place great store by the reviews and star ratings attached to products that have been bought by other people. Similarly, the decision on which hotel to stay at or restaurant to eat at could well be determined by comments on sites such as Booking.com or Trip Advisor.

  It is also estimated that bad reviews are seen by twice as many people as good reviews.

8.1 Keeping ahead of customer expectations

The question must therefore be asked: given that customer demands are evolving at such a rapid pace, how can organisations adapt so that they keep up with, or preferably ahead of, those expectations? A seemingly successful offering today could rapidly fall out of favour and lead to a reversal of the organisation's competitive advantage.

This can be avoided via the following:

- **Design thinking** – instead of designing a single product or service that can be marketed to many customers, there should be a shift in mind-set to designing many experiences for one customer. This must be mixed with the ability to constantly learn and adapt as customer needs change.

- **Experiential pilots** – this refers to the need to monitor how customers behave and to gain an appreciation of their reaction to new experiences. Questions should be asked such as "How are the customers responding to a new technology in the way they engage with it? How are customers being influenced by others? What reactions, emotional and behavioural, are we seeing through the new customer experience?"

  The organisation should be prepared to continuously take products to a new level, through innovation and developing prototypes, to be able to gauge such reactions.

- **Prototyping** – instead of waiting until a new product has been perfected before bringing it to market, an organisation should recognise that speed to market is vital. So, the first generation of a product may be only about 80% ready, but it provides vital feedback in terms of customer reactions and what needs to be done with the second version.

- **Brand atomisation** – organisations will need to design their offerings so that they can be more widely distributed and be part of the platform that is offered by other providers.

Test your understanding 4

The 'digital revolution' (sometimes known as Web 3.0) is a response to the changing expectations of customers, very often driven by advances in technology.

Required:

Identify which THREE of the following are technological advances driving change in this way.

- Increased demand for fast service provision
- Data analytics and the cloud
- Reduction in hardware cost
- Global Internet access
- Increased numbers of connected devices

Test your understanding 5

Discussion question

X is a retailer of clothes in country A.

Categorise the following issues identified by the Board of A as sources of risk facing X in the light of the increasing volatility and rate of change in the global market.

A Unemployment levels in country A

B Change of government

C Education levels

D Changing fashions

E Changing tax regimes

F Increased use of automation in production

G Shift in customer attitudes towards ethical consumerism

H Requirement for faster service provision

I Data, storage and analytics facilities increased

J Reduction in cost of IT hardware

K Increased Internet access

L Proliferation of connected devices

9 Managing in a "New World" of Business Ecosystems

As we noted earlier, the rise of business ecosystems is forcing leading organisations to think and act very differently. As ecosystems continue to develop, more will be learned but this ongoing process of learning and development is not new.

For example, in the late 1960s the standards for many business professions were agreed but continue to evolve, and then it took a further 20 years for the basic models and frameworks of "business strategy" to be developed e.g. the work of Michael Porter referred to earlier in this chapter.

Managing in this "new World" will present new challenges in terms of the risks and costs associated with success. Some examples of these are:

9.1 Creating value

Long-standing boundaries and constraints that have traditionally determined the evolution of business are dissolving, allowing new ecosystem possibilities to flourish. However, as these boundaries blur, the options for creating value are increasing substantially; "winning" increasingly requires collaboration as well as competition with others; essential capabilities need not necessarily be owned or directly controlled.

9.2 Capturing value

Capturing value is becoming more challenging, often requiring the creation of new business models. This means business strategies must be increasingly flexible and capable of rapid adaptation.

Successful business strategy will remain dependent on setting clear objectives, making well-informed and integrated choices regarding available options and developing the essential capabilities to support these ambitions.

Business leaders will have to adopt new approaches to strategy, for example, approaches to strategy are likely to evolve as a consequence of technological changes, in a variety of ways that are already becoming evident. Similarly, more emphasis will be placed on designing and renewing business models that take fuller account of the importance of relationships outside the firm.

For example, The Internet of Things (IoT), 3D printing, and other technologies are driving a further blurring of the physical and digital worlds. Further transformations are likely as lifelike digital worlds become increasingly accessible through virtual reality technology.

9.3 Creating value and society

Participating in evolving ecosystems will necessitate new alliances to address major pressing societal challenges or "wicked problems" through new solutions, generating both profits and social value at the same time.

Illustration 14 – Unilever

Market development, a traditional strength of great firms, has been well documented over the years in, for example, the sales of hygiene products. So it is perhaps no surprise that Unilever would spot the missing market responsible for the deaths of some 1.5 million children a year by severe and chronic diarrhoea.

The prevention, of course—known for centuries now—is hand-washing. HUL, Unilever's subsidiary in India, knew it had a product capable of saving lives. The problem was that even simple bars of soap were unaffordable to families earning less than a dollar a day. **The solution was to engage an entire ecosystem.**

Once the NGOs, banks, and schools concerned with keeping India's poor healthy agreed on the health benefits of cleansing products, they collectively created the market for them—while also lifting women from poverty with microloans and jobs, improving public health and sanitation, enhancing public health awareness through educational campaigns, and more.

For Unilever, making more soap-buying possible is "a marketing program with social benefits." The company now has over 50,000 women selling its products in more than 635,000 villages, making rural India a $100 million-plus market for Unilever.

These "wicked problems" of the world (such as in the example above) can therefore be addressed. It will however require decision makers and stakeholders who are committed not only to business success but also to achieving social goals and are able to work effectively with external partners to do so.

It will similarly rely on investors who are open to taking the broadest view of challenges, and willing to convene the whole of the community seeking to overcome them. It will also take government leaders who see the potential of prizes and challenges, social impact bonds, and pay-for-success approaches to spur innovation, and the power of using large-scale procurement and supply chains (see later) to create markets for them.

9.4 Regulation

As ecosystems enable more rapid, innovation, regulators will be challenged to create policies and solutions that protect the public's interests but which are also flexible enough to keep pace with innovation. This will be a tough challenge and will necessitate maintaining an effective balance between protecting the public's interest and enabling the new markets and solutions which fast-evolving ecosystems make possible.

Effective regulation depends upon the regulators' understanding of the solutions being offered by businesses, their efficacy, and their possible unintended consequences. Constant innovation makes that very hard. To respond to innovation, and also to enable it, regulatory bodies must find ways to act with greater agility, historically difficult for bureaucracies.

Regulators will need to recognise that future customers will wish for constant improvement as well as scrupulous policing of any new innovations. The regulatory "mind-set" or the basic rules followed by policy makers will need to evolve in this context as although innovation, dynamism, and flexibility come to matter to our society so will its desires for stability, control, and compliance. This will inevitably create a need for new skills and capabilities on regulatory teams.

9.5 Delivering value – supply chains

A conglomeration of changes and developments have worked together to help transform the business environment, resulting in changes to the way that supply chains are configured. In this way their strategic significance has been increased creating new leadership issues and decisions for the years ahead.

Supply chains are increasingly referred to as "value webs" which span and connect whole ecosystems of suppliers and collaborators. These "value webs" when properly activated can play a critical role in reshaping business strategy and delivering superior results. "Value webs" can be more effective by reducing costs, improving service levels, mitigating risks of disruption, and delivering feedback-fuelled learning and innovation.

The development of these webs is likely to accelerate as new technologies generate more data, provide greater transparency, and enable enhanced connectivity with a wider range of suppliers and business partners. This change will create new challenges for the supply chain profession but also extraordinary opportunities for them to play a central strategic role in shaping the future of business ecosystems.

Advances in information and communications technologies have drastically reduced the transaction costs of dealing with outside entities, so that, many assets that had made sense to own and activities traditionally performed in-house were now often better sourced from external suppliers.

This reduction of corporate dependence on ownership of key assets contributed to the creation and development of many new external resources and capabilities and an explosion of new actors ready and able to contribute. New technological developments, continuous innovation and global dissemination of new technologies are directly enabling new connectivity, collaboration, and co-creation across multiple businesses.

For example, as previously noted the rise of the Internet of Things (IoT) is greatly enhancing the creation of and access to data, and producing ever-increasing transparency. Substantial technological changes unfolding today in manufacturing, including 3D printing and new robotics, are set to transform many production processes and may significantly disrupt today's distribution models.

The speed and scale of these changes are creating new opportunities for many supply chain professionals and also putting increased pressure on them to adapt. They are being positioned as increasingly strategic leaders discovering fundamentally different ways of creating and delivering new value, driving continuous innovation and learning, and sustaining enterprise growth.

Since their inception, supply chains have generally been tightly associated with risk management and business continuity planning. It is important to note that this emphasis on collaboration is an addition to, not a replacement of, traditionally more closed, contractual arrangements. Clear commitments to meet rigorously regulations, monitored standards and service-level agreements will remain critical.

Having said that, globally extended production and distribution arrangements are often subject to risk factors beyond anyone's control, for example political events to natural disasters.

Illustration 15 –Dachangjiang

Chinese motorcycle manufacturer Dachangjiang deliberately pursued both value web and supply chain arrangements by breaking its design into multiple modules, awarding several suppliers responsibility and substantial latitude for each, and actively encouraging collaboration between them to promote innovation, while also imposing aggressive performance targets regarding pricing, quality, and timing of production.

9.6 Delivering value – assets

Firms have traditionally used mergers and acquisitions (M&A) to accelerate their entry into new businesses and markets and to build their competitive strengths. Business ecosystem thinking is making strategists value assets differently, and think differently about whether those assets need to be owned.

The traditional reasons for such strategic options has focused on some key business goals e.g. synergy, market share, cross selling, economies of scale, tax advantages, geographical expansion, diversification, and vertical integration. Similarly, firms have also always sold assets, The traditional, rationale for selling has often been as simple as the need to raise cash or remove a chronically underperforming business.

Largely due to fast evolving technologies enabling information flow and communications, options have increased for firms to make productive use of assets with or without owning them. Those options are further developed by for example, market transparency, and IP protection which allow ecosystems to take shape, often reconfiguring entire industries as they do. The "transaction costs" that once made it uneconomical to buy many components from outside suppliers have also dropped dramatically.

In the current ecosystem environment, a management team can decide to produce a specific solution for a customer with elements procured from specialist firms, with very little capital investment required on their own firm's part, saving considerable costs.

This flexibility has however brought with it further changes. Due-diligence reviews of proposed acquisitions now take on many new kinds of questions and risks. Transactions need to be assessed in terms of more complex ecosystem consequences, for example a traditional acquisition involved a detailed review of the performance of the target business, coupled with an assessment of the future cash flow benefits. Pursuing an ecosystem strategy may need the organisation to conduct more sophisticated assessments, exploring how any new acquisition (or divestment) might affect the health and productivity of an ecosystem and the firm's position within it.

9.7 Delivering value – building platforms

Business platforms can help create and capture new economic value and scale the potential for learning across entire ecosystems.

What is a platform?

Platforms help to make resources and participants more accessible to each other on an as-needed basis. Properly designed, they can become powerful catalysts for rich ecosystems of resources and participants.

A couple of key elements come together to support a well-functioning platform:

- A governance structure, including a set of protocols that determines who can participate, what roles they might play, how they might interact, and how disputes get resolved.
- An additional set of protocols or standards is typically designed to facilitate connection, coordination, and collaboration.

Platforms are increasingly supported by global digital technology infrastructures that help to scale participation and collaboration, but this is an enabler, rather than a prerequisite, for a platform.

For example In the early development of Li & Fung's platform for the apparel industry, it relied on very limited technology, largely the telephone and fax machine, and instead focused on defining the protocols and standards that made it possible to deploy a loosely coupled, modular approach to business process design.

In the past, sellers have been limited by the economics of production and distribution to "push based approaches," meaning that they simply made an efficient batch size of what they sold and placed it onto the marketplace. This "push based" strategy depended on anticipating what the customer demand might be, using that to create a sales forecast, and then procuring the right resources and people to produce the appropriate quantity of goods.

A push-based approach is as such very efficient if the forecast is accurate and can be profitable if the marketer is able to alter demand with its pricing and advertising. In the "new World", these constraints have however become much bigger problems.

The deployment of digital technology infrastructures and the long-term public policy trend globally toward economic liberalisation, are long-term trends which have been transforming the business landscape and are essentially eliminating the conditions in which push-based approaches can work.

The cost of three core digital technology capabilities, computing power, data storage, and bandwidth relative to their performance has been decreasing exponentially and at a faster rate than that of previous technological advances such as electricity and telephones. At the same time, global trade has increased at about 7 percent per annum on average (or twice the growth rate of global GDP) for almost three decades.

Together, these produce what Deloitte's Centre for the Edge call "The Big Shift." or a period of time in which the foundations that everything is built upon are reshaped, and potentially changes.

These changes will reorient operations such that nothing happens until actual demand signals are received from real buyers. Business leaders' must enable the "pull-based" approaches which have long been seen as the future of serving customers profitably and for sellers to move to pull-based approaches.

Students of lean manufacturing and pull-based inventory systems know the theory and have seen the advantages that can be gained from this reorientation. The full potential of pull-based systems has yet to be realised, because these early efforts have been applied only to small numbers of companies within well-defined supply chains.

Market-spanning platforms offer ways to take these pull-based approaches to scale.

9.8 Delivering value – transforming business

Rethinking the fundamentals of how a business creates and captures value was not a priority in an era of slow change and stable industries, but has now become essential during a time of rapid convergence of enabling technologies, customer desires, and business ecosystems.

Businesses now need to change more frequently and in more fundamental ways. The Deloitte Center for the Edge's Shift Index suggests that they are experiencing intensifying competition, an accelerating pace of change, and growing uncertainty stemming from the increasing frequency of unanticipated extreme events.

Fast, large-scale change is however enormously risky. We often hear stories of audacious initiatives which flew too close to the sun and fell flat, at enormous expense. One often-referenced study concludes that over 70 percent of all major transformation initiatives fail.

Summary diagram

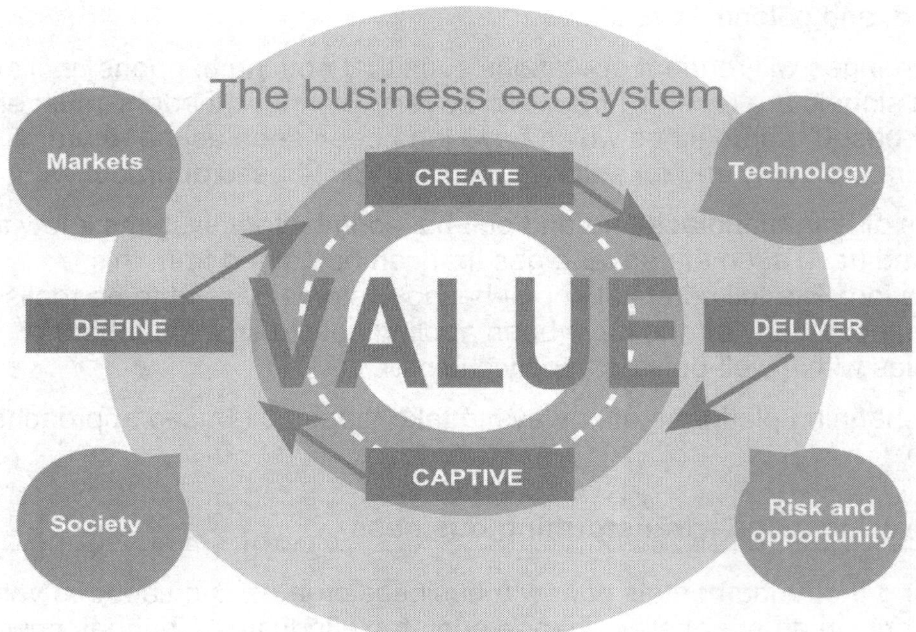

10 Chapter summary

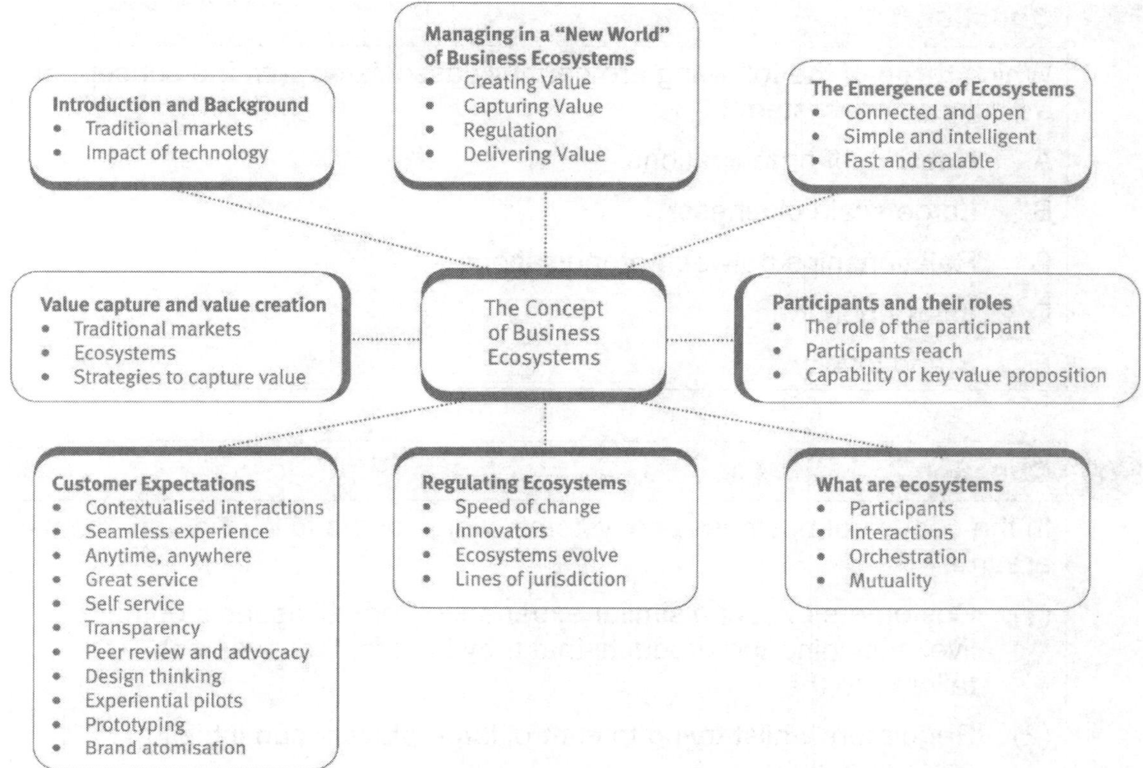

End of chapter questions

Question 1

Which **three** of the following are normally associated with the concept of a business ecosystem?

A Network of organisations

B Large scale business

C Relationships between organisations

D Interdependency

E Brand loyalty

Question 2

In the context of business ecosystems, which of the following statements are true?

(1) Customers expect a similar experience from all aspects of their lives including the products that they buy; fast, convenient and tailored to them.

(2) Regulators whilst trying to control large players can inhibit emerging players.

A (1) only

B (2) only

C Both are true

D Neither are true

Question 3

In the context of value creation in an ecosystem, which of the following statements are true?

(1) Although the value created as a whole maybe greater with collaboration, an individual player will often be worse off.

(2) End to end solutions, where different elements of the supply chain cooperate is likely to create more value for all players.

A (1) only

B (2) only

C Both are true

D Neither are true

Question 4

When buying a train ticket through an orchestrator (such as Trainline), which is usable through any train operator, as far as the train operator is concerned, this is known as:

A Direct value capture

B Indirect value capture

Question 5

The future retail environment is expected to feature ever decreasing barriers to entry and, within the confines of what is safe and legal, players are free to introduce or trade with any product that they wish.

In this situation, which is the recommended strategy?

A Fly with the hornets

B Jump with the sharks

C Roar with the lions

D Dance with the wolves

Test your understanding answers

Example of traditional analysis

Matching items – correct matches	Force	Effect	
A	Bargaining power of suppliers	Remain stable	**3**
B	Bargaining power of customers	Remain stable	**3**
C	Rivalry	Decrease	**2**
D	Threat of new entrants	Decrease	**2**

As Charlton already has mutually-beneficial relationships with customers and suppliers, the adoption of an ecosystem approach is unlikely to have any significant effect on those forces. The most likely impact, if successful, would be to gain Charlton advantage over rivals, as none of them currently take this approach, thus decreasing rivalry. Due to the cost and time involved in establishing an ecosystem approach, a barrier to entry would be created, thus decreasing the threat of new entrants.

Test your understanding 1

Option 1	Interaction	
Option 2	Orchestration	X
Option 3	Mutuality	X
Option 4	Communication	
Option 5	Conflict	

Orchestration and Mutuality are characteristics of an ecosystem. Interaction and Communication would exist in either an ecosystem or a traditional linear supply chain. Conflict would only be a characteristic of a traditional supply chain.

Test your understanding 2

Option 1	Franchising	
Option 2	Ecosystem development	X
Option 3	Upstream supply chain management	
Option 4	Customer relationship management	

A business ecosystem is "an economic community supported by a foundation of interacting organisations and individuals — the organisms of the business world."

Test your understanding 3

Option 1	New legislation is expensive to develop	
Option 2	Speed of change	X
Option 3	Data protection is a major issue	
Option 4	Ecosystems evolve	X
Option 5	Innovations cross lines of jurisdiction	X

Regulatory frameworks are being challenged by ecosystems on several fronts – these include

- Speed of change – effective regulation depends upon the regulators' understanding of the solutions being offered by businesses, their efficacy, and their possible unintended consequences.
- Ecosystems evolve and new and clever business models proliferate, the sheer diversity of competitors and competitive modes is yet another complicating factor for regulators.
- Innovations cross lines of jurisdiction and in business ecosystems, product definitions, market boundaries, the traditional distinction between digital and physical goods blur.

The high cost of new legislation and the need for data protection are both general challenges that are not specific to regulating ecosystems.

Test your understanding 4

Option 1	Increased demand for fast service provision	
Option 2	Data analytics and the cloud	X
Option 3	Reduction in hardware cost	
Option 4	Global Internet access	X
Option 5	Increased numbers of connected devices	X

The following are identified as key factors:

Mobile and internet penetration – the increasing rate of mobile phone ownership, combined with access to the internet (with mobile beginning to exceed broadband).

Connected devices – the number of connected devices are expected to grow from 2.5 billion in 2009 to 30 billion by 2020. This will help enable real-time customisation of products and services.

Data analytics and the cloud – the increasing use of e-commerce platforms, social networks, apps etc. will result in increased need for automated data analytics.

User interfaces – advances in how human beings interact with machines (e.g. through voice recognition or motion-tracking systems) means that carrying out tasks becomes quicker and more efficient for humans.

Global accessibility – rising living standards in developing economies means that more and more people are gaining access to the internet and so increased connectivity.

Increasing urbanisation – the growing percentage of people who live in urban as opposed to rural areas.

The increase in demand for fast service provision is social, NOT technological. Reducing hardware *costs* are financial, NOT technological.

Test your understanding 5

Risks could be categorised as:

A is economic

B is political

C is social

D is social

E is political

F is technological

G is social

H is social

I is technological

J is technological

K is technological

L is technological

Question 1

A, C and D

The terms network, relationships and interdependency are all normally associated with business ecosystems.

Question 2

C

Customer expectations are cross fertilising and what they get in one aspect of their lives is becoming a requirement in others. If we can put a man on the moon then surely we can…….. Regulations tends to react to abuse by large players and any new rules can become too onerous on the smaller emerging businesses.

Question 3

B

Most studies and past experience show that cooperation leads to more value for all.

Question 4

B

The value is captured by a third party and is therefore indirect as far as the train operator is concerned.

Question 5

B

This is a turbulent environment which tends to encourage a highly competitive stance being taken by the players. It has loose orchestration and low complexity.

Chapter

2

Alternative approaches to business models

Chapter learning objectives

Lead	Component
A2: Explain the elements of business models	(a) Concept of value and the business model (b) Defining value (c) Creating value (d) Delivering value (e) Capturing and sharing value

Topics to be covered

- Stakeholders and relevant value
- Stakeholder analysis
- Resources, process, activities and people in creating value
- Products, services, customer segments, channels and platforms to deliver value
- Distribution of value to key stakeholders.

1 Session content diagram

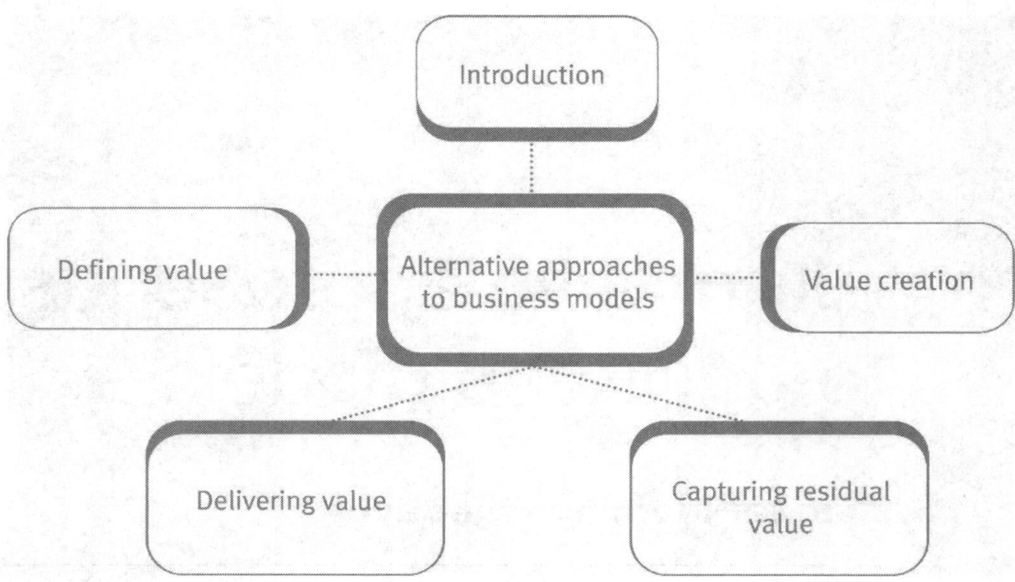

2 Introduction

As we have seen in the earlier chapter, the traditional business model is being challenged by changes in the way business enterprises operate depicted by the business ecosystem.

What is a business model?

According to KPMG any description of the business model must include how the firm is structured, the markets in which it operates, how it engages with those markets, its main products and services, its main categories of customers, and its main distribution methods.

In more common terminology – "Business models are also stories that explain how firms work, including how they make money and how they deliver value to customers at an appropriate cost" (Magretta, 2002).

The Strategy Journey 2020 – Christison and Choo

Developed by Christison and Choo in "The Strategy Journey 2020", the framework is comprised of 5 Models. These models provide the tools and techniques for businesses to navigate their strategy journeys and transform their business operating models in the digital age with value-driven, customer co-created and network-connected services to overcome the transformational challenges that could disrupt and lead to business failure.

The **'Mission Model'** describes the core purpose of an enterprise providing laser focus on the target *mission* that it seeks to achieve, while enabling the business to pull followers and people toward its future *vision*.

The **'Business Model'** describes WHAT constitutes and drives a business, giving it the means to make profit as well as growing the value of the business itself. It encompasses customers, *value propositions,* and details of what makes the business grow.

The **'Value Model'** describes what constitutes value for an enterprise or a customer, encompassing where the value is created, the exchange of value between different stakeholders, and most importantly, how to find new opportunities to create value in the wider global business ecosystem.

The **'Operating Model'** describes HOW the business runs to support the design, build, testing, and delivery of its *value propositions*. Comprising processes, data, technology systems, people and governance of the business's capabilities to operate at a cost to achieve business outcomes.

The **'Transformation Model'** describes the effort in time, resources, costs and the governance of the roadmap associated with the transformation journey of an enterprise, as it executes changes to its capabilities and improves its business agility, for continued value delivery and growth.

Each of the 5 models correspond as enablers to the 5 different stages of the lifecycle of a business, that is, the business's strategy journey.

If this is accepted then the business model depicts not only how a business creates value but also how it delivers value.

The traditional business model therefore has four key aspects:

- **define value** – firms look at who they create value for and what counts as value for them
- **create value** – firms look at how resources are sourced and turned into outputs that customers and others desire
- **deliver value** – firms find ways to get value to those it was created for
- **capture residual value** for themselves and others to share between the firms, their shareholders and others (i.e. stakeholders).

It is important to recognise that each part of the business model is aimed at a wide range of stakeholders.

Stakeholders can be defined in many ways e.g. **Freeman defines stakeholders as "any person or group that can affect or be affected by the policies or activities of an organisation**" and are all in view when firms define value.

It will depend on the industry, business and circumstances as to which stakeholder(s) take priority, although the customer is often prioritised as the most important e.g. in retail.

Those who provide resources and help turn them into outputs (e.g. suppliers and employees) are key when creating value. They also receive value from the firm at the same time. Customers are the ones to whom value is delivered.

The firm captures residual value to share among the providers of financial capital, government, senior executives and for reinvestment. The parts of the business model are linked and aligned to each other.

Value is therefore at the heart of business models and can be:

- **Financial or non-financial** and must be differentiated from price, cost, profit or cash flow. These are related concepts but they are not the same as value but they are important because they act as measures or stores of value.
- **Tangible and intangible** e.g. the move from an industrial economy to a knowledge- and information-based economy increased the importance of intangible value to firms.
- Value affects **the past present and the future**. Past value is often used in reporting, present value in operational management and future value in investment appraisal.
- **Short term and the long term** the short term is important because firms must survive for them to have any long-term prospects. However, short-term value must not undermine long-term value.

High level depiction of a business model.

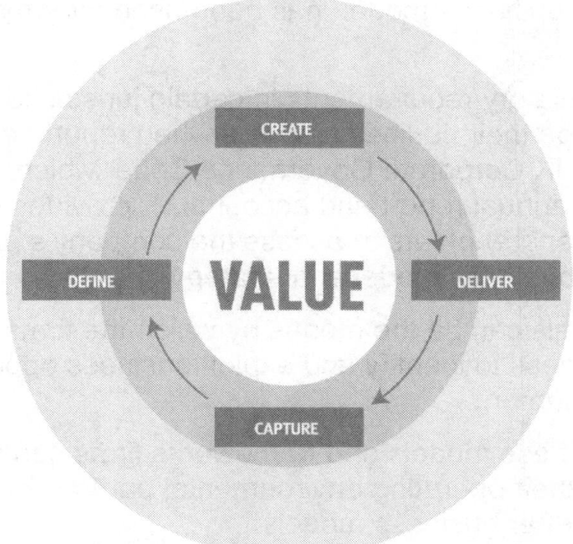

Illustration 1 – Tesco

Tesco's business model has four parts that correspond to the four parts of the business model above:

1 **Customers:** "Tesco exists to serve customers and our business model has customers as our number one priority. Our scale and reach mean we have the expertise to really understand our customers; allowing us to focus on the delivery of an offer with real value in all areas of price, quality, range and service. This focus means that we will champion our customers at every level and earn their loyalty." (Define value).

2 **Product:** "The product we create for customers is developed by our product team. They work with our suppliers to source the best possible range of quality products that meet and anticipate our customers' needs. Our relationships with suppliers are crucial to meeting our customer offer."(Create value).

3 **Channels:** "To bring the best products to customers easily, we work through a range of channels … As part of improving our offer we will invest in making our channels even more efficient and convenient for our customers." (Deliver value).

4 **Reinvest:** "Our clear priority is to improve Tesco for customers. As we do this, we have committed to reinvest any savings or outperformance into further improvements in our shopping trip." (Capture value).

In summary:

The concept of the "business model" has been used over many decades for three main reasons.

- Legal and regulatory requirements in certain jurisdictions require some firms to describe their business models when reporting to shareholders. For example, UK Corporate Governance Code, which requires directors to "state that the annual report and accounts … provides the information necessary for shareholders to assess the company's position and performance, business model and strategy".
- Business models can be the means by which the firms create long-term value and success to identify and exploit business opportunities in the external environment.
- By the use of these models and frameworks firms can respond to disruptions in their operating environments, particularly from firms who have new or better business models.

Test your understanding 1

The 'digital revolution' (sometimes known as Web 3.0) is a response to the changing expectations of customers, very often driven by advances in technology, which can change or influence the business model.

Required:

Identify which **THREE** of the following are technological advances driving change in this way.

- Increased demand for fast service provision
- The Cloud and data analytics
- Reduction in hardware cost
- Global Internet access
- Increased numbers of connected devices world wide

3 Defining value

Before creating value firms have to decide who they are creating value for, with and why. Firms therefore create value with providers of resources and services for the benefit of their customers in order to earn returns for their investors while acting within the law.

To do this firms identify their stakeholders, specify their roles and prioritise them in terms of the firms response to the "stakeholder claim" i.e. the demands that the stakeholder makes of an organisation. They essentially 'want something' from an organisation (see section 3).

3.1 Stakeholder Analysis

The traditional approach to stakeholder analysis is depicted by the use of Mendelow's Matrix:

Stakeholder mapping: The Mendelow model

Interest			
Power		Low	High
	Low	Minimal Effort	Keep informed
	High	Keep Satisfied	Key Players

Stakeholder identification is necessary to gain an understanding of the sources of risks and disruption. It is important in terms of assessing the sources of influence over the objectives and outcomes for the business decisions or projects (such as identified in the Mendelow model).

In strategic analysis, stakeholder influence is assessed in terms of each stakeholder's power and interest, with higher power and higher interest combining to generate the highest influence.

There is similarly a moral case for knowledge of how decisions affect stakeholders both internal and external to the organisation.

Mendelow model

The matrix was designed to track interested parties and evaluate their viewpoint in the context of some change in business strategy.

Power relates to the amount of influence (or power) that the stakeholder group can have over the organisation. However, the fact that a group has power does not necessarily mean that their power will be used.

The **level of interest** indicates whether the stakeholder is actively interested in the performance of the organisation. The amount of influence the group has depends on their level of power.

Low interest – low power

These stakeholders typically include small shareholders and the general public. They have low interest in the organisation primarily due to lack of power to change strategy or influence corporate governance.

High interest – low power

These stakeholders would like to affect the strategy or influence corporate governance of the organisation but do not have the power to do this. Stakeholders include staff, customers and suppliers, particularly where the organisation provides a significant percentage of sales or purchases for those organisations. Environmental pressure groups would also be placed in this category as they will seek to influence company strategy, normally by attempting to persuade high power groups to take action.

Low interest – high power

These stakeholders normally have a low interest in the organisation, but they do have the ability to affect strategy and/or influence corporate governance should they choose to do so. Stakeholders in this group include the national government and in some situations institutional shareholders. The latter may well be happy to let the organisation operate as it wants to, but will exercise their power if they see their stake being threatened.

High interest – high power

These stakeholders have a high interest in the organisation and have the ability to affect strategy and/or influence corporate governance. Stakeholders include directors, major shareholders and trade unions.

Applying the concept of value to stakeholder analysis however engenders a slightly different approach.

Critical to the decision and action to create value, it is vital that organisations decide who they are creating value for, with whom and why they are so doing.

To do this a firm may apply a four step to this process:

- **Identify** the stakeholders for and with whom they seek to create value. For example customers, suppliers, shareholders etc.
- **Prioritise** and rank the stakeholders. (NB for most firms, the customer is given the highest priority).
- **Establish and identify** the needs of the high priority stakeholders.
- **Formulate value propositions** that meet the needs of the high priority stakeholders.

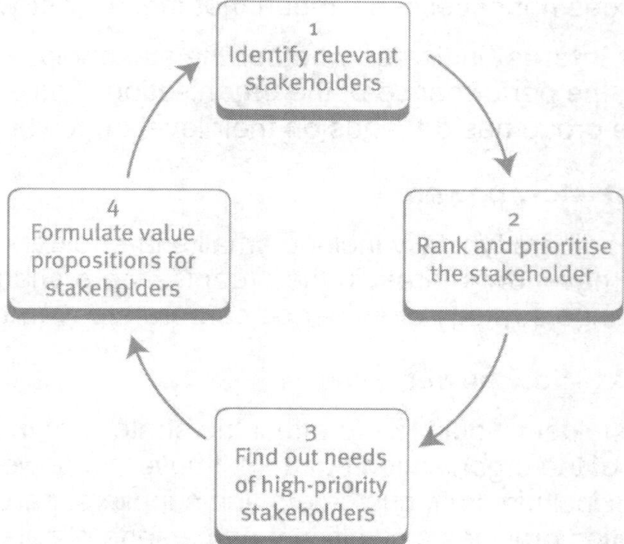

Each stakeholder is ranked on the following attributes:

- Power – ability to impose their will
- Legitimacy – according to the norms and values of the firm and society
- Urgency – the need for immediate action in the light of a stakeholder claim.

Once they have been identified and ranked, the needs of the stakeholders, their contribution and benefit to the firm can be established.

For example:

- Customers – need good services and experiences, they contribute loyalty and the benefit to the firm is financial (higher revenue) and non-financial (enhanced brand value).
- Suppliers – need custom, loyalty and cash flow, they contribute resources and the benefit to the firm is resource availability and lower cost of sales.
- Investors – need an appropriate risk-adjusted return on investment.

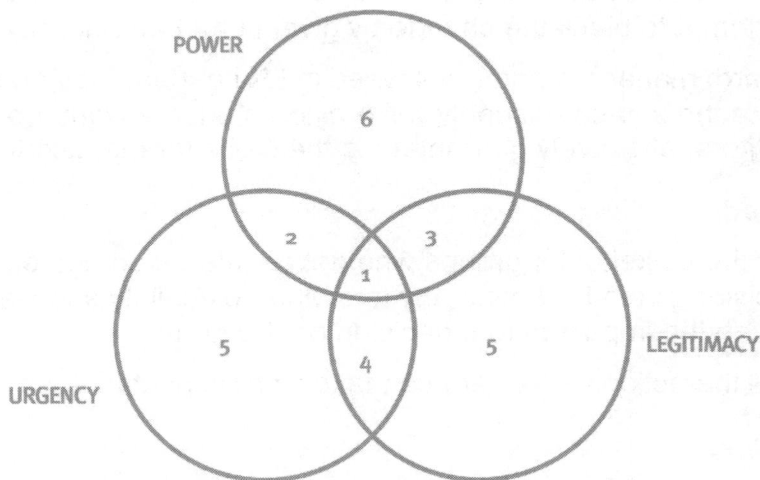

Based on the identification of needs (examples above) stakeholders are then prioritised (indicated by the numbers in the above diagram) as to how these relevant stakeholders affect or can be affected by business decisions. The process therefore aims to identify those stakeholders that are critical for business success.

Test your understanding 2 – Discussion question

The LKJ company is a distributor of electricity in a large country. In effect, LKJ purchases electricity from companies making electricity and then distributes this through a network of cables to companies and private individuals throughout the country. Electricity is generated from a variety of sources including burning coal and natural gas, nuclear power and a small amount from renewal resources such as wind and wave power.

LKJ's shares are owned by three other companies, who take an active interest in the profitability of LKJ. There are three other electricity distribution companies in the country LKJ operates in.

The board of LKJ are currently considering the proposal to purchase electricity from another country. This source of supply is quoted as being cheaper from those within LKJ's home country, although the electricity is generated by burning coal. If this supply is taken, LKJ will stop purchasing electricity from an old nuclear power station and some of the expensive wind power plants. The Clean-Earth environmental group has learnt of the proposal and is currently participating in a media campaign in an attempt to block the change by giving LKJ bad publicity.

The board, managers and employees in LKJ appear indifferent, although changing the source of supply will provide a price advantage over LKJ's competitors, effectively guaranteeing their jobs for the next few years.

Required:

Identify the stakeholder groups who will be interested and/or affected by the decision of the LKJ company to change electricity suppliers, evaluating the impact of that decision on the group.

Discuss the actions the board can take with respect to each stakeholder group.

(15 minutes)

4 Value creation

The creation of value is a common theme in the description of the purpose of business models.

For example – the FRC definition supports this assumption by defining business models as "how the entity generates or preserves value over the longer term".

In this context as we have noted in section 1 value is:

- financial or non-financial
- tangible and intangible
- not limited to the past
- covers both the short term and the long term.

Value however is also **about people**. It is about how their needs are met. It is created by people, with people and for people. Value goes beyond shareholder value to **creating shared value**.

For example, organisations such as Nestlé now produce shared value reports annually indicating that value is co-created by different stakeholders and not just the domain of shareholders.

Illustration 2 – Nestle Shared Value Report 2019 (Extract)

Creating Shared Value is about ensuring long-term sustainable value creation for shareholders while tackling societal issues at the same time. Companies that create shared value demonstrate that business can be a force for good.

We focus our work on three interconnected impact areas: the individuals and families who place their trust in our products and brands; the communities where we operate; and the planet.

We are driven by our purpose to enhance quality of life and contribute to a healthier future.

Our 2030 ambitions are:

- For individuals and families, to help 50 million children lead healthier lives.
- For our communities, to improve 30 million livelihoods in communities directly connected to our business activities.
- For the planet, to strive for zero environmental impact in our operations.

In order to achieve these ambitions, we have formulated a series of public commitments that we operationalize across our business. We report on our progress every year. Particular emphasis is on global initiatives to promote healthier lives for children, help young people access economic opportunities and demonstrate our protection of water resources. We also act decisively to tackle the current plastic pollution challenge and are working to become carbon neutral.

Our purpose

Nestlé's purpose is enhancing quality of life and contributing to a healthier future.

Our approach creates value not only for our business, but also for individuals and families, for our communities and for the planet.

Creating value

Within the boundaries of cost control, there are five key elements that must connect and align to create value at an appropriate cost. By way of comparison this can be referred to as the operating model of the firm.

- **Partners** – these include suppliers, employees, contractors and other partners (high priority stakeholders) who provide access to resources, markets and technologies. Firms must build relationships, earn their trust and reward them appropriately for their contribution to value creation.

  According to PwC, firms need to orchestrate the interactions of both the different players in their operating environment and the customers to maximise the value delivered, make money out of that for all players and give the firms a fair share of that value. The key performance drivers are relationship management and trust building.

Illustration 3 – Unilever

Unilever used its Partner to Win programme to enhance partner relationships. Its "2015 Strategic Report" stated the following: "We work with our partners in our supply chain, through our Partner to Win programme, to create innovations in products and packaging. 69 per cent of our innovations are associated with supplier-sourced technology".

Unilever's Partner with Purpose (UPWP) programme, which launched in 2020, is taking purpose-led partnerships to a whole new level to fuel industry-leading innovations, protect and regenerate nature and make sustainable living commonplace.

Unilever stated – "UPWP is an evolution in the way we partner that allows us to continually respond to new and emerging consumer trends. We are getting even closer to our partners through this programme by encouraging more responsible and transparent innovation to deliver on our ambitious commitments and generate mutual growth together".

- **Resources** – firms use their relationships with their suppliers to source and secure the right resources to make products or services that satisfy their customers. These are both tangible and intangible inputs. For critical resources long-term availability is also a primary objective.

Illustration 4 – SAB Miller

Brewery giant SABMiller identified water as a critical resource. This is how they put it in their 2015 annual report: "Water is fundamental … to SABMiller's value chain ... The accessible supply of freshwater is finite and … both water quantity and quality is in decline as populations surge and demand grows from agriculture, energy generation, industry and households … Many of our breweries are in areas of water risk. To help us better understand the nature and extent of local risk … we launched a bespoke water risk assessment process which … allows us to investigate risks more deeply, building detailed … site-by-site picture of our water exposure

> … The data enables our facilities to identify and prioritise risks and develop mitigation plans."
>
> SABMiller is a founding signatory of the UN CEO Water mandate, an initiative to help companies in the development, implementation and disclosure of water sustainability policies and practices. it is also a member of the World Economic Forum Water Project and the Water Footprinting Network.
>
> SABMiller has developed a water strategy based on the 5rs (protect, reduce, reuse, recycle and redistribute), a comprehensive, risk-based approach to managing water in its business and in the value chain. This model provides a consistent approach, regardless of the local issues and circumstances facing their businesses around the world.

- **Processes** – firms need to design, develop and deploy processes that provide the infrastructure to convert resources (inputs) into goods and services (outputs). High-quality processes can lead to improved cycle times, productivity, quality and costs.

  The balanced scorecard (discussed in Chapter 6) identifies three types of processes that are relevant to this stage: operations management processes, innovation processes and regulatory and social processes.

- **Activities** – firms and their partners engage in activities that use the processes to convert resources into goods and services. They depict what is done and where know-how, skills, learning and culture come together to make things happen, capturing how valuable the people element is in value creation. Effectiveness and efficiency are the key measures of success in this context.

- **Outputs** – resources are converted through activities and processing into outputs which can be products, services and experience, all of which aim to meet the customer value proposition. This is done via the product attributes (including the product features, quality and style/design) and pricing.

  Different combinations of these appeal to different types/segments of customers and the firm must be aware of this.

Examples of the tools and techniques that can be used to analyse ways of creating value are:

- Value chain analysis.
- Supply chain analysis.
- Various costing techniques, e.g. ABC.
- Quality management tools: six sigma, cost of quality.

5 Delivering value

Firms deliver value to customers and earn revenue from customers only when customers receive and/or use the goods and services. It is therefore imperative that firms understand their different customer segments and the channels by which they can reach each of these segments.

Customer segments can be based on any aspect of demographics e.g. gender, geography or social behaviour e.g. income, lifestyle etc.

For example:

Traditional segmentation focuses on identifying customer groups based on a number of variables that include:

- Geographic variables, such as region of the world or country, country size, or climate
- Demographic variables, such as age, gender, sexual orientation, family size, income, occupation, education, socioeconomic status, religion, nationality/race, and others
- Psychographic variables, such as personality, life-style, values and attitudes
- Behavioural variables, such as benefit sought (quality, low price, convenience), product usage rates, brand loyalty, product end use, readiness-to-buy stage, decision-making unit, and others.

Value-based segmentation looks at groups of customers in terms of the revenue they generate and the costs of establishing and maintaining relationships with them.

Whatever method is chosen, the segment must be:

- Measurable and meaningful
- Mutually exclusive
- Stable
- Substantial
- Easy to understand.

Illustration 5 – Bain and Co

Research by consultants Bain and Co suggests that to achieve the greatest benefit from segmentation firms must:

- Divide the market into meaningful and measurable segments according to customers' needs, their past behaviour or their demographic profiles.
- Determine the profit potential of each segment by analysing the revenue and cost impacts of serving each segment.

- Target segments according to their profit potential and the company's ability to serve them in a proprietary way.
- Invest resources to tailor product, service, marketing and distribution programmes to match the need of each target segment.
- Measure performance of each segment and adjust the segmentation approach over time as market conditions change decision-making throughout the organisation.

Channels firms deliver value to customers through communication, distribution and sales channels. In this context the advent and growth of technology has opened up many channels for firms to connect with their customers, for example phones, tablets and social media.

Illustration 6 – M&S

According to M&S "technology continues to shape how customers shop. The proliferation of different channels – stores, online, tablet, mobile – is turning shopping into a seamless experience. Mobile is increasingly the first port of call for consumers' research and the number of shoppers using smartphones to search for clothing has increased by more than half over the past year. Visits to M&S.com via mobile were also up 51 per cent" (M&S "2015 Strategic Report")

In the Annual Report and Financial Statement 2022, M&S stated: "We have nearly doubled our Clothing & Home online penetration from 18% to 34% and driven a focus on M&S app downloads to reach 4m users. The nascent 'Brands at M&S' offer has been established, giving customers more reasons to visit M&S.com.

According to Oracle firms must adopt the following key actions to data on customers

- **Collect** data on customers which may be "locked" in, for example, promotional offers and also differ by channel
- **Clean** the data to gain a complete view of your customer as customer information is often not consistent
- **Connect** every customer interaction across all of your channels
- **Transform** and personalise your customer's journey, deliver the right answers to recognise, personalise and reward your high-value customers

This will hopefully facilitate seamless personalisation of customer needs across the different channels. These channels must be integrated despite their variety and customer expectations.

Failure to connect across all channels will eventually erode the firm's brand reputation, ability to completely satisfy its customers and hence loss of competitive advantage.

Illustration 7 – Oracle Report

An Oracle report on cross-channel customer experience indicated that customers "might start the buying process based on the recommendation of a friend, online product research, or an email or text message offer.

They might then touch and feel the product in a retail store but ultimately buy it from the comfort of their home via a tablet or other device in the small hours of the night."

They expect the buying journey to be relevant and personalised, to reveal consistent features, offers and experiences based on where they've been, what they want and how they choose to get it. On average, Oracle's consumer research shows that more than three-quarters of consumers use two or more channels to browse for, research and purchase products.

More importantly, 85 per cent of shoppers expect a consistent and personalised shopping experience.

In that respect therefore organisations must develop a multi-channel integrative customer model that delivers customer value and a significant return on investment.

Illustration 8 – Deloitte and M&S

A Deloitte (2010) study showed that engaged consumers delivered twice the spend value and three times subsequent sale through advocacy value. Firms earn their revenue when they deliver value to customers through their preferred channels. It is important that the revenue is turned to cash very quickly.

M&S state in their Annual Report and Financial Statement 2022 – "We will offer our customers a truly seamless experience across all our channels wherever we trade around the world, using our data and insight to improve personalisation capability"

The following techniques can be used to facilitate delivering value:

- Segment analysis, identifying common characteristics, allowing the business to segment customers or products into different groups
- Channel profitability, the financial performance of sales channels
- Matrix (channel × product offering) to increase, for example, average order value.
- Customer relationship management to help companies stay connected to customers, streamline processes, and improve profitability.

Test your understanding 3

Anji is considering buying a new laptop. She is doing some Internet research, and has found a site called 'techchoice.com', which contains descriptions of various laptops together with their technical specifications and expert reviews. Anji has been asked to enter details about where she lives, and why she wishes to buy a laptop. As a result, Anji has identified the make and model of laptop she thinks she wishes to purchase, because it precisely meets her needs and is available in her area. The webpage has a link to another site, which provides independent user reviews of that model. There are also links to the relevant pages on the websites of the three retailers in Anji's country currently offering the lowest prices for that model.

According to the World Economic Forum/Accenture analysis, there are a number of factors that drive customer demands in the digital era.

Required:

Examine the above statement and **select which TWO of the following** 'drivers of customer demands in the digital era' are being described.

- Contextualised interaction
- Self-service
- Peer review
- Seamless experience
- Transparency.

6 Capturing and sharing residual value

Value is captured when revenue earned from delivering value exceeds the costs of creating value.

The difference between the two creates a surplus, the size of the surplus will depend on market conditions but will also reflects the decisions made when defining value and the success with which firms execute those decisions.

Firms will share this surplus with stakeholders who contributed to and have been part of the value creation process but have not yet received any value themselves.

There are three main issues to consider when capturing value.

Cost model – this is established when defining value. It is influenced by the value proposition to customers and the partnerships that firms use to create and deliver value.

The total cost will be established by four key factors:

- Efficiency of the processes.
- Levels of activity.
- Resources consumed during activities.
- Price paid for resources.

Revenue model – **r**evenue is earned when goods and services are delivered to customers and any prices charged should accurately reflect the customer segments that the firm addresses, the market conditions in which it trades and any regulatory control in place.

In addition the firm will also need to establish a collection policy which dictates the speed which revenue is converted to cash. Both pricing and collection policy (i.e. terms of trade) are affected by these factors.

Sharing residual value – is based on the principle of creating shared value, which comprises shareholder value and the value delivered to other stakeholders. The priority of these stakeholders will depend on the environment on which they operate. For example:

- government (taxes)
- shareholders (dividends)
- incentives for executives (performance-related pay)
- the firm (retained income for reinvestments).

The sharing has to be sensitive to the interactions in the operating environment avoiding any harm to the firm's reputation, the creation and delivery of further value and will be dependent on the strategy of the firm in terms of for example its bonus schemes, dividend policy and investment opportunities.

The following techniques can be used for capturing and sharing:

- Cash flow and operating cycle modelling/analysis.
- Cost modelling.
- Revenue modelling.
- Incentive analysis.

Conclusion

The traditional business model has been significantly affected by changes in technology, the operating environment of the firm and, as result the strategy that the firm should adopt.

The key aspect is that different parts should connect to and align, both with each other and to the operating environment. Significant misalignment will affect the performance of the organisation.

This new approach is depicted in CIMA's ® business model.

The CIMA Business Model

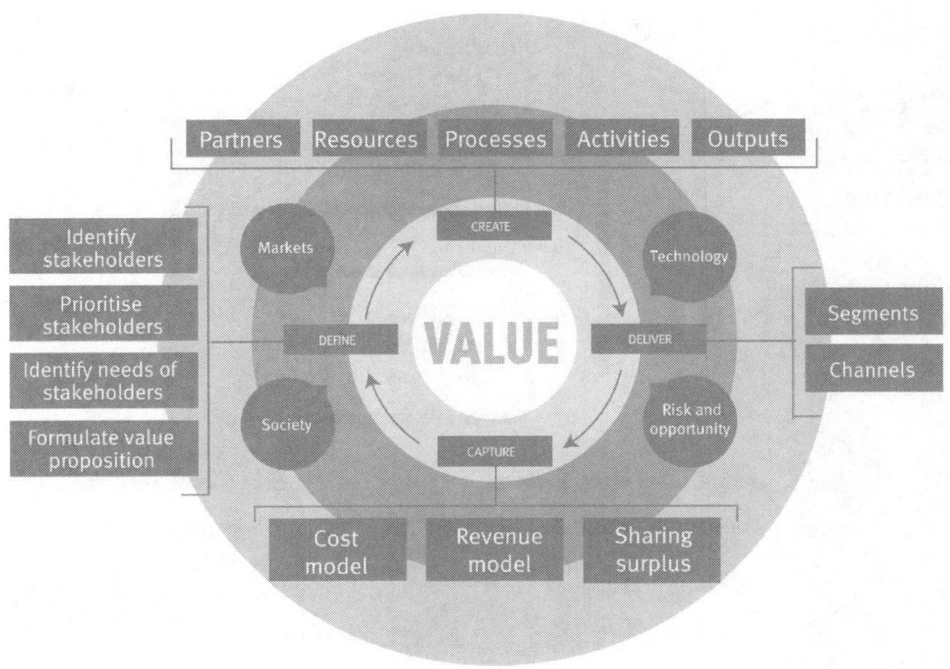

7 Chapter summary

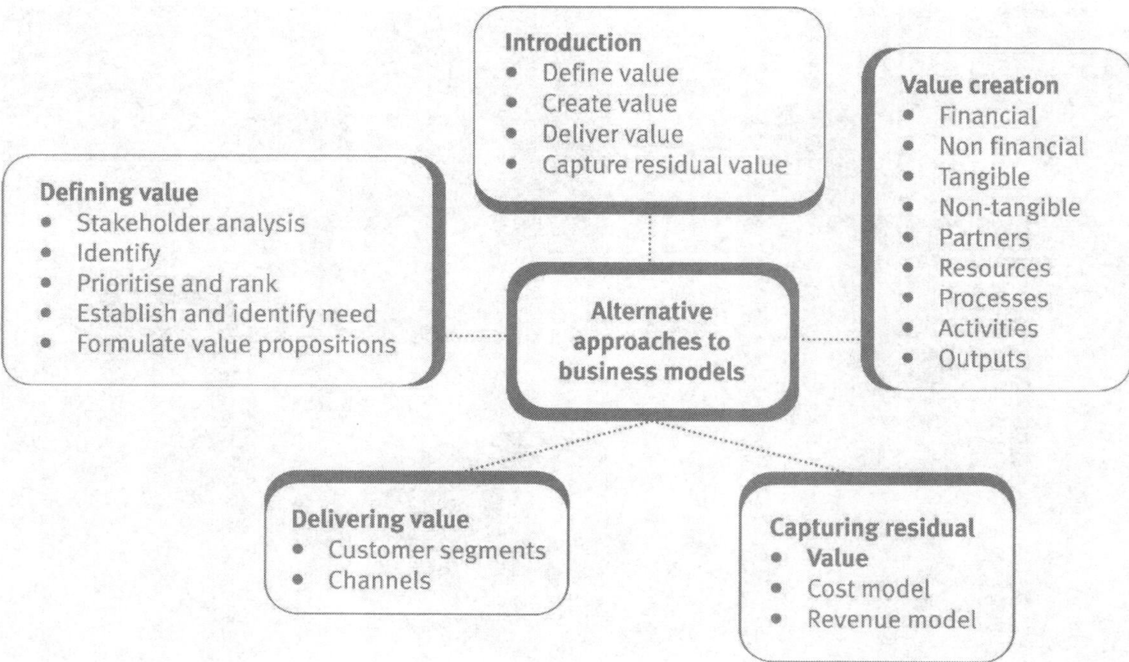
Introduction
Define value
Create value
Deliver value
Capture residual value
Value creation
Financial
Non financial
Tangible
Non-tangible
Partners
Resources
Processes
Activities
Outputs
Defining value
Stakeholder analysis
Identify
Prioritise and rank
Establish and identify need
Formulate value propositions
Alternative approaches to business models
Delivering value
Customer segments
Channels
Capturing residual
Value
Cost model
Revenue model

End of chapter questions

Question 1

An insurance company is regulated by the Financial Conduct Authority, it has many rules that must be obeyed if penalties are to follow.

How should this stakeholder be dealt with within Mendelow's matrix?

A Keep informed

B Obeyed as a key player

C Keep satisfied

D With minimal effort

Question 2

In the diagram below, where, under normal circumstances, should a business focus its value effort?

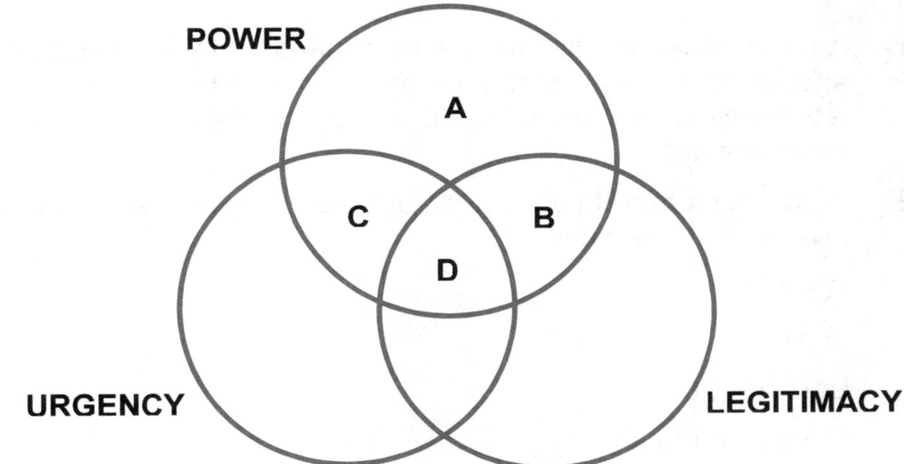

A

B

C

D

Question 3

In relation to value propositions, which of the following statements are true?

(1) Value propositions for principal stakeholders should remain unchanged for long periods to ensure trust is gained.

(2) A good value proposition doesn't have to meet the needs of a stakeholder as long as it is measurable.

A (1) only

B (2) only

C Both are true

D Neither are true

Question 4

In relation to the concept of value, which of the following statements are true?

(1) A short-term reduction in training expenditure will increase profit and so will enhance long term present value of expected future returns where perfect knowledge exists of the reason for the profit improvement.

(2) Businesses report past values but assess future values in investment appraisal.

A (1) only

B (2) only

C Both are true

D Neither are true

Question 5

Match the contribution that each stakeholder would be most likely to make to a successful business:

Stakeholder	Contribution
Customer	Advocacy Know how Capital
Investors	Advocacy Know how Capital
Employees	Advocacy Know how Capital

Test your understanding answers

Test your understanding 1

Option 1	Increased demand for fast service provision	
Option 2	Data analytics and the cloud	X
Option 3	Reduction in hardware cost	
Option 4	Global Internet access	X
Option 5	Increased numbers of connected devices	X

The following are identified as key factors:

Mobile and internet penetration – the increasing rate of mobile phone ownership, combined with access to the internet (with mobile beginning to exceed broadband).

Connected devices – the number of connected devices are expected to grow from 2.5 billion in 2009 to 30 billion by 2020. This will help enable real-time customisation of products and services.

Data analytics and the cloud – the increasing use of e-commerce platforms, social networks, apps etc. will result in increased need for automated data analytics.

User interfaces – advances in how human beings interact with machines (e.g. through voice recognition or motion-tracking systems) means that carrying out tasks becomes quicker and more efficient for humans.

Global accessibility – rising living standards in developing economies means that more and more people are gaining access to the internet and so increased connectivity.

Increasing urbanisation – the growing percentage of people who live in urban as opposed to rural areas.

The increase in demand for fast service provision is social, NOT technological. Reducing hardware costs are financial, NOT technological.

Test your understanding 2 – Discussion question

Large institutional investors

The main strategy of the board regarding a large institutional investor is communication with the need for change followed by participation in strategy determination. Most codes of corporate governance indicate the bi-lateral approach to be taken. The large investor is interested in the success of the organisation while at the same time having the ability to adversely affect the organisation if their shareholding is sold. The organisation must therefore keep the stakeholder informed regarding important strategic decisions. Similarly, there is a responsibility on the part of the stakeholder to take an interest in the activities of the organisation and to use their influence responsibly.

The three investors in LKJ are likely to be keen for the electricity to be purchased from the different country as this will increase the return on their investment.

A dialogue should be established between the chairman and large shareholders, as a minimum by discussion at the annual general meeting. However, more frequent meetings throughout the year are also expected. The chairman needs to ensure that the expectations of return from LKJ are congruent with the investing companies.

Environmental pressure group

The pressure group will attempt to influence other groups with high power to change the strategy of the organisation. The board of LKJ therefore need to communicate with the group with the aim of explaining and educating them in respect of the actions being taken by LKJ.

Currently Clean-Earth are attempting to influence the strategy of LKJ by the media campaign. The basis of this campaign is likely to be the fact that obtaining electricity from coal is more harmful to the environment than renewable sources and possibly nuclear generation. Explanation of the reason for change in terms of increased profit may not, however, be acceptable.

However, the board must be prepared to learn from the pressure. Many pressure groups do have responsible and knowledgeable people within the group. Not to listen may mean that valuable advice and assistance is rejected on grounds of prejudice against this type of stakeholder. While it is likely that advice from the group will be biased towards renewable resources, they may have ideas regarding cost efficiency that LKJ can use.

Directors/managers/employees of LKJ

The directors of LKJ are stakeholders in the organisation. In terms of corporate governance, they have the responsibility to act in the best interests of the company and its shareholders. In this sense, there is no conflict in the decision to source electricity supplies from another country; LKJ profits are forecast to increase while there is job security for the directors. While the directors have high power and interest in LKJ, this power appears to be being used correctly.

Similarly, the actions of the directors appears to meet the requirements of the managers and employees of LKJ in that their jobs are protected.

However, the environmental impact of their action may be a cause for concern. If LKJ, and therefore the directors, are considered not to be acting ethically then customers may choose alternative suppliers. This action will mean that the profit forecasts are incorrect and the directors may need to consider alternative courses of action.

Test your understanding 3

Option 1	Contextualised interaction	X
Option 2	Self-service	
Option 3	Peer review	
Option 4	Seamless experience	X
Option 5	Transparency	

According to the World Economic Forum/Accenture analysis:

From being made aware that a product or service exists, to doing the research about the product or service, to then taking the decision to purchase, customers expect a seamless service throughout the process. This can also be extended to how the customer pays and takes delivery of the goods. This is known as **'seamless experience across channels'**.

Contextualised interaction means that customers expect a product or service that is tailored to their own specific needs. The video streaming service Netflix helps meets this demand by making recommendations on programmes that are likely to be of interest to the viewer based on historic patterns.

Question 1

C

Although the rules must be obeyed Mendelow defined a regulator as having low levels of interest (unless provoked) and high levels of power and should therefore be kept satisfied.

Question 2

D

Under normal circumstances the correct answer is D. Clearly there are situations where an urgent situation arises and might take precedence for example.

Question 3

D

We live in a VUCA environment with change part of our almost daily lives and whilst consistency is important the focus might have to change regularly. Meeting the needs of a stakeholder is paramount, making something measurable is a "nice to have".

Question 4

B

A short term profit improvement in a perfect knowledge environment is likely to damage expected long-term future returns.

Question 5

The correct match ups are:

Customer – Advocacy

Investors – Capital

Employees – Know how

Chapter

3

Business models in digital ecosystems

Chapter learning objectives

Lead	Component
A3: Analyse new business models in digital ecosystems	(a) Analyse digital business models and their related operating models

Topics to be covered

- Disruption
- Ways to build disruptive and resilient business models
- Creating digital operating models
- Types of digital operating models.

1 Session content diagram

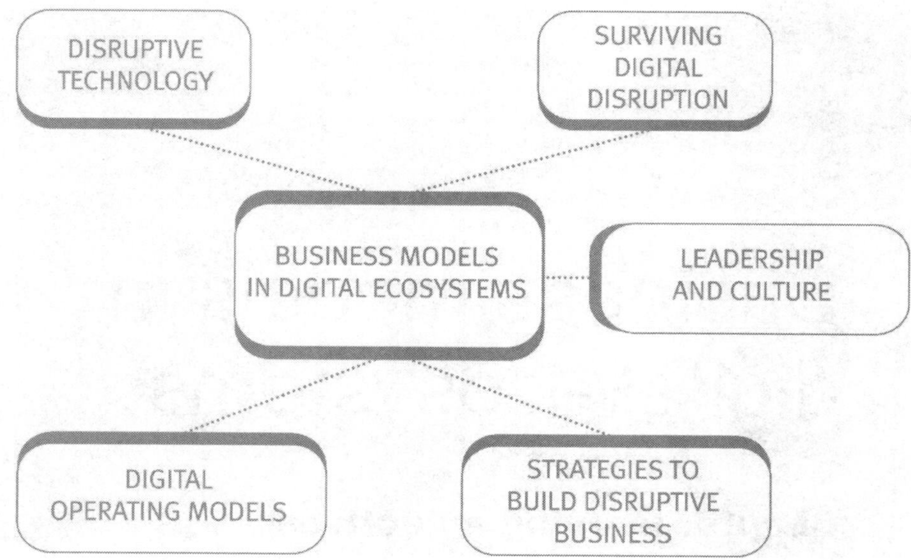

2 Introduction

Throughout the preceding chapters, reference has been made to 'the digital economy' and to a number of digital technologies. It therefore stands to reason that students need to be aware of modern digital technologies and how they can represent both an opportunity and a threat to business ecosystems.

3 Digital disruption/Disruptive technology

Digital disruption describes the change that happens when new digital technologies, services, capabilities, and business models affect and change the value of the industry's existing services and goods.

These new elements change or disrupt the status quo, forcing businesses to re-evaluate the current market regarding goods and services and possibly adjust.

Disruptive technology relates to instances where technology is used to fundamentally change and 'disrupt' the existing business model in an industry.

Digital disruption, can be a challenging and painful process, but does offer significant business benefits. For example:

- It can contribute toward increasing customer satisfaction.

  Customers today want more variety, more innovation, more choices, and all of it delivered immediately. As a result of social media (itself a beneficiary of digital disruption) today's customers are more informed, and more discerning. Digital disruption has resulted in businesses needing to rise to the challenge of today's consumers by staying ahead of the technology and incorporating the latest changes faster. For example, one outcome of digital disruption big data and analytics, allows businesses to gain more sales by gaining insights into customer buying habits. Digital disruption has therefore made marketing more manageable and effective, resulting in a healthier company overall.

- It can help business growth.

  "A business at rest is a business falling behind the competition". Digital disruption brings about radical change, taking traditional businesses out of their comfort zone, moving them forward and allowing them to grow by, for example, gaining a greater understanding of customers and their needs. A business that refuses to adapt and change, especially if its competition is doing so, is potentially doomed to fail.

- It assists in evolving and improving the workplace.

  Digital disruption brings innovations and new technology to the workplace. Workflow management tools, collaboration software, mobile devices, and cloud technology that have driven digital disruption are just a few examples. If you need a relevant example, look at how revolutions in work-from-home technology have helped companies remain functional during the global pandemic of 2020/2021.

An example of a disruptor

An example of a disruptor is the passenger service Uber which created a business model using technology which avoided the need for licensed drivers, a vehicle fleet, local booking services etc. Instead, customers use their internet connected device to hail a ride and all payments are handled by a smartphone app.

Uber has disrupted the existing business model for traditional passenger services. Uber was set up in San Francisco in the United States and its initial key competitor was the Yellow Cab Co-operative, but whilst Uber has grown to a business worth over $60bn, the Yellow Cab Co-operative has since filed for bankruptcy.

The key reason for the growth of new disruptive businesses is from technology. Not only from the technology that they employ in order to cut costs and improve efficiency, but also in the access that consumers now have to technology in the modern on-demand economy. For example, many disruptive businesses rely on smartphone applications or have internet-only based transactions.

The two largest growth sectors for disruptive technology are in health services and financial services. Financial technology (commonly known as Fintech) is, for example, completely disrupting the traditional banking sector – long seen as a highly technical, highly regulated industry dominated by giant banks.

Fintech businesses exist which can provide investment advice, offer banking services, transfer money internationally, provide mortgages and loans, exchange currency etc. These are typically big earners for traditional financial institutions. Goldman Sachs estimates that upstarts could steal up to $4.7 trillion in annual revenue, and $470 billion in profit, from established financial services companies.

Fintech examples

Fintech is empowering consumers to take charge of their financial lives, leading to much greater financial literacy than ever before by tearing down the old silos and helping to advance the consumers' financial situation and outcomes by leveraging advanced technology.

Some well-known companies such as Personal Capital, Lending Club, Kabbage (acquired by American Express in 2020) and Wealthfront are examples of Fintech companies that have emerged in the past decade, providing new twists on financial concepts and allowing consumers to have more influence on their financial outcomes.

Kabbage was acquired by American Express in 2020 and has since created a name for its streamlined application process in which borrowers can get a decision in just minutes after connecting their business checking accounts.

Lending Club, via peer-to-peer lending, lets users loan each other money (P2P lending) for business ventures without the involvement from a traditional financial institution. Some borrowers and lenders who use peer-to-peer markets suggest that they do this for ethical reasons. They argue that traditional banks often have unethical practices and a peer-to-peer system avoids giving big banks more profits.

Each of these innovations is made possible through the use of Big Data and advanced analytics across digital platforms.

In the growing field of credit reporting, Credit Karma is an example of a Fintech that's providing a service (free credit reports) in exchange for the ability to advertise loans and credit cards tailored to the specific needs of its customers.

New entrants into the market such as Funding Circle are now offering a similar service for business customers with larger loans and longer periods.

Another example of a Fintech is a company called Betterment. Betterment aims to become a financial portfolio management platform – taking business away from the typically person-to-person financial advisers. Users can use a smartphone app to get investment advice and manage their investment portfolio.

Here is an extract from Betterment's mobile app description:

Why we're here

Betterment is an online financial advisor with one purpose: to help you make the most of your money. We're taking investment strategies that have worked for decades and using technology to make them more efficient. Our goal: to increase your long-term returns.

What we do for you

We make tailored recommendations, from how much to invest to how much risk to take on in your portfolio. Then, we invest your money in a globally diversified portfolio of low-cost ETFs and help lower taxes in ways many traditional investment services can't match.

Seek higher returns:

- Automated portfolio management
- Globally diversified portfolio of ETFs
- Tax efficient investing features, like tax loss harvesting and asset location.

Get a better investing experience:

- Sync your external investments
- Customer support 7 days per week
- Access to CFP® professionals and licensed financial experts.

Invest and save with transparency:

- Low-cost, straightforward pricing plans
- Low fund fees
- No trading or rebalancing fees.

The advantages that Fintechs have are:

- better use of data – providing better understanding of their customer and giving customers a wider choice
- a frictionless customer experience using elements such as smartphone apps to provide a broad and efficient range of services
- more personalisation of products/services to individual customers
- the lack of a physical presence (with associated overheads and operating costs)
- access to cheap capital to fund growth – much like when internet based businesses first came to prominence in the 1990's, investors want to get in on the growth potential that Fintechs offer. This gives Fintechs a wide scope for raising cheap finance in order to fund their future expansion.

Test your understanding 1

What potential defences might be employed by traditional financial services businesses to defend themselves against Fintech?

Further examples of disruptive technology

Cryptocurrencies

These aim to be a digital form of money, meeting the attributes of a store of value, unit of account and medium of exchange. That is not to say that all cryptocurrencies irrefutably meet these criteria, but their main purpose is to achieve this status.

Hundreds of cryptocurrencies now exist, originating with bitcoin, each providing different attributes – "zcash", for example, offers privacy guarantees.

Blockchain

Blockchain is a distributed database existing on multiple computers at the same time. It is constantly growing as new sets of recordings, or 'blocks', are added to it. Each block contains a timestamp and a link to the previous block, so they actually form a chain.

The database is not managed by any particular body; instead, everyone in the network gets a copy of the whole database. Old blocks are preserved forever and new blocks are added to the ledger irreversibly, making it virtually impossible to manipulate by faking documents, transactions and other information.

All blocks are encrypted in a special way, so everyone can have access to all the information but only a user who owns a special cryptographic key is able to add a new record to a particular chain. As long as you remain the only person who knows the key, no one can manipulate your transactions. In addition, cryptography is used to guarantee synchronisation of copies of the blockchain on each computer (or node) in the network.

For example, think of blockchain as a digital medical record. Every record is a block which has a label stating the date and time when the record was entered. The medical history is extremely important for diagnosis and treatment purposes, so neither the doctor nor the patient should be able to modify the records already made. Nevertheless, the doctor owns a private key that allows him to make new records, and the patient owns a public key that allows him to access the records anytime. This method makes the data both accessible and secure. So, blockchain is by definition independent, transparent, and secure. The advantages of such a distributed ledger are obvious: being cost and risk reduction, data security, and/or transactions transparency; companies from most industries can benefit from this new technology.

We are all pretty much used to sharing information through a decentralised interactive platform – the Internet, but when it comes to sending money or other valuables we usually have to use the same old services provided by centralised financial institutions (i.e. banks). There are methods of making payments via the Internet (the most obvious example is PayPal), but they usually require integration with a bank account or credit card; otherwise they cannot really be used. Blockchain technology offers an attractive opportunity to get rid of this "extra link". It's perfectly designed to take on all three most important roles of the traditional financial services: registration of transactions, identity verification and contracting.

The financial services industry is the world's largest market in terms of capitalisation. If some part of those services will switch to using blockchain, this will certainly disrupt the industry, but at the same time it will significantly improve the efficiency of those services.

As transactions are completed directly between the parties with no intermediary and in digital form, settling a deal can be faster than ever.

The benefits noted below of perfect transparency, traceability and security provide further reasons to understand its potential. Moreover, blockchain can be used not only for sending digital money but as well for tracking physical goods in a supply chain, helping companies to monitor their suppliers in real time.

Test your understanding 2

Missfits is a fashion retailer, specialising in the online sale of clothing for females aged 14–28. Missfits has a large warehouse in its home country, Homelandia, from where it dispatches ordered goods to customers worldwide. As a result, Missfits holds a significant level of finished goods inventory, which incurs high storage costs and restricts cashflow for expansion of the business.

During a recent competitor analysis exercise, Ali Dan (an accountant working for Missfits) was performing ratio analysis on competitors' accounts. He noticed that one major competitor, Girlwear, seems to have very low inventory levels.

Reading elsewhere in Girlwear's annual report, Ali found reference to the fact that Girlwear shares order details with suppliers by means of an extranet, enabling them to manufacture to order and dispatch direct to Girlwear's customers. Each item of clothing is tracked through the production and delivery processes by means of a Radio Frequency Identification (RFID) tag. This allows the exact location of the garment to be determined automatically.

> **Required:**
>
> Examine the above scenario and identify which of the following is being used by Girlwear.
>
> - Fintech
> - Disaggregation
> - Competence sharing
> - Disruptive technology

4 Surviving digital disruption

So how might management ensure that their organisations survive digital disruption and rethink their business models so that they can thrive in a digital age?

The consultancy group Accenture wrote a report in 2015 called Accenture Technology Vision, which highlighted five emerging trends that were shaping the digital landscape for organisations and which business leaders should focus on in developing digital strategies:

1 **The Internet of Me** – users are being placed at the centre of digital experiences through apps and services being personalised.

2 **Outcome economy** – organisations have an increased ability to measure the outcomes of the services that they deliver; customers are more attracted to outcomes than just simply to products, and this is what organisations should focus on.

3 **The Platform (r)evolution** – global platforms are becoming easier to establish and cheaper to run. Developments such as cloud computing and mobile technology offer huge potential for innovation and quicker delivery of next-generation services. The rate of evolution is only going to increase.

4 **The intelligent enterprise** – using data in a smart way enables organisations to become more innovative and achieve higher degrees of operating efficiency.

5 **Workforce reimagined** – whilst greater use is made of smart machines, the role of human beings is not being removed altogether; they are simply being used in a different way. Ways need to be identified in which man and machines can work effectively together to create better outcomes.

Emerging trends

The consultancy group Accenture in a 2022 report called Accenture Technology Vision, "Meet me in the Metaverse" outlined some fascinating detail as to future trends in digital disruption.

"The Metaverse Continuum is a spectrum of digitally enhanced worlds, realities, and business models poised to revolutionize life and enterprise in the next decade.

From Metaverse and Web3, to digital twins and conversational AI, efforts to reimagine the future of technology are giving rise to new worlds and realities businesses will soon need to operate across – stretching from digital to physical and encompassing consumer experiences and enterprise business models alike".

"Over the next decade, nearly every environment that businesses currently operate across will transform as the Metaverse Continuum matures. Leaders will need to reimagine every dimension of their enterprise, from operating models to their core value proposition – and some are already starting today".

Examples are:

A Chinese news agency, Xinhua, has unveiled a virtual newsroom with an AI news anchor who can deliver breaking news to audiences 24 hours a day.

Amazon Sidewalk was activated, instantly creating smart neighbourhoods, and extending the reach of existing smart devices far beyond their original range.

Vail Ski Resort built a digital twin with details like real-time snowfall, past weather data, and critical mountain infrastructure. It's also automating the physical mountain with remote monitoring and automatic snow guns that activate based on weather.

AI is a big story for all kinds of businesses, but some companies are clearly moving ahead of others. McKinsey's "State of AI in 2022" survey showed that adoption of AI models has more than doubled since 2017—and investment has increased apace.

What's more, the specific areas in which companies see value from AI have evolved, from manufacturing and risk to include:

- marketing and sales
- product and service development
- strategy and corporate finance

There are also a number of myths about digital transformation that are common. This is perhaps understandable given the rate of change that has been seen in many industries over the last few years, but such impressions need to be shown as misleading if management are to see digital transformation as an opportunity as opposed to a threat.

Myth 1 – those organisations that are not digital already have missed their chance

It is true that a number of recently-formed businesses have achieved huge valuations in a very short space of time, and successfully attacked traditional markets (Uber, AirBnB, Amazon etc.). This is because they have successfully exploited new technologies and understood the changing tastes of consumers.

However, existing businesses that have been around for a long time have substantial assets – know-how, customer relationships, brands, distribution channels, data – and should look to leverage these to their advantage. The business model simply needs to adapt.

Myth 2 – becoming a digital business is an administrative exercise that focusses on achieving operational efficiencies

The reality is that successful organisations today are not just looking to cut costs through using technology; they are looking to increase the revenue sources available to them. Using technology is an important way to achieve this.

Myth 3 – digital transformation can be successfully achieved just by creating a digital business unit headed up by a Chief Digital Officer

Whilst such business units and roles may be created, the process of digitisation will impact on all employees in the business. Digital transformation needs to be driven at the very top of the organisation, with the CEO taking responsibility for it and achieving buy-in from everybody else.

The lesson from the above myths is that organisations need to recognise how technological development requires them to question their business model, to enquire how adopting such technologies can bring benefits, and to understand how employees and their roles are also evolving and how to get the best out of them.

Test your understanding 3

Option 1	The Internet of Things	
Option 2	The Internet of Me	
Option 3	The learning organisation	
Option 4	The intelligent enterprise	
Option 5	The outcome economy	

The consultancy group Accenture wrote a report in 2015 called Accenture Technology Vision, which highlighted five emerging trends that were shaping the digital landscape for organisations and which business leaders should focus on in developing digital strategies.

Required:

Identify which **THREE** of the following, according to Accenture, are among those trends

- The Internet of Things
- The Internet of Me
- The learning organisation
- The intelligent enterprise
- The outcome economy

5 The roles and responsibilities of the board and senior leadership

In order for an organisation to properly take advantage of a move to digital, or to survive digital disruption within its industry, the executive leadership team will need to demonstrate a number of abilities:

1 **Inspirational leadership** – digitisation will be an exercise in change management, but probably on a bigger and quicker scale than the organisation will typically be used to. The leadership team will need to energise the workforce and inspire confidence that digitisation is the right way forwards and is being carried out in the right way.

   The move to digital will only succeed if those at the top of the organisation take ownership and persuade others to commit to the change.

2 **Competitive edge** – not only will the leadership need to motivate others within the organisation to see the digital transformation as the right strategy; they will also have to persuade people to potentially change their mind-set. The need to adopt an inquisitive attitude, to be prepared to innovate and think outside the box, to experiment and to learn from failures may not be second nature to some, but is likely to be critical in transforming successfully to digital.

3 **Establishing a strategic direction** – this is probably something that the business has done for a long time, but a digital strategy may require it to be done in a different way. For example, the planning horizon may need to be shortened, or greater flexibility introduced – perhaps a move away from the rational model discussed in chapter 1 to a more emergent approach, which would enable the business to adapt as time passes.

4 **Influence external parties** – for example, providers of finance. Raising capital is likely to be necessary, but showing how that capital may be applied and the value that will result might be more problematic. Will investing in cloud technology deliver increased shareholder wealth? If so, how much? And when? There will be greater uncertainty over outcomes, and the leaders of the business will need to be persuasive and articulate a compelling value proposition.

5 **Collaboration** – as has already been mentioned earlier in this text, the organisation will need to see itself as part of a wider ecosystem if it is to deliver the requisite value. This will require careful thought on who to collaborate with and how each part of the ecosystem will contribute.

6 **Business judgement** – what sort of business model will the organisation need to put in place? It is probable that an altogether different model to what has worked in the past will be required.

7 **Execution** – having determined what technologies can help to drive the business forwards, thought must then be given to how these can be used most effectively by the people within the business. People and technology need to work in harmony to produce the desired outcomes.

Careful thought must also be given to how the execution of the digital strategy and transformation is to be managed. For example, what sort of metrics (or KPIs) need to be put in place? What benchmarks should be adopted as a successful outcome?

8 **Building talent** – it will be critical to identify the skills that staff will need to demonstrate and to manage training/recruitment to ensure that the business has those skills. New roles are likely to be required, including at the most senior level – for example, perhaps a new board position of Chief Digital Officer.

Test your understanding 4

Mac is CEO of Keel Her, a large manufacturer of smartphones and tablets. Mac has recently attended an 'all staff' meeting, at which he passionately outlined his personal vision for the future of Keel Her, and launched two new products which will be taken to market within the next two weeks.

In order for an organisation to properly take advantage of a move to digital, or to survive digital disruption within its industry, the executive leadership team will need to demonstrate a number of abilities.

Required:

Examine the description above, and identify which of those abilities is being demonstrated by Mac from the list below.

- Establishing a strategic direction
- Building talent
- Collaboration
- Inspirational leadership

6 Strategies to build disruptive business models

Firms looking to become digital enterprises face two main challenges.

- The business model that served them well for decades has been disrupted by digital innovation and no longer works as desired.
- All attempts to create a new, viable business model for the digital age will flounder unless a company is willing to disrupt itself.

This conundrum has been termed "the innovator's dilemma".

A fear of cannibalising profits is just one obstacle standing in the way of organisations looking to launch new business models. Such organisations often have a risk-averse culture that focuses on the present rather than the future.

For example, managers often are very adept at running existing business units but do not have the creativity to identify radically different business models or the decisiveness to commit resources to experiment.

Illustration 1 – iPods, iTunes – the innovators dilemma in action

For firms, the dilemma can be particularly testing as the disruptive technology may directly compete with their profitable existing business. This could be reduced to one sentence: "In the years before the launch of the iPod and iTunes in 2001, both Nokia and Sony had similar products under development but chose not to proceed with them, for fear of disrupting their existing business. "In fact, an IMD/Cisco report published in 2015 found that only a quarter of the companies surveyed said that they would be willing to disrupt themselves in order to compete.

So the key message is not to be afraid of change and disruption.

Illustration 2 – Amazon

From its start as a seller of paper books, Amazon has had the courage to disrupt itself and cannibalize its products and services. This happened when Amazon launched the Kindle e-book reader at the expense of its physical books sales. In 2010, the Kindle accounted for 62.8% of all e-readers worldwide.

Amazon is now the leader in promotion and sales of digital content in an e-book market worth estimated at $16.42 billion in 2023, expected to reach $20.74 billion by 2028, growing at a CAGR of 4.78% during the forecast period (2023–2028).

Amazon also disrupted itself with the launch of Amazon Prime, which undermined its DVD sales. Moreover, Amazon has made other long-term bets with the potential to further disrupt, such as Amazon Web Services, Fire smartphones and delivery drones.

Amazon's success is mainly driven by bold leadership of the CEO and an innovative corporate culture, defined by a relatively high degree of autonomy and by putting the customer in the centre.

Illustration 3 – Michelin

Michelin has adapted its business model, from being a manufacturer and seller of tangible goods (tyres) to selling outcomes (a promise of performance that is backed by a guaranteed refund if not satisfied).

Michelin offers a package that is has branded EFFIFUEL, which includes sophisticated telematics, training in how to drive efficiently, and a tyre management system. It claims that purchasing such a service can save significant costs in operating trucks (fuel and replacing tyres) and also in terms of carbon dioxide emissions.

Illustration 4 – Apple

Apple, one of the world's largest technology companies, selling consumer electronics such as iPhones and Apple Watches, as well as computer software and online services. Apple uses artificial intelligence and machine learning in products like the iPhone, where it enables the FaceID feature, or in products like the Air Pods, Apple Watch, or HomePod smart speakers, where it enables the smart assistant Siri.

Apple is also growing its service offering and is using AI to recommend songs on Apple Music, help you find your photo in the iCloud, or navigate to your next meeting using Maps.

Illustration 5 – IBM

IBM has been at the forefront of artificial intelligence for years. It's been more than 20 years since IBM's Deep Blue computer became the first to conquer a human world chess champion. The company followed up that feat with other man vs. machine competitions, including its Watson computer winning the game show Jeopardy. The latest artificial intelligence accomplishment for IBM is Project Debater. This AI is a cognitive computing engine that competed against two professional debaters and formulated human-like arguments.

Illustration 6 – IBM

IBM has been at the forefront of artificial intelligence for years. It has been more than 20 years since IBM's Deep Blue computer became the first to conquer a human world chess champion. The company followed up that feat with other man vs. machine competitions, including its Watson computer winning the game show Jeopardy.

The latest artificial intelligence accomplishment for IBM is Project Debater. This AI is a cognitive computing engine that competed against two professional debaters and formulated human-like arguments.

The decision to entirely rethink an existing business model is a difficult one to take, but once it has been made, an organisation needs to find the most effective way to disrupt itself.

Illustration 7 – The World Economic Forum White Paper:

Digital Enterprise (suggested three-step plan)

1 **"Innovate on the periphery"** Inspire innovation at the edge of your company rather than the core business. Look to projects on the periphery of your company that are focusing on new products, services or customer segments that are aligned with disruptive trends in your industry.

Rather than funding this project generously, keep investment to a minimum, so that the project team is forced by necessity to focus on leveraging external resources, tying it into the ecosystem.

2 **"Hire digital savvy individuals"** These teams work with a low profile in the organisation. Examples of these types of organizations include Netflix Chaos Monkey. Such an approach helps them establish start-ups and to achieve a twofold goal: to both defeat and disrupt the "mother ship".

3 **"Copy successful firms"** The most holistic approach, consisting of establishing an internal accelerating technology lab to focus on big ideas (as Google does with life extension, Google Glass, self-driving vehicles or with Project Loon) and of creating a fast-track partnering program with accelerators, incubators (see later) and hackerspaces.

Good examples are Y Combinator (Uber and Dropbox), Tech Shop, or bolt.io.

Efforts to disrupt will also need to be underpinned by a culture that is open to innovation.

Companies need to have a mind-set that can cope with constant change. For example, the World Economic Forum suggest the following methodologies to develop new business models.

Illustration 8 – World Economic Forum

Scenario-based design – Creates future business models in response to disruptive industry trends.

Epicenter-driven design – Uses strengths and weaknesses of the existing business model to generate ideas.

Unorthodox design – Forms business models by challenging existing industry logic and company clichés.

Customer-centric design – Builds business models through customers' eyes based on the question: Does this solve their problems?

Mirrored design – Based on the finding that 90% of new business models are not actually new, this creatively imitates business model patterns from other industries.

Companies need to fundamentally change the way they identify, develop and launch new business ventures. They have to enhance and develop their strategic toolkit.

Research at the World Economic Forum on "Digital Transformation of Industries" suggests that they need to adopt one of five approaches or a combination of build, **buy, partner, invest and incubate/accelerate**.

- **Build**

  Building new business models might be the best route when an opportunity is related to the company's core business. The benefits are that it typically maximises control and minimises costs in markets that a company must own because of their strategic importance. If companies decide to go for the build route, they can benefit by creating and developing new products and services.

Illustration 9 – GE

GE historically made most of its revenues by selling industrial hardware and repair services, but with the pace of advances in digital technology, GE was at risk of losing out to competitors. In 2011, GE launched its Industrial Internet initiative to move toward an outcome-based business model focused on optimizing asset performance and operations with the help of big data and analytics. Digitally enabled and outcomes based approaches helped GE generate more than $800 million in incremental income in 2013.

In 2015, GE made the next step, with dramatic changes to its strategy and operations, to emphasize and capitalize on its digital capabilities with the creation of GE Digital.

This move has helped GE bring together all the digital capabilities from across the company into one organization with a bold ambition to create a digital show site and grow software and analytics enterprise from $6 billion in 2015 to become a top 10 software company by 2020.

- **Buy**

  Buying another company is usually the most appropriate path when there is a strategic imperative to 'own' a market and may be the only viable option if a significant change market is imminent, hiring the right talent is not possible and the new opportunity bears little relation to the firm's current business model may provide reasons to buy. Similarly engaging early with a digital disruptor is important to wrong-foot the competition and minimise the investment needed.

Illustration 10 – Jungheinrich AG

German intralogistics provider Jungheinrich AG acquired Arculus, a developer of modular production AI software for factories and warehouses, in 2021. Jungheinrich believed the addition of automation to the intralogistics process would give its customer new levels of flexibility and control. In 2023, the company attributed record revenues to "very strong growth in the automated systems business."

Facebook acquiring Oculus Rift and WhatsApp, or BMW, Audi and Daimler buying Nokia's digital mapping service HERE, with the aim to better position themselves in the battle for self-driving and connected cars.

- **Partner**

  A firm can use partnering with a digitally disruptor to learn more about the market and its partner's model. A partnering approach is sensible when it makes sense to learn about emergent opportunities, with an eye toward deeper partnerships or acquisitions in the future. Companies need to develop a more flexible and open mind-set toward partnerships; which are expected to play an important role in the digital transformation of market players.

Illustration 11 – Novartis and Google

Novartis and Google have joined forces to work on a smart contact lens that monitors blood sugar levels and corrects vision in a new way. This helps open up new revenue streams for Novartis, moving away from selling pills to a more holistic offering for patients by enabling them to better monitor their own health and reduce the cost of managing chronic diseases.

Adidas has partnered with Spotify to launch Adidas Go, the first running app that uses iPhone's accelerometer to instantly match a runner's favourite music to their workout.

- **Invest**

  Investing in interesting start-ups is often a valid option, allowing an established company to connect with the right skills and capabilities. It will also avoid hindering entrepreneurial forces with a setup focused on internal governance and reporting.

- **Incubate/accelerate** Investment and incubation/acceleration might seem similar endeavours. The latter however represents a closer relationship to the funding company, deploying corporate internal capabilities, infrastructure and resources to the start-ups. Incubators and accelerators will however need to precisely outline both internal benefits and suitable incentives for start-ups and their entrepreneurs. In addition they will need a clear strategy and vision.

Test your understanding 5

Ben's Bits was founded in 1982 by Ben Bentley. Mr Bentley had been a car mechanic, specialising in classic and vintage Italian car restoration. He had become increasingly frustrated by how much time and effort he was spending to track down spare parts for car models that were no longer in production. Ben took a long lease on a large warehouse and began to visit dealers and vintage car events.

Having managed to obtain about half a million spare parts for classic Italian car brands, Mr Bentley offered them for sale to enthusiasts and mechanics by mail order. In 1998, Mr Bentley's son, Ben junior, computerised the inventory system. This made it easier to identify what parts were held.

Between 2000 and 2015, the company acquired over two hundred small independent car parts retail businesses, as their owners retired. Ben's Bits now has over twenty million stock items, for more than thirty classic car marques from around the World, and sells globally through its website. The business is still owned by Ben and his son.

Research at the World Economic Forum on "Digital Transformation of Industries" suggests that companies need to adopt one of (or a combination of) build, buy, partner, invest and incubate/accelerate if they wish to identify, develop and launch new business ventures.

Required:

Identify which of these was pursued by Ben's Bits between 2000 and 2015 from the list below

- Build
- Invest
- Buy
- Partner

7 Digital operating models

An operating model can be defined as the clear, 'big picture' description of the key relationships between business functions, processes and structures that are required for the organisation to fulfil its mission.

It is a description of how people, teams and organisational units interact and is the critical link between strategy definition and execution.

As we have already discussed, digital innovation is reshaping industries by disrupting existing business and operating models, but it is also having a profound impact on society, presenting a series of opportunities and challenges for businesses and policy-makers.

To compete, companies will have to change their business models and how they deliver that business model by re-examining every aspect of their operations.

Many businesses are already making these changes, with 90% of organisations saying that they have significantly adjusted their operations. This could involve introducing a digital operating model or adopting new technologies to find operational efficiencies.

In traditional thinking however, technology is often viewed purely as a cost. It can however also be an important enabler of revenue generation. Many business leaders now recognise this. For example, a recent PwC survey found that 45% of business and IT executives across 51 countries saw growing revenue through digital enablement as a top priority.

The successful adoption of new technology and integrating it into a company's operations and value chain has considerable potential to bring about efficiencies.

Illustration 12 – Cross-industry operational efficiencies

HR. Key technologies include virtual collaboration, peer-to-peer reputation systems and digital interviews. The use of talent portals for hiring was found to reduce talent and HR costs by 7%.

Finance. Innovations will include cloud accounting systems and AI to automate procedures. It is forecasted that these technologies will reduce the costs of the finance function by 40%.

IT. The most significant technologies include cloud computing, SaaS, AI, big data security, and, in the future, also quantum computing. Cloud computing alone can lead to IT costs savings of 25 to 50%.

Supply chain management/procurement. Key technologies will include autonomous transport and drones, sensors for monitoring supply chains and 3D printing. Digitally enabled companies will incur procurement costs of 0.22% of net revenue, less than half of those of their peers (0.5%).

R&D. Crowdsourcing, AI and robotics are leading the shift toward the R&D of tomorrow, which could lead to key measures of R&D performance improving by as much as 20 to 40%.

The World Economic Forum on the Digital Transformation of Industries identified five successful digital operating models. They replace rigid approaches to technology, data and processes with flexibility, while also encouraging a culture that is open to innovation and interaction with customers and partners.

- **Customer-centric.** This model focuses on making customers' lives easier and emphasizes front-office processes. Leading exponents include the UK retailer Argos, but it can be applied across industries. It works best with a culture that puts the client first and a decentralized structure that empowers frontline staff.

- **Extra-frugal.** This model thrives on a culture of 'less is more' and a standardized organizational structure. By optimizing manufacturing, supply and support processes, it can provide a high-quality service at a low cost. A prime example of this model is tire manufacturer Michelin.
- **Data-powered.** This model is built around prowess in analytics and software intelligence. Epitomized by Google and Netflix, data-powered companies have an agile culture focused on innovation through empirical experimentation.
- **Skynet.** Named after the conscious, artificial general intelligence of the Terminator films, this model makes intensive use of machines to increase productivity and flexibility in production. Pioneered by enterprises such as Amazon and Rio Tinto, Skynet organizations are characterized by an engineer-led culture dedicated to automation.
- **Open and liquid.** This model looks outward with a view to creating an ecosystem that can enrich the customer proposition. Built around a sharing customer, all processes in organizations of this kind are characterized by a constant flow of dialog with the outside world. Examples include Facebook and PayPal.

Illustration 13 – Haier

Haier is the world's largest maker of white goods with a 10.2% retail market share in 2014 and more than 70,000 employees. By focusing on innovation, CEO Zhang Ruimin turned a state-owned fridge maker on the verge of bankruptcy into the world's largest manufacturer.

Haier uses digital trends and technologies to diversify its products, optimize business processes, reduce the distance to the consumer and develop new products. The company created a community management system (called HOPE), which is an open-innovation ecosystem in which 670,000 users communicate with suppliers and other customers searching for new business opportunities.

Employees are encouraged to bring fresh ideas and rewarded for innovative thinking. Haier reorganized employees into 2,000 ZZJYTs – a Chinese acronym for independent, self-managed units, each with their own profit and loss – to create an organizational structure that emphasizes autonomy.

These operational changes have paid off with Haier Group's global turnover growing by 11% and profits increasing by 39% from a year earlier.

Illustration 14 – Xiaomi

Xiaomi focuses on low-end Android smartphones. In 2014, it sold 61 million handsets, bringing in annual revenues of more than $12 billion. Xiaomi promotes an entrepreneurial culture, fostering a family-like setup, focused on mentoring, collaborations and adhocracy.

Xiaomi's flat structures consist of its core founders, department leaders and 4,300 employees with an intense focus on performance and quality. The company engages with customers in an informal way by involving fans in discussions on product design, product development and promotions. The results of this approach are illustrated by the fact that Xiaomi itself developed only three iOS languages; the remaining 22 were developed through crowdsourcing.

Employees are required to spend 30 minutes every day interacting with customers. Xiaomi also established a peer-to-peer customer service platform.

Xiaomi's innovative approach is paying off. In 2014, its year-on-year sales of smartphones tripled and since June 2012, the company's market valuation has increased tenfold to $45 billion.

Developing the right technological capabilities is just the first step in a company's digital transformation. Successfully identifying and implementing the most suitable flexible operating model will depend on other changes, particularly to strategy development and culture.

Test your understanding 6

Simple Minds is a high-street toy and game retailer. It has developed a business model based around putting the customer first and making their life easier. Simple Minds has a very simple organisation structure, which allows staff in the shops to do pretty much anything they choose to ensure that the customer is delighted. This includes giving discounts, demonstrating toys, playing games with customers and dressing up as characters from popular games.

The World Economic Forum project on the Digital Transformation of Industries (DTI) identified five successful digital operating models. They replace rigid approaches to technology, data and processes with flexibility, while also encouraging a culture that is open to innovation and interaction with customers and partners.

Required:

Examine the above description, and identify which of the DTI operating models is being used by Simple Minds from the list below

- Skynet
- Data-powered
- Customer-centric
- Open and liquid

8 Leadership and culture

The business will need to ensure that it has staff with the right skills, that it can attract new recruits as necessary, that the appropriate leadership style is adopted, and that a digital culture is properly fostered.

These will now be looked at in turn.

8.1 Attracting and retaining talent in the digital age

With increasing levels of digitisation in the workplace, 2 features have become apparent with regards to employing staff.

1 There is much greater transparency about employment opportunities for those seeking a new challenge, with applicants becoming more and more informed thanks to increased levels of "inside information". This has come about because of the presence of agencies and peer reviews.

Illustration 15 – Glassdoor

One of the fastest growing jobs and recruiting sites in the world, Glassdoor keeps over 8 million reviews on more than 423,000 companies. Information such as CEO approval ratings, interview reviews and questions, office photos, benefits and salary reports etc. can be accessed. This is all provided by employees through a peer-to-peer network.

Businesses are realising that transparency needs to be encouraged, and that a mind-set of "we have nothing to hide" needs to be adopted. Research shows that fostering such a business culture actually results in a more productive workforce and lower levels of staff turnover.

2 The competition for digital talent is increasing; there is a global skills shortage in this area to cope with the increasing demand.

So what do organisations need to do to attract and retain the necessary talent? Firstly, they need to take great notice of what their staff are saying about their organisation, which can be done by monitoring social platforms such as Glassdoor, LinkedIn, and Twitter.

Secondly, they should look to introduce a referral programme. This means incentivising current staff to use such online networks to refer potential new employees; if employees are incentivised in the right sort of way to champion their employer's digital referral programme, attracting the right calibre staff becomes much easier.

8.2 Becoming an employer of choice

It stands to reason that the latest generation of employees, the so-called "millennials", should be the main target for organisations looking to embrace a digital strategy; after all, these are the people who have grown up in the digital era – they see digital as the norm, they have the necessary skills with digital technology, and they also understand what younger customers are looking for in products and services.

Millennials represent a generation that feels empowered to choose where and how they work, and employers must recognise this if they are to offer an attractive working proposition. Technology will be an important part of that proposition; the provision and use of technology is considered one of the most important factors in determining job satisfaction. However, it is not the only factor.

Illustration 16 – Zappos

Zappos is an online clothing retailer. It has a reputation for a strong corporate culture that employees identify with that makes them want to work for the company. This includes having a management structure that is task-orientated, rather than a more formal structure. Employees are encouraged to deal with customers in whatever way is felt appropriate, to use the Zappos Twitter account to air their thoughts, and to work wherever will let them be most creative, such as coffee bars and co-working spaces.

So how does an organisation become an employer of choice in the digital era? The World Economic Forum proposes the following:

- **Formulate a long-term working strategy for millennials** – identify the relevant positions that employees will occupy during their career with the company and then create suitable promotional opportunities.
- **Work with staff to formulate company values together** – this means listening to, and taking note of, the aspirations of those working for the business. Senior management should do this in person, not just as a communication sent company-wide.
- **Empower the workforce** – and give them incentives to perform e.g. via long term company share plans, project leadership responsibilities or training opportunities.
- **Build workspaces that attract digital talent** – this relates to the physical layout and appearance of the working environment. Flexibility and a dynamic appearance in the workplace inspires creativity and collaboration. Thought should also be given to allowing staff to work from home on occasions and flexible working hours.
- **Create policies that support collaboration and knowledge-sharing tools** – this can include encouraging staff to use platforms such as Facebook@work, Yammer or Sprinklr, or hardware preferences such as being to use your own laptop in the workplace.

8.3 Creating a workforce with digital skills

In a recent survey conducted by PwC, almost three quarters of CEOs cited skills shortages as a threat to their businesses, and 81% claimed to be looking for a broader range of skills when recruiting. Digitisation is leading to new roles being created in companies, which demand different skills sets.

The table below shows roles that might now be relevant for certain aspects of an organisation:

Commercial	Technology	Web	Marketing	Facilitation	HR
E-business manager	Scrum master	Web project manager	Digital marketing professional	Service design thinker	Design learning manager
Digital account manager	Data scientist	Web designer	Digital copywriters	Content curator	Digital work experience officer
Digital product manager	Chief Data Officer (CDO)	Webmaster	Media acquisition manager	Editorial manager	Employer brand director
Fraud manager	Data protection officer	Developer	User experience designer	Chief Listening Officer	

In order to create a workforce with the right digital skills, organisations need to collaborate with educational establishments – universities, colleges, schools – with a long term view to giving students the right skills and confidence to be the employees of the future.

Illustration 17 – Lockheed Martin

The American aerospace and defence company Lockheed Martin has a programme whereby its engineers, scientists and IT professionals volunteer to meet with schoolchildren between the ages of 9 to 12 with a view to building their interest and confidence in science and technology. This is then sustained throughout school and college.

Organisations also need to focus on making in-house training a critical activity within their talent management programme. This will included the following:

- **Develop required competencies within the workforce** – this can be done by considering the skills that are currently needed and creating training strategies that are adapted to these. The organisation should look ahead and question where the high value work is likely to be in, say, 3 years' time compared to today, and train accordingly.
- **Mine your own organisation for hidden talent** – this will incorporate assessing employees' abilities and matching these to skills required.

- **Bring new skills into the organisation** – this can be done by either hiring new, digitally-competent staff, or running exchange programmes with other digital companies and sharing insights. Rotating staff internally to give them exposure to other aspects of the organisation is also common practice within tech giants such as Google and Amazon.

8.4 Bringing leadership to the digital age

In order for digitisation to work, leaders need to adapt. This may mean a different approach to establishing a corporate structure and also fostering an alternative culture in the workplace. Leaders need to show that they are forward-thinking and progressive, and not just rely on business practices that worked in years gone by.

A traditional approach to structure might be hierarchical and autocratic – roles and responsibilities are clearly defined and work on a top-down basis. In the digital age leaders need to accept that this traditional approach will not attract people of the right skills and will certainly not get the best out of them.

As Steve Jobs once commented: "We run Apple like a start-up. We always let ideas win arguments, not hierarchies. Otherwise, your best employees won't stay. Collaboration, discipline and trust are vital".

It would therefore appear that flatter organisational structures are key to making digital work.

Furthermore, a culture of being more risk-tolerant is to be encouraged. Instead of focussing on the mistakes of employees, the organisation should be encouraged to accept failures and to persuade staff to take higher amounts of risk. This will necessarily mean changing the focus on how the organisation performs – it cannot restrict itself to just short term goals, with failure to hit annual targets being seen as career-threatening. Management need to take a longer view of performance, and instil a culture that promotes this.

According to the World Economic Forum, CEOs should fulfil six key roles in the digital age:

- **Creator of vision and mission** – the company's mission statement should be expanded to encompass a transformation purpose.
- **Strategic planner** – this is nothing new, but the focus will change. There should be a move from 5 year to 1 year planning cycles, driven by data and analysis. Greater focus should be on experimentation rather than long-term planning.
- **Driver of information-based business models** – find and develop new products that are (fully) data- and information-based for scalability.
- **Enabler of the shift to on-demand operating models** – the CEO should champion the benefit that can be gained from communities in the workplace, crowdsourcing and staff on demand.
- **Innovation promoter.**
- **Operational excellence driver** – identify ways in which automation can be introduced into processes in all departments of the organisation.

8.5 Fostering a digital culture

Culture can be defined as the shared set of beliefs, values and mind-sets that guide a group's behaviours. Having the right sort of culture in place can give the organisation a sustainable competitive advantage, as competitors will find it very difficult to replicate. Mention has already been made in previous sections of this chapter about the need for a different sort of culture in the digital era, but how can this be created and adopted?

To answer this question, leaders must first recognise what factors distinguish a digital culture from others. These include:

- Having a strong mission statement and a clear sense of purpose
- Lean business structures, with small, cross-functional teams as opposed to individual divisions working as separate siloes
- A diverse workforce with good digital skills.

Leaders can then focus on four key areas in order to move towards a digital culture:

- **Communication** – communication by digital means needs to be encouraged. This should certainly not replace face to face conversations completely, but staff should be encouraged to communicate with each other in an honest and open style using all available digital channels – social media, blogs, forums, webcasts and videos, shared mailboxes etc.
- **Journey management** – the leadership team needs to be at the forefront of the cultural change. In order for this to take effect at the operational level, middle management need to be encouraged to think in different ways. Creativity needs to be released, and training should be provided so that middle managers recognise how to achieve this. Further support can come from implementing the right HR policies, rules etc.
- **Make changes visible** – visual aids such as diagrams and charts on office walls, highlighting the "journey" that the business is undertaking.
- **Continuous change monitoring** – using tools such as feedback surveys and performance monitoring to highlight gains made.

8.6 Create environments where human and robots can work successfully together

In the event that jobs are threatened by automation, employers will have to assess whether it is possible to reskill workers, either to work alongside robots or in new roles.

8.7 Integrate your on-demand workforce

Integrate your on-demand workforce. The most effective way to recruit on-demand workers is through online talent platforms. The extended workforce can help improve the overall quality of the talent pool.

All of this can be accelerated through appointing to a senior position someone who is already well-versed in digital culture.

Test your understanding 7

Obongjayar is a bank but has chosen a disruptive approach which allows it operate without branches and with a significant number of 'bots' (automated process applications, using artificial intelligence). In order to stop this being a barrier to recruitment, Obongjayar has established a 'fast-track' development programme for its graduate recruits. The bank also offers prizes to employees if they propose a radically-different way of performing any standard banking process.

The World Economic Forum Digital Transformation of Industries project (DTI) proposed a 7-step process to build a 'digital workforce'.

Required:

Examine the above description and identify which TWO of the steps proposed by the DTI are being described from the list below

- Attract and retain talent
- Foster a digital culture in the enterprise
- Create a workforce with digital skills
- Become an employer of choice for millennials
- Bring leadership into the digital age

9 Chapter summary

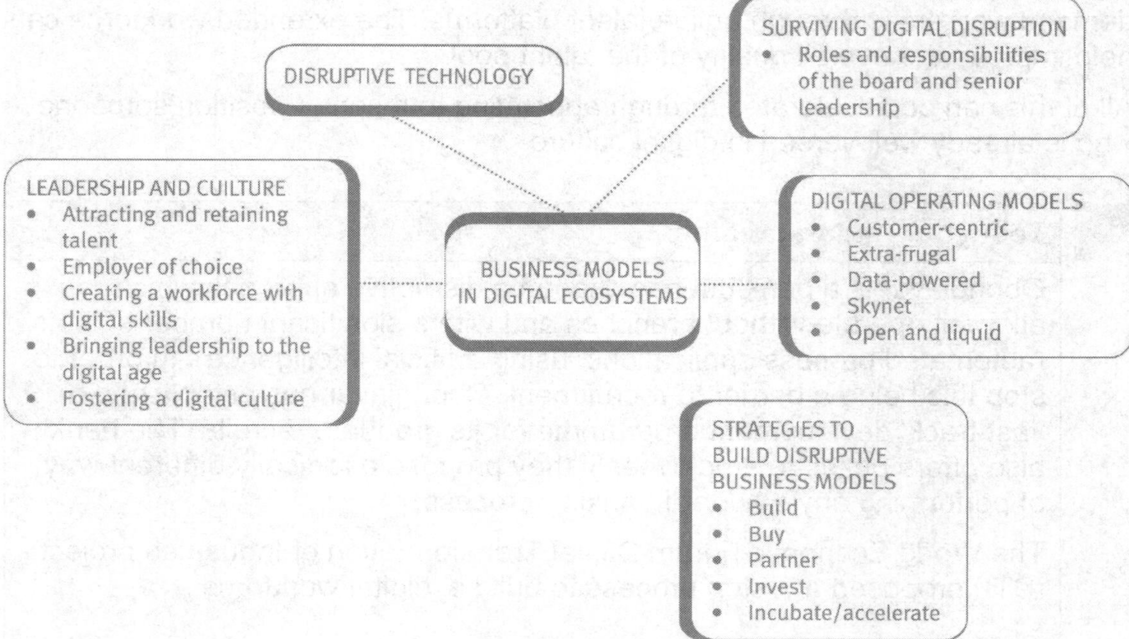

End of chapter questions

Question 1

Sonny and the Bear (SatB) is a leading children's fashion brand. Although SatB has high-street stores, it also has a vibrant and diverse e-commerce platform which it launched in 2015. SatB also pursued organic backward vertical integration, opening a design studio and fabric manufacturing factory.

None of those extensions to its business model was an acquisition, as SatB is cash-rich and chooses to pursue organic growth. It has, however, taken minority stakes in a number of small children's fashion brands, which are given access to the SatB online platform. Other than providing a cash injection, and allowing partners to sell through its e-commerce system, SatB provides no further support.

Research at the World Economic Forum on "Digital Transformation of Industries" suggests that companies need to adopt one of (or a combination of) build, buy, partner, invest and incubate/accelerate if they wish to identify, develop and launch new business ventures.

Examine the information above, and identify which **TWO** of these are being pursued by SatB.

Option 1	Build	
Option 2	Buy	
Option 3	Partner	
Option 4	Invest	
Option 5	Incubate/accelerate	

Question 2

Arlo Search (AS) began in 2001 as a search engine. Following its rapid growth, in this developing market sector, AS diversified into travel planning, cloud services and big data analytics. These moves were made by a combination of acquisition and organic growth.

In 2011, AS opened its 'Media Lab' to encourage its employees to be 'intrapreneurs'. Any AS employee with a good idea is encouraged to submit a detailed Business Case to the innovation committee of AS. If successful, the employee is provided with resources and finance, and can spend up to 2 years developing their idea. If it is successful, the intrapreneur is appointed CEO of a new AS business unit to take the idea to market. If AS does not see a future for the innovation, the employee is permitted to buy it from AS and run it as a stand-alone business. If AS sees an external start-up with high potential, its founder(s) are offered cheap finance and the opportunity to join the Media Lab. In return, AS obtains the right to acquire all or part of the business, should that business prove successful.

In 2018, AS formed a joint venture (AS-SD) with SearchDog Inc, another leading search engine provider. The joint venture aims to provide a completely safe search and email platform for users under the age of 16, free from any unsuitable content and secure from SPAM and phishing.

Research at the World Economic Forum on "Digital Transformation of Industries" suggests that companies need to adopt one of (or a combination of) build, buy, partner, invest and incubate/accelerate if they wish to identify, develop and launch new business ventures.

Examine the information above, and identify which of these is/are being pursued by AS. **Select ALL that apply.**

Option 1	Build	
Option 2	Buy	
Option 3	Partner	
Option 4	Invest	
Option 5	Incubate/accelerate	

Question 3

The World Economic Forum project on the Digital Transformation of Industries (DTI) proposed a 7-step process to build a 'digital workforce'.

Prioritise the following steps into the sequence proposed by the DTI.

Step 1	Create a workforce with digital skills	
Step 2	Foster a digital culture in the enterprise	
Step 3	Integrate your on-demand workforce	
Step 4	Attract and retain talent	
Step 5	Create environments where humans and robots can work successfully together	
Step 6	Bring leadership into the digital age	
Step 7	Become an employer of choice for millennials	

Question 4

Aldous Harding is an online provider of fitness information services. Named after its founder, a successful athlete who won a gold medals at three successive Paralympics, Aldous Harding sells its services through a subscription-only smartphone application.

Since its foundation, Aldous Harding has widened its service offering considerably. Originally only tracking 'steps', and mapping users' walking and running, the app now integrates with most commercially-available smart watches and fitness trackers, as well as the modern equipment used in up-market gyms. The app is also able to track users playing sports as diverse as football and golf, analysing their performance and recommending a tailored fitness regime. Gym users particularly like the way that the Aldous Harding app sets them daily challenges and helps them to achieve their fitness goals.

The Aldous Harding app, in common with others available, gathers a huge volume of data from other systems. However, the Aldous Harding app is characterised by the way it encourages feedback and suggestions from subscribers. In return for suggesting changes and improvements, Aldous Harding subscribers are rewarded with discounts on their app subscription and on fitness-related goods. 'Power users' (those who make a lot of suggestions) also receive Aldous Harding branded sportswear. An Aldous Harding cap is widely regarded as a prestige possession, as it cannot be purchased.

The World Economic Forum project on the Digital Transformation of Industries (DTI) identified five successful digital operating models. They replace rigid approaches to technology, data and processes with flexibility, while also encouraging a culture that is open to innovation and interaction with customers and partners.

Examine the above description, and identify which of the DTI operating models is being used by Aldous Harding.

Option 1	Customer-centric	
Option 2	Extra-frugal	
Option 3	Data-powered	
Option 4	Skynet	
Option 5	Open and liquid	

Question 5

Cate is a Non-Executive Director of King Tubby, and Chair of its Risk Committee. The Board is currently discussing a major proposed investment in 'cloud and mobile' technologies.

Cate has strongly made the case for the investment, stressing the argument that King Tubby needs a radical change to its business model if it is to deter the foreign competition currently threatening entry into King Tubby's market.

In order for an organisation to properly take advantage of a move to digital, or to survive digital disruption within its industry, the executive leadership team will need to demonstrate a number of abilities.

Examine the description above, and identify which of those abilities is being demonstrated by Cate.

Option 1	Inspirational leadership	
Option 2	Business judgement	
Option 3	Influence external parties	
Option 4	Collaboration	

Test your understanding answers

Test your understanding 1

Traditional financial services providers need to meet the threat from Fintech head on. There are a number of defences that they are employing to fight back against this emerging threat such as:

- Improving their own services in order to, for example, promote a more personal service that differentiates from the impersonal Fintech products.
- Offering more flexible products that are tailored to individual needs.
- Offer additional services not available via Fintech (such as the ability to use a physical location for cashing services).
- Seek out legislative help – the financial services industry is heavily regulated but many Fintech businesses fall outside the scope of current legislation. Traditional banks want to have more and tougher legislation of Fintechs, arguing that this will level the playing field for everyone.
- Relying on technophobia and hoping that a few bad actors in the Fintech market will destroy consumer confidence and bring consumers back to the relative safety of traditional lenders (though there is no evidence yet that this will happen).
- Better environmental analysis so that Fintech opportunities and threats are recognised and acted upon much earlier.
- Launching their own Fintech divisions or acquiring growing Fintech businesses.

Test your understanding 2

Option 1	Fintech	
Option 2	Disaggregation	
Option 3	Competence sharing	
Option 4	Disruptive technology	X
Explanation	Disruptive technology relates to instances where technology is used to fundamentally change and 'disrupt' the existing business model in an industry.	

Test your understanding 3

Option 1	The Internet of Things	
Option 2	The Internet of Me	X
Option 3	The learning organisation	
Option 4	The intelligent enterprise	X
Option 5	The outcome economy	X

The consultancy group Accenture wrote a report in 2015 called Accenture Technology Vision, which highlighted five emerging trends that were shaping the digital landscape for organisations and which business leaders should focus on in developing digital strategies:

1 The Internet of Me – users are being placed at the centre of digital experiences through apps and services being personalised.

2 Outcome economy – organisations have an increased ability to measure the outcomes of the services that they deliver; customers are more attracted to outcomes than just simply to products, and this is what organisations should focus on.

3 The Platform (r)evolution – global platforms are becoming easier to establish and cheaper to run. Developments such as cloud computing and mobile technology offer huge potential for innovation and quicker delivery of next-generation services. The rate of evolution is only going to increase.

4 The intelligent enterprise – using data in a smart way enables organisations to become more innovative and achieve higher degrees of operating efficiency.

5 Workforce reimagined – whilst greater use is made of smart machines, the role of human beings is not being removed altogether; they are simply being used in a different way. Ways need to be identified in which man and machines can work effectively together to create better outcomes.

The IoT is the connected network of consumer and industrial non-IT hardware. It includes, but is not limited to, vehicles, factory machinery, domestic appliances and buildings.

The learning organisation was a concept proposed by Senge, in the 1990s.

Test your understanding 4

Option 1	Establishing a strategic direction	
Option 2	Building talent	
Option 3	Collaboration	
Option 4	Inspirational leadership	X

In order for an organisation to properly take advantage of a move to digital, or to survive digital disruption within its industry, the executive leadership team will need to demonstrate a number of abilities:

1 **Inspirational leadership** – digitisation will be an exercise in change management, but probably on a bigger and quicker scale than the organisation will typically be used to. The leadership team will need to energise the workforce and inspire confidence that digitisation is the right way forwards and is being carried out in the right way. The move to digital will only succeed if those at the top of the organisation take ownership and persuade others to commit to the change.

2 **Competitive edge** – not only will the leadership need to motivate others within the organisation to see the digital transformation as the right strategy; they will also have to persuade people to potentially change their mind-set. The need to adopt an inquisitive attitude, to be prepared to innovate and think outside the box, to experiment and to learn from failures may not be second nature to some, but is likely to be critical in transforming successfully to digital.

3 **Establishing a strategic direction** – this is probably something that the business has done for a long time, but a digital strategy may require it to be done in a different way. For example, the planning horizon may need to be shortened, or greater flexibility introduced – perhaps a move away from the rational model to a more emergent approach, which would enable the business to adapt as time passes.

4 **Influence external parties** – for example, providers of finance. Raising capital is likely to be necessary, but showing how that capital may be applied and the value that will result might be more problematic. Will investing in cloud technology deliver increased shareholder wealth? If so, how much? And when? There will be greater uncertainty over outcomes, and the leaders of the business will need to be persuasive and articulate a compelling value proposition.

5 **Collaboration** – as has already been mentioned earlier in this text, the organisation will need to see itself as part of a wider ecosystem if it is to deliver the requisite value. This will require careful thought on who to collaborate with and how each part of the ecosystem will contribute.

6 **Business judgement** – what sort of business model will the organisation need to put in place? It is probable that an altogether different model to what has worked in the past will be required.

7 **Execution** – having determined what technologies can help to drive the business forwards, thought must then be given to how these can be used most effectively by the people within the business. People and technology need to work in harmony to produce the desired outcomes. Careful thought must also be given to how the execution of the digital strategy and transformation is to be managed. For example, what sort of metrics (or KPIs) need to be put in place? What benchmarks should be adopted as a successful outcome?

Building talent – it will be critical to identify the skills that staff will need to demonstrate and to manage training/recruitment to ensure that the business has those skills. New roles are likely to be required, including at the most senior level – for example, perhaps a new board position of Chief Digital Officer.

Test your understanding 5

Option 1	Build	
Option 2	Invest	
Option 3	Buy	X
Option 4	Partner	

Buy

Buying another company is usually the most appropriate path when there is a strategic imperative to 'own' a market and may be the only viable option if a significant change market is imminent, hiring the right talent is not possible or the new opportunity bears little relation to the firm's current business. Similarly engaging early with a digital disruptor is important to wrong-foot the competition and minimise the investment needed.

Test your understanding 6

Option 1	Skynet	
Option 2	Data-powered	
Option 3	Customer-centric	X
Option 4	Open and liquid	

The five DTI business models are:

- **Customer-centric.** This model focuses on making customers' lives easier and emphasizes front-office processes. Leading exponents include the UK retailer Argos, but it can be applied across industries. It works best with a culture that puts the client first and a decentralized structure that empowers frontline staff.
- **Extra-frugal.** This model thrives on a culture of 'less is more' and a standardized organizational structure. By optimizing manufacturing, supply and support processes, it can provide a high-quality service at a low cost. A prime example of this model is tire manufacturer Michelin.
- **Data-powered.** This model is built around prowess in analytics and software intelligence. Epitomized by Google and Netflix, data-powered companies have an agile culture focused on innovation through empirical experimentation.
- **Skynet.** Named after the conscious, artificial general intelligence of the Terminator films, this model makes intensive use of machines to increase productivity and flexibility in production. Pioneered by enterprises such as Amazon and Rio Tinto, Skynet organizations are characterized by an engineer-led culture dedicated to automation.

Open and liquid. This model looks outward with a view to creating an ecosystem that can enrich the customer proposition. Built around a sharing customer, all processes in organizations of this kind are characterized by a constant flow of dialog with the outside world.

Examples include Facebook and PayPal.

Test your understanding 7

Option 1	Attract and retain talent	
Option 2	Foster a digital culture in the enterprise	X
Option 3	Create a workforce with digital skills	
Option 4	Become an employer of choice for millennials	X
Option 5	Bring leadership into the digital age	

2 Become an employer of choice for millennials. Initiatives to boost the recruitment of millennials include identifying where their digital skills will best fit in the organization, **offering career development programmes** and building workspaces designed to attract digital talent.

5 Foster a digital culture in the enterprise. Factors that set a digital company's culture apart include a strong sense of purpose and a diverse high-quotient digital workforce. **Leadership needs to release people's creativity** and apply lean start-up methodologies such as hackathons and design thinking.

Question 1

Option 1	Build	X
Option 2	Buy	
Option 3	Partner	
Option 4	Invest	X
Option 5	Incubate/accelerate	

Build

Building new business models might be the best route when an opportunity is related to the company's core business. The benefits are that it typically maximises control and minimises costs in markets that a company must own because of their strategic importance. If companies decide to go for the build route, they can benefit by creating and developing new products and services.

Invest

Investing in interesting start-ups is often a valid option, allowing an established company to connect with the right skills and capabilities. It will also avoid hindering entrepreneurial forces with a setup focused on internal governance and reporting.

Question 2

Option 1	Build	X
Option 2	Buy	X
Option 3	Partner	X
Option 4	Invest	X
Option 5	Incubate/accelerate	X

Build

Building new business models might be the best route when an opportunity is related to the company's core business. The benefits are that it typically maximises control and minimises costs in markets that a company must own because of their strategic importance. If companies decide to go for the build route, they can benefit by creating and developing new products and services.

Buy

Buying another company is usually the most appropriate path when there is a strategic imperative to 'own' a market and may be the only viable option if a significant change market is imminent, hiring the right talent is not possible and the new opportunity bears little relation to the firm's current business model may provide reasons to buy. Similarly engaging early with a digital disruptor is important to wrong-foot the competition and minimise the investment needed.

Partner

A firm can use partnering with a digital disruptor to learn more about the market and its partner's model. A partnering approach is sensible when it makes sense to learn about emergent opportunities, with an eye toward deeper partnerships or acquisitions in the future. Companies need to develop a more flexible and open mind-set toward partnerships; which are expected to play an important role in the digital transformation of market players.

Invest

Investing in interesting start-ups is often a valid option, allowing an established company to connect with the right skills and capabilities. It will also avoid hindering entrepreneurial forces with a setup focused on internal governance and reporting.

Incubate/accelerate

Investment and incubation/acceleration might seem similar endeavours. The latter however represents a closer relationship to the funding company, deploying corporate internal capabilities, infrastructure and resources to the start-ups. Having said that, incubators and accelerators need to precisely outline both internal benefits and incentives for start-ups and entrepreneurs, and a clear strategy and vision.

Question 3

Step 1	Create a workforce with digital skills	3
Step 2	Foster a digital culture in the enterprise	5
Step 3	Integrate your on-demand workforce	7
Step 4	Attract and retain talent	1
Step 5	Create environments where humans and robots can work successfully together	6
Step 6	Bring leadership into the digital age	4
Step 7	Become an employer of choice for millennials	2

1 Attract and retain talent. Attracting and retaining talent starts by listening to what employees are saying about a firm, both externally and internally. Referred employees perform better, so enterprises should incentivize their employees to use online networks to refer potential employees.

2 Become an employer of choice for millennials. Initiatives to boost the recruitment of millennials include identifying where their digital skills will best fit in the organization, offering career development programmes and building workspaces designed to attract digital talent.

3 Create a workforce with digital skills. Organizations need to actively develop the skills they need in-house by making training a critical component of their talent management strategy. Bring new skills into the organization by hiring digital leaders and digital natives.

4 Bring leadership into the digital age. Leaders need to hire people with digital mind-sets and a willingness to challenge the status quo. A possible way for organizations to facilitate change at the top is by creating technology immersion workshops or advisory committees for boards.

5	Foster a digital culture in the enterprise. Factors that set a digital company's culture apart include a strong sense of purpose and a diverse high-quotient digital workforce. Leadership needs to release people's creativity and apply lean start-up methodologies such as hackathons and design thinking.
6	Create environments where humans and robots can work successfully together. In the event that jobs are threatened by automation, employers will have to assess whether it is possible to reskill workers, either to work alongside robots or in new roles.
7	Integrate your on-demand workforce. The most effective way to recruit on-demand workers is through online talent platforms. The extended workforce can help improve the overall quality of the talent pool.

Question 4

Option 1	Customer-centric	
Option 2	Extra-frugal	
Option 3	Data-powered	
Option 4	Skynet	
Option 5	Open and liquid	X

The five DTI business models are:

- **Customer-centric.** This model focuses on making customers' lives easier and emphasizes front-office processes. Leading exponents include the UK retailer Argos, but it can be applied across industries. It works best with a culture that puts the client first and a decentralized structure that empowers frontline staff.
- **Extra-frugal.** This model thrives on a culture of 'less is more' and a standardized organizational structure. By optimizing manufacturing, supply and support processes, it can provide a high-quality service at a low cost. A prime example of this model is tire manufacturer Michelin.
- **Data-powered.** This model is built around prowess in analytics and software intelligence. Epitomized by Google and Netflix, data-powered companies have an agile culture focused on innovation through empirical experimentation.

- **Skynet.** Named after the conscious, artificial general intelligence of the Terminator films, this model makes intensive use of machines to increase productivity and flexibility in production. Pioneered by enterprises such as Amazon and Rio Tinto, Skynet organizations are characterized by an engineer-led culture dedicated to automation.
- **Open and liquid.** This model looks outward with a view to creating an ecosystem that can enrich the customer proposition. Built around a sharing customer, all processes in organizations of this kind are characterized by a constant flow of dialog with the outside world. Examples include Facebook and PayPal.

Question 5

Option 1	Inspirational leadership	
Option 2	Business judgement	X
Option 3	Influence external parties	
Option 4	Collaboration	

In order for an organisation to properly take advantage of a move to digital, or to survive digital disruption within its industry, the executive leadership team will need to demonstrate a number of abilities:

1 **Inspirational leadership** – digitisation will be an exercise in change management, but probably on a bigger and quicker scale than the organisation will typically be used to. The leadership team will need to energise the workforce and inspire confidence that digitisation is the right way forwards and is being carried out in the right way. The move to digital will only succeed if those at the top of the organisation take ownership and persuade others to commit to the change.

2 **Competitive edge** – not only will the leadership need to motivate others within the organisation to see the digital transformation as the right strategy; they will also have to persuade people to potentially change their mind-set. The need to adopt an inquisitive attitude, to be prepared to innovate and think outside the box, to experiment and to learn from failures may not be second nature to some, but is likely to be critical in transforming successfully to digital.

3 **Establishing a strategic direction** – this is probably something that the business has done for a long time, but a digital strategy may require it to be done in a different way. For example, the planning horizon may need to be shortened, or greater flexibility introduced – perhaps a move away from the rational model to a more emergent approach, which would enable the business to adapt as time passes.

4 **Influence external parties** – for example, providers of finance. Raising capital is likely to be necessary, but showing how that capital may be applied and the value that will result might be more problematic. Will investing in cloud technology deliver increased shareholder wealth? If so, how much? And when? There will be greater uncertainty over outcomes, and the leaders of the business will need to be persuasive and articulate a compelling value proposition.

5 **Collaboration** – as has already been mentioned earlier in this text, the organisation will need to see itself as part of a wider ecosystem if it is to deliver the requisite value. This will require careful thought on who to collaborate with and how each part of the ecosystem will contribute.

6 **Business judgement** – what sort of business model will the organisation need to put in place? It is probable that an altogether different model to what has worked in the past will be required.

7 **Execution** – having determined what technologies can help to drive the business forwards, thought must then be given to how these can be used most effectively by the people within the business. People and technology need to work in harmony to produce the desired outcomes. Careful thought must also be given to how the execution of the digital strategy and transformation is to be managed. For example, what sort of metrics (or KPIs) need to be put in place? What benchmarks should be adopted as a successful outcome?

Building talent – it will be critical to identify the skills that staff will need to demonstrate and to manage training/recruitment to ensure that the business has those skills. New roles are likely to be required, including at the most senior level – for example, perhaps a new board position of Chief Digital Officer.

Chapter

4

Leadership and management

Chapter learning objectives

Lead	Component
B1: Compare and contrast different types of leadership and management styles	(a) Different leadership concepts (b) Types of leadership (c) Leadership in different contexts

Topics to be covered

- Power, authority, delegation and empowerment
- Contingent and situational leadership
- Transactional and transformational leadership
- Leadership of virtual teams
- Leadership and ethics.

1 Session content diagram

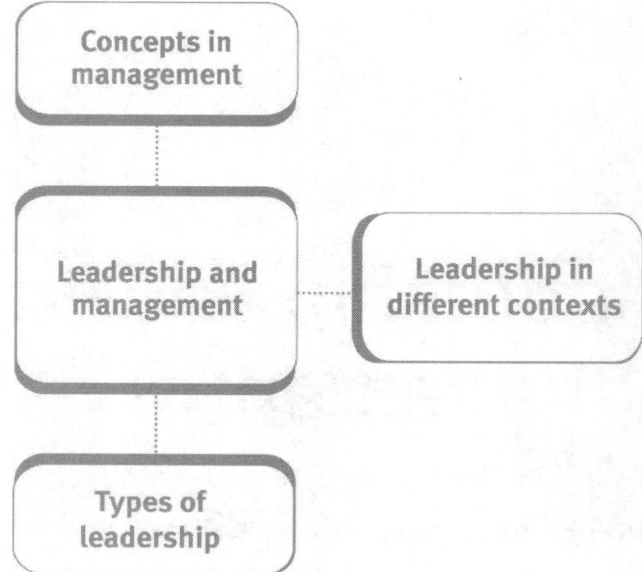

2 The difference between leadership and management

Sometimes the terms management and leadership are used interchangeably. There is, however, a difference between the two and it does not follow that every leader is a manager, or that every manager is a leader.

Leadership

Leadership can be viewed as providing direction, creating a vision, and then influencing others to share that vision and work towards the achievement of organisational goals. Leadership can be seen as 'getting other people to do things willingly' and can occur at all different levels within the organisation.

We will look at leadership in more detail later in the chapter.

Management

Management is the process of getting things done through the efforts of other people. It focuses on procedures and results. Managers tend to react to specific situations and be more concerned with solving short-term problems. Management suggests more formality and the term 'manager' refers to a position within a structured organisation with prescribed roles.

A century ago, in 1916, **Fayol** identified the common features of management. These are still relevant to management today.

He identified the common features as:

- **Planning**
- **Organising**
- **Co-ordinating**
- **Commanding**
- **Controlling**.

More recently, in 1989, **Mintzberg** identified the ten roles which managers fulfil in the course of their job. These are divided into three groups:

- Interpersonal
- Informational
- Decisional.

Interpersonal	
Figurehead	Symbolic role in which the manager is obliged to carry out social, inspirational, legal and ceremonial duties.
Leader	This relates to the manager's relationship with subordinates, especially in allocating tasks, hiring, training and motivating staff.
Liaison	The manager must develop a network of contacts outside the chain of command through which information and favours can be traded for mutual benefit.
Informational	
Monitor	The manager collects and sorts out information which is used to build up a general understanding of the organisation and its environment as a basis for decision making.
Disseminator	The manager is responsible for distributing information to those who need it.
Spokesperson	The manager is responsible for transmitting information to various external groups by acting in a PR capacity, lobbying for the organisation, informing the public about the organisation's performance, plans and policies.
Decisional	
Entrepreneur	The manager should be looking continually for problems and opportunities when situations requiring improvement are discovered.
Disturbance handler	The manager has to respond to pressures over which the department has no control.

Resource allocator	The manager must choose from among competing demands for money, equipment, personnel and management time.
Negotiator	The manager must take charge when their organisation engages in negotiations with others. In these negotiations, the manager acts as a figurehead, spokesperson and resource allocator.

3 Important concepts in management

Individuals within the workplace have different relationships with each other. To be able to analyse the nature of management relationships it is necessary to understand a number of important concepts.

- Power
- Authority
- Responsibility
- Accountability
- Empowerment
- Delegation.

Power

Power is **the capacity to exert influence**, to make someone act according to your own preferences.

Types of power

French and Raven identified five possible bases of a leader's power:

- **Reward power**. A person has power over another because they can give rewards, such as promotions or financial rewards.
- **Coercive power**. This power enables a person to give punishments to others: for example, to dismiss, suspend, reprimand them, or make them carry out unpleasant tasks.

  Reward power and coercive power are similar but limited in application because they are limited to the size of the reward or punishment that can be given. For example, there isn't much a manager could get a subordinate to do for a $5 reward, but there are many, many things they might do for a $50,000 reward.

- **Referent power**. This is based upon the identification with the person who has charisma, or the desire to be like that person. It could be regarded as 'imitative' power which is often seen in the way children imitate their parents. Think of the best boss you've ever had and consider what you liked about them and if it encouraged you to act in a similar way.

  Psychologists believe that referent power is perhaps the most extensive since it can be exercised when the holder is not present or has no intention of exercising influence.

- **Expert power**. This is based upon doing what the expert says since they are the expert. You will have a measure of expert power when you join CIMA® . People will do as you suggest because you have studied and have qualified. However expert power only extends to the expert's field of expertise.

- **Legitimate power**. This is based on agreement and commonly-held values which allow one person to have power over another person. For example, an older person, or one who has longer service in a company. In some societies it is customary for a man to be the 'head of the family', or in other societies elders make decisions due to their age and experience.

Case study style question 1

G, the senior partner of LMN, a medium sized accountancy firm, has worked for LMN for over twenty years and has a sound knowledge and understanding of the different activities of the company's business. Over the years, G has become known for his fairness in how he manages staff. He is also well liked and respected for his enthusiastic approach. He always has time to encourage and mentor younger members of staff.

The company has recently invested in new technology which will improve the effectiveness of its office systems, but will mean the roles and responsibilities of the support staff will change. G has taken on the unenviable role of leading the project to introduce the technology and new working practices. He knows that the project will be met with resistance from some members of staff and he will need to draw on various sources of power to ensure the changes are successfully implemented.

Required:

Write an email to G explaining the different sources of power that he has which will help him in introducing the changes.

(15 minutes)

Authority

Authority is the **right to exercise power** such as hiring and firing or buying and selling on behalf of the organisation; the right that an individual has to require certain actions of others; the right to do or act.

Max Weber proposed that authority legitimises the exercise of power within the structure and rules of the organisation. Hence, it allows individuals within an organisation to issue instructions for others to follow. Weber defined three bases for such authority as follows:

Charismatic authority. Here the individual has some special quality of personality which sets them apart. Because the charismatic power in the organisation is so dependent on the individual, difficulties arise when he or she has to be replaced. Unless someone else is available, who also possesses the necessary charisma, the organisation could start to fail or may have to change to another form.

Traditional authority. This authority is based upon custom and practice. The personality of the individual is irrelevant as he or she inherits their authority because of the long-standing belief in the natural right to 'rule' which is sometimes handed down.

Rational-legal authority. Here the authority comes from the individual's position in the organisation chart. The ability to perform particular functions and their operations is based on following a set of written rules. This authority is not personal but is vested, impersonally, in the position held. This is Weber's classic bureaucracy which will be considered later in the chapter.

The link between authority and power bases

Weber's three types of authority (charismatic, traditional and rational-legal) can be linked to the French and Raven power bases as follows:

Power base	Authority base
Coercive and Legitimate	Traditional
Reward and Referent	Charismatic
Expert	Rational-legal

Responsibility

Responsibility involves **the obligation of an individual who occupies a particular position in the organisation to perform certain duties, tasks or make certain decisions**.

Responsibility means the right to hold subordinates accountable for personal performance and achievement of the targets specified by the organisation's plans. It is the obligation to use authority to see duties are performed.

The scope of responsibility must correspond to the scope of authority given.

All managers should have both responsibility and authority appropriate to their role. If these are not in balance, it can cause serious problems.

Responsibility without authority. This may occur when a manager is held responsible for, say, timekeeping, but does not have the authority to discipline subordinates who are regularly late. The manager is likely to become frustrated and demotivated as they lack the power and authority needed to meet the targets they have been made responsible for.

Authority without responsibility. This may occur where an HR department has the authority to employ new members of staff, but are not held responsible for the quality of the employees that they have selected. Managers who are not made accountable for their decisions and actions may act irresponsibly, as they do not expect to suffer any negative consequences.

Accountability

Accountability describes **the need for individuals to explain and justify any failure to fulfil their responsibilities to their superiors** in the hierarchy. It refers to being called to account for one's actions and results.

Empowerment

Employee empowerment is where **employees are given autonomy and responsibility to undertake tasks without being directed at each step by management**. To be able to empower staff, management has to have trust in their capabilities and be willing to allow employees to make decisions, within set limits.

Companies can benefit from empowering staff as the managers will not feel the need to micro-manage every aspect of the employees behaviour, which should free up management time. From the point of view of the employees, they will feel valued and motivated.

To promote empowerment, managers should:

- Set clear boundaries and ensure employees know what is expected from them
- Actively encourage employee development
- Communicate openly with employees and adopt and open-door policy
- Allow employees to contribute and listen to their views
- Offer regular feedback
- Lead by example.

Delegation

Delegation is one of the main functions of effective management. It is the process whereby managers assign part of their authority to a subordinate to fulfil their duties. However, delegation can only occur if the manager initially possesses the authority to delegate.

 **Responsibility can never be delegated.**

A superior is always responsible for the actions of his subordinates and cannot evade this responsibility by delegation.

Benefits of delegation

There are many practical reasons why managers should delegate:

- Without it the chief executive would be responsible for everything and individuals have physical and mental limitations.
- Allows for career planning and development, aids continuity and cover for absence.
- Allows for better decision making; those closer to the problem make the decision, allowing higher-level managers to spend more time on strategic issues.
- Allowing the individual with the appropriate skills to make the decision improves time management.
- Gives people more interesting work, increases job satisfaction for subordinates; increased motivation encourages better work.

Reluctance to delegate

Despite the benefits many managers are reluctant to delegate, preferring to deal with routine matters themselves in addition to the more major aspects of their duties. There are several reasons for this:

- Managers often believe that their subordinates are not able or experienced enough to perform the tasks.
- Managers believe that doing routine tasks enables them to keep in touch with what is happening in the other areas of their department.
- Where a manager feels insecure they will invariably be reluctant to pass any authority to a subordinate. They may fear that the subordinate will do a better job than they can.
- Some managers do not know how or what to delegate.
- Managers fear losing control.
- Initially delegation can take a lot of a manager's time and a common reason for not delegating is that the managers feel they could complete the job quicker if they did it themselves.

Effective delegation

Koontz and O'Donnell state that to delegate effectively a manager must:

- define the limits of authority delegated to their subordinate.
- satisfy themselves that the subordinate is competent to exercise that authority.
- discipline themselves to permit the subordinate the full use of that authority without constant checks and interference.

In planning delegation therefore, a manager must ensure that:

- Too much is not delegated to totally overload a subordinate.
- The subordinate has reasonable skill and experience in the area concerned.
- Appropriate authority is delegated.
- Monitoring and control are possible.
- There is not a feeling of 'passing the buck' or 'opting out'.
- All concerned know that the task has been delegated.
- Time is set aside for coaching and guiding.

Methods of delegation

There are different methods of delegation, which vary in effectiveness:

- **Abdication**. This leave issues without any formal delegation, which is very crude and usually an ineffective method.
- **Custom and practice**. This is an age-old system, the most junior member of staff opens the mail, gets the coffee and so on.
- **Explanation**. The managers brief subordinates along the lines of how the task should be done. (not too little and not too much – a fine balance that requires judgement).
- **Consultation**. Prior consultation is considered to be important and very effective. People, if organised, are immensely powerful; by contributing or withholding their cooperation they make the task a success or failure. Managers admit that sometimes good ideas come from below. In fact the point of view of the person nearest the scene of action is more likely to be relevant.

Case study style question 2

H has for some time been in charge of a department which was producing satisfactory results before he took over. However, recently, several of his staff have asked whether similar jobs in other departments are available. There have also been a number of unexpected mistakes, and information has not been transmitted properly.

You are H's manager. As a result of your concern you have been keeping an eye on the situation. You have found that H comes in early every day, stays late, takes large amounts of work home with him, and is showing definite signs of strain. In the meantime, his staff appear bored and disinterested. You have arranged a meeting with H to discuss these issues.

Required:

Write briefing notes for the meeting covering the following:

(a) Describing the possible causes of this situation.

(10 minutes)

(b) Explaining the principles for effective delegation.

(10 minutes)

(c) Commenting on the advantages to both manager and subordinate of effective delegation.

(10 minutes)

4 Classical and contemporary theories of management

The study of management theory and development of ideas on effective management practice helps in providing an understanding of the principles underlying the process of management and which in turn influences management behaviour in organisations. The main schools of management thinking can be grouped according to their broad approaches as shown below:

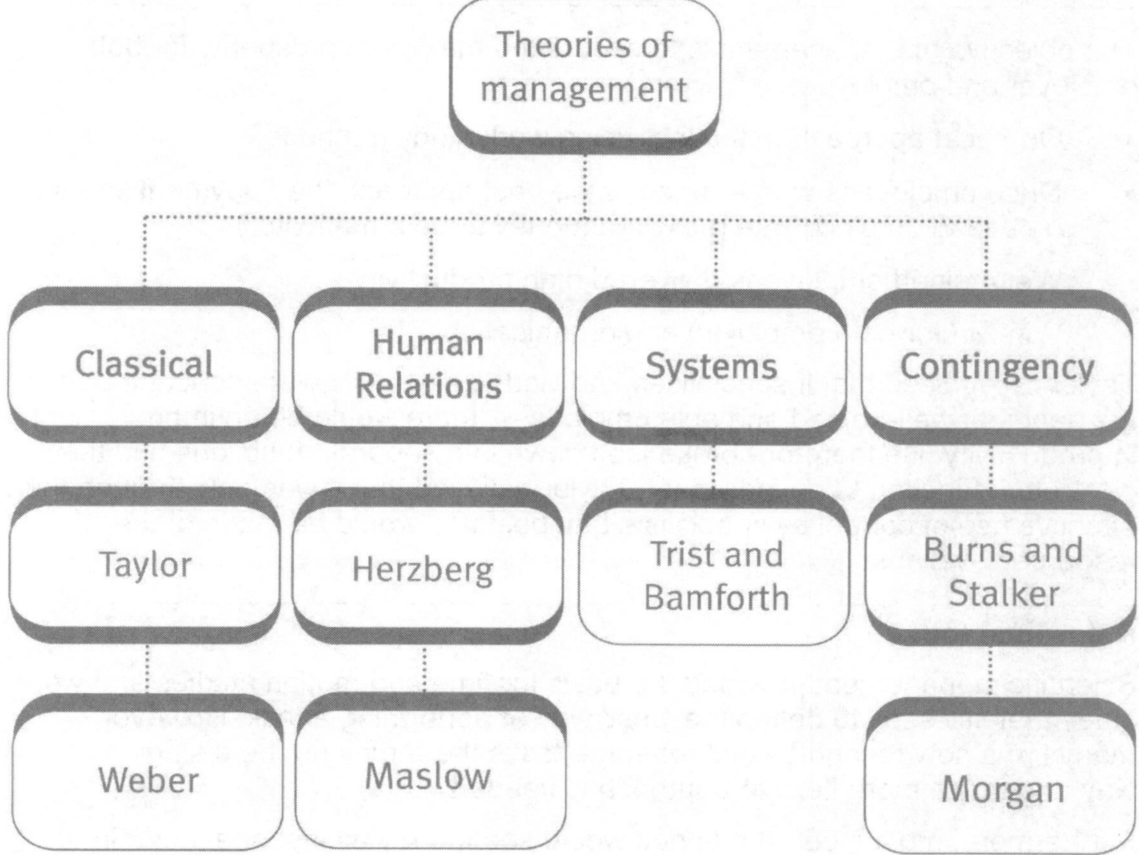

Classical theories

The classical approach to management emphasises the technical and economic aspects of organisations. It assumes that behaviour in organisations is rational and logical. There are different approaches within the Classical School which can be identified as Scientific Management (**Taylor**) and Bureaucracy (**Weber**).

The foundation on which the various theories developed was that management could be learnt and codified. These ideas were developed in an era when mass production and economies of scale were viewed as central to business success. Although some of these theories were developed over a century ago they do continue to inform management practice today.

There are some common interests that all these different perspectives focus on:

- The purpose and structure of organisations and planning of work.
- The technical requirements of each job.
- The principles of management.

Scientific management (Taylor)

The objective of management is to secure the maximum prosperity for both employer and employee:

- One best approach to the job, using work study methods
- Once employees were trained in the best approach then payment should be based on piece-rate (believed money to be a motivator)
- Well-trained employees delivered high productivity
- Win:win for both employee and organisation.

Taylor recognised that if specialised knowledge and skills were concentrated in the hands of well-trained and able employees, there would be an improvement in productivity. He therefore broke jobs down into separate functions and then gave each function to an individual. Taylor believed that it was only through the effective use of control by specialists that best use would be made of the resources available.

Relevance today

Scientific management provided the basis for time and motion studies and work study that still seek to define the 'best' way of performing a task. However, many firms now recognise that for some tasks there may not be a single best way and that a more flexible approach is needed.

Furthermore, most modern theories would see money as just one factor in a more complex understanding of motivation.

Bureaucratic management (Weber)

Max Weber developed his model of the 'ideal type' of bureaucracy, in which he explored the characteristics of a rational form of organisation. Today, the term bureaucracy tends to have many negative connotations, but Weber used it to describe what he believed to be potentially the most efficient form of organisation.

Weber's bureaucracy is based on formalisation and standardisation.

- Based on hierarchy of authority
- Strict rules and regulations govern decision making
- Specialisation in duties, segregated 'offices' and levels.

Relevance today

Nowadays, most large organisations will have some levels of bureaucracy, particularly where repetitive administrative tasks are performed. Because of the formal nature of this type of organisation, the main disadvantages are:

- slow response to change, as many rules have to be followed
- lack of speedy communication owing to the segregated 'offices' and levels
- little need for involving staff in decision-making
- rules stifle initiative and innovative ideas, preventing development
- no recognition of very important informal relationships.

This type of organisational culture is **not suitable if the firm operates in a dynamic changing environment**.

The main characteristics of bureaucracy

Weber listed the main characteristics of bureaucracy:

- **Specialisation**. Clear division of labour, so that each member has well-defined roles and responsibilities.
- **Hierarchy**. A hierarchy of authority, in which offices are linked through a clear chain of command.
- **Rules**. Strict rules and procedures govern decision-making and conduct.
- **Impersonality**. Objective and rational decisions rather than personal preferences.
- **Appointed officials**. Managers are selected by their qualifications, education or training.
- **Career officials**. Managers pursue their career within the bureaucracy and work within a defined salary structure.
- **Full-time officials**. Professionalism requires commitment.
- **Public/private division**. Money is used in a limited liability framework to prevent family money being used, as this creates conservatism because of personal risk.

5 The human relations school

In the 1930s researchers started studying the behaviour of people in groups. While the classical theories viewed workers as components in the system, and focused on processes and procedures, these researchers started looking at the effects of social interaction on motivation and productivity. This was the beginning of Human Relations School.

Herzberg

Frederick Herzberg looked at the identification of the motivational needs of individuals. His two factor theory describes motivational and hygiene factors.

- **Hygiene factors** are based on a need to avoid unpleasantness. They do not provide any long-term motivating power. A lack of satisfaction of hygiene factors will demotivate staff.
- **Motivational factors (motivators)** satisfy a need for personal growth. Satisfaction of motivator factors can encourage staff to work harder.

Herzberg believed that only motivators can move employees to action, the hygiene factors cannot. They can only prevent dissatisfaction.

In order to motivate the workforce management must avoid dissatisfaction and put in place motivators to encourage the staff.

Hygiene factors

To avoid dissatisfaction there should be:

- Policies and procedures for staff treatment.
- Suitable level and quality of supervision.
- Pleasant physical and working conditions.
- Appropriate level of salary and status for the job.
- Team working.

Motivational factors

In order to motivate staff managers should provide:

- Sense of accomplishment (achievement) through setting targets.
- Recognition of good work.
- Increasing levels of responsibility.
- Career advancement.
- Attraction of the job.

Herzberg felt that **'you can't motivate dissatisfied people'**. Satisfiers or motivators will only generate job satisfaction if the hygiene factors are present.

Herzberg's theory of motivation illustration

CDE Local Authority employs around 8,000 members of staff. It operates as a traditional, formal governmental type of organisation. Over the last few years it has recognised a problem regarding its junior Management Level in that many of them are failing to meet the expected level of performance.

A team has been set up to investigate the problem and they have decided to hold a series of meetings with all levels of management. Initially they found that the junior managers were reluctant to participate in the meetings, saying that they could see no real value in them. 'We have seen it all before' was a typical response. After the meetings, the team produced a report which identified three main problem areas.

Firstly, it became apparent that the level of morale for all staff was low. Lack of facilities and pressure of work appeared to be the main grievance. There appeared however to be a deeper problem, that of mistrust between the staff as a whole and senior management. The reason for this was unclear.

The second problem appeared to be that junior managers were regarded by staff as poor at managing their sections. In response, the junior managers said that their positions in general were unclear; there were no clear lines of authority, command or responsibility which allowed them to make decisions for their departments. In addition many quoted their roles as being menial and highlighted funding shortages, unrealistic targets, little recognition of their position, no job descriptions and lack of training as problems.

Job security was the third issue. Financial cutbacks and changes in service levels had led to rumours of substantial cutbacks in staff. Rumours were especially strong amongst the junior management. It was felt that new, younger staff would be better trained and would be likely to replace them.

In all, the problems had shown themselves in high labour turnover, which in addition to the problems already outlined, were blamed on low salaries, little opportunity for personal advancement and poor working conditions.

Using Herzberg's theory of motivation, the attitude of the junior managers can be explained as follows:

The case illustrates Herzberg's motivation theory, which attempts to explain those factors which motivate the individual by identifying and satisfying the individual's needs, desires and the goals pursued to satisfy these desires.

This theory is based upon the idea that motivation factors can be separated into hygiene factors and motivation factors and is therefore often referred to as a 'two need system.' These two separate 'needs' are the need to avoid unpleasantness and discomfort and, at the other end of the motivational scale, the need for personal development.

A shortage of those factors which positively encourage employees (motivating factors) will cause those employees to focus on other, non-job related factors, the so called 'hygiene' factors. These are illustrated in the case with the attitude of the junior management to senior management and their concerns for example with shortages, targets, recognition and training and 'we've seen it all before'.

The most important part of this theory of motivation is that the main motivating factors are not in the environment but in the intrinsic value and satisfaction gained from the job itself. It follows therefore that the job itself must have challenge, scope for enrichment and be of interest to the job holder. This is not the case in the scenario; there appears to be little or no intrinsic satisfaction from the junior manager's work, illustrated by them regarding themselves and their role as menial and their lack of responsibility and decision making powers within their own departments.

Motivators (or 'satisfiers') are those factors directly concerned with the satisfaction gained from the job itself, the sense of achievement, level of recognition, the intrinsic value felt of the job itself, level of responsibility, opportunities for advancement and the status provided by the job. Motivators lead to satisfaction because of the need for growth and a sense of self achievement. Clearly, none of this applies to the junior managers of CDE Local Authority.

A lack of motivators leads to over concentration on hygiene factors; that is those negative factors which can be seen and therefore form the basis of complaint and concern.

Hygiene (or maintenance) factors lead to job dissatisfaction because of the need to avoid unpleasantness. They are so called because they can in turn be avoided by the use of 'hygienic' methods i.e. they can be prevented. Attention to these hygiene factors prevents dissatisfaction but does not on its own provide motivation. Hygiene factors (or 'dissatisfiers') are concerned with those factors associated with, but not directly a part of, the job itself. These can be detected in the scenario; salary and the perceived differences with others, job security, working conditions, the quality of management, organisational policy and administration and interpersonal relations.

Understanding Herzberg's theory identifies the nature of intrinsic satisfaction that can be obtained from the work itself, draws attention to job design and makes managers aware that problems of motivation may not necessarily be directly associated with the work.

Maslow's hierarchy of needs

Maslow developed a hierarchy of needs, shown below.

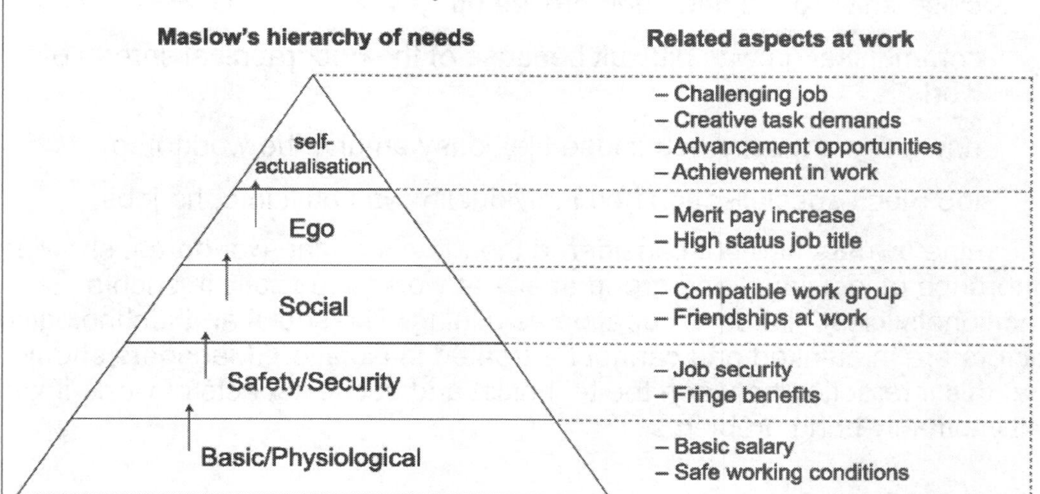

According to the model, each individual has a set of needs which can be arranged in a hierarchy. The above diagram has shown the hierarchy in a business context. The largest and most fundamental needs, such as basic pay and safe working conditions are shown at the bottom, and the need for self-actualisation/self-fulfilment is at the top, moving through aspects such as job security, friendships at work and status.

The lowest needs must be satisfied first, only then can an individual move to the next level. This can be used as a motivational tool, if the management can determine where individuals are on the hierarchy, they will know that the next level can be used in motivating staff.

6 Systems theory

Systems theory is an approach to organisational work design which takes account of social aspects and technical aspects. It looks at the interaction between people and technology within the organisation.

Trist and Bamforth

Trist and Bamforth developed a socio-technical systems theory. While he was working at the Tavistock Institute, Trist's most famous research was into the structure and operation of the 'longwall' method of mining in County Durham in the 1940s as it highlighted the interaction between social needs and technological activities. The 'longwall' method introduced new cutting equipment which widened the narrow coal 'face' into a 'longwall'. But very soon the low morale, high absenteeism and deteriorating relationships were so serious that the Tavistock Institute was invited to investigate causes and possible solutions to the problems.

Trist and Bamforth diagnosed that although the new methods had been introduced 'scientifically':

- close-knit groups had been broken up
- communication was difficult because of the geographical spread of workers
- new payment schemes caused jealousy among the workforce
- too much specialisation and individuality was built into the jobs.

The mine owners had not considered the effects on the workforce, showing an ignorance of individual and group needs at work, especially in such a traditionally close-linked occupation as mining. The social and technological factors are interlinked and cannot be treated in isolation. Managers should note that this interaction between the technical and social aspects of work, if ignored, will inevitably bring problems.

7 Contingency theory

Managers, researchers and consultants often found that the methods suggested by the classical management schools did not always work. The idea of one approach being right, whether it be the school of scientific management, classical, human relations or systems, is rejected in favour of contingency. The contingency view suggests that the effectiveness of various managerial practices, styles and techniques will **vary according to the particular circumstances of the situation**.

Mechanistic versus Organic Organisations (Burns and Stalker)

Burns and Stalker (1961) distinguished between mechanistic and organic organisations. Burns is quoted as saying: 'The beginning of administrative wisdom is the awareness that there is no one best way of designing a management system.' Burns and Stalker studied the way in which high-technology industries were being introduced into Scotland. The difficulties experienced by low-technology companies in the conversion process to high technology highlighted many organisation structural problems.

Burns and Stalker's studies led them to distinguish between two major types of organisations (mechanistic and organic). However, they considered these two systems to be located at opposite ends of a continuum, with various combinations in between.

Features of a mechanistic organisation:

- High degree of task specialisation.
- Responsibilities and authority clearly defined.
- Coordination and communication – a responsibility of each Management Level.
- Selectivity in the release of top-level information to subordinates.

- Great emphasis on the organisational hierarchy's ability to develop loyalty and obedience.
- Employees are often locally recruited.
- The mechanistic system was seen to be appropriate in fairly stable conditions where the management of change was not seen to be an important factor. The relationship with Weber's bureaucracy is obvious.

Features of an organic organisation

- Skills, experience and specialist knowledge recognised as valuable resources.
- Integration of efforts via lateral, vertical and diagonal communication channels.
- Leadership based on consultation and involvement in problem-solving.
- Commitment to task achievement, survival and growth more important than loyalty and obedience.
- Employees are recruited from a variety of sources.
- The organic system is seen to be more responsive to change, and is therefore recommended for organisations moving into periods of rapid changes in technology, market orientation, or tasks.

The appropriateness of organisational structure to its environment is a cornerstone of contingency theory.

Contemporary perspectives

Gareth Morgan has argued that we can view organisations in different ways as we try to understand them. We are rarely aware of the image of organisations we take for granted but, just like the photographs of the Parthenon from different perspectives, they fundamentally influence what we see and the explanations we put forward to make sense of it. However, the Parthenon can be approached from different directions, though not all are equally easy. Different angles will give different perspectives, and by arriving very early in the morning you could get a photograph with unusual lighting and fewer people in it.

The same is true of the way we look at organisations and the process of management.

From one perspective it is helpful to think of organisations as machines, in which the various jobs and departments are carefully designed to work smoothly together to perform certain functions effectively. This is certainly the view implicit in the early classical theories such as scientific management.

The view of organisations as machines provides some useful insights, but also imposes limitations, which in some circumstances can be severe. For example, the use of basic costing techniques in large multi-product firms may result in misleading information for decision-making. In this type of situation, more sophisticated models which recognise the more complicated nature of the organisation, may be more appropriate.

The limitations of mechanistic perspectives on organisations are as follows:

- They can create organisational forms that have great difficulty adapting to changed circumstances.
- They can result in mindless and unquestioning bureaucracy.
- They can have unanticipated and undesirable consequences as the interests of those working in the organisation take precedence over the goals the organisation was designed to achieve.
- They can have dehumanising effects upon employees, especially those at the lower levels of the organisational hierarchy (Morgan, 1986).

Morgan goes on to argue that there are other ways of viewing organisations that lead to different insights. It is not possible to go into all of those here, but two other perspectives he identifies are the view of organisations as organisms and organisations as cultures. It is important for managers to be able to examine organisational problems from more than one perspective in their search for effectiveness.

8 Leadership

Leadership is influencing others to do what he or she wants them to do; it involves human interaction and is often associated with the willing and enthusiastic behaviour of followers. The ability to influence needs the permission of those to be influenced. Leadership is related to motivation, interpersonal behaviour and the process of communication.

Leadership is a **dynamic process** and is very important at all levels within the organisation, from the board room to the shop floor. It does not necessarily take place within the hierarchical structure of the organisation. A leader may have no formal title at all and may rely on personal traits and style to influence followers.

Leadership comes about in a number of different ways:

- Some leaders are **elected** such as in politics and trade unions.
- Other leaders **emerge** by popular choice and through their personal drive and qualities.
- Within an organisation a manager is **appointed** to a position of authority. Leadership is a function of the position.

Types of leaders

- **Charismatic**. The influence springs mainly from personality.
- **Traditional**. The influence stems from accepted social order, such as a director runs a company.
- **Situational**. The influence can only be effective by being in the right place at the right time.
- **Appointed**. The influence arises directly from a position/status, e.g. most managers and supervisors. This is the bureaucratic type of leadership, where legitimate power springs from the nature and scope of the position within the hierarchy.
- **Functional**. The influence comes from the individual securing the position by doing what he or she does well.

The benefits of leadership

There are many benefits from good leadership, including the following:

- Reducing employee dissatisfaction.
- Encouraging effective delegation.
- Creating team spirit.
- Helping to develop skills and confidence in the group.
- Helping to enlist support and co-operation from people outside the group or organisation.

The skills of a leader

The skill of leadership seems to be a compound of at least four major ingredients:

- The ability to use power effectively and in a responsible manner.
- The ability to comprehend that human beings have different motivation forces at different times and situations.
- The ability to inspire.
- The ability to act in a manner that will develop a climate conducive to responding to and arousing motivations.

Differences in attitudes between managers and leaders

There are differences in attitudes towards goals, conceptions of work, relations with others, self-perception and development between leadership and management.

- Managers tend to adopt impersonal or passive attitudes towards goals. Leaders adopt a more personal and active attitude towards them.
- In their relationships with other people, managers maintain a low level of emotional involvement. Leaders have empathy with other people and give attention to what events and actions mean.
- Managers perceive themselves as regulators of the existing order of affairs within the organisation. A leader's sense of identity does not depend upon membership or work roles. Leaders tend to search out opportunities for change.
- Management may be seen more in terms of planning, organising, directing and controlling the activities of subordinates. Leadership, however, is concerned more with attention to communicating with, motivating, encouraging and involving people.
- Management reacts. Leadership transforms – making a difference.

Theories of leadership

In the search to explain why some leaders are more effective than others, the following approaches can be identified:

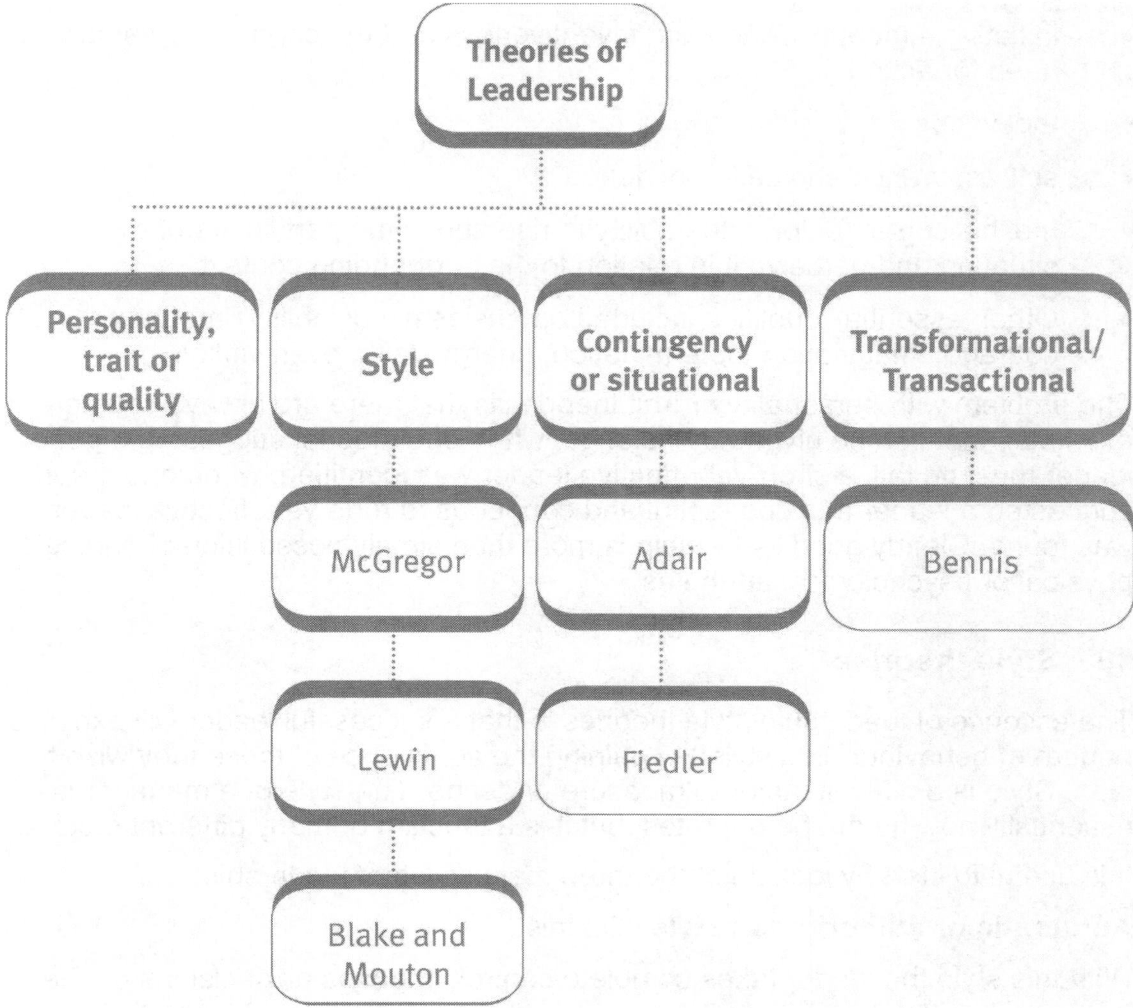

9 Personality, trait or qualities theories

Early studies focused on the qualities required by effective leaders. Lists were compiled of required leadership qualities including:

- physical traits, such as drive, energy, appearance and height
- personality traits, such as adaptability, enthusiasm and self-confidence; and
- social traits, such as co-operation, tact, courtesy and administrative ability.

Certain other writers selected other personal qualities which were thought to be desirable in leaders, who are '**born and not made**' Many great leaders were considered to have:

- above-average intelligence
- initiative – independence and inventiveness and the capacity to perceive a need for action
- motivation
- self-assurance and self-confidence
- the 'helicopter factor' – the ability to rise above the particulars of a situation and perceive it in relation to the surrounding context
- Other 'essential' qualities included enthusiasm, sociability, integrity, courage, imagination, determination, energy, faith, even virility.

The problem with personality or trait theories is that there are always counter-examples that can be given, for instance, when one theorist suggested a good leader must be tall, a short yet effective leader was identified; when one theorist suggested a leader must be tactful and courteous, a rude yet effective leader was found. Clearly good leadership is more than simply possession of particular physical or psychological attributes.

10 Style theories

The essence of leadership style theories is that a successful leader will exhibit a pattern of behaviour (i.e. 'style') in gaining the confidence of those they wish to lead. Style is a difficult factor to measure or define. The style of a manager is essentially how he or she operates, but it is a function of many different factors.

It is useful to start by looking at the three main styles of leadership:

Autocratic or authoritarian style. 'Do this'

With this style the leader takes complete control, imposes all decisions on the group and neither asks for or listens to the opinions of others. Autocratic leaders tend to distrust the members of the group and as a result closely supervise and control the actions of the group.

While in many circumstances this style can cause resentment, in other situations it can be necessary. For example, in the military, or where safety and security is paramount.

Democratic or participative style. 'Let's work together to solve this'

With this style there is open discussion between the leader and the group. Ideas from the group are encouraged and while the leader will still ultimately make the decisions, the reasons for the decisions will be explained to the group.

This style is more likely to encourage innovation and creativity and group members are normally more motivated under a democratic leader.

Free rein or delegative style. 'You go and sort out the problem'

With this style, the leader provides little or no leadership and expects the group to make decisions and solve problems on their own.

Like the autocratic style, this style of leadership can also lead to resentment within the group.

There are a number of theories dealing with style approaches to leadership. It is important that students have knowledge of a wide variety of theories.

- McGregor – Theory X and Theory Y
- Lewin
- Blake and Mouton – the managerial grid.

As you go through these models, it can be useful to consider the similarities in each and identify if the positions in each model fit under the three main styles of leadership discussed above.

Model	**Autocratic style**	**Democratic style**	**Free rein style**
McGregor			
Lewin			
Blake and Mouton			

Douglas McGregor – Theory X and Theory Y

Independently of any leadership ability, managers have been studied and differing styles emerge. The style chosen by a manager will depend very much upon the assumptions the manager makes about their subordinates, what they think they want and what they consider their attitude towards their work to be. McGregor came up with two contrasting theories:

- **Theory X** managers believe:
  - employees are basically lazy, have an inherent dislike of work and will avoid it if possible
  - employees prefer to be directed and wish to avoid responsibility
  - employees need constant supervision and direction
  - employees have relatively little ambition and wants security above everything else
  - employees are indifferent to organisational needs.

Because of this, most people must be coerced, controlled, directed and threatened with punishment to get them to put in adequate effort towards the achievement of organisational objectives. This results in a leadership style which is **authoritarian**. This is indicted by a tough, uncompromising style which includes tight controls with punishment/reward systems.

- **Theory Y** managers believe:
  - employees enjoy their work; they are self-motivated and willing to work hard to meet both personal and organisational goals
  - employees will exercise self-direction and self-control
  - commitment to objectives is a function of rewards and the satisfaction of ego
  - personal achievement needs are perhaps the most significant of these rewards, and can direct effort towards organisational objectives
  - the average employee learns, under proper conditions, not only to accept, but to seek responsibility
  - employees have the capacity to exercise a relatively high degree of imagination, ingenuity and creativity in the solution of organisational problems.

This theory results in a leadership style which is **democratic**. This will be indicated by a manager who is benevolent, participative and a believer of self-controls.

Of course, reality is somewhere in between these two extremes.

Most managers do not give much conscious thought to these things, but tend to act upon a set of assumptions that are largely implicit.

Kurt Lewin

The first significant studies into leadership style were carried out in the 1930s by psychologist Kurt Lewin. His studies focused attention on the different effects created by three different leadership styles.

- **Authoritarian**. A style where the leader just tells the group what to do.
- **Democratic**. A participative style where all the decisions are made by the leader in consultation and participation with the group.
- **Laissez-faire**. A style where the leader does not really do anything but leaves the group alone and lets them get on with it.

Lewin and his researchers were using experimental groups in these studies and the criteria they used were measures of productivity and task satisfaction.

- In terms of productivity and satisfaction, it was the **democratic** style that was the most productive and satisfying.
- The **laissez-faire** style was next in productivity but not in satisfaction – group members were not at all satisfied with it.
- The **authoritarian** style was the least productive of all and carried with it lots of frustration and instances of aggression among group members.

Relevance today

While Lewin's leadership models could be viewed as being simplistic, his work emphasises how critical the quality of leadership is for teams and organisations and that leadership can be taught, learned, and adapted.

Furthermore, the terminology and ideas are still useful, although some of the conclusions need to be seen in context.

For example, you could argue that Warren Buffett (an extremely successful and high profile investor) has a hands-off, laissez-faire management style that is highly successful because he focuses on hiring very capable people, and the autonomy of these executives is key to the success.

On the other hand, Steve Jobs (Apple) was well known for his authoritarian approach and reluctance to delegate, so could be described as having an autocratic approach. Lewin's work indicated that this style was the least effective, but according to Forbes, Apple was the world's most valuable brand in 2019, and was also the 6th largest company in the world.

Blake and Mouton – The Managerial Grid

Effective leaders will have concern both for the goals ('tasks') of their department and for the individual ('people').

Blake and Mouton designed the managerial grid, which charts people-orientated versus task-oriented styles. The two extremes can be described as follows:

- **Task-centred leadership** – where the main concern of the leader is getting the job done, achieving objectives and seeing the group they lead as simply a means to the end of achieving that task.
- **Group-centred leadership** – where the prime interest of the leader is to maintain the group, stressing factors such as mutual trust, friendship, support, respect and warmth of relationships.

The grid derived its origin from the assumption that management is concerned with both task and people. Individual managers can be given a score from 1 to 9 for each orientation and then plotted on the grid.

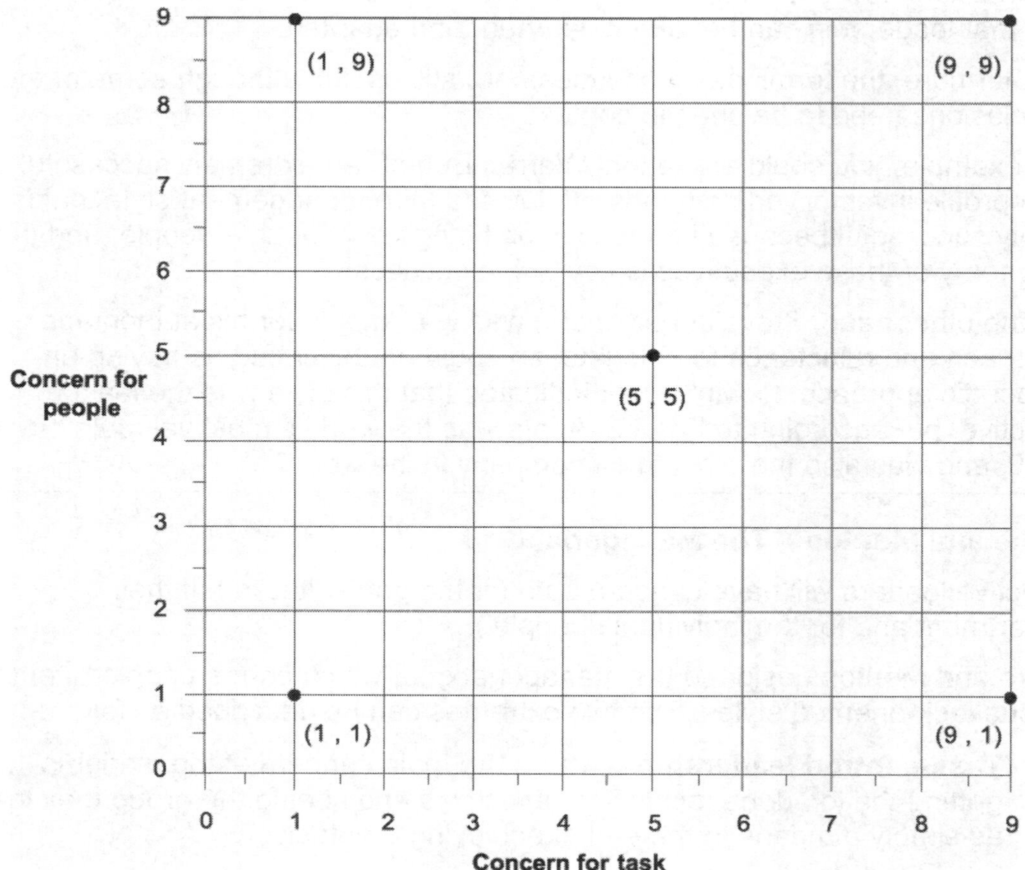

- The **task-orientated** style (9,1) is in the best Taylor tradition. Staff are treated as a commodity, like machines. The manager will be responsible for planning, directing, and controlling the work of their subordinates. It is a Theory X approach, and subordinates of this manager can become indifferent and apathetic, or even rebellious.
- The **country-club** style (1,9) emphasises people. People are encouraged and supported and any inadequacies overlooked, on the basis that people are doing their best and coercion may not improve things substantially. The 'country club' has certain drawbacks. It is an easy option for the manager but many problems can arise from this style of management in the longer term.

- The **impoverished** style (1,1) is almost impossible to imagine occurring on an organisational scale but can happen to individuals e.g. the supervisor who abdicates responsibility and leaves others to work as they see fit. A failure, for whatever reason, is always blamed down the line. Typically, the (1,1) supervisor or manager is a frustrated individual, passed over for promotion, shunted sideways, or has been in a routine job for years, possibly because of a lack of personal maturity.
- The **middle road** (5,5) is a happy medium. This viewpoint pushes for productivity and considers people, but does not go 'over the top' either way. It is a style of 'give and take', neither too lenient nor too coercive, arising probably from a feeling that any improvement is idealistic and unachievable.
- The **team** style (9,9) may be idealistic; it advocates a high degree of concern for production which generates wealth, and for people who in turn generate production. It recognises the fact that happy workers often are motivated to do their best in achieving organisational goals.

Style theories – is there one best style?

The difficulty with style theories, even when they attempt to reflect the multidimensional nature of leadership, is that they ignore the important influence of the **context** in which the leader is operating. From the discussions on the leadership styles theories, it should be apparent that there is no one best style of leadership that is equally effective for all circumstances. The best leadership style is the one that fulfils the needs of the group the most, while at the same time satisfying the needs of the organisation.

Case study style question 3

Management development

You are running a management development course for six supervisors from a finance department. One of them, A, has reported his proposals about a case, which they have been studying. The other five have rated A by placing crosses on Blake and Mouton's managerial grid. The results are as shown.

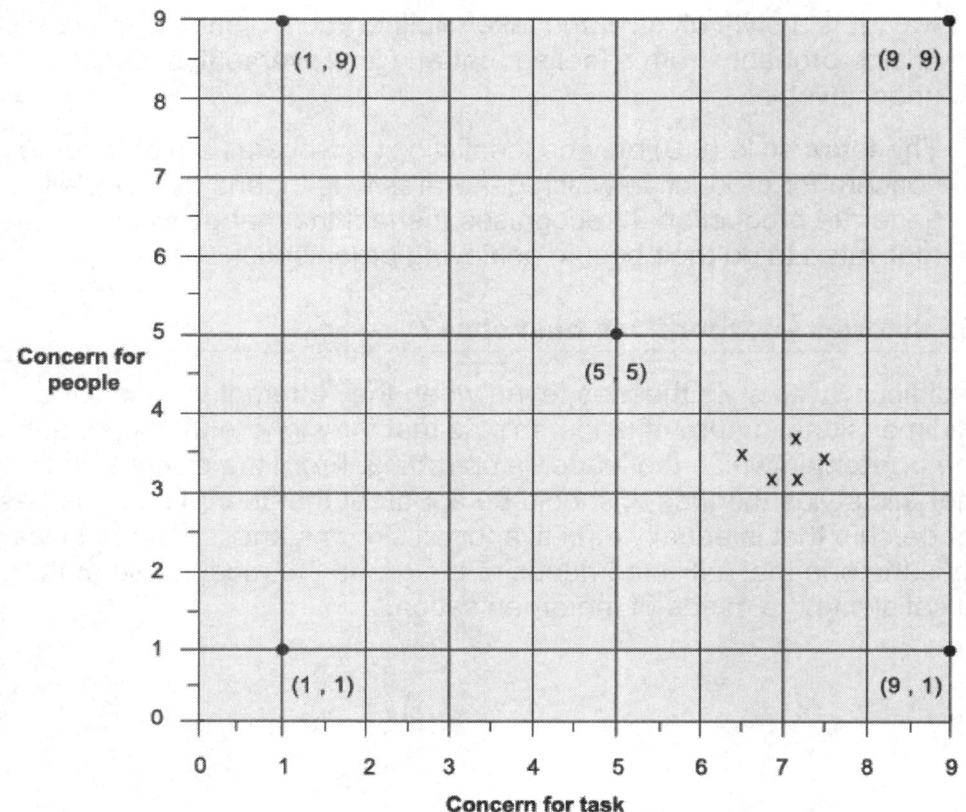

Required:

As part of the course discussion on this topic, what should you tell the group about the significance of the result and what suggestions could you make to A as to how he could improve his management style.

(15 minutes)

11 Contingency or situational theories

Contingency theory suggests that here is that there is no one best approach to leadership, either in terms of trait or style. A good leader will change their style to suit the situation. The best leadership style is the one that fulfils the needs of the individual, the group, and the organisation.

A more advanced version of simple trait theories is **situational leadership**. The theory here is that leaders are products of particular situations. Where a given set of factors exists e.g. economic depression, weak government, high unemployment and disenchantment with traditional politics the theory suggests the emergence of a leader, who recognises the problems and has characteristics or traits that fit the needs of the situation. This can be seen where a company is in financial difficulties and "going concern" is in danger, a new, more experienced CEO may be brought in to make the hard decisions required to ensure the survival of the company.

Theories dealing with contingency or situational approaches to leadership:

- Adair – action centred leadership
- Fielder – contingency model.

Adair – Action-centred leadership

Adair's action-centred leadership takes Blake and Mouton's ideas one step further, by suggesting that effective leadership regards not only task and group needs as important, but also those of the individuals making up the group:

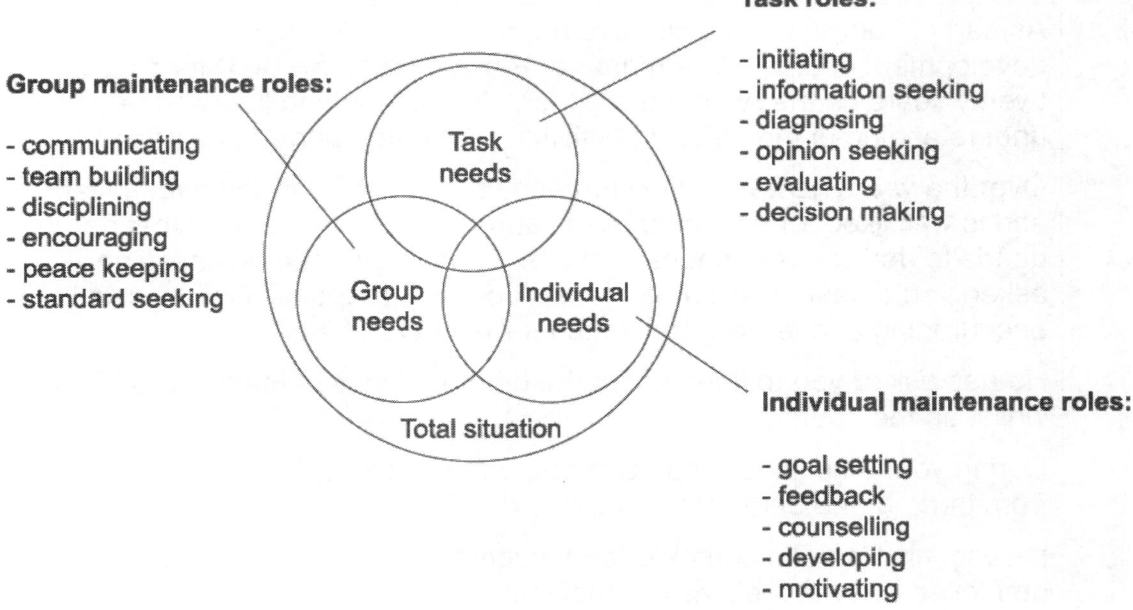

Adair's model stresses that effective leadership lies in what the leader does to meet the needs of task, group and individuals.

- Task achievement is obviously important for efficiency and effectiveness, but it also can be valuable for motivating people by creating a sense of achievement.

- Teams, almost by definition generate synergy out of the different skills and knowledge of individuals.
- Where individuals feel they have opportunities to satisfy their needs and develop, they are more likely to contribute to creativity and effectiveness.

The key task for the action-centred leader is to understand these processes and bond them together because otherwise there will be a tendency for the organisation to remain static.

However, the three elements can conflict with each other, for example, pressure on time and resources often increases pressure on a group to concentrate on the task, to the possible detriment of the people involved. But if group and individual needs are forgotten, much of the effort spent may be misdirected. In another example, taking time creating a good team spirit without applying effort to the task is likely to mean that the team will lose its focus through lack of achievement.

It is important that the manager balance all three requirements.

Relevance today

Adair's ideas still form a key element of many management and leadership training programmes. However, the model does not stand alone but it must be part of an integrated approach to managing and leading.

Case study style question 4

As part of your training, you have been sent on a leadership development course. Your manager P has worked for BCD for over twenty years as the Accounts partner. He has a sound knowledge and understanding of the different activities of the company's business.

Over the years he has demonstrated fairness in how he manages staff and is well liked for his enthusiastic approach. P has decided that he needs to dedicate more time and energy managing the business and asked you to take over some of his leadership responsibility especially encouraging and leading the younger members of staff.

He has asked you to think about the different types of leader at BCD whilst on the course.

During your time so far you have noted the following leadership styles from three of the partners:

L treats his staff like computerised machines and doesn't consider his employees views, feelings or ambitions.

J barely vacates his office and leaves his employees to get on with the workloads themselves.

R gives and takes. She is neither lenient nor too coercive.

Upon your return, P has asked for a report on certain matters.

Required:

Write a report to P, covering the following:

(a) Providing a definition of leadership.

(5 minutes)

(b) Describing the managerial grid and the five extreme scores identified by Blake and Mouton. Relating what you have learnt to the BCD leadership styles.

(15 minutes)

(c) Briefly explaining Adair's action centred leadership theory.

(10 minutes)

(d) Explaining whether you feel one style of leadership is effective in all circumstances.

(10 minutes)

Fiedler – contingency model

The development of the contingency approach marked the bringing together of the personality and situational approaches. Fiedler's contingency model is the best example of an attempt to integrate individual characteristics with the structural and task properties of the situation.

First, he identified two distinct styles of leadership:

Psychologically distant managers (PDMs)

- seek to keep their distance from subordinates by formalising roles and relationships within the team
- are withdrawn and reserved in their interpersonal relationships
- prefer formal communication and consultation methods rather than seeking informal opinions
- are primarily task oriented.

Psychologically close managers (PCMs)

- do not seek to formalise roles and relationships
- prefer informal contacts to regular staff meetings
- are primarily person oriented rather than task oriented.

Fiedler suggested that the most effective style of leadership would be determined by the situation, which would be influenced by three factors:

- **Leader/member relations** – the nature of the relationship between the leader and the group
- **Task structure** – the extent to which the task is structured
- **Leader position power** – the degree of formal authority/ responsibility allocated to the position.

In terms of leadership style, Fiedler intimates that the leader can be high on only one aspect at a time – either people oriented or task oriented, but not both.

Fiedler suggested that a PDM approach works best when the situation is either very favourable or very unfavourable to the leader and the PCM approach works best when the situation is only moderately favourable for the leader.

12 Recent thinking on leadership

Transformational/transactional leadership

Bennis proposed that there were two types of leaders:

- **Transactional leaders** see the relationship with their followers in terms of a trade: they give followers the rewards they want in exchange for service, loyalty and compliance.
- **Transformational leaders** see their role as inspiring and motivating others to work at levels beyond mere compliance. Only transformational leadership is said to be able to change team/organisational cultures and move them in a new direction.

Transactional leaders tend to be more passive and transformational leaders more proactive. While a transactional leader would work within the confines of the organisational culture, the transformational leader would seek to change and improve the culture. Transformational leadership enhances the motivation, morale, and job performance of followers. They act as a role model and inspire others to develop and innovate. They would advocate empowerment, encouraging followers to take greater ownership for their work.

Transformational leadership has become more important in recent years. The dynamic nature of the environment facing many organisations today means that there is a constant need to innovate and change. It is suggested that to cope with this type of environment, leaders need to have vision and creativity, be innovative and capable of inspiring others. The distinguishing feature of transformational leadership is the ability to bring about significant change.

Also bear in mind that leadership styles are not only relevant within business. Nelson Mandela was a prime example of a transformational leader who spearheaded change on a very large scale by inspiring others.

Skills required by transformational leaders

The new kind of transformational leader needs a different range of skills from those suggested by traditional management theories.

These new skills according to **Boyd** encompass:

- **anticipatory** skills providing foresight in a constantly changing environment
- **visioning** skills whereby persuasion and example can be used to induce the group to act in accordance with the leader's purpose or the shared purpose of a larger group
- **value-congruence skills** – which enable the leader to be in touch with individuals' economic, psychological, physical and other important needs in order to be able to engage them on the basis of shared understanding
- **empowerment** skills involving the willingness to share power and to do so effectively
- **self-understanding** so that the leader understands his or her own needs and goals as well as those of the followers.

Boyd believes that there is a need to develop such skills in organisations and to create the conditions in which this type of leadership can emerge.

Distributed leadership

Another more modern perspective on leadership is distributed leadership. While traditional leadership has been viewed as the role of one person in charge of others, a distributed, or shared, leadership perspective recognises that there are multiple leaders.

Case study question 5

Before taking up her position as Head of the Finance department of QRS, T had enjoyed a career in the Army where she had attained the rank of major. The military style of command had suited T's personality. She is by nature an assertive kind of individual, so giving orders is something that comes naturally to her.

The start of her new post as Head of Finance has not been easy. She has found that her previous style of management has not been well received by her new staff. Her enthusiasm for improving the way things are done in the department is not matched by that of her staff. In fact, if anything, an air of resentment seems to exist in the department. More generally, T is finding it difficult to adjust to the whole way of operating in QRS. In her view, so much time seems to be spent in meetings and in consultation generally that she wonders how the organisation manages to compete in the market place as successfully as it does.

Required:

Using any appropriate theory of management style, write an email to T explaining why she is experiencing the difficulties described in her new post, and recommend the kind of management style that might be more appropriate.

(15 minutes)

13 Leadership in virtual teams

As organisations become more global and cost-conscious, virtual teams have become more widely used.

A virtual team is a team made of members with complementary skills working towards a common purpose, but which is separated physically and must interact electronically. The teams do, however, meet up in person from time to time.

Virtual teams can eliminate the expenses of travelling, relocating and acquiring property allowing companies to bring employees at different locations together to work on the same projects. Virtual teams help increase productivity and maximise profit while reducing cost.

There are many operational reasons why businesses are now increasingly reliant on virtual teams to achieve their project and business aims. Virtual teams are now an established and increasingly important part of the global business environment. Virtual teams can potentially offer a range of benefits such as greater flexibility, higher productivity and increased job satisfaction for employees.

This will inevitably present challenges to the leadership and management of these teams. It is vital to overcome these challenges and work effectively and successfully in virtual environments. As a result managers of virtual teams need to adapt or change their approach and develop new and existing behaviours and skills in order to generate optimum levels of individual and organisational performance.

Virtual teams are likely to become a more common feature of working life, so it's increasingly important that managers are as adept at leading in the virtual world as they are in the physical one. The growth of virtual teams has been possible because of significant achievements in communication technologies.

However they also produce unique challenges for both managers and their team members, such as communication challenges, cultural sensitivities and performance management.

It would be incorrect to assume that the characteristics that make a good leader are the same no matter where that leader is located. However, managing virtual teams effectively requires a set of skills that is different from managing teams located under the same roof. In addition to excelling at the execution-oriented practices that define any good leader, virtual leaders must also juggle the interpersonal, communication and cultural factors that define virtual teams.

Leaders of virtual teams must see themselves as leaders as well as managers. Managers' roles involve ensuring the business aspects of the team's work are undertaken correctly, that timesheets and documentation are delivered correctly and on time and to ensure the right skills are made available to the project at the right times. All of these activities still need to be undertaken, and often are done or overseen by the leader, but to be an effective leader you also need to see yourself as a leader and take responsibility for setting the culture, tone and pace of the team. The team will look to the leader for guidance and leadership more than for management. This is critical to ensure that the motivation needed to succeed in this environment is not subdued; resulting in the achievement of goals and objectives being challenged.

Virtual team leadership skills are therefore more complex. The leader of a virtual team must be able to inspire and lead their team without meeting them, without seeing them each and every day and without being able to model appropriate and desirable behaviour in a physically visible way.

Leadership skills in virtual teams are different to leadership skills needed in a co-located team. Leaders of co-located teams need to be able to inspire and direct a team they see around them every day; they can lead by example and by modelling in ways that all of their team members can see visually each day. They develop their communication skills to be effective in face to face environments and in casual discussions around the office, their external communication skills are typically honed around dealing with suppliers, subcontractors and clients.

The effective leader of a virtual team must also be able to deal with higher levels of ambiguity, understand and lead across cultural boundaries and lead a distributed team of personnel who, themselves, may never meet and rely on communicating using electronic media. In short, the skills required to effectively lead a virtual team are all those of a leader of co-located personnel with many additional skills added on.

Illustration 1 – SAP

SAP holds the title of the world's largest inter-enterprise software company. With more than 30,000 employees in 60 countries, virtual team collaboration is critical to the company's success. The company has structured itself in a strategic way, with global headquarters in Germany and large R&D centres in India, China, Israel and the United States. Each centre has a specific area of expertise it shares with the entire company, which reduces costs. Managers can assemble virtual teams that include employees from each of these specialty groups, making each team more well-rounded.

SAP has also enhanced its virtual team performance by creating an ongoing team building initiative with the help of an organisational development consulting company. This initiative began with a training program in which teams worked together to build a community through a blend of online learning, conference calls, briefings, and coaching sessions.

14 Leadership and ethics

Business ethics is defined as the set of moral rules that govern how businesses operate, how business decisions are made and how people are treated.

In business, there are many different stakeholders to answer to e.g. customers, shareholders and clients. Law often guides business ethics, while other times business ethics provide a basic framework that businesses may follow to gain public acceptance.

To facilitate this acceptance, leaders need to create a healthy culture that influences employee actions, decision-making and behaviour. This takes time and requires awareness, sensitivity, patience and resources. One of the key dangers in this context is that unethical behaviour may be ingrained into a company's culture or industry to be considered as 'the way business is done around here', and so may not be considered unethical at all.

Illustration 2 – Examples of poor business ethics:

For example, in a company that sells cereals with all-natural ingredients, the marketing department must temper enthusiasm for the product versus the laws that govern labelling practices in the pursuit of market share. Some competitors' advertisements advertise high-fibre cereals that have the potential to reduce the risk of some types of cancer. The marketing department cannot make dubious health claims on cereal boxes without the risk of litigation and fines. Even though competitors with larger market shares of the cereal industry may use shady labelling practices, that doesn't mean every manufacturer should engage in unethical behaviour.

Nestle

The World Health Organization found children in developing countries who fed on Nestle's infant-formula had mortality rates five to ten times greater than that of breast-fed children. The problem was Nestle's sinister campaign of appointing uniformed nurses to distribute the baby formula to poor mothers for free, long enough for lactating mother's milk to dry up. The mother and child now became entirely dependent on Nestle's infant formula, and since most of them could not afford the formula, they gave their children an insufficient quantity of the formula. The formula also required clean water, which most mothers could not access.

ASDA (owned by US company WalMart) is a retail colossus. It has monumentally failed to embed corporate responsibility into its operations and supply chains around the globe. This has led to workers' rights abuses at supplier factories, accusations of discrimination by staff, and a host of other charges.

Excellence in leadership means having the ability to influence others and directing them down a particular course of action. A good leader will have a strong following and a strong sense of ethics. There is a direct link between leadership and ethics. A leader must display an ethical approach to everything that they do if they want others to follow their actions.

So how does an organisation ensure that it is developing its business leaders to become ethical activists?

- **To create and maintain** a strong ethical culture, core ethical values need to be identified and integrated into everything the organisation does – from external processes such as buying and selling to internal ones such as governance and accounting. From the first interview to their last day of work, employees should feel that the company's core values form the basis of every decision it makes.
- **The role of managers** at all levels is critical to the process of embedding ethics throughout any organisation. Line managers have an essential role in communicating ethics messages and acting as role models. Ethical acumen is a key competence for 21st-century business leadership.
- **The quality and style** of the leadership will influence the tone of the entire organisation. While the collective 'tone from the top' of the organisation is of utmost importance, there are also 'leaders' at every level, who others will naturally try to emulate.
- **'Tone from the middle'** is as important as 'tone from the top'. Research into embedding ethics in the workplace indicates that employees consider their line manager as the biggest enabler and teacher of ethics in their organisation. Data from the Ethics at Work survey shows that, in Britain, 71% agree that their line manager 'sets a good example of ethical business behaviour' and 69% feel supported by their line manager in 'following [the] organisation's standards of ethical behaviour'.

The challenge lies with not only enforcing ethical behaviour amongst leaders and followers but instilling it. In many cases when instances of fraud and illegal practices are uncovered the board of directors were unaware that these activities were taking place. Although directors can create a set of values and principles that they think define the business, they are useless if they are not being implemented by employees. In order for these guidelines to be effective an organisation must rely on its business leaders to set the example.

Ethical leadership is all about the CEO and board leading by example; only then can you truly have an ethical culture in an organisation.

15 Leadership in context

Summary of thoughts on leadership

Throughout this chapter we have viewed a range of theories and models discussing how to be a good leader. Some theories, especially 'classical' ones, suggested that there was one best approach but many others support a more modern view of leadership that suggests that there is no single best approach. Instead a situational/contingency approach is taken that argues that leadership approaches need to be adapted to the context within which it operates.

Summarising some of the models already covered:

Theory/model	Contextual variable	Recommendation
Fiedler	• How favourable the situation is to the leader, based on leader/member relations, task structure and leader position power	Fiedler suggested that a PDM (Psychologically distant manager) approach works best when the situation is either very favourable or very unfavourable to the leader and the PCM (Psychologically close manager) approach works best when the situation is only moderately favourable for the leader.
Bennis	• Business environment	In a dynamic business environment, a transformational leadership approach is more likely to facilitate the change required.

Daniel Goleman

Another useful model in this context is the work of psychologist Daniel Goleman. He identified six key types of leadership styles and argued that effective leaders move across these styles in a situational manner and use the style that works best for the specific context.

Leadership style	Description	When suitable
Visionary	• Leader has good communication skills, see the big-picture and has a forward-looking focus. • Can inspire teams to shared goals by outlining where the organisation is going, but not necessarily how it will get there. • Example: Steve Jobs (Apple).	• The company or team needs to shift in a new direction.

Coaching	• Objective is to develop people for the future. • Style is one-on-one and instructional, guiding the employee on how they can improve.	• You have an employee with strong initiative who wants to develop professionally.
Affiliative	• Designed to create strong bonds and connections between people. • Gives positive feedback and promotes team building.	• When there is a need to improve harmony, morale, communication and repair trust.
Democratic	• (See also Lewin's concept of democratic leadership). • Builds consensus by encouraging participation, encouraging ideas from others and communal decision making.	• Most effective when direction is weak and the organisation can benefit from tapping into the skills, talents, and opinions of staff. • Inappropriate for a crisis.
Pacesetting	• Leads by example and sets high standards. • Expect team members to be self-directed and follow their lead.	• Can help motivate staff to achieve strict deadlines and tight schedules. • However, should be used sparingly given its potential to "poison the climate" – i.e. affect morale and team members' sense of achievement.
Commanding	• Military style where the leader demands compliance. • Rarely offers praise but focusses on criticism, coercion, and prescription.	• Should be used only in crises requiring rapid redirection and change.

16 Summary diagram

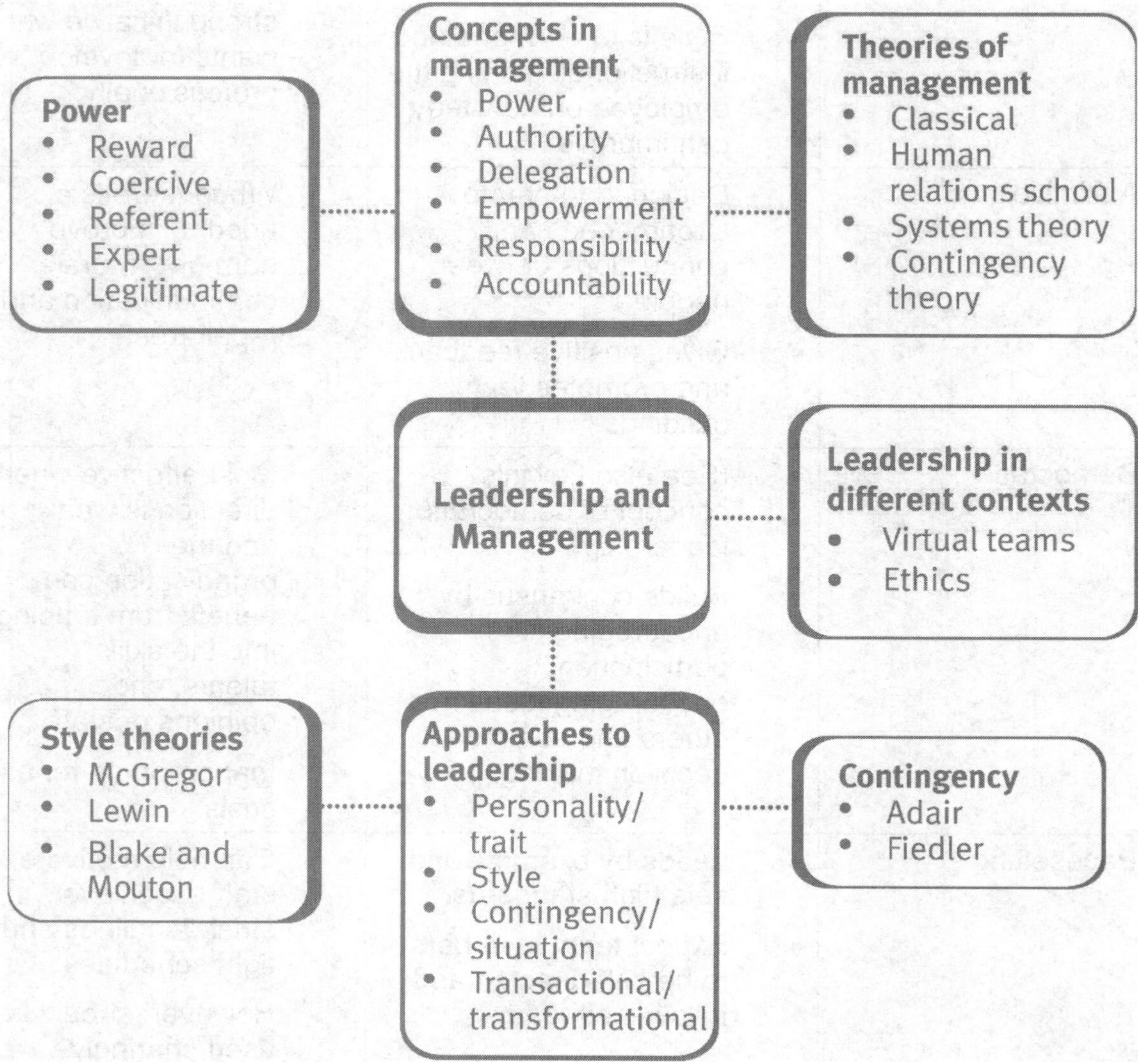
Power
• Reward
• Coercive
• Referent
• Expert
• Legitimate
Concepts in management
• Power
• Authority
• Delegation
• Empowerment
• Responsibility
• Accountability
Theories of management
• Classical
• Human relations school
• Systems theory
• Contingency theory
Leadership and Management
Leadership in different contexts
• Virtual teams
• Ethics
Style theories
• McGregor
• Lewin
• Blake and Mouton
Approaches to leadership
• Personality/ trait
• Style
• Contingency/ situation
• Transactional/ transformational
Contingency
• Adair
• Fiedler

End of chapter questions

Question 1

Identify the correct definition for each of the following management concepts.

Accountability
Delegation
Responsibility
Power

Getting others to do things willingly
Being called to account for one's actions and results
The right to exercise power
The obligation to perform certain duties, tasks or make certain decisions
The assignment of tasks or duties to another member of staff
The ability to exert influence

Question 2

Insert the correct word into the sentences.

- Referent
- Coercive
- Reward
- Legitimate
- Expert

Where a member of staff undertakes a task because they believe their manager has knowledge about the subject, the manager is said to have ________________ power.

A manager who uses threats to get compliance from staff is using ________________ power.

Where a member of staff undertakes a task for their manager because they have respect for them, this would indicate ________________ power.

Question 3

Authority which is based on custom and practice is known as?

A Charismatic authority

B Traditional authority

C Expert authority

D Rational-legal authority

Question 4

Which of the following statements are correct? Select all that apply.

A Authority can never be delegated

B The scope of responsibility must correspond to the scope of authority given

C Accountability is the ability to exercise influence

D Responsibility is the right to exercise power

E Responsibility can never be delegated

F Authority is the right to exercise power

Question 5

Which three of the following are common features of management as identified by Fayol?

A Contracting

B Commanding

C Communicating

D Co-ordinating

E Controlling

F Coercing

Question 6

Complete the sentences using the phrases provided.

- Psychologically distant managers
- Psychologically close managers
- Transformational leaders
- Transactional leaders
- Bureaucratic management
- Scientific management

The idea of there being one best approach to doing a job, arrived at from work study methods, comes from ____________________ theory.

Leaders who keep their distance from subordinates by formalising roles and relationships with their team are known as ____________________.

____________________ see their role as inspiring and motivating others.

____________________ is based on a hierarchy of authority with strict rules and procedures.

Question 7

Using Herzberg's theory of motivation, match the items to whether they are hygiene or motivating factors.

- Team working
- Career advancement
- Increasing levels of responsibility
- Pleasant physical working conditions
- Suitable level and quality of supervision

Hygiene factor	Motivating factor

Question 8

With reference to Burns and Stalker's theory, match the following features to whether they relate to a mechanistic or an organic organisation.

A High degree of task specialisation

B Most suitable under stable conditions

C Employees recruited from a variety of sources

D Emphasis on loyalty and obedience

E Emphasis on task achievement

F More responsive to change

Question 9

Which of the following statements would relate to a Theory X manager? Select all that apply.

A Employees dislike work and will avoid it if possible

B Employees will exercise self-direction and self-control

C Employees accept and seek responsibility

D Employees need constant supervision

E Employees are indifferent to organisational goals

F Employees can exercise creativity to solve organisational problems

Question 10

In the Blake and Mouton managerial grid, shown below, match the styles to the correct place on the grid.

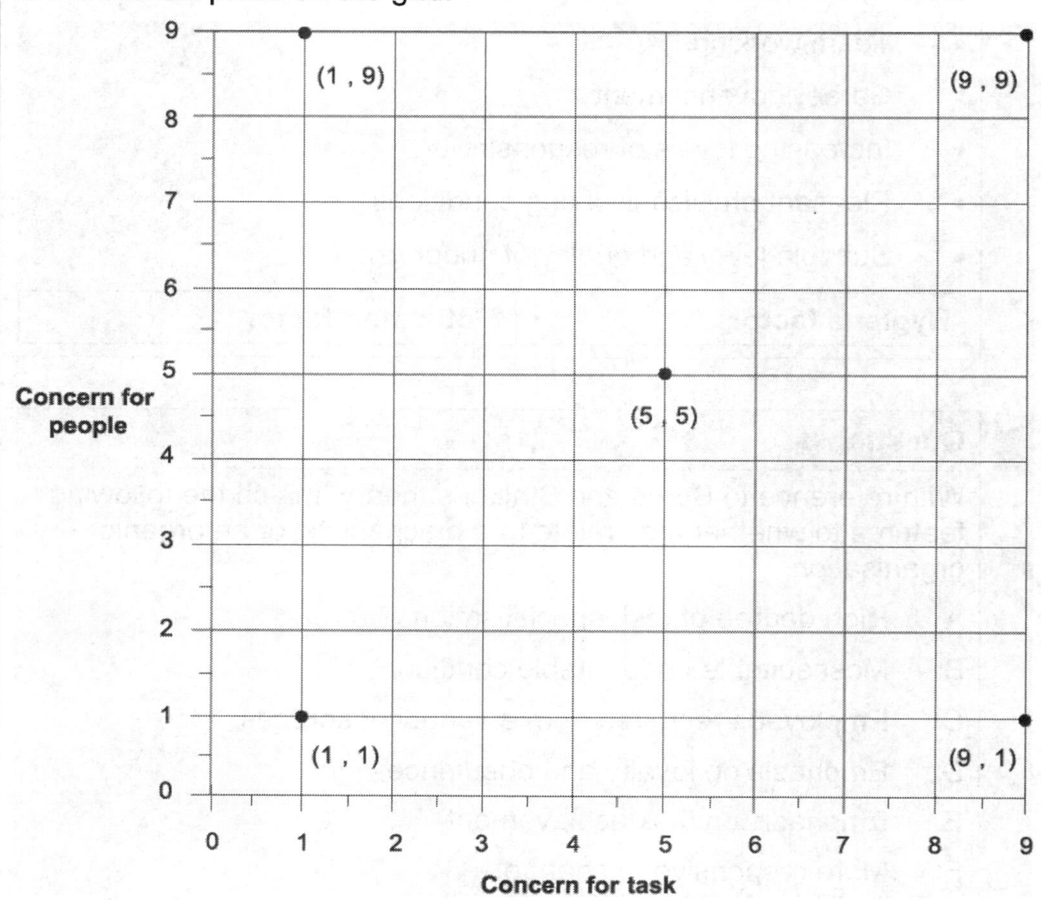

- Task orientated
- Country-club
- Impoverished
- Team style
- Middle road.

Test your understanding answers

Case study style question 1

EMAIL

To: G

From: Management accountant

Date: today

Subject: Sources of power

A useful framework that can be used to discuss the different sources of power is that proposed by French and Raven and includes referent, reward, coercive, expert and legitimate power.

Referent power is sometimes termed charismatic power and is derived from one's admiration or respect for an individual that can inspire followers. This is gained by the personal qualities of the individual and when followers believe that the leader has desirable characteristics that should be copied, or has inspiration charisma. You are known for your fairness and are well liked and respected for your enthusiastic approach. It is therefore likely that you will have referent power which will help you in implementing the changes to working practices.

Reward power is where the leader is able to directly influence the intrinsic or extrinsic rewards available to followers. For example, the ability to provide incentives for individuals to behave in a particular manner and has control over the organisation's resources such as salary, bonuses or promotion. This type of power is usually used in a positive manner, although it can be used in a negative way through the threat of removal of rewards. As senior partner, you will have reward power that you could use to encourage people to adopt the new working practices. As well as financial rewards, you could use intrinsic rewards such as verbal praise and recommendation for promotion.

Coercive power, as the term implies, is the ability to punish or deprive people of things that they value and where the leader uses penalties or sometimes physical punishments to enforce compliance. It is based on fears and the use of the 'stick' or sanction, making life unpleasant for people. The receiver is unlikely to respond to this type of power. Whilst the immediate response might be compliance, it is unlikely to result in long term commitment. It is doubtful that you would want to resort to using this type of power, unless there is strong resistance to the changes, in which case you may have no choice.

Expert power is based on the followers' belief that the leader has certain expertise and knowledge relevant to a particular problem or issue. It will only work if others acknowledge that expertise. You will probably have this power given the time you have worked for the organisation and your sound knowledge and understanding of the firm's different business activities. This experience will be of great help in the drive to introduce new technology and working practices into the organisation and should encourage respect from staff.

Legitimate power, sometimes referred to as position power, is the power which is associated with a particular job. It is when followers accept that the leader has the right to influence them in certain areas or aspects of behaviour. This is often based on the individual's formal position in the organisation. Since you are a senior partner and leader of the project you will be deemed to have legitimate power in managing the changes and hence the right to issue instructions to staff.

I hope you have found the above helpful. Please do not hesitate to get in touch if you require any further information.

Case study style question 2

BRIEFING NOTES FOR MEETING WITH H

(a) **Causes of the situation**

- The main reason for the situation in H's department is his **inability or unwillingness to delegate work**.
- **What should he delegate?** – the day-to-day operational activities to his staff, instead of doing it himself.
- **Explain why**. This leaves his **time** free for organising and planning the medium-term activities of the department – putting the strategic decisions made by his superiors into place.
- **Why does H not delegate**? Whether he does not delegate because he **does not trust his staff** to do the work properly or he **does not know how to**, is a matter only H can clarify. As staff are trying to leave, H may even feel more pressure to carry most of the work load instead of having to pass it on to inexperienced staff in the future. There may have been changes or reorganisations in the department resulting in a higher workload for H, and thus inadequate time for managing his subordinates.
- **Any external factors**? The problems seem to have started recently, therefore, it must be established whether or not H is experiencing any external problems, domestic for instance, that are affecting his performance at work.

(b) **Principles of delegation**

- **Explain what delegation should be**. Delegation is the passing on to someone else of the freedom and authority to carry out a job for which the delegator is accountable.
- **Go through the process**. Ideally, the process should include a careful and thorough briefing of the subordinate by the senior covering the following points:
  (i) the required performance levels
  (ii) agreement of the actual tasks assigned
  (iii) agreement of the resources allocated
  (iv) delegation of authority to do the job
  (v) recognition of the responsibility by the senior.

Although there is no single approach to delegation, it should be well planned and ensure that the content is appropriate and understood.

- **Explain the main principles**. The following principles are essential for delegation to be effective:
  - The range of the authority delegated must be clearly understood by both parties and must be within the scope of the delegator's authority.
  - It is the manager's responsibility to ensure that the subordinate has sufficient ability and experience to carry out the task. If necessary, training and an initial period of close supervision must be given.
  - The manager must have the authority to delegate before he or she does so and must delegate sufficient resources to complete the task.
  - The subordinate should have only one immediate superior, so that there is no confusion concerning his or her (space) accountability and responsibility.

(c) **Advantages of effective delegation**

In any large complex organisation, management must delegate some authority and tasks simply because of the limitation (physical and mental) of the workload on any individual and the need for specialisation of certain tasks.

- **Explain the Benefits:**
  (i) Workloads of managers and supervisors are relieved with the subsequent reduction in stress.
  (ii) Managers are left free to carry out non-routine tasks while passing on more routine activities to subordinates.
  (iii) Specialists are able to develop their specialisms.

(iv) Training of subordinates is assisted by the delegation of tasks. The right opportunity to do a job is a very effective method of training.

(v) Management succession is aided, as subordinates are able to gain experience and become accustomed to working at the higher level of management.

(vi) Decisions can be made sooner by managers with delegated authority on the spot that can respond to changing events.

(vii) The subordinate's work experience is enriched with subsequent increase in job satisfaction leading on to better work.

(viii) The opportunity exists to evaluate the performance of a subordinate before being permanently promoted.

- **Explain the problems/disadvantages:**

(i) Decisions taken at a lower level may not be to overall advantage of the organisation.

(ii) The organisation must be able to meet the aspirations through eventual promotion of subordinates who accept delegated duties.

(iii) There may be an increase in costs due to additional payments to the extra member of staff with delegated authority.

Case study style question 3

You should tell the group the following:

- That supervisor A is perceived to have a high 'concern for production'. In this context that could refer to the case they have been studying. It could also refer to insights others have gained into how A does their job. Either way this high concern for the job would be seen as a positive attribute of A.
- However, A is perceived to have a low 'concern for people'. Again this could refer to how the other supervisors felt they were treated on the course or how they feel A supervises his staff at work.
- This would be viewed as a potential problem with A being too task-orientated.
- These findings are reinforced by the fact that that everybody saw supervisor A in a similar light.

In terms of how A could improve his management style, you could suggest any of the following:

- Attending a further training course.
- Delegating more work to subordinates.
- Within this, using more trust rather than explicit control.
- Involving staff in more discussions.
- Asking staff for more feedback concerning his management approach.
- Treating staff more as adults.
- Using more group discussions to make decisions.
- Adopting an 'open door' policy.
- Adopting more 'management by walkabout'.
- Give staff more feedback on the quality of work done.

Case study style question 4

REPORT

To: P

From: Management accountant

Date: today

Subject: Management styles

Introduction

This report will cover the definition of leadership and look at two management models, namely the Blake and Mouton managerial grid and Adair's action centred leadership. It will also cover whether one style of leadership will be effective in all circumstances.

(a) **Definition of leadership**

Leadership is a conscious activity and in business is about setting goals and inspiring people to give a commitment to achieve the organisation's goals. It is a relationship through which one person influences the behaviour or actions of others.

Leadership is seen as 'a social process in which one individual influences the behaviour of others without the use or threat of violence'.

Leadership can be viewed from three standpoints:

- an attribute of a position e.g. your role at BCD as Finance Director
- a characteristic of a person e.g. you are a natural leader, well-liked by all
- a category of behaviour e.g. your enthusiastic approach to everything.

From the position of leadership at work, the latter standpoint is most applicable and can be considered as something one person does to influence the behaviour of others. It is all about moving people and things on, getting them from 'a' to 'b' by improving performance, changing the way things are done, making a new product or creating a new or better service.

There are different levels of leadership from the top down to small team leaders, but they will still share the same function – to get people to do the job. How they do that will depend on their attitudes, their perceptions of what motivates people and the prevailing culture of the organisation. If the designated leader cannot communicate the why, how and when of moving from 'a' to 'b' then he or she will neither behave like a leader, nor succeed in the task.

(b) **Blake and Mouton's Managerial Grid**

Blake and Mouton, observed two basic ingredients of managerial behaviour, namely: concern for production and concern for people. Concern for production includes the manager's attitude towards procedures, processes, work efficiency, and volume of output. Concern for people includes personal commitment, sustaining the esteem and trust of the group, maintaining interpersonal relationships and ensuring good working conditions.

They recognised that it was possible for concern for production to be independent of concern for people. It was therefore possible for a leader to be strong on one and weak on the other, strong on both, weak on both or any variation in between. They devised a series of questions, the answers to which enabled them to plot these two basic leadership dimensions as the axes on the following grid structure:

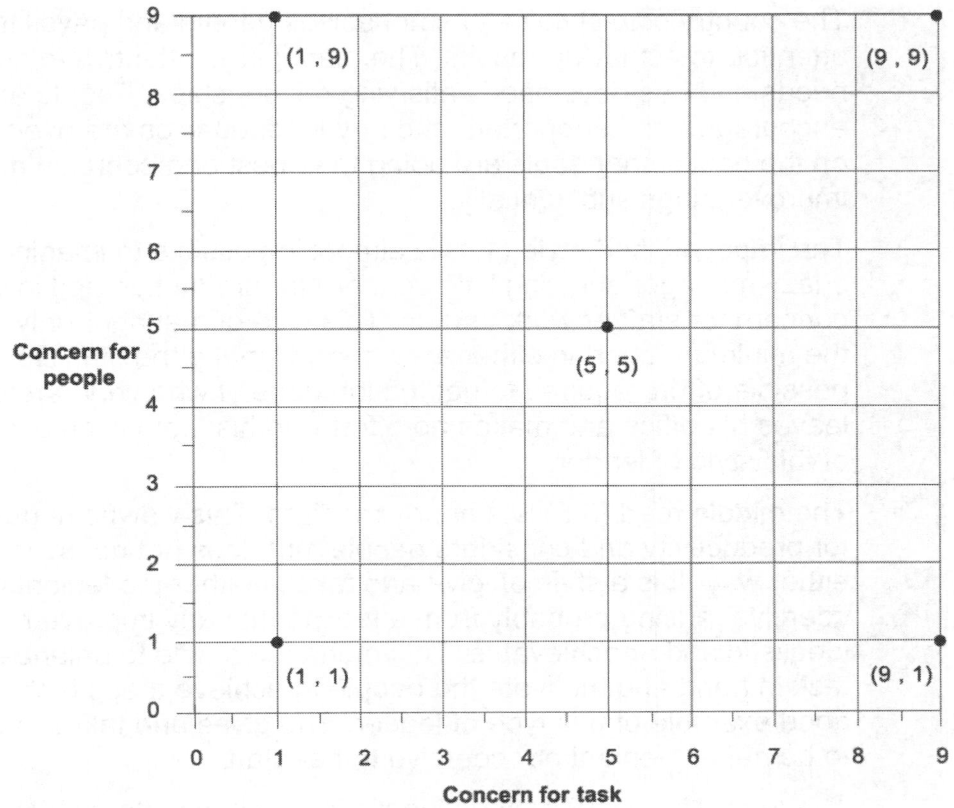

A high concern for production will score 9 and a high concern for people will also score 9, the two co-ordinates on the grid indicating the proportion of each concern present. Blake and Mouton picked out these two elements of a manager's job as characterising the leadership role. The implication is that managers should aim for the 9.9 combination; a goal-centred team approach that seeks to gain optimum results through participation, involvement, commitment and conflict solving where everyone can contribute. According to Blake and Mouton, individuals can adapt their style to become more effective personally and, working in a team, can build the synergy needed to raise output above the level that could be achieved individually.

Although there are 81 points of reference in the managerial grid, only five positions are precisely identified and described.

The task-orientated style (9,1) is almost totally concerned with production and has a low concern for people. Subordinates are treated as a commodity, like machines. Their needs are virtually ignored and conditions of work are arranged so that people cannot interfere to any significant extent. This is very similar to L who treats his staff like computerised machines and fails to consider their views.

The country club style (1,9) emphasises people and pays little attention to achieving results. The manager is attentive to staff needs and has developed satisfying relationships. People are encouraged and supported, and any inadequacies are overlooked, on the basis that people are doing their best and coercion may not improve things substantially.

The impoverished style (1,1) is almost impossible to imagine, with a lazy manager showing little concern for production and low concern for staff or work targets. This type of manager only makes the minimum effort in either area and will make the smallest possible effort required to get the job done. J who very rarely leaves his office and makes no effort with his team is an example of this style of leader.

The middle road (5,5) is a happy medium. This viewpoint pushes for productivity and considers people, but does not go 'over the top' either way. It is a style of 'give and take', neither too lenient nor too coercive, arising probably from a feeling that any improvement is idealistic and unachievable. This manager is able to balance the task in hand and motivate the people to achieve these tasks. R is a good example of this type of leader. She gives and takes and likes to be neither lenient nor coercive to her staff.

The team style (9,9) may be idealistic as it advocates a high degree of concern for production and for people. This manager integrates the two areas to foster working together and high production to produce true team leadership. You are the only manager that matches this description. You are the one to follow.

(c) **John Adair (1983)**

Adair put forward a model of action centred leadership, which is based on the premise that effective leadership requires a bringing together of task, team and individual needs. Adair's action-centred leadership takes Blake and Mouton's ideas one step further, by suggesting that effective leadership regards not only task and group needs as important, but also those of the individual subordinates making up the group.

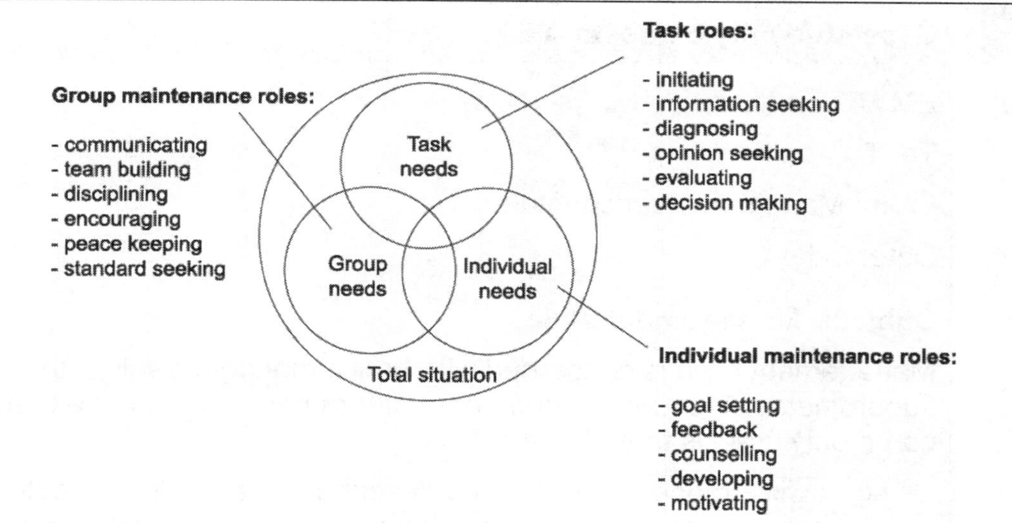

Adair's model stresses that effective leadership lies in what the leader does to meet the needs of task, group and individuals.

Task achievement is obviously important for efficiency and effectiveness, but it can also be valuable for motivating people by creating a sense of achievement. Effective teams generate synergy out of the different skills and knowledge of individuals. Where individuals feel that they have opportunities to satisfy their needs and develop, they are more likely to contribute to efficiency and effectiveness.

The key is for us to understand these processes and bond them together because otherwise there will be a tendency for the organisation to remain static.

(d) **One best style**

From discussions of leadership it is clear that there is no one style that is equally effective in all circumstances and no one style has proved to be universally superior to the others. The best leadership style is the one that fulfils the needs of the group the most, whilst at the same time satisfying the needs of the organisation.

The variables that define the successful style include:

– The personality of the leader
– The situation of the group – calm or crisis
– The situation within the group – cooperative or militant
– The people within the group – intelligence and interest.

Conclusion

This report has shown that there are many ways to look at leadership and a number of models available to help explain the different approaches. Styles of leadership should be adaptable to the situation to ensure that the leadership is always effective.

Case study style question 5

EMAIL

To: T

From: Management accountant

Date: today

Subject: Management style

Management style is concerned with how a manager deals with subordinates. There are a number of different models but one that is commonly used is that of Lewin.

Using Lewin's model, you could be described as adopting an autocratic style of management. This means that you are telling the subordinates what to do. This style of management probably comes naturally to you since it is the style adopted in the armed forces where subordinates are trained to not question their orders. Since you have spent a long time in this environment it is, understandably, the style you are used to.

The workers that you are supervising in the Finance department however may well be professionally qualified people used to carrying out tasks in their own way without a great deal of supervision.

With this kind of worker an autocratic style is unlikely to be successful, since the workers will resent the reduction in the amount of decision-making they are allowed. You may find it more useful to adopt a more democratic management style in which decisions are discussed with the employees rather than being imposed. This should lead to greater worker contentment with resulting gains in productivity and morale.

There will probably be a number of difficulties in changing your management style. You are used to doing things in 'the army way' (which you clearly did successfully having risen to the rank of major) and you are a naturally assertive person to whom an autocratic style of management is probably most comfortable.

Another factor that could cause problems is the potential for you to feel that you are 'losing face' by changing to suit your subordinates. You might question the effect this will have on your authority both now and in the future, for example, what happens if they dislike something else, will you be expected to adapt to them again?

Although there are many practical difficulties surrounding this change in style they are not insurmountable. You may have to gradually change your style over time, perhaps by getting key subordinates more involved now and gradually extending this.

An alternative solution would be to involve another senior manager from a different department to help mentor you. This would involve working with a mentor who could help you discuss practical ways in which your style can evolve.

The above measures are likely to be unsuccessful unless you recognise that it is in your interests as well as that of your sub-ordinates and the company to change your style.

I hope you have found the above helpful. Please do not hesitate to get in touch if you require any further information.

Question 1

Power	**The ability to exert influence**
Accountability	**Being called to account for one's actions and results**
Delegation	**The assignment of tasks or duties to another member of staff**
Responsibility	**The obligation to perform certain duties, tasks or make certain decisions**

The right to exercise power is **authority**.

Getting others to do things willingly is **leadership**.

Question 2

Where a member of staff undertakes a task because they believe their manager has knowledge about the subject, the manager is said to have **expert** power.

A manager who uses threats to get compliance from staff is using **coercive** power.

Where a member of staff undertakes a task for their manager because they have respect for them, this would indicate **referent** power.

French and Raven suggested five sources of power:

- Expert power where the holder has specialist knowledge
- Coercive power where the holder has the ability to punish
- Reward power where the holder has the ability to reward
- Legitimate power where the holder has power due to the position held
- Referent power where the holder has charisma and makes others desire to like them.

Question 3

B

According to Weber there are three bases for authority:

- Authority based on custom and practice is known as traditional authority.
- Charismatic authority is based on the individual's personality.
- Rational-legal authority comes from the individual's position in the hierarchy.

Question 4

B, E and F

When delegating, authority must always be delegated but responsibility can never be delegated.

Accountability is being called to account for one's actions and results. The ability to exercise influence is power.

Responsibility is the obligation of an individual to perform certain duties, tasks or take certain decisions.

Question 5

B, D and E

Fayol suggested five principles of management, the other two are Planning and Organising.

Question 6

The idea of there being one best approach to doing a job, arrived at from work study methods, comes from **scientific management** theory.

Leaders who keep their distance from subordinates by formalising roles and relationships with their team are known as **psychologically distant managers**.

Transformational leaders see their role as inspiring and motivating others.

Bureaucratic management is based on a hierarchy of authority with strict rules and procedures.

Question 7

Hygiene factor	Motivating factor
Team working Pleasant physical working conditions Suitable level and quality of supervision	Career advancement Increasing levels of responsibility

According to Herzberg, hygiene factors can avoid dissatisfaction and these factors must be in place before motivating factors will take effect.

Question 8

A High degree of task specialisation – **mechanistic**

B Most suitable under stable conditions – **mechanistic**

C Employees recruited from a variety of sources – **organic**

D Emphasis on loyalty and obedience – **mechanistic**

E Emphasis on task achievement – **organic**

F More responsive to change – **organic**

Burns and Stalker identified two major types of organisation which they felt were at the opposite ends of a continuum.

Mechanistic organisations show many of the features of Weber's bureaucracy and are seen as being more suitable under fairly stable conditions.

Organic organisations are more responsive to change and more suitable for organisations moving through periods of rapid change.

Question 9

A, D and E

Theory X managers believe that people need to be coerced, controlled and directed. This results in an authoritarian approach to leadership. Theory Y managers would adopt a more democratic style of leadership.

Question 10

Task orientated – **(9,1)**

Country-club – **(1,9)**

Impoverished – **(1,1)**

Team style – **(9,9)**

Middle road – **(5,5)**

Chapter

5

Controlling performance – part 1

Chapter learning objectives

Lead	Component
B2: Analyse individual and team performance	(a) Employee performance objective setting (b) Employee appraisals (c) Coaching and mentoring (d) Managing workplace environment

Topics to be covered

- Target setting and employee alignment
- Employee empowerment and engagement
- Performance reporting and review
- Rewards and sanctions in managing performance
- Different approaches to coaching and mentoring to improve performance
- Diversity and equity practices
- Health and safety
- Organisational culture.

1 Session content diagram

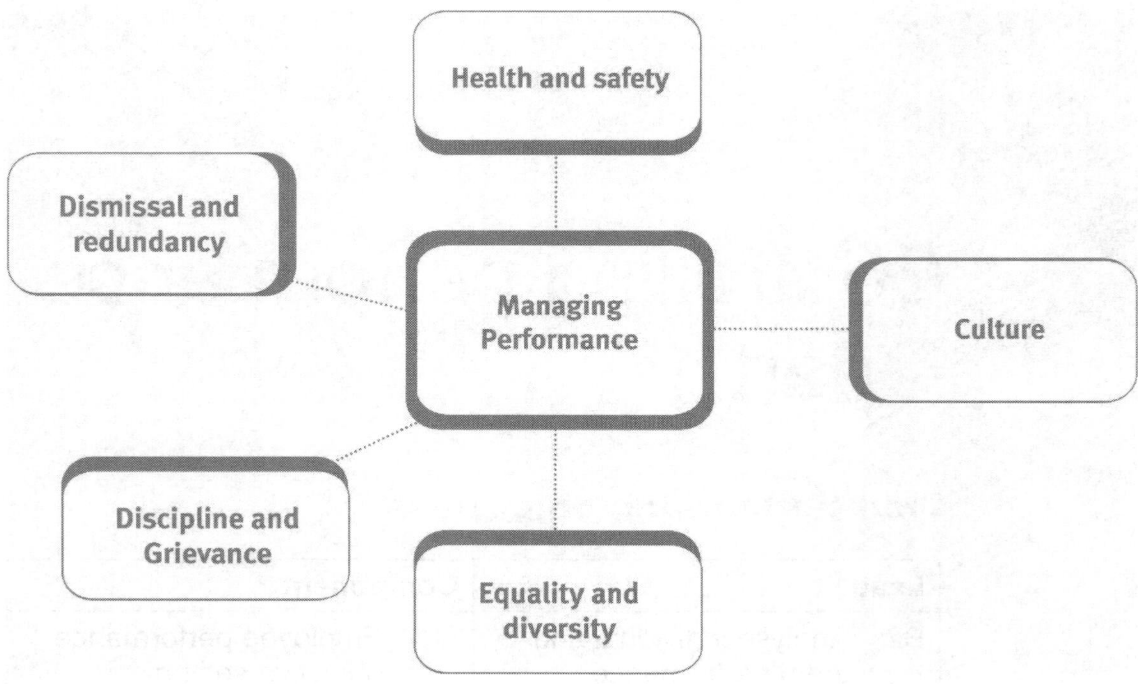

2 The purpose of Organisational Control

Fundamental to the achievement of organisational strategy is the contribution of the human element of the organisation. In this respect human resources are seen as valuable assets for the organisation however benefits obtained from these assets come at a cost. The recruitment, retention and training of employees is costly, especially where their knowledge, skills and experience are expected to generate competitive advantage.

Hence, the effective management of human resources is a vital part of organisational success. In many organisations, particularly service organisation, the investment in human resources is significant. CMAs will be involved in ensuring that the investment being made in human resources is worthwhile and is generating value and advantage for the organisation.

Human resource management in its broadest sense is concerned with management decisions and practices associated with people. The management accountant needs to understand the importance of good managerial practices and how to make the best use of people. This encompasses recruiting and selecting staff, development and reward, and performance management as well as ensuring that all legal requirements relating to human resources are adhered to.

Human resource management involves ensuring that the right people are recruited for the organisation and that they develop their knowledge, skills and experience so that they perform to the best of their abilities to help the organisation achieve its strategy. At the same time, they must control the behaviour of the people within the organisation to ensure that they are doing the right things in the right way within the rules of the organisation and any statutory rules imposed upon the organisation.

3 Management control

An underlying feature of the relationship between managers and their subordinates is management control. Most definitions of management include control as a function, it is essentially a means of ensuring that the objectives of the organisations are met. One definition of control is:

Control is a primary task and is the process of ensuring the operations proceed according to plan.

This chapter looks at the human resource management approaches to control. Behavioural aspects of control will be covered in the next chapter.

Within the context of human resources management, control will require to be exercised over the recruitment of staff, their performance and legal requirements connected with employment.

Note: all legal requirements referred to in this chapter are based on UK legislation.

Control systems in practice

Internal control systems exist to enhance the achievement of organisational objectives. They promote the orderly and efficient conduct of business, help keep the business on course, and help it change safely.

In CIMA's ® framework of control, the control system is seen as consisting of:

- **The control environment.** This includes management philosophy, operating style and management policies
- **Control procedures**. This includes control mechanisms such as segregation of duties, authorisation, reconciliation and so on.

In today's organisations, one of the most important systems of control is the human resources system. The quality of an organisation's employees is fundamental to its success. It is essential for the organisation to get its people system right.

Human Resources are largely responsible for ensuring a number of employment practices are in place in the organisation. These should all contribute to the effectiveness of the organisation.

- Appraisal system
- Health and Safety
- Discipline and Grievance
- Dismissal and Redundancy
- Fairness in the workplace – Diversity and Equal Opportunities.

Some of these, such as appraisal systems, are management controls, while others are legal requirements. Appraisal systems will be covered in the next chapter, while the rest of these control systems will be discussed in this chapter.

Policies, procedures and best practice

For many organisations the main mechanisms of control and influence relate to setting up HR policies and procedures.

For example, legislation on equality and diversity is translated into a set of policies and procedures that make it much easier for managers to follow, thus ensuring that legislation is adhered to.

Similarly clear procedures for grievance and disciplinary action are established to ensure that managers do not unwittingly break the law, leaving the organisation exposed to the risk of legal action, but also to ensure that employees' rights are protected.

Most organisations will insist that employees undergo training to ensure that they are aware of the policies and procedures, have a system where this is acknowledged and link this to disciplinary policies.

For example, suppose a company has clear policies on appropriate use of company laptops and an employee then breaks those rules. It would be very difficult for the employee to make a defence against resulting disciplinary procedures if they have already signed something stating that (1) they were aware of the policies and (2) they accepted and understood that breaking them was a disciplinary offence.

4 Management by Objectives

One of the economic points of leadership is to leverage the more 'drone-like' resources of staff with lesser skills by giving them guiding frameworks of what they are setting out to achieve. Poor delegation means the job is done twice – and by a more expensive resource.

MBO supports delegation by setting a more global sense of direction while leaving it up to staff to sort out the minutiae of how they actually do the work. It is linked with the idea of empowerment, with decisions being taken lower down the organisation.

MBO could be defined as 'setting a clear direction and aims without necessarily predetermining how that will be achieved and delegating much of the responsibility for making the 'how' decision'.

Empowerment is about encouraging staff wherever possible to be proactive and creative and solve problems with support and coaching from above, rather than just waiting to be told what to do.

MBO was popularised by management expert Peter Drucker decades ago. His idea has the virtues of relevance and simplicity, and helps combat micromanagement. Its relevance can be observed frequently in everyday management situations.

One of the key jobs of an MBO leader is thus to set objectives and to coach staff to achieve them, like a football manager, rather than dictating exactly how the ball should be kicked.

NB MBO will be covered in more detail in Chapter 6.

5 Health and Safety

A legal requirement which management must adhere to is health and safety legislation. Management have a responsibility to manage the health and safety risks in their workplace. They must think about what, in their organisation, might cause harm to people and ensure that they are doing enough to prevent that harm.

Management must identify the health and safety risks within their organisations and decide how to control them and put the appropriate measures in place.

Benefits of health and safety controls

- Employers' legal obligations for health and safety are being met.
- Cost savings. Accidents and illness cost the employer money in legal damages and operating costs.
- Company image. The company does not want to be associated with a poor health and safety record.
- To preserve the well-being of employees and others, improves employee morale, trust and motivation.

The Health and Safety at Work Act (HASAWA)

In the UK, the Health and Safety at Work Act 1974 (HASAWA) requires every organisation employing five or more persons to prepare and regularly revise a health and safety policy statement of:

- their policy for health and safety
- the organisation to enforce it
- the arrangements to implement it

and bring it to the attention of the employees.

The following are key areas:

- Provision and maintenance of risk-free plant and systems of work.
- Ensuring the safety in use, handling, storage and transport of articles and substances.
- Provision of information, training, instruction and supervision.
- Maintenance of a safe workplace.
- Provision of means of entry and exit.
- Provision of a safe working environment.
- Adequate facilities.

A **senior member** of the organisation should be responsible for implementing the policy and may be supported by safety officers.

Employees also have basic responsibilities in this regard.

Most companies have a **safety committee and representatives** who have some experience, are entitled to training and are consulted about arrangements to ensure the effectiveness of the health and safety policy implementation.

The Health & Safety Executive (HSE)

The Health & Safety Executive is an independent regulator with the duty to make adequate provision for the enforcement of the HASAWA. The main function of the HSE is providing workplace inspections to ensure compliance with the law and enforce the legal requirements, if necessary. The HSE also provides an advisory service to employers and unions.

Safety committee and meetings

One rule requires organisations to have a method of communicating and evaluating safety and health issues brought up by management or employees in their workplace. Larger employers must establish a safety committee. Smaller employers have the choice of either establishing a safety committee or holding safety meetings with a management representative present.

There is a difference between a safety committee and a safety meeting:

- A safety committee is an organisational structure where members represent a group. This gives everyone a voice but keeps the meeting size to an effective number of participants.
- A safety meeting includes all employees and a management person is there to ensure that issues are addressed. Typically, the safety committee is an effective safety management tool for a larger employer and safety meetings are more effective for a smaller employer.

Health and safety training

The Health and Safety at Work Act imposes a duty on employers to provide training to ensure a healthy and safe workplace. As well as being a way to obtain compliance with health and safety regulations, safety training enhances employees' knowledge, understanding and commitment.

Organisations implement safety training because it improves job knowledge and skills and ensures optimum employee performance at a specified level. In health and safety training, specified performance standards include attention to safety rules and regulations regarding safe work behaviour.

- First, problems or training needs are identified by inspection, by accident reports and through discussion at the health and safety committee.
- Next, the planning, execution and evaluation of the training takes place.
- Because training programmes only have a short-term effect on employee's behaviour, regular refresher courses should be organised.
- Top management support is a key ingredient in the availability and success of health and safety courses.

All new staff under **induction** must receive training that ensures their safety both in normal working conditions and in cases of emergency.

Monitoring policy

Safety specialists argue that the safety policy should reflect the employer's commitment to develop safe systems of work and to pursue a healthy work environment.

There is a growing awareness that, in practice, many employers are turning a blind eye to health and safety requirements.

Furthermore, many safety policies are not that helpful in practice because of the failure to monitor their relevance to workplace arrangements, inadequate training, and supervisors and safety officers lacking authority to make decisions.

A proactive approach would involve Human Resources regularly checking to ensure that safety policies, management procedures and arrangements are working and are changed to suit new developments or work structures in the workplace.

Case study style question 1

PQR has recently been taken over by RST. RST has always been very concerned about health and safety however this is not an area that PQR has paid much attention to. The previous managing director of PQR has always said that as they are not a manufacturing company, then they don't really have to comply with health and safety. The management team of RST have arranged a presentation about health and safety for the managers and staff of PQR. You have been asked to present part of the presentation.

Required:

Write briefing notes for your presentation. These notes should cover:

(a) An outline of the main features of health and safety legislation.

(8 minutes)

(b) An identification of those responsible for ensuring that the organisation is a safe place in which to work.

(10 minutes)

6 Discipline

The word discipline is used and understood in several different ways. It brings to mind the use of authority or force. To many, it primarily carries the disagreeable meaning of punishment. However, there is another way of thinking about discipline, based on the meaning of the original Latin distipulus meaning a learner or pupil.

Discipline means learning

Maintaining discipline (learning) among employees is an integral function of management. Discipline is present when the members of the enterprise follow goals or objectives sensibly without overt conflict and conduct themselves according to the standards of acceptable behaviour.

Discipline therefore can be considered as positive when employees willingly follow or go beyond the rules of the enterprise. Discipline is negative when employees follow the rules over-strictly, or disobey regulations and violate standards of acceptable behaviour.

The main purpose of taking disciplinary action is to achieve a change in behaviour of employees so that future action is unnecessary.

The stages involved in a disciplinary process

Employees need to be aware that certain actions will lead to disciplinary action.

There are several situations where work norms might not be adhered to and which would cause problems if there were no remedial action:

- leaving work early, lateness, absenteeism
- defective and/or inadequate work performance
- breaking safety or other rules, regulations and procedures
- refusing to carry out a legitimate work assignment
- poor attitudes which influence the work of others or which reflect on the public image of the firm, such as improper personal appearance.

Rules will normally cover issues such as absence, timekeeping and holiday arrangements, health and safety, use of the organisation's equipment and facilities, misconduct, sub-standard performance, discrimination, bullying and harassment.

Rules and procedures should be clear, and should preferably be put in writing. They should be known and understood by all employees.

Process for handling disciplinary procedures:

- The informal talk.
- The oral warning.
- The written or official warning – first and second.
- Suspension.
- Demotion.
- Dismissal.

Standards need to be set for the right to appeal against these procedures.

In a well-managed organisation disciplinary procedures may not be needed very often. But if a problem does arise then they are vital. Good procedures can help organisations to resolve problems internally – and avoid employment tribunal claims.

The statutory procedures and the Code of Practice

Although organisations can be flexible about how formal or extensive their procedures need to be, there is a statutory procedure they must follow as a minimum if they are contemplating dismissing an employee – or imposing certain kinds of penalty short of dismissal such as suspension without pay or demotion. Unless employers follow the statutory procedure, employment tribunals will automatically find dismissals unfair.

The statutory procedure involves the following three steps:

- A statement in writing of what it is the employee is alleged to have done.
- A meeting to discuss the situation.
- The right of appeal.

The statutory procedure is the minimum standard. Employment tribunals expect employers to behave fairly and reasonably.

Disciplinary procedures are an aid to the effective management of people, and should not be viewed primarily as a means of imposing sanctions or as leading to dismissal. Where dismissal does occur, employees may make a complaint to an employment tribunal if they believe they have been unfairly dismissed, although ordinarily the employee must have one year's service.

It is for the employer to show the reason for the dismissal and that it was a fair reason.

The tribunal will determine whether the dismissal was fair or unfair and will take into account the size and administrative resources of the employer in deciding whether they acted reasonably or unreasonably. The tribunal consider how far the statutory procedures have been followed. Employment Tribunals expect employers to behave fairly and reasonably.

ACAS code of practice

In the United Kingdom, there exists a set of advisory booklets about various employment practices published by the Advisory Conciliation and Arbitration Service (ACAS). These are often used as yardsticks against which internal disciplinary procedures are judged to be fair or reasonable. The disciplinary code of practice states that disciplinary procedures should:

- be in writing
- specify to whom they apply
- provide for matters to be dealt with quickly
- indicate the disciplinary actions which may be taken

- specify the levels of management which have the authority to take the various forms of disciplinary action
- provide for individuals to be informed of the complaints against them and to be given an opportunity to reply
- give individuals the right to be accompanied by a trade union representative or by a fellow employee
- ensure that, except for gross misconduct, no employees are dismissed for a first breach of discipline
- ensure that disciplinary action is not taken until the case has been carefully investigated
- ensure that individuals are given an explanation for any penalty imposed
- provide a right of appeal and specify the procedure to be followed.

Handling discipline

Encourage improvement

The main purpose of operating a disciplinary procedure is to encourage improvement in an employee whose conduct or performance is below acceptable standards.

Act promptly

Problems dealt with early enough can be 'nipped in the bud', whereas delay can make things worse as the employee may not realise that they are below standard unless they are told. The manager should arrange to speak to the employee as soon as possible – the matter may then be able to be dealt with in an informal manner and not as part of the disciplinary process.

Gather the facts

Whilst maintaining satisfactory standards and dealing with disciplinary issues requires firmness on the part of the manager, it also requires fairness. The manager must be as objective as possible, keep an open mind, and do not prejudge the issues.

Having gathered all the facts, the manager or supervisor should decide whether to:

- drop the matter – there may be no case to answer or the matter may be regarded as trivial.

- arrange counselling/take informal action – this is an attempt to correct a situation and prevent it from getting worse without using the disciplinary procedure.
- arrange a disciplinary meeting – this will be necessary when the matter is considered serious enough to require disciplinary action.

Stay calm

All enquiries, investigations and proceedings must be conducted with thought and care.

Be consistent

The attitude and conduct of employees may be seriously affected if management fails to apply the same rules and considerations to each case.

Consider each case on its merits

While consistency is important, it is also essential to take account of the circumstances and people involved.

Follow the disciplinary procedure

The disciplinary procedure must be followed and the supervisor or manager should never exceed the limits of his or her authority.

If the employee is dismissed or suffers a disciplinary penalty short of dismissal – such as suspension without pay – the statutory minimum procedures must have been followed.

Suspension with pay

Where there appears to be serious misconduct, or risk to property or other people, a period of suspension with pay should be considered while the case is being investigated.

Self-discipline

Self-discipline is based upon socialisation, producing norms which follow reasonable standards of acceptable behaviour. Positive self-discipline is based upon the premise that most employees want to do the right thing. Most people accept the idea that following instructions and fair rules of conduct is part of the work ethic.

Once employees know what is expected of them and feel that the rules are reasonable, self-disciplined behaviour becomes a part of collective attitudes and group norms (i.e. the way in which employees behave as a work group), enabling 'responsible autonomy'. When new rules are introduced, the manager must try to convince employees of their purpose and reasonableness. If the work group as a whole accepts change, a strong sense of group cohesiveness on the employees' part will usually exert group pressure on possible dissenters, thus reducing the need for corrective action.

Douglas McGregor's 'hot stove rule'

This rule draws a comparison between touching a hot stove and experiencing discipline. When one touches a hot stove, the reaction is immediate, consistent, impersonal and with warning. The burn is immediate, with no questions of cause and effect. There is a warning, because everyone knows what happens if one touches a stove when the stove is hot. The result is consistent; every time a person touches a hot stove, they are burned. The result is impersonal; whoever touches a hot stove is burned. One is burned because of what they do, because the stove is touched, not because of who the person is. The comparison between the 'hot stove rule' and disciplinary action is that discipline should be directed against the act and not against the person.

Immediacy means that after noticing the offence, the supervisor proceeds to take disciplinary action as speedily as possible, normally the preliminary informal investigation.

For example, emotional incidents such as arguments in public or insubordination often require immediate response.

Case study style question 2

EFG was established three years ago. Since then, the company, which provides online financial advice, has experienced rapid growth, and the management has not really had the time to get all management systems and procedures into place.

The chief executive officer has recruited you to look at the way in which the company deals with its disciplinary problems and procedures.

Required:

Write a report to the CEO covering the following:

(a) Explaining why EFG should have a formal disciplinary procedure.

(5 minutes)

(b) Recommending guidelines for drawing up a disciplinary procedure.

(10 minutes)

7 Grievance procedures

Grievance procedures are not the same as disciplinary procedures. A grievance occurs when an employee feels superiors or colleagues are wrongly treating him or her; e.g. unfair appraisal, discrimination, prevented from advancing, being picked on, etc.

The grievance procedure often follows this sequence:

- The employee discusses the grievance with a colleague, staff or union representative.

- If the grievance is warranted, it is taken to the employee's immediate superior.
- If that superior cannot help, then it is referred to the superior's manager, at which stage the HR or Personnel department should be informed.
- Distinction should be made between an individual and a collective grievance.
- The colleague, staff or union representative should be permitted to be involved.
- Time-frames and deadlines should be stated to resolve the issue or submit an appeal.

Tribunals

A company may find that an employee is not happy with the outcome of a grievance procedure and that the individual wants to make a claim to an employment tribunal.

Employment tribunals are independent judicial bodies, less formal than a court, established to hear and determine claims to do with employment matters. Their aim is to resolve disputes between employers and employees over employment rights.

Examples include:

- unfair dismissal
- breach of contract
- discrimination
- equal pay.

Resolving disputes without a tribunal

In some cases it is possible to resolve disputes without the need for a tribunal. The following techniques may be used:

Arbitration

With arbitration, an independent arbitrator hears the case and delivers a legally binding decision in favour of one party. It is used to decide cases of alleged unfair dismissal or claims under flexible working legislation.

Benefits include:

- Speedy private informal hearing.
- No cross-examination.
- Limited grounds for review of the arbitrator’s decision.

Mediation

With mediation an impartial third party facilitates discussion between the parties and encourages them to reach a mutually satisfactory conclusion.

Benefits include:

- Speedy resolution
- Avoids the stress of a formal hearing
- Parties can express their views directly to each other.

Conciliation

This can be used to settle a dispute before it gets to a tribunal hearing. It involves trying to build a positive relationship between the disputing parties.

Benefits include:

- Confidentiality.
- Avoid time, stress and cost of attending a tribunal.
- Lessening damage to the employment relationship.
- Reaching an agreement that satisfies both parties.

Benefits of discipline and grievance procedure

- Employer's legal obligations are being met.
- Cost savings. Fewer costs for legal damages and lower operating costs.
- Company image. The company does not want to be associated with a discipline and grievance record.
- To preserve the well-being of employees and others, improves employee morale, trust and motivation.

Case study style question 3

P has worked in the customer services department of LMN company for two years. Last week he was sent to meet with M, a senior Human Resources manager.

At the meeting, which lasted less than ten minutes, P was told that the company were very unhappy with his performance and that his attitude was ‘not as it should be’. He was informed that, in accordance with the company's discipline code, he was being demoted to a lower graded role in the credit control department and that this was with immediate effect.

P was shocked by this as he had never been informed of the company's unhappiness with him before and he was confused about the comment about his attitude. He had always enjoyed his job, and thought he got on well with his colleagues. He had also never heard of the company's discipline code.

Required:

Write an email to P discussing what LMN have done wrong in the handling of his case and explain the actions which are available to him regarding this decision.

(20 minutes)

Case study style question 4

S, who was recently appointed as Head of Human Resources (HR) in a small but growing business, reviewed the company HR policies and decided that they need updating. The company has existing documents covering Equal Opportunities, a Company Code of Conduct, Disciplinary Procedures and Grievance Procedures. Several members of staff did not know the difference between grievance and disciplinary procedures and were unaware that the company had policies on these matters.

Required:

Write an email to be sent to all members of staff explaining the difference between 'grievance' and 'discipline' and briefly describing the disciplinary process.

(20 minutes)

8 Dismissal and redundancy

Dismissal

Under UK law, dismissal is described as **termination of employment** with or without notice by the employer, or in the case of constructive dismissal, resignation by the employee because the conduct of the employer was sufficient to be deemed to have terminated the contract by the employer's actions. Dismissal without notice is usually wrongful dismissal, that is breach of the contract of employment; it may or may not also be unfair dismissal.

Dismissal is normally fair only if the employer can show that it is for one of the following reasons:

- a reason related to the employee's **conduct**.
- a reason related to the employee's **capability** or qualifications for the job.

- because a **statutory duty** or restriction prohibited the employment being continued.
- some **other substantial reason** of a kind which justifies the dismissal and that the employer acted reasonably in treating that reason as sufficient for dismissal.
- because the role was **redundant**.

Types of dismissal

- Constructive dismissal is resignation by the employee because the conduct of the employer was sufficient to be deemed to have terminated the contract by the employer's actions.
- Wrongful (unfair) dismissal is dismissal without notice, a breach of the contract of employment.

For a dismissal to be fair, the employer must show that the reason for the dismissal is of a type acceptable under statute.

Redundancy

Redundancy is a type of dismissal. The grounds of redundancy may be justified on any of the following grounds:

- cessation of business
- cessation of business in the place where the employee was employed
- cessation of the type of work for which he or she was employed.

The law relating to redundancy

For the purposes of the right to be consulted, which applies when an employer proposes to make 20 or more employees redundant over 90 days or less, the law defines redundancy as: 'dismissal for a reason not related to the individual concerned or for a number of reasons all of which are not so related'. This definition might include, for example, a situation where dismissals are not related to the conduct or capability of the individuals but are part of a reorganisation.

Case study style question 5

DEF, a national airline carrier, has made a net loss for the last five years. While its major competitors have pursued programmes of modernisation, DEF has been left behind and is reported to have administrative costs and average salary costs that are, respectively, 35% and 25% higher than those of its competitors. The use of outdated and fuel-inefficient aircraft, as well as a reluctance to make use of modern Internet systems for online reservation, have been among the factors that have contributed to DEF's decline.

The board of DEF has produced a restructuring plan that includes 5,000 job cuts out of a workforce of 50,000; new, more demanding employment conditions; the sale of non-core assets; the establishment of twelve profit centres; a reduction in routes flown; replacement of its ageing fleet with fewer but more fuel-efficient aircraft and a complete overhaul of its reservation system.

Fierce confrontation is expected with the fourteen airline unions, but the board of DEF is committed to the implementation of the restructuring plan.

Required:

Your manager, the Finance Director, has asked you to prepare some notes for her on this matter for the next board meeting. Your notes should identify the key problems associated with making large-scale redundancies and discuss the ways in which redundancies can be managed to minimise these problems for DEF.

(15 minutes)

9 Equality and diversity

Globalisation has changed the nature of companies in many ways. In terms of staff, it has meant:

- The end of the "job for life" ideal.
- A move from employee's effort due to loyalty to the company towards effort expecting appropriate rewards.
- Employees willing to look outside of the company for advancement opportunities.

Obtaining employee commitment is often seen as the key to competitive performance, but due to the above factors, commitment from employees is becoming more difficult for companies to obtain.

Rosseau and Greller's psychological contract

Rosseau and Greller looked into the relationship between what the employees believed was expected of them and what they expected in return from the employer. They called this the **psychological contract**. They defined three types of psychological contract:

- **Coercive** where employees feel forced to contribute and view rewards as inadequate.
- **Calculative** where employee acts voluntarily and works in exchange for an identifiable set of rewards.
- **Cooperative** where employees contribute more than would normally be expected from them. They actively seek to contribute further to the achievement of company goals.

In coercive contracts, motivation and commitment would be low, or even negative. In calculative contracts, motivation and commitment could be increased if the rewards were increased. In cooperative contracts motivation and commitment would be linked to achievement. Motivation was found to be highest when the contract was viewed in the same way by the organisation and the individual, that is where the employee perceived the practices of the company towards them to be fair.

Salomon

Salomon looked at the difficulty in achieving equity in relation to pay, there are many considerations:

- A living wage (compare employee needs and their income)
- Rate for the job (compare employees carrying out the same role)
- Output reward (compare the output of employees working in the same area)
- Responsibility (compare the responsibilities of employees at different levels of the organisation)
- Differentials (compare employees carrying out different roles within the organisation)
- Comparability (compare employees carrying out the same roles in different organisations)
- Status (compare employees carrying out different roles in different organisations)
- Contribution (compare the employee's pay to the profitability of the organisation)
- Supply and demand (compare the organisation's ability to pay and its need for labour).

Equality and diversity are important concepts in human resources management. They cover the legal obligation of organisations to protect against discrimination and to ensure that all individuals are treated fairly and equally.

Equality

In the UK, **The Equality Act** (2012) is the most significant piece of equality legislation to be introduced for many years. It is there to strengthen protection, advance equality and simplify the law. The Equality Act brings together, and significantly adds to and strengthens, a number of previous existing pieces of legislation, including race and disability. One of the key changes is that it extends the protected characteristics to encompass:

- age
- disability
- gender reassignment
- marriage and civil partnership
- pregnancy and maternity
- race
- religion or belief
- sex
- sexual orientation.

Diversity

Every business wants the best person for the job. Unequal treatment, prejudice or harassment discredits businesses and can be very costly. The owner or manager of a business may also be held responsible for discriminatory action by its employees.

Under the Equality Act (2012) it is unlawful to discriminate on the grounds of someone's sex, sexual orientation, status as a married person or a civil partner, race, colour, nationality, ethnic origin, religion, beliefs or because of a disability, pregnancy or childbirth, or subsequent maternity leave or because they are a member or non-member of a Trade Union. It is also unlawful to discriminate against part-time workers.

Equal opportunities

The object of providing equal opportunities on the workplace is to:

- ensure fair and non-discriminatory treatment is given by management to all job applicants and existing employees.

A positive approach to equal opportunities should:

- secure the best recruits from the widest available range of candidates.
- ensure the best use is made of the skills and abilities of all employees.
- reinforce the professionalism and image of the organisation itself.

The implementation of equal opportunities policies is important to all organisations. Unfair or unlawful discriminatory practices not only lead to resentment on the part of those who suffer from them; they also adversely affect public perceptions of the organisation. A genuine belief in equal opportunities, coupled with the knowledge that unfair or unlawful discriminatory practices will not be tolerated, should yield benefits within the organisation itself and lead to a more positive public belief in its fairness and professionalism and an improved relationship with its stakeholders.

Equal Opportunities Policy

The main points of a typical Equal Opportunities Policy should be as follows:

- Equal opportunities shall mean fairness for all; the recognition, development and use of everyone's talents.
- This fairness will run through recruitment, selection, training, promotion, specialisation and career development generally. It should also govern the relationship of all employees with each other.
- Equal opportunity does not just relate to sex or marital status, but the fact that people can be particularly disadvantaged for those reasons is reflected in legislation.
- No job applicant or employee shall receive unfavourable treatment directly or indirectly on the grounds of gender, sexual orientation, marital status, race, nationality, ethnic origin, religious beliefs and, where applicable, trade union membership, age or disability.
- Selection criteria and procedures will be frequently reviewed to ensure that individuals are selected, promoted and dealt with on the basis of merit, fitness and competence, subject only to the restrictions imposed by law.
- Training is an important part of the implementation of the Equal Opportunities Policy. Training programmes will be arranged to ensure that staff are fully aware of their roles and responsibilities and have the opportunity to develop and progress within the organisation.

The differences between equal opportunities and diversity:

Equal opportunities	Diversity
Removing discrimination	Maximising potential
Issue for disadvantaged groups	Relevant to all employees
A Human Resources role	A managerial role
Relies on proactive action	Does not rely on proactive action

10 Organisational culture

What is culture?

Organisational culture is an important concept since it has a widespread influence on the behaviours and actions of employees. It represents a powerful force on an organisation's strategies, structures and systems, the way it responds to change and ultimately, how well the organisation performs.

Handy described culture as:

'the way we do things around here'

By this Handy means the sum total of the **belief, knowledge, attitudes, norms** and **customs** that prevail in an organisation.

Levels of culture

According to Edgar Schein (1992)

Culture exists at three different levels:

1 **Artefacts**. These are the things that can be seen, heard and observed. This is largely the view of the organisation that the public experience. It can include items such as:

- Dress codes. Is the dress code formal or informal, for example are uniforms worn?
- Patterns of behaviour. This is the way people within the organisation are seen as acting.
- Physical symbols. This could include logos and branding.
- Office layout. This includes the facilities and furnishings.

2 **Espoused Values**. These can be identified from stories and the opinions of those within the organisation. It can include items such as:

- Language. This is the way people communicate both within and outside the organisation.

- Behaviour. This shows what the people in the organisation feel is important.
- How people justify what they do. These values can be deep rooted, many will take for granted that their behaviour is acceptable without questioning it.

3 **Basic assumptions**. These beliefs are so deeply embedded in a culture that members are no longer consciously aware of them. It can include:

- Beliefs on environmental issues. If this is important, it will be part of every aspect of the work done.
- How people should be treated. This will include human relations policies, customer relationships etc.

As you go through the levels, the elements become less visible and more ingrained. At the third level, those within the organisation may not even be aware of their beliefs, they have become so fundamentally part of their way of being.

For an organisation, understanding this helps them to anticipate problems with their culture and allows them to see how difficult it may be to change. Changing level one items, such as dress codes or office layouts, is relatively easy, but changing values and beliefs can be very difficult. This may also lead to differences between the levels, for example what the organisation says and does may be different to how it is perceived by the outside world. The public may view certain acts as superficial and often do not believe that the underlying beliefs of the organisation have really changed.

The organisational iceberg

The idea of hidden elements in culture is often referred to as the organisational iceberg.

The iceberg describes two levels at which culture operates:

- Formal aspects (visible) above the water
- Behavioural aspects (hidden) below the water.

The elements of culture above the surface would include:

- goals
- technology
- procedures
- structure
- skills.

The hidden elements represent the larger part of the iceberg which is below the water, and that would include:

- attitudes
- style
- communication patterns
- values
- feelings
- beliefs.

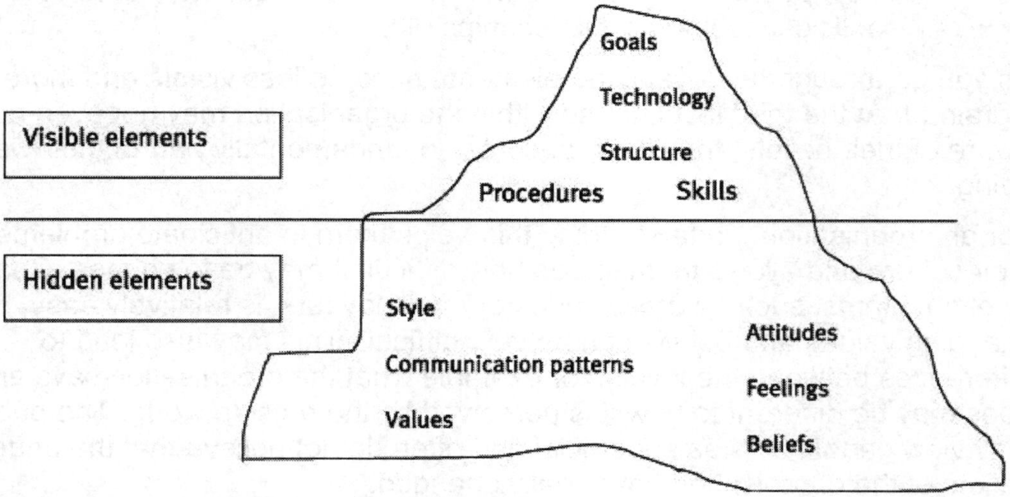

The diagram shows that what the public, customers, suppliers and others outside of an organisation see is only a small part of the picture. Much of what makes the organisation what it is, is intangible or hidden from view. It suggests that it is really only possible to fully understand the workings and culture of an organisation from within.

Why is culture important?

Culture is that invisible bond, which ties the people of a community together. It refers to the pattern of human activity. The importance of culture lies in its close association with the way of living of the people. The different cultures of the world have brought in diversity in the ways of life of the people inhabiting different parts of the world.

Culture is related to the development of one's attitude. The cultural values of an individual have a deep impact on his/her attitude towards life. They shape an individual's thinking and influence his/her mindset.

- It gives an individual a unique identity.
- The culture of a community gives its people a character of their own.
- Culture shapes the personality of a community. This includes the language that a community speaks, the art forms it hosts, its staple food, its customs, traditions and festivities comprise the community's culture.

Advantages of having a strong culture

An organisation's culture has a significant bearing on the way it relates to its stakeholders (especially customers and staff), the development of its strategy and its structure. A strong culture will:

- facilitate good communication and co-ordination within the organisation.
- provide a framework of social identity and a sense of belonging.
- reduce differences amongst the members of the organisation.
- strengthen the dominant values and attitudes.
- regulate behaviour and norms among members of the organisation.
- minimise some of the perceptual differences among people within the organisation.
- reflect the philosophy and values of the organisation's founder or dominant group.
- affect the organisation's strategy and ability to respond to change.

Disadvantages of having a strong culture

A strong culture that does not have positive attributes in relation to stakeholders and change is a hindrance to effectiveness. Other disadvantages of a strong culture are:

- Strong cultures are difficult to change, beliefs which underpin culture can be deep rooted.
- Strong cultures may have a blinkered view which could affect the organisation's ability or desire to learn new skills.
- Strong cultures may stress inappropriate values. A strong culture which is positive can enhance the performance of the organisation, but a strong culture which is negative can have the opposite effect.
- Where two strong cultures come into contact e.g., in a merger, then conflicts can arise.
- A strong culture may not be attuned to the environment e.g., a strong innovative culture is only appropriate in a dynamic, shifting environment.

Influences on culture

The structure and culture of an organisation will develop over time and will be determined by a complex set of variables, including:

Size How large is the organisation in terms of turnover, physical size and employee numbers?

Technology How technologically advanced is the organisation either in terms of its product, or its productive processes?

Diversity How diverse is the company either in terms of product range, geographical spread or cultural make-up of its stakeholders?

Age How old is the business or the managers of the business? Do its strategic level decision makers have experience to draw upon?

History What worked in the past? Do decision makers have past successes to draw upon; are they willing to learn from their mistakes?

Ownership Is the organisation owned by a sole trader? Are there a small number of institutional shareholders or are there large numbers of small shareholders?

When analysing an organisation, look for clues given as to the culture of the organisation using these main areas, although there are many other influences, including the leadership style adopted.

Other influences on culture

As well as the main influences on culture listed above, there are other, more subtle influences:

- The degree of individual initiative – is it encouraged or are decisions always referred upwards?
- The degree of risk tolerance – are managers only allowed to follow low-risk strategies?
- Clarity of direction – is there a clear focus; are these clear objectives and performance expectations?
- The degree of integration between groups – are different units encouraged to work together? Are management aloof or approachable; is communication clear to lower level staff?
- The reward system – are individuals rewarded for succeeding, i.e. are rewards based on performance criteria?
- Conflict tolerance – are employees encouraged to air grievances?
- Communication patterns – is there a formal hierarchy or an informal network?
- Formalisation of clothing and office layout – are there strict rules over this?
- The kind of people employed – are they graduates, young, old, etc.?

11 Summary diagram

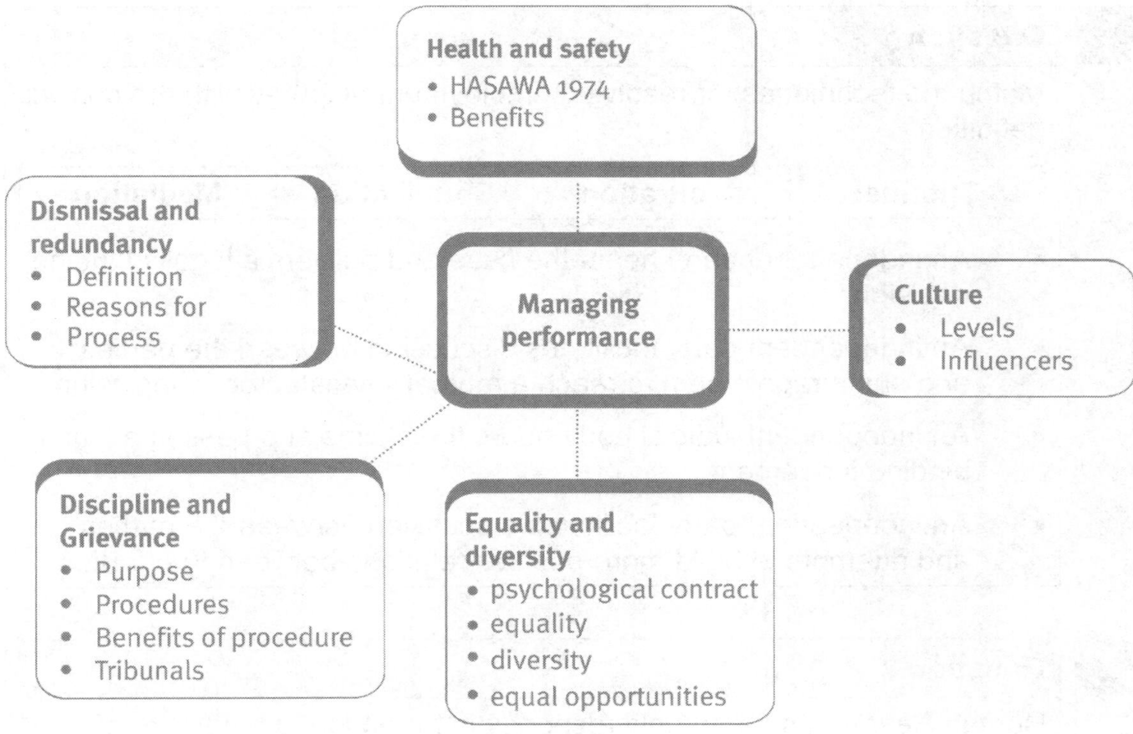
Health and safety
• HASAWA 1974
• Benefits
Dismissal and redundancy
• Definition
• Reasons for
• Process
Managing performance
Culture
• Levels
• Influencers
Discipline and Grievance
• Purpose
• Procedures
• Benefits of procedure
• Tribunals
Equality and diversity
• psychological contract
• equality
• diversity
• equal opportunities

End of chapter questions

Question 1

Match the techniques for resolving employment disputes with the correct definition:

Tribunal	Arbitration	Conciliation	Mediation

- An independent party hears the case and delivers a legally binding decision
- An independent party facilitates discussion between the parties and encourages them to reach a mutually satisfactory conclusion
- An independent judicial body hears the claims and passes a legally binding judgement
- An independent party facilitates discussion between the parties and attempts to build more positive relations between the parties

Question 2

Human Resources are largely responsible for ensuring a number of employment practices are in place in the organisation. One of these is health and safety. Health and safety legislation is a legal requirement in the UK.

Which of the following statements are true in relation to health and safety? Select all that apply.

A Health and safety is solely the responsibility of management

B The Health and Safety at Work Act 1974 applies to all organisations in the UK

C Organisations can save costs through health and safety compliance

D Health and safety issues should be covered during the induction of new members of staff

E Adhering to health and safety legislation can improve a company's reputation

F All large organisations in the UK must have an up to date health and safety policy statement

Question 3

Insert the correct words in the sentences below (words can be used more than once).

- Discipline
- Grievance
- Dismissal
- Tribunal
- Redundancy

A __________ occurs when a member of staff feels they are being treated unfairly.

The objective of _____________ is to change behaviour.

Where an employee has been subject to _________ they may wish to take their case to a ___________________.

Unfair ___________ would be grounds to take a case to a ___________.

_____________ is a form of ____________ which would be allowed if the business ceased trading.

Question 4

Which of the following statements about discipline are true? Select all that apply.

A There are no legal requirements regarding disciplinary procedures; organisations can be flexible about how formal their disciplinary procedures are.

B Where a member of staff feels that they are being unfairly treated by colleagues or managers, they may initiate disciplinary action.

C Douglas McGregors's 'hot stove rule' suggests that disciplinary action should be taken immediately after the offence is noticed.

D Persistent lateness or absenteeism would be unfair grounds for disciplinary action.

E Disciplinary action will normally follow a process including verbal and written warnings before dismissal would be considered.

F The purpose of a disciplinary procedure is to change behaviour.

Question 5

Using Rosseau and Greller's model of psychological contract, match the words to the definitions.

Calculative	Cooperative	Coercive

- Employees feel forced to contribute and view rewards as inadequate
- Employees contribute more than would normally be expected from them
- Employee acts voluntarily and works in exchange for an identifiable set of rewards

Question 6

Which of the following is NOT covered by the Equality Act 2012?

A Pregnancy and maternity

B Sexual orientation

C Physical appearance

D Religion or belief

Question 7

Which of the following would be seen as fair grounds for dismissal? Select all that apply.

A The member of staff was known as a troublemaker

B Company restructuring

C The role had become redundant

D Gross misconduct, such as theft or violence

E Long term absenteeism due to ill health

F Statutory restriction prohibiting continued employment

Question 8

Match the statements to whether they relate to equal opportunities or diversity.

A Human Relations role
Objective of maximising potential
Objective of removing discrimination
Relevant to all employees
A management role

Equal opportunities	Diversity

Question 9

Which **three** of the following statements regarding equality are correct?

A It is unlawful to discriminate against part-time workers

B Equal Opportunities is a managerial role

C Diversity is about removing discrimination

D Equal opportunities is an issue for disadvantaged groups

E The UK Equality Act 2012 makes it illegal to discriminate on the grounds of age

Test your understanding answers

Case study style question 1

BRIEFING NOTES

Presentation on Health and Safety for PQR

(a) The **Health & Safety at Work Act (HASAWA)** was designed to have far-reaching consequences upon employers' premises and methods of work. The main provisions of the Act require an employer to provide a safe and healthy working environment in which to work. This includes the duty to provide training and appoint individuals responsible for maintaining safety at work, for example, safety representatives and trained safety officers.

The **Health & Safety Executive (HSE).** The Commission, together with the Secretary of State makes appointments to the Health & Safety Executive whose duty it is to make adequate provision for the enforcement of the HASAWA. The main function of the HSE is providing workplace inspections to ensure compliance with the law and enforce the legal requirements, if necessary. The HSE also provides an advisory service to employers and unions.

(b) **Managerial responsibilities**. Health and safety at work is the responsibility of both employers and employees. Legislation can only provide the underpinning to safe working practices, ultimately, it is how the legislation is translated in practice that determines whether a workplace is safe, or not. There are a number of ways in which managerial responsibility can be discharged to make work safe. The management of an organisation carry the prime responsibility for implementing a policy they have laid down, and they also have responsibility under the Act for operating the plant and equipment in the premises safely and meeting all the Act's requirements whether these are specified in the policy statement, or not. Management has a duty to provide a safe and healthy working environment, which is hazard free, and to train others so that they are able to operate and maintain a safe and healthy working environment for themselves.

Employee responsibilities. For the first time in health and safety legislation a duty is placed on employees while that are at work to take reasonable care for the safety of themselves and others. The employee is, therefore, legally bound to comply with the safety rules and instructions that the employer requires. Employers are also fully empowered to dismiss employees who refuse to obey safety rules on the grounds of misconduct, especially if the possibility of such a dismissal is explicit in the disciplinary procedure. Employees need to be enabled by management to carry out their duties and responsibilities. This might take the form of communicating policies and procedures about health and safety issues, appointing safety representatives, setting up committees and providing training.

Safety representatives. To reinforce the employees' role in the care of their own health and safety, provision has been made for the appointment of safety representatives by trade unions. Safety representatives have a legal duty of consultation with employers and are entitled to paid time off for training to enable them to carry out their function. Under the HASAWA employers' are expected to set up safety committees and consult with safety representatives about the membership of that committee.

Safety committees. Although the Act does not specifically instruct employers to set up safety committees, it comes very close. Safety representatives and training officers have to be consulted about the membership of the committee, and detailed advice on the function and conduct of safety committees is provided by the Health and Safety Commission. Since the Act there has been a great increase in the number of Safety Committees in operation. It has also been noted that the effectiveness of committees has been very much dependent on the employment of trained safety officers.

Case study style question 2

REPORT

To: CEO

From: Consultant

Date: today

Report on the need for a formal disciplinary procedure for EFG.

Introduction

In this report, the need for EFG to introduce a formal disciplinary procedure will be explained and guideline for drawing up this procedure will be recommended.

Need for a formal disciplinary procedure

(a) At its most fundamental level, the existence of a written disciplinary procedure is designed to protect both the employer and the employee.

Employer perspective

The employer should be protected from facing future actions (e.g. for unfair dismissal). If the company has clearly set out what it views as unacceptable behaviour and the actions that will be taken if this behaviour is undertaken, then it becomes very hard for the employee to claim they have been mistreated.

If an employee does undertake some action that is deemed unacceptable, the sliding scale of various different punishments should mean that the employee is less likely to repeat the action.

Looking at the big picture, the point of a disciplinary scheme is to deter employees from breaking the rules; in other words, to make sure that the scheme never has to be used.

Employee perspective

The employee of an organisation benefits from having a formal disciplinary procedure since it reduces the risk that they will be arbitrarily accused and punished for their actions.

This is becoming more important as more individuals are left to their own devices at work, rather than being given detailed rules and procedures (as organisations move from a mechanistic to an organic approach). This is likely to be particularly important in a company, such as EFG which is growing and changing rapidly.

Guidelines for drawing up a disciplinary procedure

(b) Any disciplinary procedure must take account of local legislation. In the case of EFG, there are a number of steps that should be followed.

The company should write down the procedures to avoid misunderstandings, and provide all members of staff with a copy.

It should be very clear which sections apply to which staff (e.g. some parts may only be relevant to senior executives).

The procedures should state very clearly the forms of disciplinary action which can occur, e.g. verbal warnings, written warnings, etc.

The procedures should also state which levels of management are able to use certain kinds of action (e.g. only senior executives being able to issue written warnings).

Detail the steps that will be taken to investigate complaints that might lead to action being taken.

Detail the procedures of how the employee will be notified of any complaint and of any action being taken against them.

Detail the appeal procedures for workers who feel that the action taken is unmerited.

Conclusion

The establishing of a disciplinary procedure is important for EFG as it would protect the company and the employees of the company.

Case study style question 3

EMAIL

To: P

From: Management accountant

Date: today

Subject: Grievance

Dear P,

I feel that LMN have acted against the statutory procedures laid down for companies in the way they have treated you.

Companies are expected to follow the ACAS code of practice in all disciplinary and grievance procedures.

The purpose of disciplinary procedures should be to improve the behaviour of the individual before action such as suspension, demotion or dismissal takes place. These actions should only occur in cases of gross misconduct or after a number of other courses of action have been taken first. This is clearly not the case here.

The stages which would normally be undertaken in this sort of case before a demotion would be:

- Informal chat
- Oral warning
- Written warning – first then second
- Suspension.

It would appear that none of these stages had been undertaken as the meeting notifying you of the demotion was the first you knew of the company's unhappiness with your performance. You also do not appear to have been given any details, or shown any evidence about the source of their unhappiness and it would appear that you have been given no opportunity to respond to their claims.

It is also significant that you were not aware of the company's discipline code. All employees should be made aware of this code when they join the company. The code should be clear about the expectations of the company and about actions which would be taken as a result of these expectations not being met.

You have obviously never had any sort of appraisal since joining the company or these matters would have been raised, and hopefully resolved, sooner.

In this case, you would have the right to appeal the decision at tribunal. As the company have not followed the statutory rules, it is likely that you would win your case.

I hope you have found the above useful. Please do not hesitate to get in touch if you would like any more information or would like to discuss any of these issues further.

Case study style question 4

EMAIL

To: all staff

From: Management accountant

Date: today

Subject: Grievance and discipline

It has come to the attention of Human Resources management that staff may be unclear about the difference between grievance and discipline and may not be aware of the disciplinary process within the company. The purpose of this email is to clarify the differences between grievance and discipline and to outline the disciplinary process within the company.

Grievance procedures are used for considering problems or concerns that employees wish to raise with their employers.

Discipline is not about punishment, but about correcting inappropriate behaviour. When an employee breaks the company code of conduct, a disciplinary process starts so that the employee becomes aware of their mistakes and can take the opportunity to improve their behaviour. Disciplinary offences may include, but are not limited to, persistent lateness, refusal to carry out reasonable work, poor work performance, harassment of colleagues and/or misuse of company assets.

A code of conduct should be established and documented. Staff should have access to the document and be made aware of its importance and the consequences of a breach.

The disciplinary process is progressive in nature. A disciplinary offence does not automatically lead to dismissal.

The stages of the disciplinary process are:

- informal talk
- formal talk
- verbal warning
- written warning
- decision – suspension, demotion, dismissal.

At each stage of the process, the employee must be made aware of the following:

- the section of the code that has been breached
- how the behaviour can be rectified
- what will happen if there is no improvement.

In many instances an informal talk can rectify problems without the need to progress through the formal stages. It is also important to establish if there are any mitigating circumstances that might be causing problems at work. Additionally all staff should be treated in the same manner with regard to discipline in accordance with the Equal Opportunities Policy.

I hope you have found the above useful. Please do not hesitate to get in touch if you would like any more information or would like to discuss any of these issues further.

Case study style question 5

NOTES

To: Finance Director

From: Management Accountant

Date: today

Subject: Problems associated with large-scale redundancies

The key problems in any redundancy situation include that of deciding which personnel shall be made redundant, carrying out the redundancy process in a way that is fair and within the law, deciding what the redundancy package will consist of, and how to maintain the morale and motivation of the remaining workforce.

Selection for redundancy must be fair, carried out according to an agreed procedure laid down beforehand and consistently applied. This procedure does not have to be the last in first out' principle, although this is a popular method because of its ease of application.

In the United Kingdom, the ACAS Code of Practice provides a useful checklist that helps ensure that companies operate within the law and that individuals are treated fairly in the redundancy process. Other countries have similar codes of practice and these should be followed where available.

The ACAS code suggests that management should stop recruitment, reduce overtime, consider retraining or transfer of people to other jobs, retire those over normal retirement age and introduce short-time working. Where the redundancy is inevitable, as in the case of DEF, employers should give as much warning as possible, use voluntary redundancy and early retirement, and offer help in finding other work. Employers must also ensure that individuals are informed before any news leaks out, and should try to run down establishments slowly.

The redundancy package offered needs to be considered for a number of reasons. First, a basic legal minimum sum based on the number of years of employment can result in a substantial sum, and this has to be budgeted for. Second, DEF might consider paying over the legal minimum as a way of indicating to the remaining employees and the world more generally that it is a 'good' employer.

The needs of the remaining staff should also be considered. Their morale and confidence in the organisation will need to be boosted. In the case of a partial redundancy, those remaining at work may well have to change their work patterns by operating new machinery, coping with bigger jobs or changing their job location. This will need to be discussed with the trade union(s), the employees concerned and their supervisors.

The term 'outplacement' has come to be used to describe the efforts of management to place redundant employees in other economically active positions. Some consultants have become expert in revising curriculum vitae (CVs) of staff and 'selling' them to a network of contacts.

Please do not hesitate to get in touch if you would like me to prepare any additional notes on this topic.

Question 1

The correct definitions are:

- An independent party hears the case and delivers a legally binding decision – **Arbitration**
- An independent party facilitates discussion between the parties and encourages them to reach a mutually satisfactory conclusion – **Mediation**
- An independent judicial body hears the claims and passes a legally binding judgement – **Tribunal**
- An independent party facilitates discussion between the parties and attempts to build more positive relations between the parties – **Conciliation**

Question 2

C, D, E and F

All employees have responsibility for health and safety, not just management.

The HASAWA applies to all organisations which employ five or more people.

Question 3

A **grievance** occurs when a member of staff feels they are being treated unfairly.

The objective of **discipline** is to change behaviour.

Where an employee has been subject to dismissal they may wish to take their case to a **tribunal**.

Unfair **dismissal** would be grounds to take a case to a **tribunal**.

Redundancy is a form of **dismissal** which would be allowed if the business ceased trading.

Question 4

C, E and F

There are no legal requirements regarding disciplinary procedures; organisations can be flexible about how formal their disciplinary procedures are. This is incorrect as disciplinary procedures are set by law.

Where a member of staff feels that they are being unfairly treated by colleagues or mangers, they may initiate disciplinary action. This is incorrect as in this case they would initiate grievance procedures.

Persistent lateness or absenteeism would be unfair grounds for disciplinary action. This is incorrect as this would be grounds for disciplinary action.

Question 5

The correct definitions are:

Coercive – **Employees feel forced to contribute and view rewards as inadequate**

Cooperative – **Employees contribute more than would normally be expected from them**

Calculative – **Employee acts voluntarily and works in exchange for an identifiable set of rewards**

Question 6

C

The Equality Act 2012 covers:

- Pregnancy and maternity
- Sexual orientation
- Religion of belief
- Age
- Disability
- Gender reassignment
- Marriage and civil partnership
- Race
- Sex

But it does not cover physical appearance.

Question 7

C, D and F

A member of staff being known as a troublemaker is not grounds for dismissal but should be dealt with through the disciplinary process if there is evidence of troublemaking.

Company restructuring may result in redundancy but is not in itself grounds for dismissal.

Employees cannot legally be dismissed on the grounds of ill health.

Question 8

The correct matching is:

Equal opportunities	Diversity
A Human Relations role	A management role
Objective of removing discrimination	Objective of maximising potential
	Relevant to all employees

Question 9

A, D and E

Equal opportunities is a Human Resources role.

Equal opportunities is about removing discrimination, diversity is about maximising potential.

Chapter

6

Controlling performance – part 2

Chapter learning objectives

Lead	Component
B2: Analyse individual and team performance	(a) Employee performance objective setting (b) Employee appraisals (c) Coaching and mentoring (d) Managing workplace environment

Topics to be covered

- Target setting and employee alignment
- Employee empowerment and engagement
- Performance reporting and review
- Rewards and sanctions in managing performance
- Different approaches to coaching and mentoring to improve performance
- Diversity and equity practices
- Health and safety
- Organisational culture.

1 Session content diagram

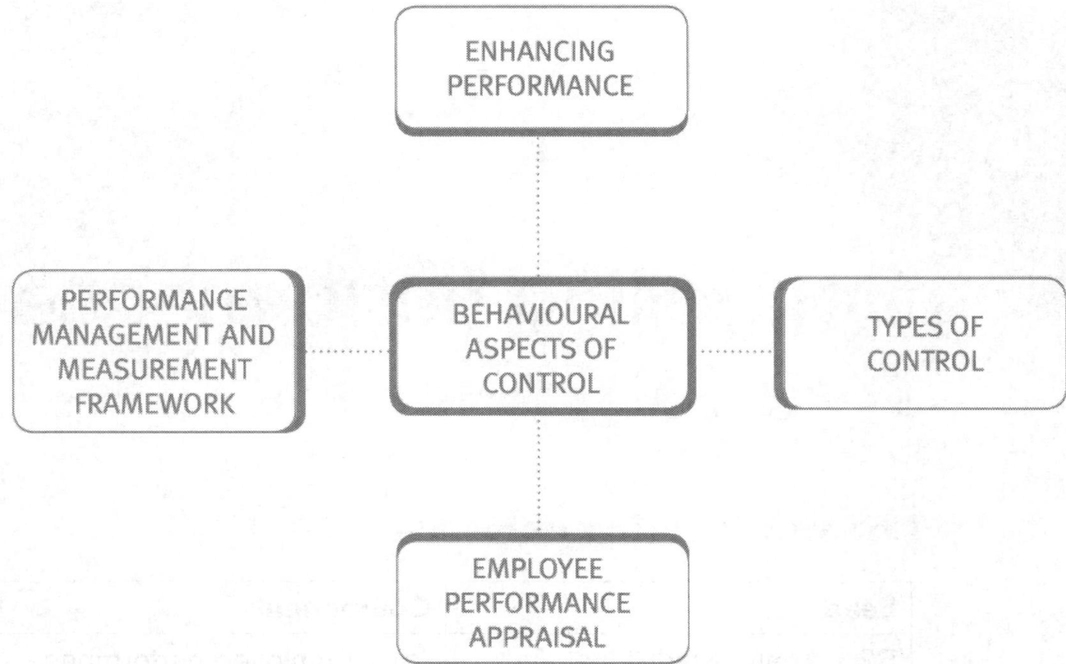

2 The wider context of control

In the previous chapter a number of control techniques were looked at. These were the responsibility of HR and were all legal requirements under UK law. Note that legal requirements in relation to employment practices may differ in other countries.

In addition to these legal requirements, organisations need to consider what other controls are necessary to manage and control the behaviour of their employees and to ensure that the organisation performs effectively.

What do we mean by 'behavioural' control?

Organisations want to influence employees' behaviour to benefit the organisation. This can involve a mixture of the following:

- Encouraging employees to adopt best practice to do 'the right thing the right way'
- Motivating employees to improve productivity
- Motivating employees to improve quality
- Preventing employees making mistakes and ensuring that mistakes are detected quickly if made
- Trying to limit the likelihood and impact of employee malfeasance, such as theft or fraud
- Encouraging employees to act ethically
- Motivating managers to make decisions that are in the best interests of the organisation.

The role of management includes trying to get the best performance from their employees as possible. This includes using control to modify the behaviour of employees. The leadership and management chapter covered a number of concepts which are used by management to control the behaviour of employees. The use of power and authority, the style of management adopted, the use of delegation and the empowerment of staff all contribute to behavioural control.

The following sections consider different ways of classifying and analysing approaches to control.

Control mechanisms

There are a wide number of ways that control can be used within an organisation, including the following:

- Organisational **structure** – breaking the organisation down into smaller units, such as having a dedicated accounts department, with clearly defined roles, responsibilities and authority. This can be reflected in many ways, such as insisting that all capital expenditure over $1,000 must be authorised by the Finance Director, for example.
- **Target** setting and budgeting – so staff know what is expected of them.
- Direct **supervision** of staff by managers.
- The **culture** of the organisation – for example, where mistakes are not tolerated.
- **Self-control** where employees are encouraged to work independently and take responsibility for their own results.
- Control **systems** – for example where actual results are compared to the budget each month and variances produced. These allow managers to identify, and focus on, areas where performance is not as expected and take corrective action, facilitating 'management by exception'.
- Specific control **processes** – for example, Creditors Ledger Control Account reconciliations may identify errors in processing purchase invoices.
- **Policies** and guidelines – for example having an ethical code to help employees recognise and deal with ethical conflicts.

Case study style question 1

Jersey Ltd is a small business that manufactures high quality portable loudspeakers. The business is small and has only twenty members of staff, with one supervisor. The work is highly skilled and complex, with staff divided into four teams – each with very different sets of required skills.

Currently there are no control procedures or any work guidance for employees, meaning that each member of staff often works in the way they individually feel is best. The twenty employees are moderately well paid, though there are few, if any, real promotion prospects and several employees have expressed their dissatisfaction with the working conditions within Jersey.

Jersey is owned and run by one person, H. She is concerned that the level of quality of production has fallen in recent months, as evidenced by an increase in wastage and a decrease in output. H is concerned about the effect this is having on the profitability of the company. As such, H is examining the possibility of introducing control processes to ensure that all units made are of adequate quality.

Task

Discuss the appropriateness of each of the following possible controls for Jersey:

(a) Direct supervision of manufacturing staff

(b) Setting performance targets for employees based on quality of output

(c) Relying on individual employees to control their own work.

Types of organisational control

The type of control used within organisations is largely dependent on the nature of the organisation, and will be influenced by the size and structure of the organisation, the number and types of employees and the work carried out within the organisation.

As well as the list of possible controls given above, there are a number of different ways of discussing or classifying controls and control systems, depending on the context or perspective being taken. Another angle considers the following four main types of organisational control.

- **Personal centralised control**. This approach is likely to be found in small owner-managed organisations where there is centralised decision-making by the owner. Control is carried out by the owner through personal supervision.

  However, as the organisation grows in size and complexity, owners may find increasing external demands on their time and will need to employ others to undertake supervision of day-to-day tasks. In this phase of growth, control moves away from personal centralised control to more bureaucratic control or output control.

- **Bureaucratic control**. Controls will be based on formalised rules, procedures, standardisation and hierarchy. This is achieved through specifications of how employees should behave and carry out their work using formal job descriptions and specification of standard methods for performance of tasks. Reward and punishment systems can be used to reinforce this control strategy.
- **Output control**. This approach is a form of control that is based on the measurement of outputs and the results achieved. It is most appropriate where there is a need for quantifiable and simple measures of organisational performance since it requires a specification of output standards and targets to be achieved. This approach facilitates delegation without the need for bureaucratic controls, because once output standards have been agreed, employees can work semi-autonomously to carry out tasks.
- **Clan or Cultural control**. This form of control requires the development of employees' strong identification with management goals, for example through professional identification and acceptance of the values and beliefs of the organisation. If employees have the necessary skills, experience and ability, they can be given freedom in deciding how to undertake their tasks. This leads to semi-autonomous working with few formal controls. This approach depends on the common agreement of objectives and shared cultural values. It will require careful selection, socialisation and development of employees.

Trust and control

Trust is the belief that someone is reliable and honest.

In an organisational context this suggests that management believe that employees can be depended upon to act ethically, with integrity and in the best interests of the organisation.

Where there is a high level of trust, management may reduce the level of formal control as they will have confidence that employees will always take the correct action. In essence, management have to find the right balance between trust and control within their organisation.

In the past, control systems within organisations were formal in nature. The system would rely on the required behaviour being specified in detail, with predictable outcomes expected. This type of approach could be seen in the classical theories of management where there was a high degree of specialisation, a hierarchical structure of authority and each employee was tasked with very specific roles.

A key feature of the scientific management school is the use of job, process analysis and time study to establish the optimum production methods and targets as to how long each task should take. The worker is not left with any discretion. The principles of scientific management make the workplace much simpler for managers to control. It is easier to measure inputs and outputs and compare the performance of workers. This approach can also be seen in McGregor's theory X model where the view held by the manager is that the employee is basically lazy and cannot be trusted. This opinion leads to an authoritarian approach to leadership.

The problem with this type of approach to management control, like the problem with the classical management theories, is that it fails to take account of the human element. A focus on this type of control could lead to:

- **Motivation problems**. Lack of morale; little worker commitment; no interchangeable skills (people are only trained to do one small part of the job); high staff turnover.
- **Quality problems**. No overall responsibility; no intrinsic satisfaction from work.
- **Little understanding of people**. People at work are not necessarily rational, for example they do not always work harder to earn more money and they are sometimes less inclined to work well if closely supervised; budgets sometimes cause problems, for example people might be inclined to purchase poor quality raw materials to stay within budget, thus causing production problems.

Today's business climate requires a far greater degree of flexibility and employees need to be more empowered to accommodate this flexibility. This suggests that an approach closer to McGregor's Theory Y approach, which was covered in the leadership and management chapter, should be adopted and managers should recognise that employees want to work and can be trusted.

The human relations approach emphasises the social organisation and the importance of informal relationships. Elton Mayo's studies on how to improve productivity revealed that work groups impose their own controls on members, such as the rate of work, working conditions and the members' interaction with managers. This control was imposed through a series of 'punishments', for example ostracising members who were persuaded to comply with the objectives of management rather than the norms set by the group.

Control is, therefore, a feature of interpersonal influences rather than close and constant supervision, recognising that people do not behave as unfeeling robots. This has an impact on control systems. There still needs to be control over the work being carried out and the manger must put in place regular reviews so that they have confidence that the objective will be met as required. Any possibility that the objective will not be met must be highlighted as soon as possible so that corrective action can be taken.

Allowing trust in controls works well for both the company and the employee. The employee is allowed to work on their own initiative and feels valued, this leads to increased motivation and increased productivity which benefits the company.

In order for control based on trust to work a number of factors must be in place.

- The manager must be confident that the employee has the knowledge and the skills to undertake the task.
- The objective must be clear and agreed by both parties.
- The employee must be motivated to work hard and use initiative to achieve the objective.

Case study style question 2

STU develops accountancy software for small-to medium-sized businesses. STU was established 15 years ago by a graduate in accounting. Despite an increasingly competitive environment, it has grown and diversified to become a global provider of specialised accountancy software.

In order to cope with the increasing size and diversity of the business, additional levels of management and control systems have been introduced, including additional policies, rules and procedures. Unfortunately, the increase in bureaucracy is having the effect of slowing down decision-making processes and limiting ideas for new software development.

The Chief Executive Officer is aware of the conflict between the structural changes and the need for continuous creativity and innovation that are critical to new software development and the future success of the business, but is not sure how to overcome the problem.

Required:

Write an email to the CEO explaining why formal control systems are increasingly necessary as an organisation grows and diversifies and why the use of bureaucratic forms of control in STU might limit creativity and innovation.

(20 minutes)

3 Employee performance appraisal

An important management control system used in most organisations is the employee performance appraisal system.

A performance appraisal system involves the regular and systematic review of performance and assessment of potential, with the aim of producing action programmes to develop both work and individuals. It aims to improve the efficiency of the organisation by ensuring that the individual employees are performing to the best of their abilities and by developing their potential for improvement.

There are different views on the purpose of performance appraisal. The purpose can be viewed as developmental or control but we will focus on the control aspect.

A performance appraisal system can bring many benefits to both the individual and the organisation.

Benefits to individuals

- Feedback about performance at work and an assessment of competence through comparison of performance against established standards and agreed targets
- Identifies work of particular merit done during the review period
- Provides a basis for remuneration
- May be used as an opportunity to discuss future prospects and ambitions
- Identifies training and development needs.

Benefits to organisation

- Provides a system for assessing competence of employees and identifies areas for improvement
- Provides a fair process for reward decisions
- Helps identify and formulate training needs
- Improves communication between managers and subordinates
- Provides clear targets linked to corporate objectives
- Provides a basis for HR planning
- Monitors recruitment and induction process against results.

The formal process of performance appraisal (TARA)

Targets. Targets must be set which employees understand and agree to. If they do not 'buy into' them, they will not put any effort in to accomplishing them, especially if they do not feel that the targets are achievable. This can lead to demotivation.

Actual results monitored. During the period, the manager should monitor the actual employee performance and provide regular feedback. Managers can offer rewards for good performance and support and help where it looks as though the employee is failing to meet their targets.

Review. At the end of the period, the manager and employee will usually have a formal appraisal interview where they discuss the employee's performance and investigate how successful the employee has been at meeting the pre-agreed targets.

Action plan. The manager and employee then agree on new targets that will be set for the coming period.

Approaches to performance appraisal

There are a number of approaches to performance appraisal, including:

The Ranking System. This is a formal structured approach which consists of the individual being assessed and analysed in terms of objectives, tasks, workflows and results achieved. These are then compared with previously agreed statements of required results and performance levels. For each of the set targets, the manager will provide a ranking as to the individual's performance. The rankings are usually based on an agreed scale, for example 1–5, with 1 being unsatisfactory and 5 being excellent.

The Unstructured Format. The unstructured format is another common approach where evaluators use an essay or short answer to grade employees. The benefit here is that any and all variables are used, from the most quantitative to the most informal. This approach tries to capture all aspects of employee performance rather than being restricted to the pre-agreed targets used in the more structured approach. Unstructured appraisals are meant to be open ended and all encompassing.

Self Rating. This approach is where the individual rates themselves on certain agreed criteria. This is then fed back to the manager who can review the individual's assessment and make their own assessment. The advantage of this approach is that that the individuals get the opportunity to consider their performance and in some cases remind management of what they have achieved in the period. It also forms the basis for the appraisal interview where both parties get the opportunity to discuss the ratings they have given and try to reach a consensus.

360 approach. In most appraisal approaches the manager appraises the individual. The individual may get some say in the appraisal, but ultimately the outcome will be decided by the manager. The 360 approach allows more participation by the individual. While the manager will appraise the individual, the individual is also given the opportunity to appraise the manager. In some systems, individuals will also appraise their colleagues. Every member of staff can be asked to give confidential and anonymous assessments on their colleagues and their manager. These assessments will help senior management to build up a more accurate pictures of the performance of departments. It also encourages individuals to work together for the good of the department.

Effective performance appraisal

To be effective, the system must:

- Be applied fairly and consistently
- Have the commitment and support from senior managers
- Be carried out with serious intent
- Relate to the main objectives of organisation
- Be clearly understood by all parties
- Be cost effective to operate.

Barriers to effective performance appraisal

One aspect of the typical performance appraisal system that can reduce its effectiveness is the appraisal interview. Poor performance appraisal interviews can be confrontational, judgemental, just a chat, a paper exercise, a substitute for the management process that should be undertaken during the year and/or out of date and irrelevant because it is only held annually.

Barriers to effective appraisal may be overcome if:

- There is commitment from all parties involved.
- There is a system of follow up and feedback.
- Recorded agreement between manager and employee about future training and development. Training should be arranged within an agreed time period.
- Alternative methods of appraisal, such as self rating or 360 approach could be used.

Case study style question 3

H joined the finance department of MNO a year ago. He is surprised that in that time, he has never been given any clear targets or objectives and he has had no opportunity to discuss his performance with his line manager, G. Other members of the department feel the same so they have discussed this with G. G was surprised and stated that if something was wrong with their work, he would have told them about it by now. G has confided in you that he has never undertaken performance appraisal in the department because he felt that it would take up a lot of his time and he was not really sure what it would achieve.

Required:

Write an email to G, explaining the benefits that MNO and the individual members of staff would obtain from having a formal staff appraisal system.

(15 minutes)

Reward systems

Linked to behavioural control is the reward system used within the organisation. In developing a reward system, organisations hope to support the goals of the organisation by aligning the goals of employees with these. Reward systems can be used to motivate employees to work in the best interest of the organisation.

A reward is something given, to an individual or group, in recognition of their services, efforts or achievements. The rewards that an organisation offers to its employees can either be intrinsic or extrinsic. Note that extrinsic rewards are closely linked to Herzberg's hygiene factors, while intrinsic factors tie in to Herzberg's motivators.

- **Intrinsic rewards** – these arise from the performance of the job itself. Intrinsic rewards include the feeling of satisfaction that comes from doing a job well, being allowed to make higher level decisions or being interested in your job.
- **Extrinsic rewards** – these are separate from (or external to) the job itself and are dependent on the decisions of others (i.e. the workers have no control over these rewards). Pay, working conditions and benefits are all examples of extrinsic rewards.

The offering of positive rewards to employees is a key motivational issue for most organisations. However, rewards systems should be carefully designed in order to ensure that they:

- are fair and consistent for all employees, even for those workers with different job sizes or required levels of skill
- are sufficient to attract and retain staff
- maintain and improve levels of employee performance
- reward progression and promotion
- comply with legislation and regulation (i.e. minimum wage laws)
- control salary costs.

Employees can be rewarded in a number of ways, including through ongoing development and training (which will boost their future career prospects). This links back to Maslow's hierarchy of needs, as continuous development will help to meet self fulfilment and ego needs. However, most employees will be particularly interested in their remuneration. One way that businesses tie the performance of their employees to their pay is through the use of incentive schemes. There are a number of incentive schemes:

- **Performance related pay (PRP)** – part of the payments received by the individuals relates to the performance of the company.
- **Piecework** – reward related to the pace of work or amount of effort. The faster the employee works, the higher the output and the greater the reward.
- **Points system** – a range of rewards is available based on a point system derived from the scale of improvement made, such as the amount of cost reduction achieved.
- **Commission** – paid on the performance of an individual and typically paid to salaried staff in sales functions, where the commission earned is a proportion of total sales made.

- **Bonus schemes** – usually a one off as opposed to PRP schemes which are usually a continual management policy. Bonuses may also be awarded to teams or groups that have met or beaten certain targets. Group bonuses can help the team to pull together and work as a cohesive unit, but may lead to conflict if some members of the team are seen to be doing less work than others.
- **Profit sharing** – usually available to a wide group of employees (often company wide) where payments are made in the light of the overall profitability of the company. Share issues may be part of the scheme.

4 Performance management and measurement systems

While a staff performance appraisal system can offer many benefits to an organisation, one of its main objectives is to manage and measure performance. Within organisations, performance can be measured at divisional, departmental and individual level, as well as at the overall organisation level.

Target setting

In order to measure performance, a target must be set to measure performance against. To be acceptable a target must be viewed as fair, measurable, achievable and controllable by the person or people being measured.

A well set target can influence behaviour in a positive way and can lead to increased level of commitment and motivation, which in turn can lead to increased productivity. It is therefore important for organisations to carefully consider the targets they set to ensure that they obtain the behaviour they desire.

Setting targets for individuals is made more complex because most jobs have many dimensions, meaning that the targets must look at a number of different criteria in order to accurately reflect the employee's performance. Targets may include the following:

- Volume of work produced
- Knowledge of work
- Quality of work
- Management skills
- Personal skills.

Drucker's Management by objectives

A model which can expand on the setting of targets within the appraisal system is Drucker's Management by objectives. Management by objectives can be defined as a type of control strategy which focuses on controlling outputs. Within this model Drucker emphasised that if corporate objectives are to be effective, they must be stated in behavioural or measurable terms, so that any deviation can be highlighted at an early enough stage to permit corrections to be made.

This is a process whereby individual goals are integrated with the corporate plan, as part of an ongoing programme of goal setting and performance review involving all levels of management.

Many people have responsibility in an organisation, but managers are held accountable for the work of others as well as their own. Managers, when setting objectives, have a responsibility to:

- agree their own departmental targets with their superiors
- discuss and agree targets for their staff that are achievable
- ensure that all targets set are measurable and possible, and that resources are made available together with some setting of priorities
- ensure that there is a balance between the goals and needs of departments and individuals
- apply the control system and discuss progress with staff at regular intervals. Where staff jointly set objectives with their manager they achieve valuable feedback on performance, a motivating factor acknowledged by Herzberg
- ensure continual review and appraisal of results.

Drucker's key objectives

Drucker argues that the nature of the business organisation requires multiple objectives to cover every area where performance and results affect the business.

Drucker suggested the following eight key objectives:

1 **Profitability**. This could be measured by growth in earnings per share. At some stage in the planning procedure, probably at the time of developing the strategic plan, this objective will need to be translated into targets for control linking sales, profit and capital employed.

2 **Innovation**. The board must determine whether it intends to lead in developing technology and products, to follow other companies or to design to meet customer needs.

3 **Market standing**. Overall marketing policies and objectives such as which products to sell and in which markets.

4 **Productivity**. Productivity targets will be set in terms of output in relation to manpower, plant, material yields and costs.

5 **Financial and physical resources**. Financing both working and long-term capital requirements through debt and shares. Physical resource objectives will include the location and acquisition of physical resources over the planning period, whether to lease or buy the assets, etc.

6 **Managerial performance and development**. Policies and objectives will cover matters such as organisation and development; measures of performance; training and development; reward systems and organisational culture.

7 **Worker performance and attitude**. Policies and objectives will cover the development of management and worker relationships.

8 **Public responsibility**. There may well be objectives relating to social responsibility and business ethics.

Not all of these will apply to all organisations, and emphasis could change in response to environmental changes. The need for balancing objectives is obvious. There has to be a balance between profit and the demands of the future (short-, medium-, and long-term).

The Balanced Scorecard

Another commonly used performance management tool is **Kaplan and Norton's** Balanced Scorecard. In developing the balanced scorecard.

The balanced scorecard provides a framework which can be utilised to develop a multidimensional set of performance measures for strategic control of the overall organisation. These measures should be in line with the overall strategic objectives and vision of the organisation.

Kaplan and Norton recognised that when measuring performance, organisations tended to focus almost exclusively on short-term financial measures. They recognised that this did not reflect the complexity and diversity of business circumstances and that organisations should use a variety of measurements, many of them non-financial to give managers a broader perspective of their business performance. Measures used should attempt to address all relevant issues of performance in an objective and unbiased fashion and should cover areas such as profitability, customer satisfaction, internal efficiency and innovation.

Kaplan likened running a business to flying a plane in that airspeed, altitude, heading and fuel level are just a few of the pieces of information needed. Yet, in many businesses, managers have to rely on a narrow set of financial indicators to support their decision making and this in an environment with many more complexities than a plane.

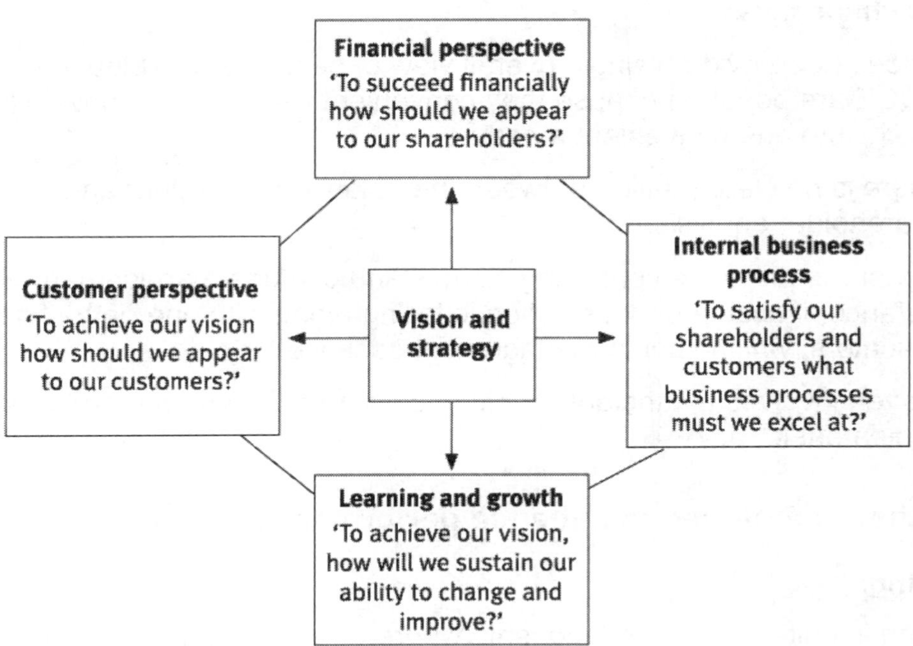

This is a powerful tool that assists in the running of an organisation. Gains in one area need to be considered with the losses that may arise in other areas and vice versa. Thus the manager's view is broadened and the tendency to concentrate on one measure is reduced, hopefully removed.

Once the balanced scorecard has been set at an organisational level, it can be cascaded down to departmental and individual levels setting appropriate targets for each depending on their role. In this way individuals can see that their efforts are contributing to the overall goals of the organisation. The scorecard approach can help management to identify any areas of weakness within the organisation. Any failure in meeting a target at an individual or department level scorecard will be cascaded up to the top level organisational scorecard. In this way, the source of any failure can be quickly identified and action can be taken to remedy it.

The main benefits are:

- It avoids management reliance on short-termist or incomplete financial measures.
- By identifying the non-financial measures, managers may be able to identify problems earlier. For example, managers may be measuring customer satisfaction directly as part of the balanced scorecard. If this changes, steps can be taken to improve it again before customers leave and it starts to impact on the company's finances.
- It can ensure that divisions develop success measures for their division that are related to the overall corporate goals of the organisation.
- It can assist stakeholders in evaluating the firm if measures are communicated externally.

The drawbacks are:

- It does not provide a single overall view of performance. Measures like ROCE are popular because they conveniently summarise 'how things are going' into one convenient measure.
- There is no clear relation between the balanced scorecard and shareholder analysis.
- Measures may give conflicting signals and confuse management. For instance, if customer satisfaction is falling along with one of the financial indicators, which should management sacrifice?
- It often involves a substantial shift in corporate culture in order to implement it.

5 Other techniques to enhance performance

Mentoring

Mentoring is quite simply a relationship where one person helps another to improve their knowledge, work or thinking. It is a very valuable development tool for both the person seeking support (the mentee) and the person giving the support (the mentor).

The benefits of mentoring include:

- Faster career progress.
- Excellent value for money for the organisation as the financial cost is relatively small.
- Enhances company image. The company does not want to be associated with a poor turnover record and encouraging learning helps staff to achieve their full potential and not look for new employment.
- Improved motivation. Employees often feel that real improvements in competences are delivered from the mentoring process. This can preserve the well-being of employees and others, improves employee morale, trust and motivation.

Who is a mentor?

A mentor should be someone who:

- Can give practical support and advice.
- Can give technical, ethical and general business guidance.
- Can help with development of interpersonal and work skills.
- Is an impartial sounding board – a mentor would generally have no direct reporting responsibility.
- Is a good guide, counsellor.
- Is a role model who can help improve career goals.

Quite often a mentor is from the same function (i.e. finance), it is unusual for them to be a direct line manager. The mentor is normally a role model, having already achieved a status (and possibly qualification) to which the subordinate aspires.

For a mentoring system to be successful, relationships should not be based on authority but rather a genuine wish by the mentors to share knowledge, advice and experience and should be one of mutual trust.

Mentoring works alongside more formal control mechanisms, such as appraisal, and is intended to provide the employee with a forum to discuss development issues which is relaxed and supportive. Mentors often discuss such issues as training, the choice of qualification, interpersonal problems and career goals.

The role of a mentor is to encourage and assist junior members of staff to analyse their performance in order to identify their strengths and weaknesses. The mentor should give honest but supportive feedback and guidance on how weaknesses can be eliminated or neutralised. The mentor could also act as a sounding board for ideas. The process should help junior staff to question and reflect on their experiences.

A mentoring system has both career-enhancing and psychological functions. The career function is concerned primarily with enhancing career advancement through exposure, visibility and sponsorship. The psychological function is more concerned with aspects of the relationship that primarily enhance competence and effectiveness in management roles. A mentoring system should help junior staff in expanding their network of contacts and gain greater exposure in the organisation.

Examples of the benefits of mentoring

Mentoring has many benefits for those involved:

Mentees will find a safe environment where they can admit gaps in knowledge and skills, raise queries and consider their strengths. Below you can see how some of our mentees felt they have gained from their mentoring relationships.

'I gained a better vision of what I want to do in the future, and what steps I must take in order to achieve my goals.'

'I gained a great deal. It was good to talk with someone who was independent of my work, college and home circumstances. I gained an alternative and dispassionate view and I have been able to make a more rational assessment of my priorities.'

'I learned about self belief, having respect for others, becoming more assertive, when to listen and when to ask questions, planning and decision making.'

'I gained a great insight into the practice of running your own business, which is what I would like to achieve myself.'

'My mentor gave a good sounding board and plenty of encouragement towards my impending exams.'

Mentors get a unique opportunity to put something back into their profession while enjoying a fresh challenge and personal and professional development of their own. Richard Garnett MAAT explains why he volunteered as a mentor:

'I felt it was time to give something back to the AAT. I think I have experience I can usefully share with those newer to the AAT. I really hope I helped my mentee to develop. I also think the scheme had some great learning for me too.'

Article by the AAT (Association of Accounting Technicians)

Case study style question 4

P is a senior manager in the finance department of PQR. He has worked for PQR for 25 years and is well respected throughout the company. PQR have decided to implement a mentoring scheme to help new recruits to the company fit in more quickly and P has been asked to be a mentor to K, who is a new management accounting trainee. K has just left university and his first placement is in the production department, but he will be moved to different areas of the company on a six monthly basis.

P has never mentored anyone before and is unsure about what would be expected of him, he is also concerned about spending time on this task as he is unsure of the benefits of mentoring.

Required:

Write an email to P, explaining what would be expected of P as a mentor and how a mentoring scheme would benefit K in his new role.

(20 minutes)

Coaching

Coaching is another method which can be used to enhance performance. Unlike mentoring, coaching focuses on achieving specific objectives, usually within a defined time period. It is more about improving the performance of someone that is already competent, rather than establishing competency in the first place.

- It is usually on a one to one basis and is set in the everyday working situation.
- It involves gently encouraging people to improve their performance, to develop their skills and increase their self confidence in order to develop their career prospects.
- Most coaching is carried out by a more senior person or manager, however the key issue is that whoever carries out the coaching must have sufficient expertise, experience and judgement to help the person being coached.

6 Summary diagram

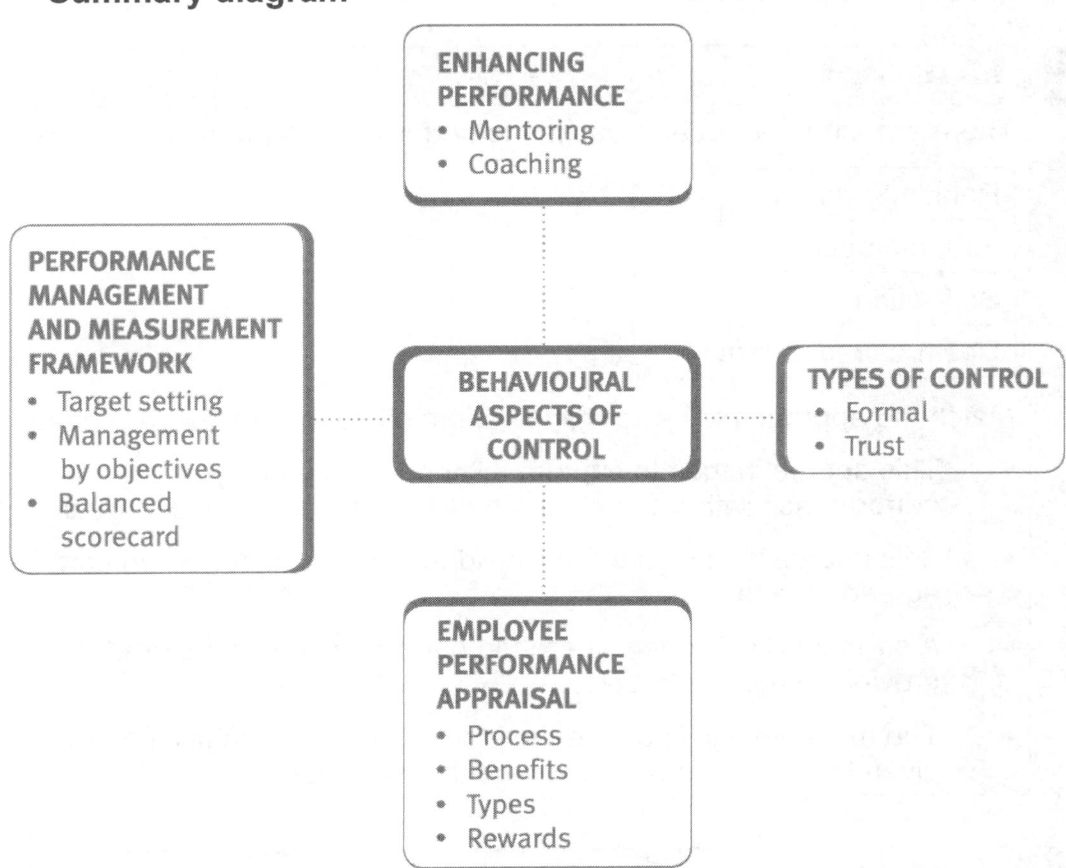
ENHANCING PERFORMANCE
• Mentoring
• Coaching
PERFORMANCE MANAGEMENT AND MEASUREMENT FRAMEWORK
• Target setting
• Management by objectives
• Balanced scorecard
BEHAVIOURAL ASPECTS OF CONTROL
TYPES OF CONTROL
• Formal
• Trust
EMPLOYEE PERFORMANCE APPRAISAL
• Process
• Benefits
• Types
• Rewards

End of chapter questions

Question 1

There are a number of approaches to performance appraisal, such as:

Ranking system
360 approach
Self-rating
Unstructured format

Match the approach to performance appraisal to the correct description.

- This approach tries to capture all aspects of employee performance rather than being restricted to pre-agreed targets.
- This approach is where the individual rates themselves on certain agreed criteria.
- A structured approach where the performance is compared to previously agreed targets.
- The manager will appraise the individual and the individual is also given the opportunity to appraise the manager.

Question 2

Complete the following sentences regarding rewards:

Intrinsic	Extrinsic

- Rewards which arise from the performance of the job itself are known as ________________ rewards.
- Herzberg's hygiene factors are closely linked to ________ rewards.
- Recognition or higher levels of responsibility would be classed as ____________ rewards.
- ____________ rewards would include pay and working conditions.

Question 3

There are a number of financial incentive schemes available for employers to motivate their staff, such as:

Piecework
Commission
Profit sharing
Bonus schemes
Performance related pay

Match the incentive scheme to the correct description.

- Reward related to the pace of work or amount of effort. The faster the employee works, the higher the output and the greater the reward.
- Payments are made in the light of the overall profitability of the company.
- Paid on the performance of an individual and typically paid to salaried staff in sales functions.
- Key results are identified for which rewards will be paid on top of salary.
- One off rewards which can be paid to individuals or groups if they meet certain targets.
- Part of the payment received by individuals relates to the overall performance of the company.

Question 4

Which THREE of the following are key objectives as suggested by Drucker?

A Customer satisfaction

B Innovation

C Productivity

D Public responsibility

E Employee satisfaction

F Ethical behaviour

Question 5

In the balanced scorecard, one of the perspectives is the financial perspective. What are the other three perspectives?

A Customer

B Training and development

C Product

D Internal Business Process

E Employee

F Learning and growth

Question 6

Which of the following statements relating to mentoring are true? Select all that apply.

A Mentoring can lead to faster career progress.

B A mentor will generally be the mentee's line manager.

C A mentor can give technical, ethical and general business guidance.

D A mentor is a role model who can help improve career goals.

E Mentoring is used as a means of measuring performance.

F Mentoring focuses on achieving specific objectives, usually within a defined time period.

Question 7

Complete the sentences to suggest the most appropriate type of control for each organisation.

- Personal centralised
- Bureaucratic
- Clan or Cultural
- Output

Small, owner managed organisations which rely on key individuals are likely to use ______________ control.

Large manufacturing companies would be most likely to use ___________________ control.

A professional firm of lawyers would most likely use ________________ control.

A large hierarchical organisation would be likely to use ______________ control.

Question 8

To achieve our vision, how will we sustain our ability to change and improve?

The above statement relates to which of the perspectives of Kaplan and Norton's balanced scorecard?

A Financial perspective

B Customer perspective

C Internal business process

D Learning and growth

Question 9

Which of the following statements regarding target setting are correct? Select all that apply.

A A well set target can improve motivation.

B Targets can only be set using financial measure.

C Volume of work would be a suitable target.

D To be accepted, target should be viewed as controllable and achievable.

E Ideally, each individual will be set just one main target.

Question 10

The balanced scorecard model provides a framework which can be utilised to develop a multidimensional set of performance measures for strategic control of the overall organisation. The model is shown below:

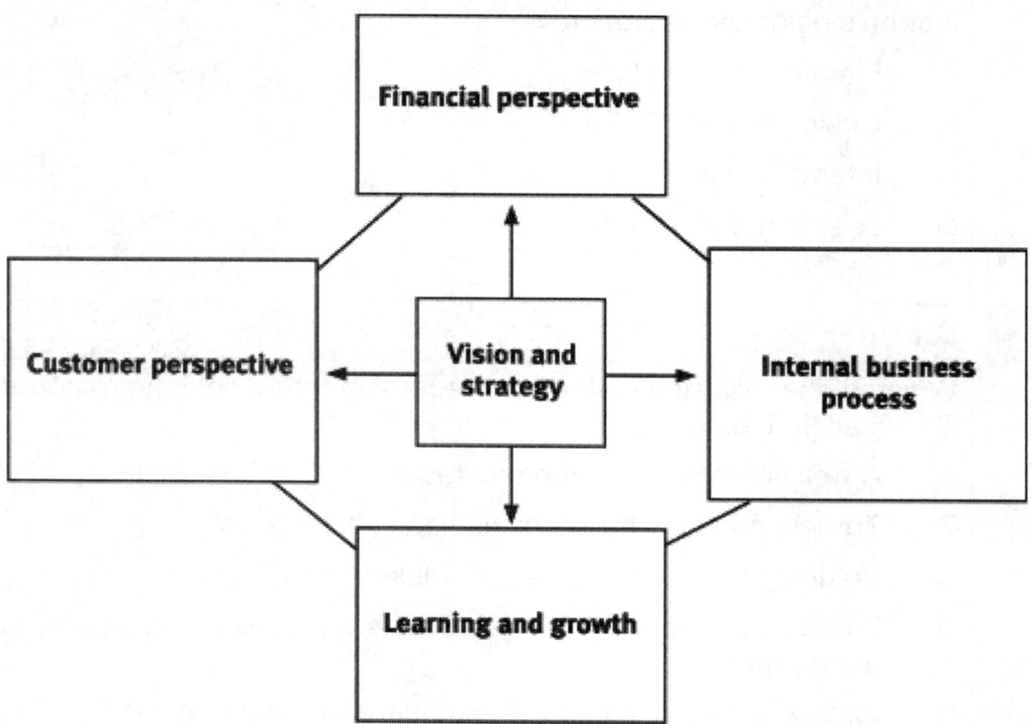

Within each perspective of the model, key metrics are used to measure the performance of the organisation.

Drag the following metrics to the most appropriate perspective on the balanced scorecard model.

- Number of complaints
- ROCE
- New products launched
- Operational efficiency
- Repeat purchases

Test your understanding answers

Case study style question 1

(a) **Direct supervision of staff**

Jersey could opt to directly monitor the activities of its staff in order to ensure their work is of appropriate quality. This could be effective at stopping the production of poor quality speakers and the associated waste that would be involved in this. The fact that Jersey only has a small number of staff would also tend to make this approach work well.

However, there would be several problems associated with this control. Firstly, each group of workers has highly specialised skills. This may make it difficult for Jersey's supervisor to understand what each group does and monitor their activities effectively. In addition, the fact that each worker may undertake the same job as their colleagues but using a different technique, will increase the complexity of the monitoring role.

While the workforce is small, there is only one supervisor. They may have insufficient time available to supervise all staff. Hiring of additional supervisors would have cost implications for Jersey.

Finally, additional supervision may have a negative impact on the motivation of employees, who are used to having autonomy over the way they perform their jobs. A sudden change to being closely monitored could cause further job dissatisfaction.

(b) **Performance targets**

Setting performance targets could be of great use to Jersey. This would likely involve offering incentives for staff (such as pay rises and bonuses) depending on how well they perform their jobs. For Jersey, the number of defective units produced by each employee could be measured and a bonus could be offered if this was below a pre-agreed level.

This could be a very practical approach for Jersey, as it links employee rewards with the objectives of the company itself. It should be easy to implement and would prevent the production of units that were defective, reducing waste. The offer of an additional bonus or extra pay may also help to improve general motivation as workers are currently only adequately paid and have few other benefits or prospects.

Note that this may not improve the output of each worker, which is another issue for Jersey. Workers may spend longer on each unit in order to ensure the quality and thus receive their bonus, leading to a further fall in productivity.

(c) **Reliance on self-control of workers**

Relying on individual staff to monitor their own activities may be problematic. It has the advantage of being cheap for Jersey, as it does not require any further staff to be hired. In addition, the staff are clearly skilled at their jobs, making it easier for them to understand the best way to approach individual tasks.

However, staff seem to be relatively de-motivated. This means that they are less likely to be concerned about the quality of their output. Unless they are offered an incentive by Jersey, there is no reason why they would focus on higher quality production.

In addition, there is no agreed 'best practice' for each of the four teams. Each worker is likely to see their method as superior to those of their colleagues, whether this is in fact correct or not. This means that they are unlikely to change their working practices to ones that would improve output and quality.

Case study style question 2

EMAIL

To: CEO of STU

From: Management accountant

Date: today

Subject: The necessity of formal control systems

For any organisation like STU, the growth and diversification of the business poses an increasing problem of control. As the number of levels in the organisation is increased and the number of different kinds of tasks to be carried out multiplies, the division of labour becomes more complex. In this changing situation, it becomes increasingly difficult to ensure that members of an organisation are doing what they are supposed to be doing.

Without some attempt to control what people do in organisations, there is a danger of staff beginning, intentionally or unintentionally, to do 'their own thing' by working towards their own personal goals and perceived self-interests.

To counteract the tendencies created by the processes of differentiation, and to ensure goal congruence, there is a need to create a 'common focus' in an organisation, which will control and integrate members' diverse activities. This is why organisations introduce a variety of formal controls.

In small, simple organisations it is possible for the owner manager or senior management to supervise subordinates' activities personally and systematically. Often, in such organisations, it is possible to achieve control in an informal way by setting employees tasks and then checking that they have been carried out. Any deviations from the accepted standard of performance can be communicated directly by the owner manager to particular employees and the necessary corrective action taken. In larger organisations, however, with a complex division of labour, and a taller hierarchy of responsibility, it is not physically possible to control people in such a simple manner. In such situations, formal policies, rules and procedures have to be put into place together with a system of rewards and punishments to ensure that the policies, rules and procedures are observed.

In such hierarchical organisations, policies and objectives are typically set, or at least confirmed, by occupants of higher-level positions and are then communicated to lower-level staff, who are then charged with the responsibility to carry out the necessary actions. It is up to the higher-level managers to determine whether or not the objectives have been met and, if not, to take the appropriate steps. This is the process of control.

It is important to note, however, that there are a number of different ways of exercising control in organisations and that the effectiveness of a particular type of control system depends on a number of factors including the organisation's strategy, culture, structure, environment and the type of goods or services produced.

In the case of STU, it chose to use bureaucratic (administrative) forms of control, but as the CEO realised, such a form of control is not conducive to creativity and innovation.

Creativity, which can be defined as 'the generation of new ideas, and innovation, which is the transformation of creative ideas into tangible products or processes' varies considerably between one organisation and another. Some organisations have a reputation for creativity and innovation while other organisations hardly ever seem to generate new products or new ways of doing things.

The generation of new ideas and their translation into commercial use is a particularly important issue for an organisation like S because its future depends on a continuous supply of innovative software products. There are many factors influencing the rate of innovation in organisations, but research suggests that one reason has to do with how an organisation is structured and controlled.

Studies have found that excessive bureaucracy with its allegiance to central control and to rules and procedures discourages creativity and innovation. The focus on rules and procedures and the accompanying sanctions designed to ensure compliance means that employees 'play safe' by sticking to the rules rather than risk trying out new ideas. Rules can become 'ends in themselves'.

The division of labour that often accompanies the growth of an organisation also affects creativity and innovation because it restricts the sharing of ideas between individuals and between different units, departments or divisions. The case of STU illustrates well the problems facing all large organisations at some time in their development – that of balancing the need to ensure adequate direction and control of staff and yet allowing sufficient freedom and discretion of middle managers and other employees to contribute their particular knowledge and expertise to the organisation. Too little direction and control can result in wasted effort and inefficiencies as the departments and divisions into which an organisation is subdivided pursue their own particular goals. Too much central control and lower level staff become frustrated by rules and procedures forced upon them from on high by those who are too far from the action to make informed decisions.

I hope you have found the above useful. Please do not hesitate to get in touch if you would like any more information or would like to discuss any of these issues further.

Case study style question 3

EMAIL

To: G

From: Management Accountant

Date: today

Subject: Performance appraisal system

You are right in saying that a performance appraisal system can be time consuming, but the time spent on this can bring many benefits to both the company and to the individuals within your department. Performance appraisal can help to improve efficiency and effectiveness of a company. It should be used to review, change, inform, examine and evaluate employees.

From the company point of view, a formal appraisal system can:

- Provide a means for assessing employees and identifying areas for improvement. The system would encourage you to review the work of the individuals within your department, which would benefit you in allowing you to get to know their capabilities.
- Provide a fair basis for reward decisions.
- Aid in succession planning by identifying candidates for promotion.
- Help to plan for training needs.
- Link targets to company's strategic plans.
- Aid in human resource planning.

From the employee's point of view it can:

- Provide a fair and understandable basis for remuneration.
- Provide feedback about performance and allow an opportunity to discuss future prospects. H, and others within the department are unhappy with the lack of feedback from you. A formal appraisal system would give both you and H the opportunity to discuss his work.
- Identify training and development needs.
- Help to highlight work of high quality carried out in the period.

I hope you have found the above useful. A performance appraisal system can be very beneficial to both you as a manager, the individual members of your team and the company as a whole. Please do not hesitate to get in touch if you want to discuss any of these aspects more fully.

Case study style question 4

EMAIL

To: P

From: Management Accountant

Date: today

Subject: Mentoring

A mentor is a person who helps another person to develop. A mentor is usually a more experienced person within the organisation and they are appointed to mentor a more junior member of staff who will usually come from another part of the organisation. If the mentor is from the same department, they would not usually be a direct line manager. In this case, you are an experienced, well respected manager in the finance department, and have been asked to mentor K who is a management accounting trainee in the production department. This is a fairly typical mentoring arrangement whereby the mentor is from the same function, but not the same department.

As a mentor, you would be expected to arrange regular meetings with K, or allow K to contact you as required. When you meet, you should make it clear to K that he can discuss any issues of concern he has. Topics discussed could include study support and advice, technical or business guidance, training advice, interpersonal problems or career advice. K may also wish to use you as a sounding board for decisions he has to make. You should be able to give K impartial and independent advice.

Discussions between you and K should be confidential so that K feels that he can discuss any areas of concern he has in a safe environment.

There are many benefits from mentoring. There are career-enhancing benefits and personal developmental benefits. From a career-enhancing perspective, you can provide technical help and study support. K would be able to discuss openly areas of weakness within their role and you may be able to provide practical advice as to how to overcome these weaknesses. Going forward you could also advise K on routes for career development.

You may also be able to help K get to know other members of staff within the organisation. You have been with PQR for 25 years, so you are very likely to know many of the other managers that K will be dealing with. This is especially helpful to K as he will be moving round the organisation every six months. You may be able to give K information about the managers and staff he will be dealing with in each of the departments. As he moves around the organisation, K may come across new situations which he finds difficult to deal with. You may be able to give him general advice to help build his confidence in dealing with new situations, or may be able to help identify suitable training courses which would help him.

In addition, K would also gain from a personal point of view. He is just out of university and is not used to this working environment. You will be able to help K understand the culture of LPM which would help him to settle in more quickly. A better understanding of PQR will improve K's confidence which would help him to perform better in his role.

Over time, as he develops in his role, K may contact you less about how to handle situations and more for advice on career development.

I hope you have found the above helpful. Please do not hesitate to get in touch if you want to discuss any of these aspects more fully.

Question 1

The correct matching is:

Ranking system	**A structured approach where the performance is compared to previously agreed targets**
360 approach	**The manager will appraise the individual and the individual is also given the opportunity to appraise the manager**
Self rating	**This approach is where the individual rates themselves on certain agreed criteria**
Unstructured format	**This approach tries to capture all aspects of employee performance rather than being restricted to pre-agreed targets**

Question 2

- Rewards which arise from the performance of the job itself are known as **intrinsic** rewards.
- Herzberg's hygiene factors are closely linked to **extrinsic** rewards.
- Recognition or higher levels of responsibility would be classed as **intrinsic** rewards.
- **Extrinsic** rewards would include pay and working conditions.

Intrinsic rewards arise from the performance of the job itself while extrinsic rewards are external to the job and rely on the decisions of others.

Question 3

The correct matching is:

Piecework	**reward related to the pace of work or amount of effort. The faster the employee works, the higher the output and the greater the reward**
Commission	**paid on the performance of an individual and typically paid to salaried staff in sales functions**
Profit sharing	**payments are made in the light of the overall profitability of the company**
Bonus schemes	**one off rewards which can be paid to individuals or groups if they meet certain targets**
Performance related pay	**part of the payment received by individuals relates to the overall performance of the company**

Question 4

B, C and D

The others are:

- Profitability
- Market standing
- Financial and physical resources
- Management performance and development
- Worker performance and attitude

Question 5

A, D and F

The complete diagram is shown below:

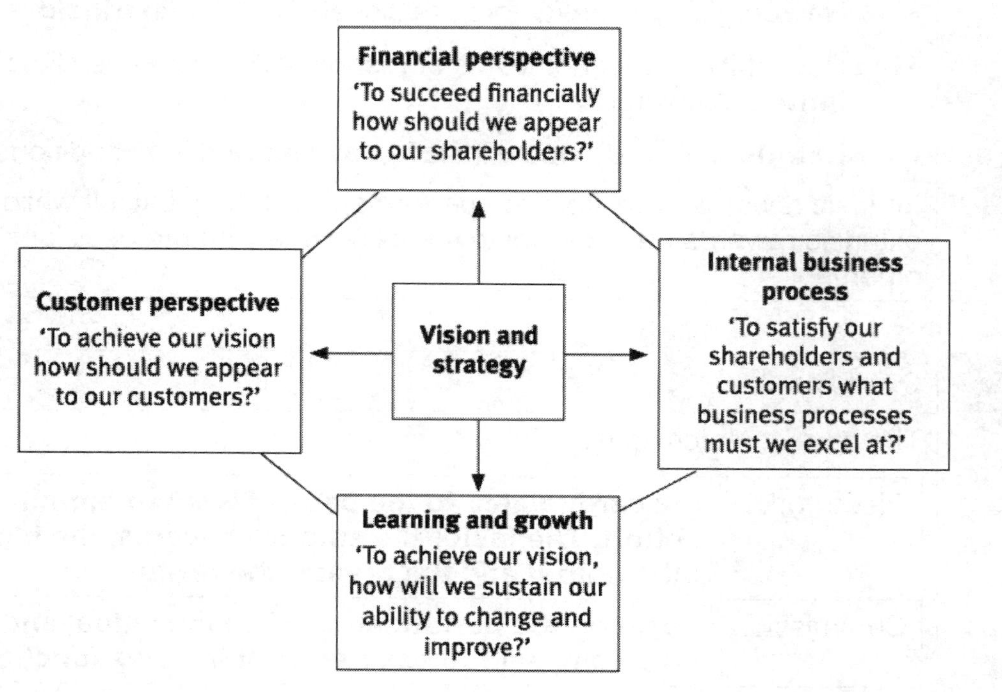

Question 6

A, C and D

A mentor will generally be the mentee's line manager is incorrect. It is generally accepted that it is better for the mentor to come from a different department.

Mentoring is used as a means of measuring performance is incorrect. Mentoring is used to enhance performance.

Mentoring focuses on achieving specific objectives, usually within a defined time period is incorrect. Mentoring an ongoing activity.

Question 7

Small, owner managed organisations which rely on key individuals are likely to use **personal centralised** control.

Large manufacturing companies would be most likely to use **output** control.

A professional firm of lawyers would most likely use **clan or cultural** control.

A large hierarchical organisation would be likely to use **bureaucratic** control.

Personal centralised control is used where there is centralised decision making by a key individual. This is usually found in small, owner run companies.

Bureaucratic control is usually found in large hierarchical organisations with formalised rules and procedures and detailed job descriptions.

Clan or Cultural control is found where employees have a strong identification with management goals.

Output control is based on the measurement of outputs and results achieved and is often used in manufacturing organisations.

Question 8

D

The learning and growth perspective looks at how an organisation manages change through development and innovation.

Question 9

A, C and D

Targets can only be set using financial measure is incorrect. Targets can also use non-financial measures. In fact, in many cases, these are better measures than financial measures.

Ideally, each individual will be set just one main target is incorrect. Most jobs have a number of dimensions meaning that multiple targets are normally required to actually assess an employee's performance.

Question 10

The completed model is shown below:

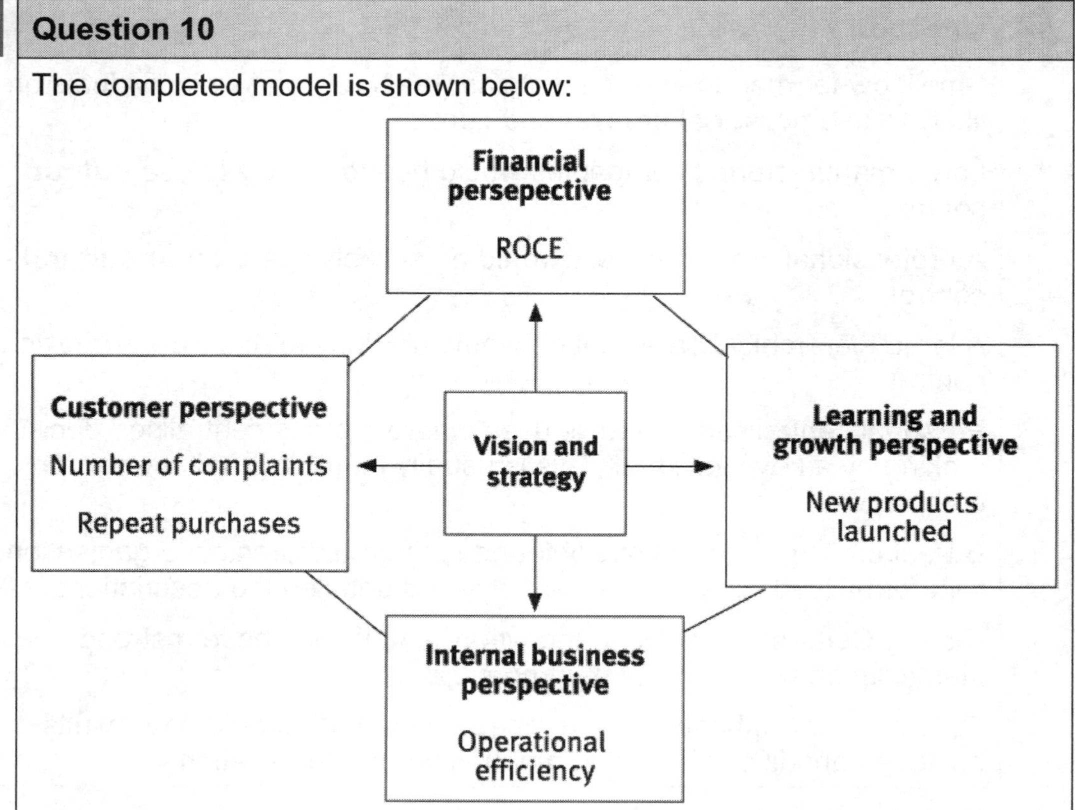

Chapter

7

Building, leading and managing teams

Chapter learning objectives

Lead	Component
B3: Explain how to manage relationships	(a) Building and leading teams

Topic to be covered

- Characteristics of high-performing teams
- Motivating team members
- Communication process
- Strategies for managing conflict.

1 Session content diagram

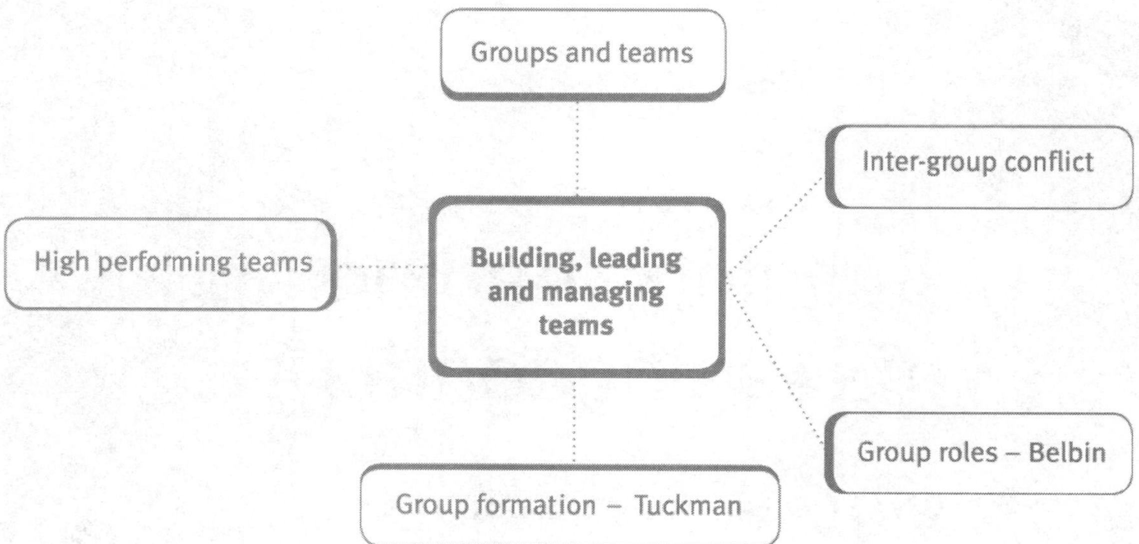

2 Group and teams

Note that throughout this chapter, the terms groups and teams are used interchangeably.

People rarely work in isolation at work, since most activities need some coordination through groups of people. Groups provide security and social satisfaction for their members. They support individual needs and promote communication, formally or informally.

There are many different definitions available to explain what constitutes a group. **Schein** suggests that a group is any number of people who:

- interact with one another
- are psychologically aware of one another; and
- perceive themselves to be a group.

Groups have power structures, leadership structures, role structures, communication structures and sociometric structures. They develop norms, ideologies, characteristic atmospheres, degrees of cohesiveness and morale.

Types of groups

- **Formal groups**. Used by organisations to carry out tasks, communicate and solve problems. Membership is normally formal, often determined or constrained by the organisation into departments or divisions.
- **Informal groups**. Individuals join groups to meet their social and security or safety needs. Membership is normally voluntary and informal. Individual members are dependent on each other, influence each other's behaviour and contribute to each other's needs.

- **Reference groups**. These are groups the individual does not currently belong to but wants to join, for example a particular work group or committee.
- **Self-directed and autonomous groups**. The ideas of these evolved from the work of Trist and Bamforth and through experiments carried out in the 70s by Swedish car manufacturers Volvo and Saab. A self-directed or autonomous group is one which is encouraged to manage its own work and working practices.

Informal groups

Managers need to pay attention to the formation of, and support for, formal groups and also realise that they cannot ignore or suppress informal groups. In relation to informal groups, it is important:

- to let employees know that managers understand and accept them while discouraging dysfunctional behaviour in such groups
- to try to anticipate how decisions will influence informal groups; and
- to keep formal decisions from unnecessarily threatening informal groups.

Work teams

A work team is a **formal group**. It has a leader and a distinctive culture and is geared towards a final result.

An effective team can be described as 'any group of people who must significantly relate with each other in order to accomplish shared objectives'.

In order to ensure that the team is truly effective, team members must have a reason for working together. They must need each other's skills, talent and experience in order to achieve their mutual goals.

Multi-skilled teams bring together individuals who can perform any of the group's tasks. These can be shared out in a flexible way according to availability and inclination.

Multidisciplinary teams bring together individuals with different specialisms so that their skills, knowledge and experience can be pooled or exchanged.

Benefits and problems with groups

Benefits of groups

Within organisations there has been an implicit belief that people working as members of a group or team perform more effectively than if they are organised as individuals. There are a number of benefits from team working:

- **Increased productivity** – working as part of a group can result in a better overall result than could be achieved if each person worked independently. By breaking a task up into its component parts, different members of the group, with different skills, can be working on different aspects of the task at the same time.
- **Synergy** – One person cannot do everything, but a team can combine all the main areas of skill and knowledge that are needed for a particular job. Synergy describes the phenomenon in which the combined activity of separate entities has a greater effect than the sum of the activities of each entity working alone – often described as a way of making **2 + 2 = 5**.
- **Improved focus and responsibility** – each member can be given the responsibility for specific tasks, avoiding overloading one person with too much responsibility which may result in a loss of focus.
- **Improved problem solving** – having a group made up of members with different abilities will mean a higher likelihood of having the appropriate knowledge and skills to solve problems.
- **Greater creativity** – the idea that two (or more) heads are better than one. Group discussions can generate and evaluate ideas better that individuals working alone.
- **Increased satisfaction** – working as part of a group can bring social benefits and a sense of belonging to its members. In addition, the group will offer support to its members and provide a facility for individual training and development needs.
- **Increased motivation** – members will work hard for the other members of the group. They will feel a collective responsibility and will not want to let the other members down.
- **Improved information flows** – there will be more effective communication through participation in group discussions.

Problems with groups

Unfortunately, groups can also have negative as well as positive effects. Subsequent research has identified a number of these negative effects, some of which are discussed below:

- **Conformity** – individuals can be persuaded by group pressures to agree with decisions which are obviously wrong, and which the person must know to be wrong.

- **The Abilene paradox** – this is a famous case, which demonstrates that the group can end up with an outcome that none of the members wanted. The story was written up as a case by a sociologist whose family all ended up in Abilene, Texas, driving 100 miles through desert heat, though none of them actually wanted to go. They all thought each other wanted to go, and no one wanted to disturb the 'consensus'.
- '**Risky shift' or group polarisation** – this is the tendency for groups to take decisions which are riskier than any that the individual members would take on their own. It now appears that there is also a tendency, under certain circumstances, for groups to take excessively cautious decisions.
- **Groupthink** – this occurs within deeply cohesive groups where the members try to minimise conflict and reach consensus without critically testing, analysing, and evaluating ideas.

In a group, there is a high level of mutual interaction and awareness which are responsible for powerful forces, which cause the individual to behave, sometimes, rather differently from the way they would behave on their own. It is important to the organisation that these forces work for the organisation and not against it.

Clearly, managers must attempt to minimise these potential problems while harnessing the many benefits of groups and teams.

Groupthink

Some symptoms of groupthink are:

- the raising of protective barriers and the illusion of impregnability.
- a negative attitude towards competing projects.
- an unwavering belief in the group and its decisions.
- a sectarian emphasis on agreement.

Groupthink can lead to disastrous results. After the initial 'Bay of Pigs' disaster, when the United States encouraged an abortive 'invasion' of Cuba via the Bay of Pigs, John F Kennedy saw clearly how to try to avoid 'groupthink' and planned his leadership accordingly by insisting on:

- critical evaluation of alternatives
- independent sub-groups to work on solutions
- external testing of proposed solutions
- the leader avoiding domination of the group (which can be unconscious)
- the avoidance of stereotypes of the opposition.

Group cohesiveness

There are a number of factors which affect the integration of organisational and individual objectives in groups, and hence the cohesiveness of the group. They include:

Membership factors

- **Homogeneity**. Similarity of members is preferred for simple tasks; it leads to easier working but less creative problem-solving. A variety of skills and knowledge is more effective for complex tasks. Homogeneity of status, both internally and externally, leads to a more cohesive group.
- **Alternatives**. If the individual has alternatives, that is he or she can leave the group easily, his or her dependence on the group is reduced. Similarly, if turnover of membership is high, the group will tend to lack cohesion. Management may, of course, deliberately keep changing the membership of awkward groups.
- **Size of group.** The importance of this factor depends on the nature of the particular task. Groups solve problems more quickly and effectively than individuals, but one should also consider cost-effectiveness. As the size of the group goes up, the average productivity of the members goes down; there is less opportunity to participate; individuals' contributions are less obvious; cliques or factions may form; less work is done; and 'social loafing' or 'social noise' may increase.
- **Membership in other groups**. This may detract from the cohesion and effectiveness of the original group.

Environmental factors

- **Task:** the nature of the task and its organisation must be compatible.
- **Isolation of the group:** external threats and incentives are lower the more isolated the group is.
- **The climate of management and leadership:** the leadership style adopted should be appropriate to the task. For example in organisations where management adopt McGregor's Theory X approach, this can lead to anti-management groups forming, even if only informally.

Dynamic factors

- **Groups are continually changing.** It should be recognised that groups are changing all the time, not just in membership but also in understanding each other and of the task.
- **Success and failure.** There can be a tendency for groups to persist in failure.

3 Team development

The level of group performance is affected by the manner in which teams come together. According to **Tuckman**, teams typically pass through four stages of development: The stages are:

- **Forming**
- **Storming**
- **Norming**
- **Performing**.

This is shown in the following diagram:

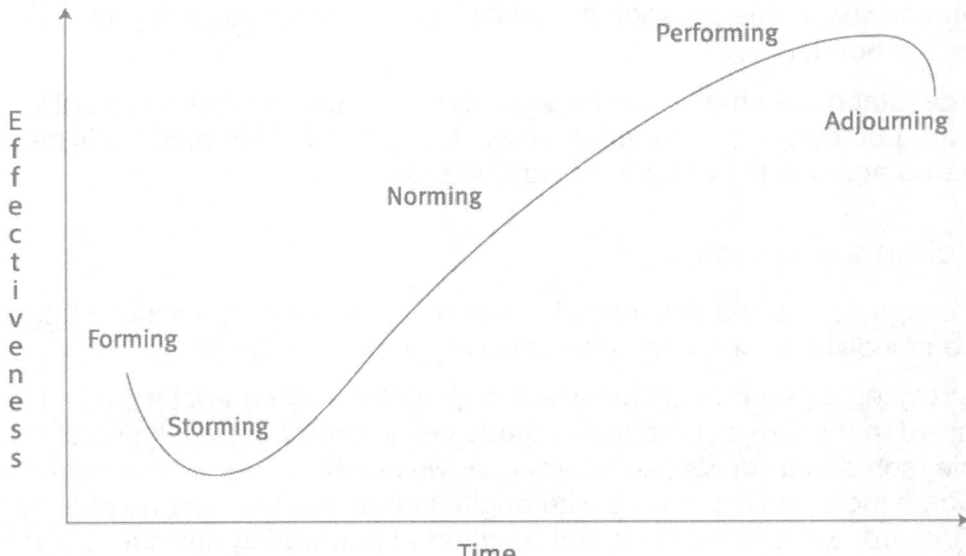

- **Forming**. At this initial stage, the team members are no more than a collection of individuals who are unsure of their roles and responsibilities until the manager clearly defines the initial processes and procedures for team activities.
- **Storming**. Most teams go through this conflict stage. As tasks get underway, team members may try to test the manager's authority and team preconceptions are challenged. Conflict and tension may become evident. The conflict resolution skills and the leadership skills of the manager are vital at this stage and he or she needs to be more flexible to allow team members to question and test their roles and responsibilities and to get involved in decision-making.
- **Norming**. This stage establishes the norms under which the team will operate and team relationships become settled. Team procedures are refined and the manager will begin to pass control and decision-making authority to the team members. They will be operating as a cohesive team, with each person recognising and appreciating the roles of the other team members.

- **Performing**. Once this final stage has been reached the team is capable of operating to full potential. Progress is made towards the set objectives and the team feels confident and empowered.

Not all teams automatically follow these four stages in this sequence and not all teams pass through all the stages. Some get stuck in the middle and remain inefficient and ineffective.

Tuckman added a fifth stage:

- **Adjourning**. If a team remains for a long time in the performing phase, there is a danger that it will be operating on automatic pilot. 'Groupthink' occurs to the extent that the group may be unaware of changing circumstances. Instead, maintaining the team becomes one of its prime objectives. In this situation it may be necessary for the group to 'adjourn' or be suspended.

These development stages can be seen clearly in project management where teams are put together to undertake a specific project. This model will be considered again in the people and projects chapter.

4 Belbin's team roles

Belbin suggests that the success of a group can depend significantly upon the balance of individual skills and personality types within the group.

Belbin devised a personality test which highlighted key character traits. He recognised that different personality types would prefer certain types of role. For example, some individuals like interaction, while others prefer to work on their own. Some individuals come up with original ideas but may not be able to take these forward, while others may not be good at generating new ideas but may be very good at progressing existing ideas. The theory suggests that if individual's characteristics are known then each individual can adopt an appropriate role for their personality type. Where individuals are working in roles which suit them, they are more likely to engage fully with the role, be more motivated and perform better.

From a group point of view, a balance of personality types is needed. A team full of shy, ideas people may be able to generate great ideas but is unlikely to be successful as it would lack the ability to take the ideas forward and communicate these ideas outside the team.

According to Belbin, a well-balanced group should contain the following nine main character types:

Character types	Role
Co-ordinator	Mature and confident. Ensures team focuses on objectives. Delegates well.
Shaper	Challenging and dynamic. Provides the drive to keep the team moving. Promotes activity.
Plant	Thoughtful and creative. Generates original ideas.
Monitor Evaluator	Logical and analytical. Evaluates options in an impartial manner.
Resource Investigator	Enthusiastic and inquisitive. Find ideas from outside to bring to the team.
Implementer/ Company worker	Practical and reliable. Deals with planning and scheduling. Drives efficiency.
Teamworker	Co-operative and diplomatic. Concerned with relationships within the team . Diffuses conflict.
Completer Finisher	Anxious and conscientious. Scrutinises the work of the team for errors. Quality control.
Specialist	Single-minded and dedicated. Brings in-depth specialist knowledge to solve technical problems.

The description of Belbin's basic nine roles does not mean that a team cannot be effective with fewer than nine members. Members can adopt two or more roles if necessary. However, the absence of one of these functions can mean a reduction in the effectiveness of the team.

Case study style question 1

N is in charge of a group of twelve people involved in complex work. The group has been working together amicably and successfully for a considerable time. Its members value N's leadership and the back-up given him by O. She often elaborates on N's instructions and deals on his behalf with group members' queries, especially when he is absent on the group's business.

Much of the success of the group has been due to P, who is very creative at problem solving, and R who has an encyclopaedic knowledge of sources of supply and information. Q is an expert on all aspects of product development, and S is invaluable at sorting out disagreements and keeping everyone cheerful. The remaining members of the group also have roles which are acceptable to themselves and to the others.

Recently O resigned for family reasons. Because the workload has been increasing, N recruited four new people to the group. N now finds that various members of the group complain to him about what they are expected to do, and about other people's failings. P and R have been unusually helpful to N but have had several serious arguments between themselves and with others.

N recently attended a presentation about effective work groups and would like to understand the issues his group is experiencing better. The presentation covered models by Tuckman and Belbin and N thinks that if he understood these models better, he could improve the performance of his team.

Required:

Write an email to N explaining the causes of these changes in the group and recommending how he can ensure that the group reverts to its former cohesiveness. The email should refer to the theories of Belbin and Tuckman.

(20 minutes)

Role theory

Role theory is concerned with the roles that individuals adopt. Developing a group means identifying distinct roles for each of its members. Any individual can have several roles, varying between different groups and activities. The role adopted will affect the individual's attitude towards other people.

Role theory assists in the understanding of how productive teams are formed and operated.

There are several terms associated with role theory.

- **Role ambiguity** arises when individuals are unsure what role they are to play, or others are unclear of that person's role and so hold back co-operation. For example this can arise when a new member joins an established group.
- **Role conflict** arises when individuals find a clash between differing roles that they have adopted. A company finance officer who uncovers fraud by senior management may feel a conflict between the roles of professional confidentiality and honest citizenship.
- **Role incompatibility** occurs when individuals experience expectations from outside groups about their role that are different from their own role expectations.

- **Role signs** are visible indications of the role. Style of dress and uniform are clear examples of role signs. These may be voluntary (a male accountant wearing a grey or blue suit and a tie) or mandatory (in military, police and hospital occupations).
- **Role set** describes the people who support a lead person in a major role, e.g. the clerk and junior barristers would form part of a senior barrister's role set.
- **Role behaviour** where certain types of behaviour can be associated with a role in an office or works. For instance, the 'crown prince' behaving as if they are heir apparent to a senior position.

5 High performing teams

A high-performing team is a group of skilled individuals who are selected to work together to meet a common objective and share responsibility for outcomes, achieving outstanding performance by making optimal use of the capabilities of each team member. The members are committed, close-knit and share a common objective.

High-performing teams are not only important at the top of the organisation and are widely used in the form of project teams and cross-functional teams. Highly effective teams can also make higher-quality decisions and accomplish more in less time and with less distraction and frustration.

Vaill – high-performance teams

Vaill said that high-performing teams may be defined as human systems that are doing dramatically better than other systems. He claimed that they have a number of common characteristics:

- Clarification of broad purposes and near-term objectives.
- Commitment to purposes.
- Teamwork focused on the task at hand.
- Strong and clear leadership.
- Generation of inventions and new methods.

Peters and Waterman – successful teams

Peters and Waterman identified five key aspects of successful teams as:

- The numbers should be **small**; inevitably each member will then represent the interest of their section/department. Larger teams would be slower and harder to manage.
- The team should be of **limited duration**, and exist only to achieve a particular task.

- Membership should be **voluntary**. Where members do not want to be part of the group, they are unlikely to participate fully.
- **Communication should be informal and unstructured**, with little documentation and no status barriers.
- It should be **action-oriented**. The team should create a plan for action not 'just a form of words'.

Building the team and improving effectiveness

Teams are not always able to achieve their goals without some outside intervention or support from management. As such, managers may attempt to create 'teambuilding' exercises for workers. Team building exercises are tasks designed to develop group members and their ability to work together. Team building exercises tend to be based around developing the team in several areas, including:

- **improved communication**, such as through the use of problem solving exercises which force all team members to discuss a problem the group is facing.
- **building trust** between team members, which will help the individual members work as a group.
- **social interaction** between the individuals in the team can help to reduce conflict and increase the cohesion of the group.

In addition to formal teambuilding exercises, managers can attempt to reinforce the individual identity of the team, strengthening team members' sense of belonging and improving the efficiency of the group. This can be accomplished in a number of ways, including giving the team its own name, its own office/space or its own uniforms.

Measuring team effectiveness

There are many possible ways of measuring team effectiveness, including:

- the degree to which the team achieved its stated objectives and the quality of its output.
- team member satisfaction.
- the efficiency of the team which can be measured by the resources used to achieve team objectives.

Management could measure these by using labour turnover or absenteeism rates or through the use of questionnaires for team members, interviews, or direct observation of the team. Team rewards could then be designed to not only motivate the individuals within the group, but also encourage cooperation and responsibility sharing between the team as a whole.

6 Distributive leadership

A distributed leadership perspective recognises that there are multiple leaders. From the leadership and management chapter it can be seen that traditionally leadership has been viewed as the role of one person in charge of others, but this view is changing.

Distributive leadership is also known as **shared**, or **collective** leadership and involves the sharing of the power base between a number of individuals. With distributed leadership, leadership is shared so that team members effectively interact with and lead each other. This form of leadership is more horizontal in nature, compared to traditional leadership which tends to be more vertical or hierarchical. This can be seen in the self directed and autonomous groups mentioned earlier in the chapter. With these groups, individuals are encouraged to manage their own work and working practices.

Carson et al proposed that shared leadership is facilitated by an overall team environment that consists of three dimensions:

- **Shared purpose**. When team members have similar understandings of their team's main objectives and take steps to ensure a focus on collective goals.
- **Social support**. The extent to which team members actively provide emotional and psychological strength to one another.
- **Voice**. The degree to which a team's members have input into how the team carries out its purpose.

The three dimensions are highly inter-related. If team members are encouraged to voice their opinions and get involved, they are more likely to start demonstrating leadership traits. If all members do this, there will be a greater focus on collective goals. This in turn leads to increased motivation within the team which encourages members to voice their opinions and get involved.

This suggests that a consequence of distributive or shared leadership is improved team performance and many studies have found a positive relationship between shared leadership and team effectiveness.

7 Inter-group and intra-group conflict

Inter-group conflict within organisations can be defined as the behaviour that occurs between organisational groups when participants identify with one group and perceive that other groups may block their group's goal achievement. While intra-group conflict occurs when there are disagreements or misunderstandings between members of a team. Conflict between team members can lead to a reduction in team productivity.

Inter-group conflict requires three ingredients.

1. **Group identification**. Employees have to perceive themselves as part of an identifiable group or department.

2 There has to be an **observable group difference** of some form. The ability to identify oneself as a part of one group and to observe differences in comparison with other groups is necessary for conflict.

3 **Frustration**. This means that if one group achieves its goal the other will not; it will be blocked. Frustration need not be severe and only needs to be anticipated to set off intergroup conflict. Intergroup conflict will appear when one group tries to advance its position in relation to other groups.

Managing inter-group conflict

Faced with inter-group conflict, the purpose of any managerial strategy will be to turn the conflict into fruitful competition or, if this is not possible, to control the conflict.

There are a number of approaches which can be used to manage intergroup conflict including:

- **Confrontation**. Occurs when parties in conflict directly engage one another and try to work out their differences. Negotiation is the bargaining process that often occurs during confrontation and that enables the parties to systematically reach a solution. Confrontation is not always successful as there is no guarantee that discussions will focus on a conflict or that emotions will not get out of hand.
- **Third-party consultants**. When conflict is intense and enduring, and department members are suspicious and uncooperative, an expert third-party consultant can be brought in from outside the organisation to meet with representatives from both departments.
- **Inter-group training**. A strong intervention to reduce conflict is intergroup training. This technique has been developed by psychologists such as Robert Blake, Jane Mouton and Richard Walton. When other techniques fail to reduce conflict to an appropriate level, or when other techniques do not fit the organisation in question, special training of group members may be required.
- **Member rotation**. It means that individuals from one department can be asked to work in another department on a temporary or permanent basis. The advantage is that individuals become submerged in the values, attitudes, problems and goals of the other department. In addition, individuals can explain the problems and goals of their original departments to their new colleagues. This enables a frank, accurate exchange of views and information.
- **Superordinate goals**. Another strategy is for top management to establish superordinate goals that require cooperation between departments. Conflicting departments then share the same goal and must depend upon one another to achieve it.

NB: Confrontation, third-party consultants and some training methods could also be used to manage intra-group conflict.

Illustration 1 – Rivalry generated by inter-group competition

The intensity of rivalry generated by inter-group competition can be seen in the well-known case documented below.

Sherif and Sherif divided boys at a summer school camp into two teams and established clear identities for each with a rivalry between the two. The immediate result was that inter-group competition increased group cohesion. Each group regarded the other as the enemy, and fraternisation and communication between the groups ceased.

Within each group it was found that:

- conformity was demanded, and group requirements outweighed individual needs
- group members encouraged a move from informal to formal and from a leadership approach of participation to an autocratic one the group became better organised.

At the end of the exercise a winning team and losing team resulted. The friction existing between the teams resisted concentrated efforts to remove it. Attempts to run joint teams and act against an outside team were of limited success. It was noted that the winning team retained its spirit and cohesion but became complacent and sought to satisfy the needs of individuals. On the other hand, the losing team sought to allocate blame both inside and outside the group. Its cohesion fell and it ignored the needs of individual members.

In summary, some degree of competition may prove beneficial but the long-term result of excessive competition is likely to result in conflict and a reduction in efficiency.

Managing inter-group conflict – training

Training is a method for managing inter-group conflict.

This training requires that department members attend an outside workshop away from day-to-day work problems. The training workshop may last several days, and various activities take place. This technique is expensive, but it has the potential for developing a company-wide cooperative attitude. The steps typically associated with an intergroup training session are as follows:

- The conflicting groups are both brought into a training setting with the stated goal of exploring mutual perceptions and relationships.
- The conflicting groups are then separated and each group is invited to discuss and make a list of its perceptions of itself and the other group.

- In the presence of both groups, group representatives publicly share the perceptions of self and other that the groups have generated, while the groups are obligated to remain silent. The objective is simply to report to the other group as accurately as possible the images that each group has developed in private.
- Before any exchange takes place, the groups return to private sessions to digest and analyse what they have heard; there is great likelihood that the representatives' reports have revealed to each group discrepancies between its self-image and the image the other group holds of it.
- In public session, again working through representatives, each group shares with the other what discrepancies it has uncovered and the possible reasons for them, focusing on actual, observable behaviour.
- Following this mutual exposure, a more open exploration is permitted between the two groups on the now-shared goal of identifying further reasons for perceptual distortions.
- A joint exploration is then conducted of how to manage future relations in such a way as to encourage cooperation between groups.

After this training experience, department employees understand each other much better. The improved attitudes lead to better working relationships for a long time.

Case study style question 2

LMN is a company which undertakes road reconstruction and maintenance. The work is carried out by teams which operate independently of each other. The team members have worked together for years and are well integrated. Each team includes a salesman who is responsible for getting additional work, ideally in the area where the team is already working. The teams draw their materials and road-surfacing and other machinery from the company pool, and obtain information on potential customers from a central sales office.

Although the company's performance has been satisfactory, the operations manager has decided to try to improve productivity by introducing competition between the teams. This will be done by drawing half of the wages of each team member from a single bonus pool for which all the teams compete.

The finance manager is concerned about these proposals as she feels that while this could improve team performance, it could also adversely affect the behaviour of the teams. She has requested a meeting with the operations manager to discuss the proposals. She has asked you to prepare some discussion points for her to use in the meeting.

Required:

Prepare a paper containing discussion points for the finance manager. The points should cover how such a policy is likely to affect the behaviour of these teams.

(15 minutes)

8 Summary diagram

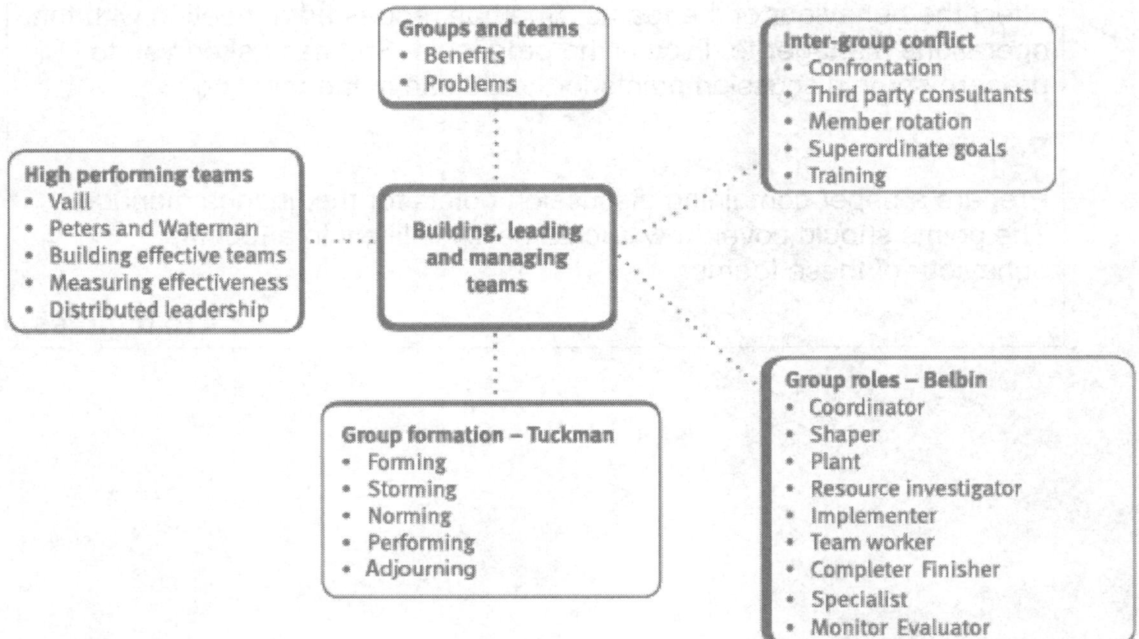
Groups and teams
• Benefits
• Problems
Inter-group conflict
• Confrontation
• Third party consultants
• Member rotation
• Superordinate goals
• Training
High performing teams
• Vaill
• Peters and Waterman
• Building effective teams
• Measuring effectiveness
• Distributed leadership
Building, leading and managing teams
Group formation – Tuckman
• Forming
• Storming
• Norming
• Performing
• Adjourning
Group roles – Belbin
• Coordinator
• Shaper
• Plant
• Resource investigator
• Implementer
• Team worker
• Completer Finisher
• Specialist
• Monitor Evaluator

End of chapter questions

Question 1

When members of a group try to minimise conflict and reach consensus without critically testing, analysing and evaluation ideas, this is known as:

A Conformity

B Risky shift

C Groupthink

D The Abilene paradox

Question 2

Using Tuckman's model, match the descriptions to the stage of team development.

Stage	Description
Storming	Members start to operate as a team and appreciate the roles of others
Performing	Team members test the manager's authority, and conflict can arise
Forming	The team is capable of operating to full potential
Norming	Team members are a collection of individuals unsure of their roles

Question 3

Using Belbin's team roles, insert the correct character type in the sentences below.

- Shaper
- Teamworker
- Monitor Evaluator
- Resource Investigator
- Plant
- Co-ordinator
- Implementer
- Completer Finisher

The ______________ is concerned with the relationships within the group.

The ________________ will promote activity within the group.

The ________________ analyses others' ideas and brings the group down to earth.

The ________________ chases progress and ensures timetables are met.

Question 4

Consider the following types of group behaviour:

According to Peters and Waterman, which of these would be characteristics of a successful group? Select all that apply.

- Avoidance of conflict
- Clear objectives
- Small number of members
- Informal and unstructured communication
- Strong pressure for group members to conform
- Voluntary membership
- Dominant individual members

Question 5

Which of the following are the three requirements for intergroup conflict?

- The groups have to have superordinate goals.
- Employees have to perceive themselves as part of an identifiable group or department.
- There has to be dominant personalities within the groups.
- There has to be weak leadership within the groups.
- There has to be an observable group difference of some form.
- There has to be a degree of frustration between the groups.

Question 6

Which THREE of the following statements about distributed leadership are true?

- Distributed leadership is facilitated by the team members having a shared purpose, social support and a voice.
- Distributed leadership is also known as transformational leadership.
- Distributed leadership tends to be more vertical in nature while more traditional leadership tends to be more horizontal.
- Distributed leadership has been found to improve motivation and team performance.
- Distributed leadership involves the power base for a team being shared between a number of team members.

Question 7

Team X is successfully run by A and has six members including A. A has been in the team for over 20 years and is very good at analysing new ideas and at keeping the group focused.

D has been in the industry for 20 years but only joined the team two years ago. She has a lot of contacts with suppliers and customers and is very good at networking.

E is very good at sorting out disputes and conflicts between team members. The main disputes happen between B, who can be aggressive and pushes people to get the job done, and F who is stable and deals with the administration and the scheduling for the team.

C tends to generate the ideas for the team and is very creative at problem solving.

Match the team members to the Belbin's tam role which they would be most suited to. A team member can have more than one role.

- co-ordinator
- shaper
- plant
- monitor evaluator
- resource investigator
- implementer
- teamworker
- completer finisher
- specialist

Question 8

Match the approach for managing inter-group conflict to its description.

Superordinate goals
Member rotation
Third-party consultants
Confrontation

- Parties directly engage with each other to attempt to work out their differences
- An expert is brought in from outside to meet with both parties
- Conflicting parties are set the same goal and must depend on each other to achieve it
- Individuals from one department can be asked to work in another department

Question 9

Which of the following statements about types of groups are true?

- Organisations should try to discourage informal groups.
- A group that an individual does not belong to but would like to join is known as a reference group.
- Organisations use informal groups to carry out tasks, communicate and solve problems.
- When making business decisions managers should always consider how these decisions will impact on informal groups.
- Individuals join informal groups to meet social and security needs.

Question 10

According to Vaill, which THREE of the following are key characteristics of high-performance teams?

- Commitment to purpose
- Functional specialism
- Eight main character types
- Strong and clear leadership
- Super-ordinate goals
- Teamwork focused on the task at hand

Test your understanding answers

Case study style question 1

EMAIL

To: N

From: Management Accountant

Date: today

Subject: Team performance

N,

Your group of twelve people is a long established and successful group. It would therefore be operating in Tuckman's fourth and final stage, which he terms 'performing'. In this stage the group is mature and individuals have evolved the roles that each will discharge and the norms of behaviour for group sessions. Such a settled group will be comfortable and familiar with each other, encouraging each individual to fulfil his/her role.

Belbin has devised a series of questionnaires whereby a person's natural role within a group can be defined. His theory further explains that a successful group has a balance of types.

Prior to the recent changes in the team, you were fulfilling the 'Co-ordinator' role; P was the 'Plant', capable of innovative solutions but may be low on practical follow through. R would have been the 'Resource Investigator', Q was an 'implementer', but may also have functioned as a 'Monitor Evaluator', providing an organising, dutiful, unemotional aspect to the group's work. S was the 'Teamworker', defined by Belbin as important in promoting team spirit. O seems to have been the 'Completer Finisher', ensuring that matters are followed through; also during your absence she may have acted as 'Shaper' in providing the drive and momentum for completion of the work. This analysis suggests that this group was well balanced in having all major team roles present.

The resignation of O could cause an imbalance within the group unless another individual develops into the 'Completer Finisher' and 'Shaper' roles. Belbin explains that people can adopt different roles in different groups and amend their behaviour to fill a vacant role. However, there will be a temporary imbalance. Furthermore, the resignation of O and her replacement by four new people means that the group reverts to the earlier stages of Tuckman's group formation i.e., forming, storming and norming.

As the group seeks to absorb new unknown people and strange roles are adopted it is inevitable that some people conflict will emerge. This could be aggravated by the increased size of the group. When the group had twelve members, a degree of cohesiveness is possible; however, this is less likely in a group of fifteen, especially when four members are new.

Since P and R have been unusually helpful, they are probably aware of this difficulty and are trying to cover O's role gap. However, the friction between them and with others highlights the need for you to take action.

To recapture group cohesiveness and efficiency you could:

- let the group evolve over time through the four stages until the performing stage is reached when group cohesiveness would be restored. This would incur the intermediate stages when the group members get to know each other, when roles develop and are accepted by others, when disagreements arise. This may feel like a safe option since eleven of the fifteen members are long standing and extra support is coming from P and R. However, you need to remember that the personality of the new group will be different from the old team – there are new people and roles involved. Also, the size of the group is significantly larger and could not operate in the same way.
- break the group into smaller teams, which may progress through the four stages of formation more quickly. A smaller team can be managed in a more personal manner and this may suit you.
- become directly involved in structuring the progression of the group through each stage of formation. You could, for example, influence the development of roles and behaviour norms through your own behaviour in recognising a particular person as the 'Shaper' in the team.
- change the group structure through delegation, assigning individual responsibilities, making some tasks team based instead of personal based. Since the tasks are complex, this may be a current practice.
- emphasise the change and need for a new approach by altering the physical layout of the office. A revised desk seating plan could create its own team influences and separate potential conflict staff.
- introduce a series of team building training sessions in which the group could analyse its own behaviour. This could involve understanding the value that each person brings to the team as well as ensuring that everyone understands the group tasks that must be completed. In the final resort this could lead to the payment of team bonuses based on team, rather than individual, performance.
- you may also have to consider whether there is a need to change your management style. Likert emphasises that the effective manager can adapt his/her management style in response to changes in staff, tasks and situation. For example, you may find it necessary to be less participative in the early stages of group formation. Or even adopt two different styles if you chooses to split the group into two smaller teams.

I hope you have found the above useful. Please do not hesitate to get in touch if you would like any more information or would like to discuss any of these issues further.

Case study style question 2

Discussion points for meeting re team bonus structure

Prepared by Management Accountant

Date: today

Introduction

Road reconstruction and maintenance work will consist of contracts where each contract is different in nature, size and location. The techniques and materials used may be common but the application will be variable. Under this pattern of work there is considerable initiative available to the work team while central control cannot be detailed.

The present teams are cohesive, successful and operate independently of each other. The introduction of competition between groups will heighten the cohesive aspect and reduce the co-operation overall, this can be concluded from the boys camp experiments of Sherif and Sherif. This will be accentuated in this example because the change in wage system means that teams are competing for a share of a single bonus pool. The operations manager's introduction of competition will change the attitude and behaviour of the teams. Some of these changes will be beneficial while others will be negative.

The positive changes in behaviour are likely to be:

- An improvement in productivity within the teams. Each team will endeavour to safeguard or increase its share of the bonus pool. The team will concentrate its attention on improving its own productivity through streamlining working practices, ignoring trade demarcation boundaries and working outside normal hours to complete the job.
- The bonus element of the wages can be calculated on a basis of contract profitability as contract time targets. If profitability is the measure then the team will be cost conscious and material wastage, equipment abuse etc. will be minimised. However, if the measure is time targets then wastage and machinery abuse will be irrelevant to the team's bonus and management will need a central system to check team behaviour and operations.
- An improvement in timekeeping and attendance should occur. Mayo, in the Hawthorne Experiment, was the first researcher to point out the strong pressure of group colleagues upon the behaviour of any individual within a group. The more cohesive the group, the stronger its peer pressure. Group names will be clearly evident covering areas of attendance, timekeeping, 'breaktimes' and individuals will be pressurised to fulfil their role within the team. As Mayo discovered, if the behaviour of an individual usurps a team name then team members exact a penalty and the offender is subjected to ostracisation, sneering comments and similar social pressure.

- Local sales effort is likely to be increased. If potential customers are logged with a central sales office then once a team has commenced work with a customer, they are likely to 'sell' extra services and develop sales to a maximum. There could be a situation where this is damaging to the organisation. For instance a major customer operating several sites could employ more than one team from the road reconstruction company. If one team disparages the work of another team or causes it to miss a deadline, in order to gain the next slice of work, then the overall company reputation is damaged. This is the potential danger in all situations of local rivalry.
- There will be a change in internal working relationships as group members become less social in behaviour and more task centred. This will increase pressure on newcomers or poor-performers, as time spent in coaching or supporting by other team members becomes resented.

The negative changes in behaviour are likely to be:

- Competition will breed selfishness and the bonus share out will create winners and losers encouraging envy and recriminations between teams and their members.
- Teams will be selective in the jobs that they undertake. A difficult or potentially low bonus job is likely to be avoided. An additional temptation would arise when a team developed a major customer and was unable to handle all the work generated in the timescale required by the customers. The team may seek to postpone the work and so safeguard future bonuses but would damage customer services in doing so.
- Fluctuating wages and internal group pressure to perform could have harmful consequences for individuals and reduce loyalty.
- There will be severe pressure on the sales person to put the interests of his team first and the company second. Sub-optimising of performance is likely as each team seeks to direct its sales person's efforts for the team's benefit. This selfishness of behaviour could extend to other areas such as machines being drawn from the company pool and not returned promptly for other teams to use. A further example could arise where one team learns of a contract which is in the immediate vicinity of a rival team's current working. The overall benefit of the company dictates that disruption and travelling costs would be minimised by the team in that locality fulfilling that work. But selfish team behaviour may block this.

In summary competition between teams will deeply affect the behaviour of individuals within groups and inter group behaviour.

Question 1

C Groupthink

Conformity is where individuals are persuaded by team pressure to agree with decisions which are obviously wrong.

Risky shift is the tendency for groups to take riskier, or more cautious, decisions than the individuals would take.

The Abilene Paradox refers to the situation where the outcome achieved was not what any of the members wanted but they all thoughts the others did.

Question 2

The correct match is:

Norming	Members start to operate as a team and appreciate the roles of others
Storming	Team members test the manager's authority, and conflict can arise
Performing	The team is capable of operating to full potential
Forming	Team members are a collection of individuals unsure of their roles

Question 3

The **teamworker** is concerned with the relationships within the group.

The **shaper** will promote activity within the group.

The **monitor evaluator** analyses others' ideas and brings the group down to earth.

The **completer finisher** chases progress and ensures timetables are met.

Question 4

- Small number of members
- Informal and unstructured communication
- Voluntary membership

Peters and Waterman also suggested that successful teams should be of a limited duration and be action orientated.

Question 5

- Employees have to perceive themselves as part of an identifiable group or department.
- There has to be an observable group difference of some form – individuals must identify themselves as part of one group.
- There has to be a degree of frustration between the groups – frustration means that one group achieving its goals will block another group from meeting its goals. Frustration only has to be anticipated to cause conflict.

Question 6

- Distributed leadership is facilitated by the team members having a shared purpose, social support and a voice.
- Distributed leadership has been found to improve motivation and team performance.
- Distributed leadership involves the power base for a team being shared between a number of team members.

Distributed leadership is also known as transformational leadership. This is false, it is also known as collective leadership.

Distributed leadership tends to be more vertical in nature while more traditional leadership tends to be more horizontal. This is false as distributed leadership tends to be more horizontal.

Question 7

A is coordinator and monitor-evaluator

B is completer/finisher

C is plant

D is resource-investigator

E is team worker

F is implementer

Question 8

The correct matching is:

- Parties directly engage with each other to attempt to work out their differences – **Confrontation**
- An expert is brought in from outside to meet with both parties – **Third-party consultants**
- Conflicting parties are set the same goal and must depend on each other to achieve it – **Superordinate goals**
- Individuals from one department can be asked to work in another department – **Member rotation**

Question 9

- A group that an individual does not belong to but would like to join is known as a reference group.
- When making business decisions managers should always consider how these decisions will impact on informal groups.
- Individuals join informal groups to meet social and security needs.

Organisations should try to discourage informal groups. This is false, they have to be aware of them and understand the need for them.

Organisations use informal groups to carry out tasks, communicate and solve problems. This is incorrect. While informal groups may contribute to these outcomes, they would generally use formal groups for these purposes.

Question 10

- Commitment to purpose
- Strong and clear leadership
- Teamwork focused on the task at hand.

In addition Vaill suggested that high performing teams would also exhibit:

- Clarification of broad purpose and near term objectives
- Generation of inventions and new methods.

Chapter

8

Managing organisational relationships

Chapter learning objectives

Lead	Component
B3: Explain how to manage relationships	(b) Communication (c) Negotiations (d) Managing conflicts

Topics to be covered

- Communication process
- Digital tools for communication
- Negotiation process
- Strategies for negotiation
- Sources and types of conflicts
- Strategies for managing conflict
- Leadership and ethics.

1 Session content diagram

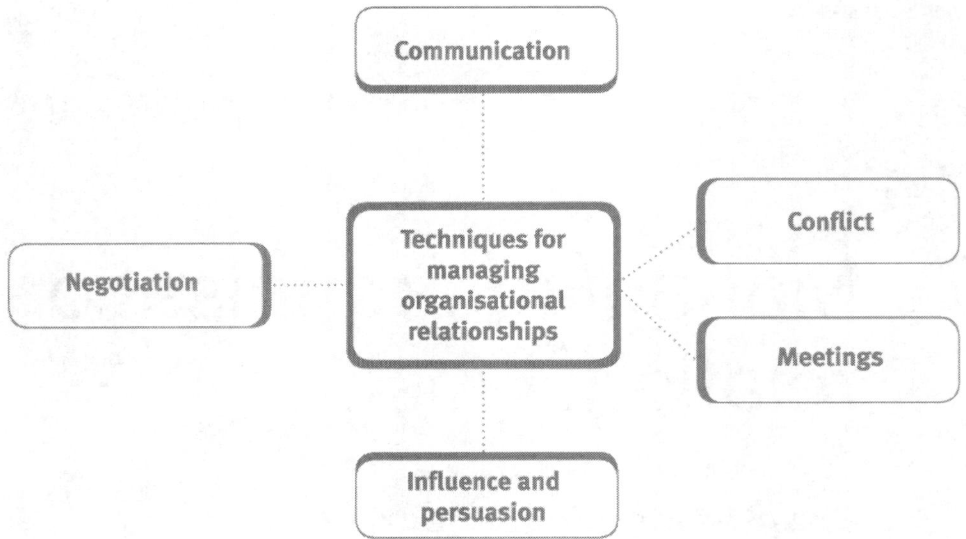

Why are these communication skills important?

In any organisation there will frequently be conflicting demands on time, or differences of opinion or attitude for which these skills are key in trying to reach agreements where all parties are happy and can work together towards the organisational goals. In certain job roles they will be more important than others, for example in any role with responsibility for customer or supplier relationships, or for managing others, these communication skills are essential.

The importance of effective communication for Chartered Management Accountants

For Chartered Management Accountants (CMAs) who are required to deal with a variety of parties, both internal and external, these skills are fundamental.

CMAs are an integral part of any business and hold a variety of positions within organisations, often senior management positions. Their roles are varied and can include (amongst others):

- formulation of policy and setting of corporate objectives
- acquisition and use of finance
- generation, communication and interpretation of financial and operating information for management and other stakeholders
- derivation of performance measures
- improvement of business systems.

To undertake these roles, they often work as part of multi-skilled management teams. They will be required to deal with other employees throughout the organisation, at all different levels, and external parties such as customers, suppliers, contractors and advisors. Effective communication skills are therefore vital for the CMA as they will be required to deal with a variety of people in order to carry out a variety of roles. Influencing, persuasion and negotiation skills will be particularly important.

2 Communication

An important aspect in all relationships within an organisation is communication. Most organisations will depend to some extent on the speed and accuracy of communication to maintain their competitive edge, and the management function relies on effective communication. Good communication skills are often included as an essential management competence, since people with good communication skills have been found to make better decisions and tend to be promoted more frequently.

Effective and regular personal communication is vital to ensure coordination and to identify problems quickly.

Types of communication

Most communication within an organisation can be classified as either formal or informal.

Formal communication

Formal communication is planned and intentional and tends to have a more professional tone. This is generally used within a work context.

Informal communication

Informal communication is more casual in nature and is generally unplanned. Informal communication is less structured with a more relaxed tone. This type of communication is generally used between family and friends.

The process of communication

The communication process can be defined as a process that is used to transmit a message from a sender to a receiver. A message can be words, numbers, gestures or non-verbal cues such as body language.

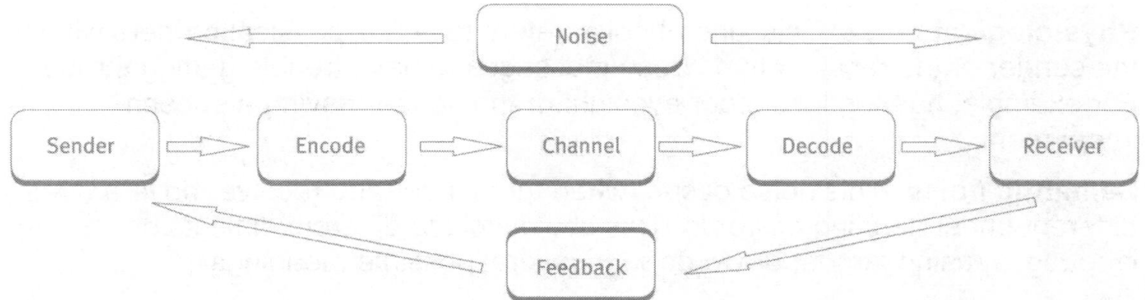

The message goes through several stages when it is sent by the sender to the receiver. These stages are as follows:

1 **Sender**. The sender is the entity that conveys or sends the message.

2 **Encoding**. Encoding is a process through which the message is symbolised.

3 **Channel**. Channel is the medium through which message is being sent. (email, face-to-face conversations, meetings, telephone calls etc).

4 **Receiver**. The receiver is the entity that receives the message.

5 **Decoding**. Decoding is the process in which the message is translated and meaning is generated out of it. (problems can occur here due to interpretation).

6 **Feedback**. Is the process through which receiver sends their response.

The importance of feedback

When a message is sent, it is important that the sender receives feedback from the receiver to let them know that the message was successfully received. Feedback can be verbal, for example acknowledgements, questions or comments or it can be non-verbal such as a smile (or a frown). Feedback can also be written, for example in replying to a text or email.

Feedback is a very important part of the communication process as it gives the sender the knowledge that the message has been received as intended, or can allow the sender to clarify the message where it appears that the receiver is confused or doesn't understand the message.

It is important that the sender asks for feedback. Assuming a message has been received and understood can be a dangerous assumption to make.

Noise

Another feature of the communication process is noise. Noise is anything which interferes with the communication process and stops the message being received and understood by the receiver as it was intended. There are many types of noise, including:

Environmental/physical noise: This noise physically disrupts communication and prevents the receiver from hearing or seeing the message clearly. For example, loud music, phones ringing, people chatting loudly or difficult-to-read fonts or colours.

Physiological noise: This kind of noise refers to actual physical barriers within the sender or the receiver that cause messages to have trouble getting through. For example, hearing loss, poor eyesight or the sender having a speech impairment.

Semantic noise: This noise occurs when the sender and receiver have a different understanding of words. This could include different dialects or languages, using jargon, or words with several possible meanings.

Psychological noise: The attitude of the sender and receiver can also make communication difficult. For example anger or sadness may cause someone to lose focus, being preoccupied with a problem or feelings of prejudice can all affect the communication process.

Barriers to communication

Sender:

- not being clear as to what has to be communicated
- omitting information
- choosing words in coding the message that do not accurately reflect the idea/concept, and or choosing words that the intended receiver cannot understand
- choosing words that provoke an emotional response
- using technical jargon
- choosing an inappropriate medium
- sending too much information
- sending mixed messages.

Receiver:

- not in an appropriate state to receive the message
- not wishing to receive the message
- filtering out elements that he or she does not wish to deal with
- information overload
- mindset that does not admit the substance of the message.

Ways to overcome the barriers:

the **sender** should:

- have a definite, clear objective
- plan the communication
- think about the receiver and their situation
- anticipate reactions to the message and cater for these
- practise using the channels of communication
- seek and work with the feedback.

the **receiver** should:

- consider their contribution
- listen attentively
- check out anything that is vague
- give feedback.

Non-verbal communication

According to Druker: **"The most important thing in communication is hearing what isn't said."**

Studies by **Mehrabian** suggested that only around 7% of a message is transmitted through the actual words said, with the other 93% being conveyed through the way the words are said and other non-verbal elements.

A great deal of communication can take place without any words at all. The raised eyebrow, the smile, the frown and the glare all say a great deal; so can more obvious physical gestures such as the hand shake, pat on the back or an arm around the shoulders.

Body language is about:

- appearance
- eye contact
- facial expression
- posture and distance
- tone.

Non-verbal actions can vary across countries and cultures. For example, in most western countries eye contact is seen as a way of indicating interest in what the other person is saying while eye contact is avoided in Japan. Pointing and other hand gestures can also be interpreted differently in different countries, with some gestures viewed as positive in some countries and offensive and rude in others.

2.1 Digital tools for communication

The traditional workplace was composed of a physical office space with employees working face-to-face, communicating via paper and meetings which were usually held on-site.

The introduction of email (first configured in the 1970's by Ray Tomlinson) and other forms communication such as video conferencing changed this format. In 1995 when the restrictions on carrying commercial traffic over the Internet ended it became the norm for employees to be working across multiple locations, hours and devices.

The workforce became more flexible and was no longer confined to a single office environment. As these diversified workplaces emerged, the need for team-based, collaborative and digitally connected work environments became critical to business efficiency and future growth.

Some examples of such digital communication tools are:

Intranet

A private hub that can be accessed by any authorised users within a business organisation. It is mainly used for effective internal communication and collaboration among colleagues, producing a more educated, skilled and engaged workforce.

With the advent of bring-your-own-device (BYOD) and telecommuting, an intranet solution will result in a more flexible workforce and ensure all employees are working towards the same goals.

Intranets enable organisations to easily share company news and build an information-rich environment, for example, news feeds can be personalised for each staff member based on their team, department and/or location to ensure the most relevant news is provided for their needs. Clearly this would need to be linked to security permissions to ensure sensitive or confidential information is protected.

Intranets can be further developed by facilitating communication among staff working in different locations or in a particular location or area of specialty facilitating interaction with the content and offering feedback in real-time.

Chat and private messaging

Collaborative spaces which provide private/group messaging and "chat functions" are often viewed as one of the best business communication tools to keep teams working together…an effective form of communication for busy employees and managers.

For example, instant messaging makes updates on projects and general team discussion much easier, which works well when employees or team members are spread across different geographical locations or different time zones. Similarly, they enable files to be shared and conversations can be accessed if needed.

Discussion forums

A discussion forum can bring together management and employees and allows for an open discussion on any topic (usually set up and monitored/moderated). It can also help in knowledge dissemination and bring the workforce together.

Forums are also effective in archiving organisational knowledge to be used by anyone as a reference. Employee morale can also be boosted by participating in regular discussion forums which will also facilitate knowledge sharing. This will enable information to be discovered by people who need it, when they need it.

Tracking and case software

An online help desk with a case tracking system enables employees and customers to submit a case or support ticket. This allows it to be assigned to the right employee and have it checked and resolved in time, helps centralise customer support queries and keep track of any open issues.

Tracking team productivity can be monitored and it enables the business to prioritise the most relevant and important queries and collect valuable customer feedback which in turn can help in improving future products, services and customer relationships.

This can also be extended to an issue tracking system which is generally used in an organisation's customer support/call centre to create, update and resolve reported customer issues or internal issues reported by employees within the company.

Internal blogs

The internal blog is a place where employees can share ideas and experiences fast and in an informal fashion.

Internal blog advantages can include:

- Broadcasting and highlighting an employee's knowledge about a certain topic or area of the organisation.
- Creating a searchable and permanent archive of articles, knowledge and expertise.
- Promotes open discussion and collaboration among the workforce. (NB there are instances where some employees will be more likely to speak up in a virtual environment than face-to-face).
- It connects employees across departments and locations.
- It keeps the staff up-to-date on important information and company updates.

2.2 Data visualisation

Data visualisation allows large volumes of complex data to be displayed in a visually appealing and accessible way that facilitates the understanding and use of the underlying data.

The growing significance of data has seen a rise in the importance of being able to access and understand the data in clear, concise way. This is where data visualisation fits in. The tools of today's market leaders Tableau and Qlik, go far beyond the simple charts and graphs of Microsoft Excel. Data is displayed in customisable, interactive 3D formats that allow uses to manipulate and drill down as required. Central to data visualisation is understanding and ease of use, the leading companies in the field look to make data easier and more accessible for everyone.

Essentially it aims to remove the need for complex extraction, analysis and presentation of data by finance, IT and data scientists. It puts the ability to find data in to the hands of the end user, through intuitive, user friendly interfaces.

The most common use of data visualisation is in creating a dashboard to display the key performance indicators of a business in a live format, thus allowing immediate understanding of current performance and potentially prompting action to correct or amend performance accordingly.

3 Meetings

Meetings can be an effective communication method for the manager. In order to ensure that meetings are effective and useful it is important to adopt the following steps:

- determine the purpose of the meeting
- establish who needs to attend
- determine the agenda in advance
- make suitable arrangements for location and time
- facilitate discussion
- manage the plan of action
- summarise
- publish results/minutes.

A rule of thumb of facilitation is that successful meetings are:

80% preparation and **20% execution**.

Roles of team members in meetings:

- The meeting requires a **chairperson/facilitator** to setting the agenda and ensuring the meeting achieves its objectives. During the meeting this person will ensure the agenda is followed.
- The meeting will require a **secretary or administrator** to take minutes.
- Team members will play various roles:
  - protagonists are positive supporters.
  - antagonists are challenging and disruptive.

All meeting members must be listened to with respect, but it is the responsibility of the facilitator to make the whole team aware of the overall objectives, and the role that each team member plays in their achievement.

If the meeting is designed to solve problems, individual team members will be called upon to offer their own expertise and advice on the situation. Other team members will take a more passive role, but will be important in providing an objective perspective on the solutions generated. It is important that a variety of skills are represented at a meeting so that those present can provide varying expert opinions upon the same problem.

NB: much of the traditional approach to meetings has been affected and to some extent superseded by technological change including an increase in the use of online meeting applications such as Zoom.

For example, Zoom can be used on your laptop, desktop, tablet, or mobile device, allowing remote workers to feel seen and is a simpler, yet more robust, way of connecting with co-workers when meeting in person is not possible.

The problems, that can exist with ensuring that the meeting fulfils its purpose however, remain.

Problems with meetings and their solution

Problems with meetings	**Actions to avoid problem**
Inappropriate chairperson.	Selection should be based on someone with the requisite range of communication skills.
The objectives of the meeting are undefined and unclear.	Ensure that an agenda is produced and circulated prior to the meeting. During the meeting, the chairperson should state the objective and must return the focus of the meeting to the points on the agenda.
Lack of enthusiasm or interest in the meeting.	For future meetings, ensure that only those with an interest in the meeting, or whose view is required, are actually invited to the meeting. For the current meeting, suggest a short break or stress the need to reach a conclusion.
Attendees talk too much without regard to the chairperson's requests.	The chairperson must impose some order on the meeting. Possible solutions include asking the participants to speak in accordance with meeting protocols such as a time constraint if necessary, or (worst case) asking them to leave the meeting altogether.

Attendees cannot reach an agreement concerning issues on the agenda.	The chairperson will need to exercise negotiation skills to try to bring the meeting to some agreement. If this is not possible, then attendees may have to agree to differ. However, some action points may be required to ensure that more information is obtained so agreement can be achieved at the next meeting.
Action points from previous meetings have not been carried out.	Assuming that minutes were issued correctly, in the current meeting, the chairperson should obtain reasons for actions not being completed. For future action points, ensure that each has a person identified as responsible for completing it. Check the minutes of the meeting to ensure that all action points are included.
Minutes are either too long (information overload) or too brief (do not include appropriate points).	Ensure that the minutes are either minutes of resolution (which contain agreed outcomes) or, if minutes of narration, that they are sufficiently edited to provide the flavour of the discussions, but not small detail.

Case study style question 1

PQR has experienced significant success over the last year and is expanding rapidly. B, the founder and managing director, feels that changes to the way the company is being run will have to be made in order to ensure future success. One area he has identified which needs improving is the communication between managers.

The main means of communication between mangers is via a monthly managers' meeting, however these meetings are generally unproductive. B feels this is due to the following reasons:

- Lack of participation. During the meetings, some managers do not contribute, many feel they have better things to do with their time, so keep quiet to speed the meeting up.
- Non-attendance. Not all managers turn up for the monthly meetings, and on some occasions the operations manager has sent a junior member of staff on his behalf.
- Decisions are rarely made at the meeting as the managers don't usually know what will be discussed at the meeting so rarely bring any documentation. Discussions can be held at the meeting, but managers can leave the meeting unclear as to what will happen next.

> - The manager of the sales department is a formidable character and the other managers are usually reluctant to disagree with him. He usually takes over the discussions within the meeting.
>
> B has employed you as a consultant for advice as to how to improve these areas.
>
> **Required:**
>
> Write a report for B discussing the problems which have been experienced in the monthly meetings and suggesting what should be done to make future meetings more productive.
>
> **(15 minutes)**

4 Influence, persuasion and negotiation skills

Influence, persuasion and negotiation are all aspects of communication. They are linked and can often be used together, but they are different.

- **Influence** is the ability to change others' attitudes, opinions or behaviour.
- **Persuasion** is the attempt to deliberately get others to change an attitude, opinion, or behaviour.
- **Negotiation** is the ability to discuss an issue with one or more other people in the attempt to establish ways to reach agreement.

Influence

Influence can be direct or indirect. Direct influence is when the person attempting to change the attitude of another speaks directly to the other person. This type of influence would be used within sales or customer services roles. Indirect influence is where the message attempts to reach its target via a third party. For example organisations may pass messages to public relations firms or analysts, in the hope that these parties will in turn influence potential customers.

Influencing techniques are used frequently by sales people to encourage us to purchase goods and services. There will also be many situations within organisational relationships where it will be important to influence other people, for example, attempting to gain support for a new product or process. When attempting to influence others it is important to consider the objective and the reasons why influencing the other party is necessary as forceful influence may be seen as manipulative.

Cialdini came up with six principles of Influence (or the six weapons of influence). These can be used whenever there is a need to influence others.

1 **Reciprocity**. Human nature can lead us to feel obliged to return favours. Therefore we may be influenced to support someone who has supported us in some way in the past.

2 **Commitment**. As humans, we desire consistency and don't like to be seen to be changing our minds. Therefore we may be influenced to follow through with our support for something if we had shown some initial interest in it.

3 **Social Proof**. This principle relies on the fact that humans tend to be influenced by peer pressure. If we see others acting in a certain way, it is likely to influence us to act in the same way.

4 **Liking**. This principle is based on the fact that as humans we are more likely to be influenced by people we like, people who are nice and friendly towards us or people who are similar to us.

5 **Authority**. Another principle of influence is based on the premise that we are more likely to be influenced by people in positions of authority. This comes from a sense of trust and respect for the position held.

6 **Scarcity**. This principle suggests that we are more likely to want something if its availability is limited. We are more likely to support something if we fear losing out if we don't.

Using the six principles of influence

Reciprocity: Identify what you want to achieve and what you need from the other person. You can then identify what you may be able to offer them, or remind them of what you have done for them in the past.

Commitment: Try to get some commitment from others at an early stage on the process. This makes it more difficult for them to withdraw their support later on.

Social Proof: Use the opinions of those already supporting you to influence others to join that support. If others are talking about your project, new people will want to be part of it.

Liking: Build relationships with those you want to influence so that they trust you. This can be difficult and can take some time, also different approaches may be required for different people.

Authority: Use your own authority and the authority of others, as influencers. Getting the backing of senior, powerful people will encourage others to back you.

Scarcity: People need to know that they could miss out if they don't act quickly. Imposing deadlines to enhance urgency can encourage people to give their support.

It is worth recognising these principles so that you can be aware when others are trying to use them to influence you.

Persuasion

Persuasion is a stronger form of influence. While influence can be direct or indirect, intentional or unintentional, persuasion is always direct and intentional. The aim of influence could be to inspire someone to buy in to an idea or make a particular decision, while the aim of persuasion is to change a person, or group's attitude or behaviour towards something or someone. The person using persuasion has a clear objective and is set on achieving it by getting others to support them. Persuasion falls short of telling or ordering someone to do something, but may use coercion as it attempts to get the other person to agree, albeit perhaps under duress.

The six principles of influence can be used in persuasion, but they may be used in a stronger form.

Negotiation

Negotiation is another important communication skill required within organisations. Negotiation can be used by managers in their relationships with not only subordinates but with other stakeholders such as suppliers and customers.

The aim of negotiation is to settle differences between people or groups, and to allow them to come to an agreement which both parties accept.

Negotiation is defined by three characteristics:

1. Conflict of interest between two or more parties. What one wants is not necessarily what the others want.
2. No established set of rules for resolving conflict, or the parties prefer to work outside of an established set of rules to develop their own solution.
3. Parties prefer to search for an agreement rather than to fight openly, to have one side capitulate, to break off contact permanently, or to take their dispute to a higher authority.

Examples of negotiations managers might need to undertake:

- on **his/her own behalf** when securing a pay rise, for instance, or an improvement in the terms and conditions of employment.
- on **behalf of a department or functional area**, e.g. securing an acceptable departmental budget.
- with the **external environment** on behalf of the organisation, e.g. obtaining planning permission for an extension to the warehouse.

The skills required by a negotiator can be summarised under three main headings:

- **Interpersonal skills**. The negotiator requires good communicating techniques such as influence, and persuasion.
- **Analytical skills**. The negotiator requires the ability to analyse information, diagnose problems, to plan and set objectives, and the exercise of good judgement in interpreting results.
- **Technical skills**. The negotiator requires attention to detail and thorough case preparation.

The process of negotiation

The negotiation process can be divided into four distinct stages:

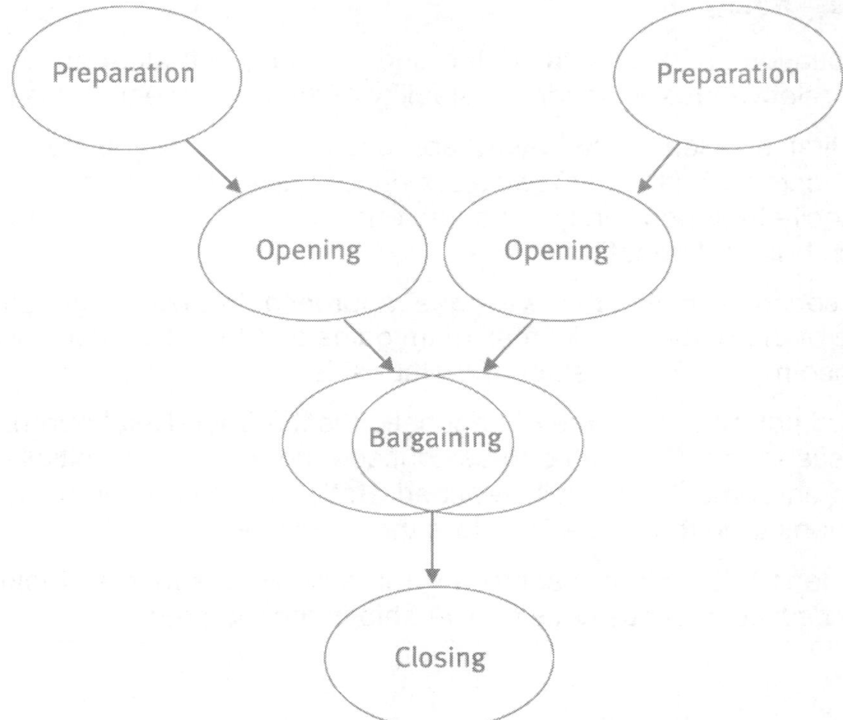

- **Preparation**. This stage involves information gathering. It is important to know the background to the problem, and the likely constraints acting on each participant.
- **Opening**. During this stage both sides present their starting positions. This is a good opportunity to influence the other party.
- **Bargaining**. The purpose of this stage is to narrow the gap between the two initial positions and to persuade other party of the strength of your case. In order to do this, you should use clearly thought out, planned and logical debate.
- **Closing**. At this stage agreement is reached and hopefully a mutually beneficial outcome has been found.

Guidance for successful negotiation

- Focus initially on each side's primary objective. Trivial negotiating points can become a distraction in the early stages (bikeshedding).
- Be prepared to settle for what is fair. If an agreement is not seen to be fair it is unlikely to be stable. Maintain flexibility in your own position, this makes it easier for the other side to be flexible as well.
- Listen to what the other side wants and make efforts to compromise on the main issues, so that both sides can begin to attain their goals.
- Seek to trade-off wins and losses, so each side gets something in return for everything they give up.

Types of negotiation

Negotiation processes can differ fundamentally in their approach and in their relative prospects for the stability of the agreement that is reached.

The first is called the **'win-win'** approach. In these negotiations, the prospects for both sides' gains are encouraging. Both sides attempt to reconcile their positions so that the end result is an agreement under which both will benefit.

The second is called the **'win-lose'** approach. In these negotiations, each of the parties seeks maximum gains and therefore usually seeks to impose maximum losses on the other side.

A third potential outcome of negotiation is the **'lose-lose'** approach. In this scenario either both parties concede more than they initially intend, or no agreement is actually reached. Both parties can end up in worse positions than they were in before the negotiation.

It is clear that a win-win solution is more likely to lead to a stable solution and a successful business relationship in the long run.

Case study style question 2

BCD is a manufacturer of building materials, supplying the house building industry. As a result of the downturn in the demand for its products and in response to difficult operating conditions in its existing market, the company is currently going through a major restructuring. It is anticipated that the restructuring plan will involve the consolidation of some business activities which will result in a number of staff having to move to different areas of the company. This could mean re-location to different sites, and other staff being made redundant.

While employee relations have in the past been good, the management of the company is aware that employees and the trade unions which represent their interests will be resistant to the changes that need to be made. The first stages of change will require skilful negotiation between the management and unions on a range of issues relating to the movement of staff jobs, the proposed job losses and, specifically, the criteria for redundancy and the redundancy package.

K, the operations director has been asked to lead the negotiations on behalf of BCD. He is not confident about this as he has never been involved in negotiations of this kind before. He has asked you for some advice.

Required:

Write an email to K, explaining the role of negotiation in the management of change in BCD, making reference to the different stages involved in the negotiation process.

(15 minutes)

5 Conflict

Conflict is a disagreement, and is when one party is perceived as preventing or interfering with the goals or actions of another. Conflict can occur in a variety of forms and at different levels, for example organisational, group or individual level.

Inter-group conflict was looked at in the previous chapter.

Conflict can arise for many different reasons, these are known as the **causes of conflict**. When conflict occurs certain behaviours can develop, these are known as the **symptoms of conflict**. There are also two main **types of conflict**. It is important that that you can distinguish between these different elements of conflict.

Causes of conflict

Mainwaring suggested that the causes of conflict generally include:

- **History**. Conflicts have a tendency for being self-perpetuating.
- **Differences**. Mainly of interests, objectives, priorities and ideologies.
- **Limited resources**. Where there are limited resources, there may be a battle for what is available.
- **Win/lose situations**. Success for one group often involves failure for others.
- **Interdependencies**. Where relationships, responsibilities or boundaries are not clearly defined, and/or where they are perceived to be unfair.
- **Misunderstandings**. These include communication failures and are common where there already exists some sort of conflict or threat.
- **Conviction beliefs**. If one group is convinced of their essential rightness or goodness, then there may be tendencies to 'enlighten' others, causing resistance.
- **Stress and failure**. If an individual, a group, or an organisation feels unable to cope with pressures and problems, then this is likely to generate fault finding, reality denial and seemingly irrational acts.
- **Change**. Individual, group, organisational and societal change creates new relationships, objectives, perceptions, problems and possibilities.

Symptoms of conflict

Certain behaviours and attitudes can manifest themselves when conflict exists. Sometimes these behaviours are overt, as when it emerges in the form of a strike, or individuals refusing to communicate with each other at all. However, the management of conflict is likely to be easier and more effective if these symptoms of conflict can be recognised and dealt with at an earlier stage. Such symptoms would probably include some of the following:

- Problems, even trivial ones, being passed up the hierarchy because no one wants to take responsibility for them.
- Hostility and jealousy between groups.
- Poor communications up and down the hierarchy, and between departments.
- Widespread frustration and dissatisfaction because it is difficult to get even simple things done efficiently.
- Problems constantly being polarised around people, usually in different groups, and personalities rather than issues.

Consequences of conflict

Daft noted that several **negative consequences** for organisations that may arise from conflict are as follows:

- Diversion of energy resulting in time and effort wasted.
- Altered judgement. Judgement becomes less accurate as focus is lost.
- Loser effects. The loser may deny or distort the reality and may seek scapegoats.
- Poor co-ordination. Under intense conflict co-ordination does not happen. Co-operation across groups decreases and groups may actively attempt to jeopardise the goals of other groups.

Types of conflict

Horizontal conflict

The first type of conflict is horizontal. Horizontal conflict occurs between groups and departments **at the same level** in the hierarchy. The main sources of horizontal conflict are:

- **Environment**. Each department or group becomes tailored to 'fit' its environmental domain and, thus, is differentiated from other groups or departments.
- **Size**. As organisations grow, members of departments begin to think of themselves as separate, and they erect walls between themselves and other departments.
- **Technology**. Interdependency creates opportunity for conflict as technology determines task allocation.
- **Structure**. Divisionalisation and departmentalisation create competition which can lead to conflict.
- **Goal incompatibility**. Each department's operative goals interfere with each other or the achievement of goals by one department may block achievement of the goals of other departments.
- **Task interdependence**. Dependence on each other for materials, resources and information. Generally, as interdependence increases, the potential for conflict increases.
- **Reward systems**. If departments are rewarded only for departmental performance, managers are motivated to excel at the expense of the rest of the organisation.
- **Differentiation**. Functional specialisation causes differences in cognitive and emotional orientations.

More on horizontal conflict

The potential for horizontal conflict exists in any situation in which separate departments are created, members have an opportunity to compare themselves with other groups, and the goals and values of respective groups appear mutually exclusive. The main sources of horizontal conflict are:

- **Environment**. Each department is geared to fit its external dynamic environment. As the uncertainty and complexity of the environment increase, greater differences in skills, attitudes, power, and operative goals develop among departments. Moreover, increased competition, both domestically and internationally, have led to demands for lower prices, improved quality, and better service. These demands exert more intense goal pressures within an organisation and, hence, greater conflict among departments.
- **Size**. As organisations increase in size, subdivision into a larger number of departments takes place. Employees feel isolated from other people in the organisation. The lengthening hierarchy also heightens power and resource differences among departments.
- **Technology**. Groups that have interdependent tasks interact more often and must share resources. Interdependence creates frequent situations that lead to conflict.
- **Structure**. Pay incentives may be based on competition among divisions. Organisation structure defines departmental groupings and, hence, employee loyalty to the defined groups.
- **Goal incompatibility**. Goal incompatibility is probably the greatest cause of intergroup conflict in organisations. A typical example of goal conflict may arise between marketing and manufacturing departments. Marketing strives to increase the breadth of the product line to meet customer tastes for variety. A broad product line means short production runs, so manufacturing has to bear higher costs.
- **Uncertainty**. When departments do not know where they stand because activities are unpredictable. When factors in the environment are rapidly changing, or when problems arise that are poorly understood, departments may have to renegotiate their respective tasks. Managers have to sort out how new problems should be handled. The boundaries of a department's territory or jurisdiction become indistinct.

- **Reward system** — the reward system governs the degree to which subgroups cooperate or conflict with one another. When departmental managers are rewarded for achieving overall organisation goals rather than departmental goals, cooperation among departments is greater.
- **Differentiation** – functional specialisation requires people with specific education, skills, attitudes, and time horizons. The underlying values and traits of personnel differ across departments, and these differences lead to horizontal conflicts.

Vertical conflict

A second type of conflict is vertical. Vertical conflict occurs among individuals and groups **at different levels** in the hierarchy. Individual employees may have conflicts with their bosses. Managers of international divisions often experience conflict with senior executives located at domestic headquarters. Many of the sources of horizontal conflict above may apply here as well. The other primary sources of vertical conflict are often about power and powerlessness and differences in status and power. Some example are:

- **Power and status**. At the bottom of the hierarchy, workers often feel alienated.
- **Ideology**. Different values held by individuals can cause conflict, e.g. free enterprise versus the right to industrial action.
- **Psychological distance**. Workers can feel isolated from the organisation.
- **Scarce resources**. Financial resources affecting remuneration and working conditions, and costs.

Destructive and constructive conflict

Management thinking and writing has generally viewed conflict as negative, unhelpful and undesirable. However it is accepted that not all conflict is harmful and a certain degree of conflict can be positive, beneficial, desirable and often inevitable. The terms destructive and constructive conflict are used to differentiate between negative or positive outcomes.

Constructive conflict

Constructive conflict is considered useful, positive and beneficial to the organisation as it does not revolve around personality and:

- creates an environment of innovation and change
- facilitates bringing problems to the surface so that they can be dealt with
- settles and defines boundaries of authority and responsibility.

Destructive conflict

Destructive conflict tends to be ad hoc and personal:

- harmful for the organisation and its involved members
- causes alienation between groups, within groups and between individuals
- can be demoralising for those involved.

Some companies have sought to promote team spirit by creating competition between work teams. In some instances this has been successful in reducing absenteeism and bad timekeeping but, when extended to include poor productivity, working relationships have tended to deteriorate. It was found that work teams concentrate on rivalry instead of the tasks to be achieved. A group would take greater interest in impeding the progress of the competing group than in achieving a better result.

6 Managing conflict – the Thomas-Kilmann Conflict Mode Instrument

A useful framework for classifying different ways of handling conflict is the **Thomas-Kilmann Conflict Mode Instrument (TKI).** It is based on two conflict-management dimensions. These are the degree of assertiveness in pursuit of one's interests and the level of co-operation in attempting to satisfy others' interests. The strength of each of these in a particular situation can suggest the ways the conflict may be resolved, as shown:

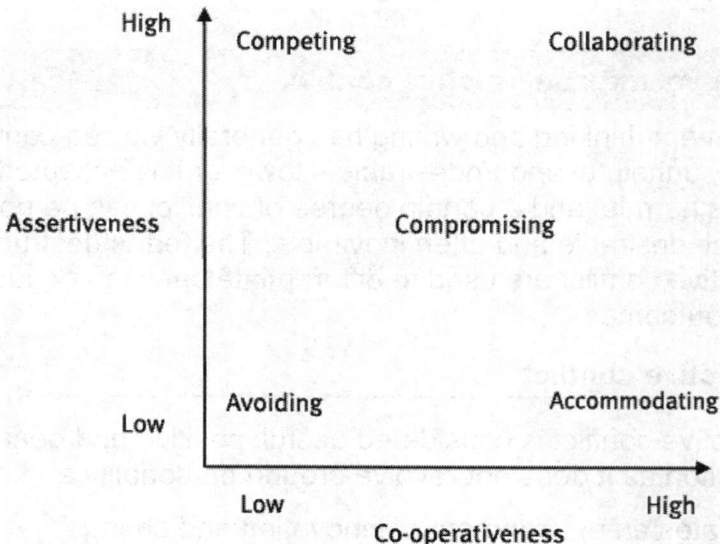

This results in five conflict-handling strategies:

- **Competing**: High assertiveness and low co-operativeness – the goal is to **'win'**. All or both parties seek to maximise their own interest and goals. They do not co-operate, creating winners and losers as well as causing damage to the organisation and one of the parties.

- **Avoiding**: Low assertiveness and low co-operativeness – the goal is to **'delay'**. One or more of the parties seeks to ignore or suppress the conflict.
- **Collaborating**: High assertiveness and high co-operativeness – the goal is to **'find a win-win solution'**. A 'win-win' situation is achieved through joint confrontation of the problem and using problem-solving techniques with creative solutions.
- **Accommodating**: Low assertiveness and high co-operativeness – the goal is to **'yield'**. One party puts the other party's interests first.
- **Compromising**: Moderate assertiveness and moderate co-operativeness – the goal is to **'find a middle ground'**. Negotiation results in each party giving up something and 'meeting half way'. The problem is each party may lose something when there may be a better alternative.

Mainwaring – Strategies for managing conflict

Mainwaring suggested four broad strategies for managing conflict in organisations:

- **Conflict stimulation and orchestration**. This approach actively **encourages conflict** as a means of generating new ideas and new approaches or of stimulating change. There are obvious dangers in generating conflict, not least that they will escalate in a destructive way. However some conflict is necessary to prevent organisations becoming fixed and unwilling to change. This approach involves the maintenance and management of constructive conflict as a means of continuous renewal.
- **Conflict suppression**. This involves the use or threatened use of authority or force, or the **avoidance of recognition that a conflict situation exists**, or smoothing over the conflict by de-emphasising the seriousness of the situation. Such strategies are essentially short-term, and are likely to be perceived as such by those involved.
- **Conflict reduction**. This involves **building on areas of agreement** and on common objectives, and changing attitudes and perceptions of the parties involved. Techniques that can be used include compromises and concessions. These can be facilitated by independent third party interventions, such as conciliation and arbitration.
- **Conflict resolution**. This seeks to **eliminate the root causes of conflict** by establishing a consensus. Attitude change is a key element, particularly regarding the possibility of 'win-win' situations where the parties involved are aware of the mutual gains to be derived from co-operation and collaboration.

The mix of strategies used will depend not only on the situation, but also on the assumptions that managers make about conflict.

Important methods to apply when dealing with organisational conflict are altering:

- the context, e.g. new procedures, reducing interdependency, changing work allocation.
- the issue in dispute by separating into smaller issues, separating people- and task- related issues.
- the proximity, i.e. physically separating the persons or groups involved.
- the individuals involved including relocation and dismissal, or changing behaviour through training or organisational development techniques.

Dealing with industrial relations conflict

Although vertical conflict can take place without the presence of trade unions, Unions highlight vertical conflict as they try to equalise power differences between workers and management where the ground rules for conflict are formalised by laws and regulations. The sources of vertical conflict reflect the reasons why workers join unions.

The first priority for representatives is loyalty to their group. These can create strategies for avoidance or individualistic approaches:

- **Union avoidance strategies** including 'double-breasting' (setting up new plants in areas of high unemployment, or low union activity), devolving collective bargaining to factory level, removing unions from annual pay rounds whilst giving the right of the union members to be consulted and represented.
- **Individualistic approaches** away from third party involvement using appraisal systems, training and development schemes, performance-related pay systems, share schemes and the same pension and health schemes for all.
- **Collective bargaining** using procedural methods (a prescribed format) ultimately leading to the substantive agreement (defining each party's rewards and responsibilities for the next two to three years) in collective negotiations between workers and management.

New approaches tend to be more co-operative including:

- **Partnership agreements**.
- **Gain sharing** based on bonuses and profit rather than fixed-rate increases.
- **Labour-management teams** based on Japanese quality circles at shop-floor levels, middle management and union leader teams, and at top management, long-term policies to avoid layoffs.
- **Employment security** rather than job security where workers are reassigned to different positions and jobs are dependent on the firm's success.

Case study style question 3

Textile company, TUV, is in a troubled state. The weavers have just been awarded a pay increase, and this has led to a claim by the mechanics, who maintain the machinery, for a similar percentage pay increase. TUV is seeking to resist the mechanics' claim on the grounds that the weavers' extra payment can be justified by increases in productivity, while the maintenance work carried out by the mechanics has not changed. The response of the mechanics has been to threaten industrial action.

The problems for TUV have been made worse by a dispute between the Weaving Department and the Cloth Inspection Department. All members of the Weaving Department receive a bonus based on the productivity of the whole department. Employees in the Cloth Inspection Department are paid a fixed salary based on proven competence and experience.

The conflict between the departments has heightened recently by the decision of the new manager of the Cloth Inspection Department to tighten up of the inspection standards. He insists that the quality of output has to improve if the company is to remain competitive. This has resulted in weaving machines standing idle more frequently than in the past while faults detected during cloth inspection are investigated.

The sight of idle machines has resulted in intense frustration among management and employees in the Weaving Department as every idle machine means a reduction in their bonus payments. The weavers' frustration is now being taken out on the Cloth Inspection Department by adopting a policy of not cooperating.

The CEO has become aware of these issues and is concerned about the effect they are having on productivity.

Required:

The CEO has asked you to write a report for him:

(a) Explaining the causes of the conflicts within TUV.

(10 minutes)

(b) Discussing how each type of conflict within TUV might be resolved.

(10 minutes)

7 Summary diagram

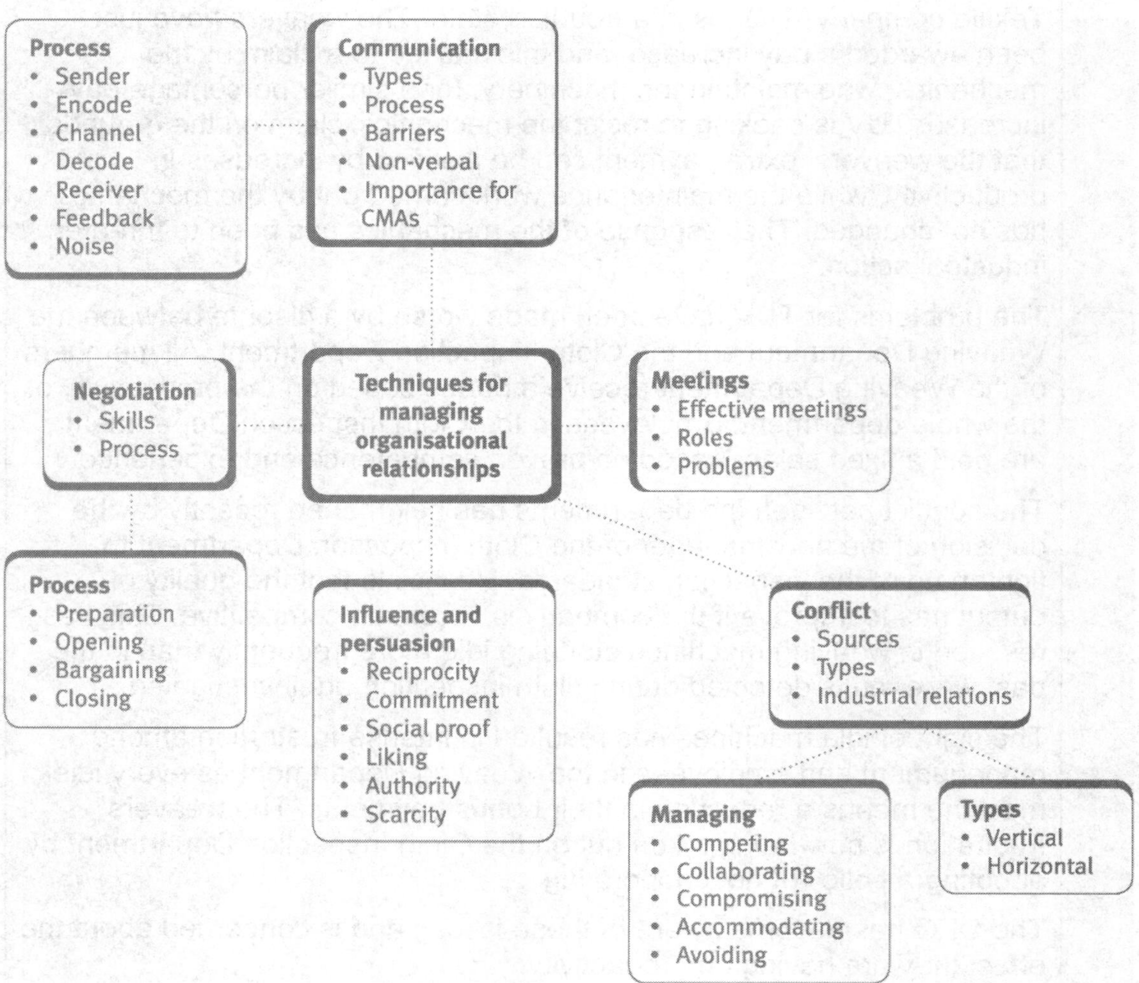

End of chapter questions

Question 1

The element in the communication process which makes it a cycle rather than a series of send-receive events is called ______________.

The process through which the message is symbolised is known as ____________________.

_____________ is anything which stops the message being received and understood as intended.

Supply the term that most accurately fills the gaps.

- Message
- Encoding
- Noise
- Feedback

Question 2

Which of the following is most likely to cause vertical conflict within an organisation?

A Psychological distance

B Goal incompatibility

C Task interdependence

D Functional specialisation

Question 3

Mainwaring suggested four strategies for managing conflict.

Match the strategy to the correct description.

Stimulation and orchestration
Suppression
Reduction
Resolution

- This approach actively encourages conflict as a means of generating new ideas and stimulating change.
- The approach seeks to eliminate the root cause of the conflict by establishing consensus.
- The approach involved building of areas of agreement and on common objectives.
- The approach involves the use, or threatened use of authority or force.

Question 4

X is trying to communicate with all the staff within his department. He has placed the information on the business intranet, but after a week very few staff members have seen the information. X has been told by several of his colleagues that they 'never really look on the intranet' and so they had failed to see X's message.

Which aspect of the communication process has caused this problem?

A X has chosen the wrong channel

B X has encoded the message poorly

C X's communication has suffered from too much noise

D X's communication has not been accurately decoded

Question 5

Match the description to the stage in the negotiation process.

Bargaining
Preparing
Closing
Opening

- Getting to know the background to the problem and the likely constraints
- Attempting to narrow the gap between the two initial positions
- Reaching agreement which is mutually beneficial
- Presenting starting positions and attempting to influence the other party

Question 6

Two key roles in a meeting are that of the chairperson and the secretary. Match the responsibilities shown to the correct role.

Chairperson	Secretary

- Ensuring all agenda items are discussed
- Preparing minutes of the meeting
- Summing up the issues discussed at the meeting
- Preparing and issuing the agenda before the meeting

Question 7

According to Cialdini, which of the following are principles of Influence. Select all that apply.

A Reciprocity

B Accountability

C Commitment

D Trust

E Assertiveness

F Authority

Question 8

Three important concepts in communication are Negotiation, Influence and Persuasion.

Match each of these to their correct definition.

- The ability to deliberately manipulate others to change an attitude, opinion, or behaviour.
- The ability to change others' attitudes, opinions or behaviour and can be direct or indirect.
- The ability to discuss an issue with one or more other people to determine ways to reach agreement and mutual satisfaction.

Question 9

The conflict management strategy recommended as a means to benefit all parties in a dispute is:

A compromising

B competing

C collaborating

D accommodating

Question 10

Place the conflict resolution strategies on the Thomas-Kilmann conflict managing grid.

- Avoiding
- Competing
- Collaborating
- Compromising
- Accommodating

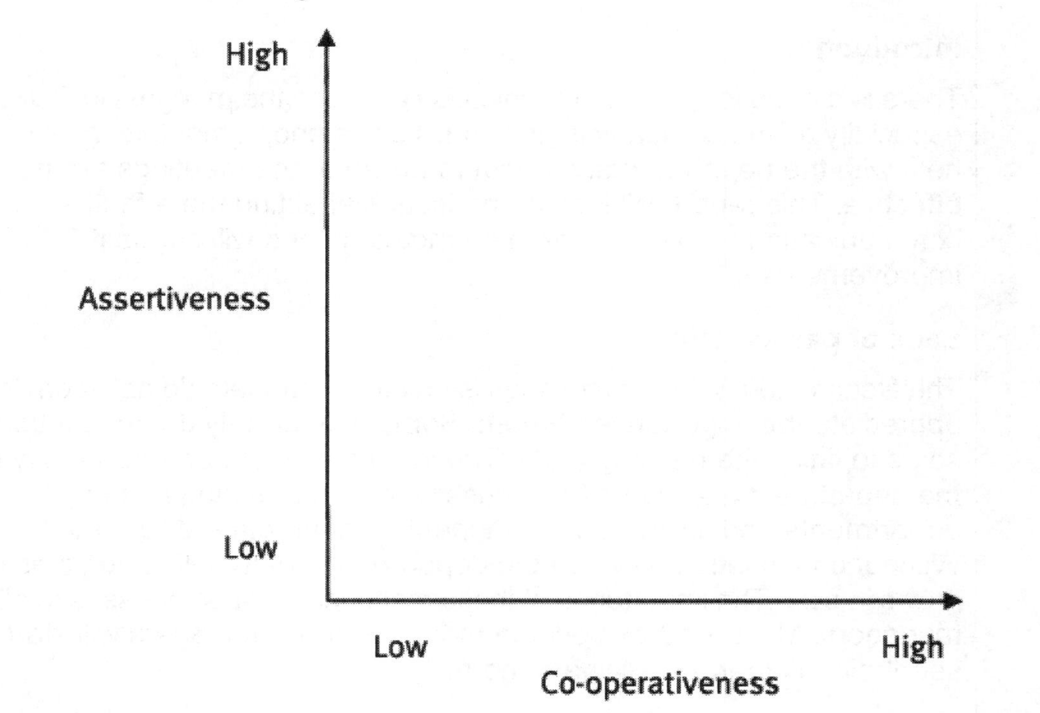

Test your understanding answers

Case study style question 1

REPORT

To: B

From: Consultant

Date: today

Subject: Management communication within PQR

Introduction

There is a need for good communication between the mangers in PQR, especially as the company is growing. To this end, a monthly meeting is held with the departmental managers however the meetings are not effective. This report will look at the issues affecting the effective communication at the management meetings and will suggest improvements.

Lack of participation

The first problem with the meetings is that the managers do not seem to appreciate the importance of them. Some deliberately do not contribute so as to finish the meeting early. These meetings are an opportunity for the department managers to discuss what is happening in their departments and learn what is happening in the other departments. Without coordination between the departments, PQR will struggle as it grows in size. The importance of these meetings must be stresses to all managers. Maybe if they become more effective, managers will start to see their value and participate more.

Non-attendance

For a meeting to be effective, the right people must attend. Every manager must attend these meetings where possible. The meetings should be scheduled at a regular time and place and managers should give priority to attending these meetings. Where a manager cannot attend, they could send a representative if this is appropriate and acceptable to the other managers, but this person should be of a senior enough level to participate in the meeting. Sending a junior member of staff is unacceptable as it would be difficult for the more junior members to talk out at the meeting. Sending a junior member shows that the operations manager does not view the meeting as important.

No agenda

Managers do not know what is going to be discussed at the meeting which suggests that there is no agenda. For a meeting to be successful, all participants must prepare for the meeting and bring along any relevant documentation. This is only possible if an agenda is drawn up and circulated in advance of the meeting. This also gives managers the opportunity to add items to the agenda which they would like discussed.

Action points not recorded

Decisions must be made at the meetings. Attendees should leave the meeting with a clear understanding of what has been agreed and any action points which they have to take away with them. It appears that there is no secretary at the meetings as nothing appears to be being recorded. A secretary should attend the meeting taking notes of proceedings and documenting decisions made. The minutes of the meeting should be sent to all attendees soon after the meeting to ensure that everyone is aware of the decisions made.

No Chairperson

There appears to be no one chairing the meetings. The sales manager is domineering and others are not contributing. A chairman should be selected to chair each meeting. The chairman must be a strong character and must be able to keep all attendees in line, they must ensure that all attendees are given the opportunity to speak at the meeting. The chair should ensure that an agenda is available for the meeting and that it is followed. This would avoid the meeting becoming unproductive and going off topic.

Conclusion

The monthly management meetings held at PQR are important in terms of communication between the managers, however a number of improvements are required in order to make this form of communication more effective.

Case study style question 2

EMAIL

To: K

From: Management Accountant

Date: today

Subject: Negotiation

Negotiation is an activity that seeks to reach agreement between two or more conflicting starting positions. The aim in any negotiation is to achieve a settlement that is acceptable to the other parties concerned but which also comes as close as possible to one's own desired outcome.

In the case of BCD the two parties involved and their objectives are as follows:

- Management is seeking to restructure the organisation to ensure business survival and long-term profitability. This will involve cutting costs through redundancies and staff relocations.
- Trade unions will represent employees' interests and will thus be acting to minimise job losses, and to enhance relocation and redundancy packages.

There is thus a clear conflict over job cuts and how much the company will pay to the employees affected. Negotiation is essential in this situation as the alternative is likely to be a strike, which would benefit neither party in the short term. Such a scenario could precipitate a collapse of the company, ultimately affecting all employees' jobs.

Most writers on negotiation argue that the aim is to achieve a 'win-win' situation where both parties feel that they have gained from the negotiation process.

Most negotiation processes go through four stages: preparation, opening, bargaining and closing. These can be applied to BCD as follows:

Preparation: The preparation stage involves each side gathering information to gain insights into the conflict. This could include trying to understand the other party's key concerns and finding out who will be involved in the negotiating process. In the case of BCD, the union will seek to understand the business case for redundancies, explore possible alternative strategies that the company could undertake and will ensure it is fully up to date on employment law. This will help it see how strong its bargaining position is.

Similarly management will try to obtain details of how many employees will be affected, their ages and likelihood of getting other jobs. For example, the option of early retirement sounds better than redundancy, even though it is still a job cut. The time for negotiation will also be agreed.

Opening: During this stage each party presents its position to the other, hoping to gain influence early on. Management will presumably want to emphasise that redundancies are inevitable to save the company. It will try to move the negotiation onto what support is given rather than whether job cuts are needed. Similarly the union may present the case that it wants to prevent any job cuts and will initially reject all management proposals in this respect.

Bargaining: During the bargaining phase both parties will try to narrow the gap between the two positions and to seek a win-win solution. Usually this will involve a degree of compromise by each party. The main focus during this phase is the ability to argue and persuade the other side that your arguments are stronger than theirs to ensure that they compromise more than you. Given the circumstances involved, it is likely that the negotiations for BCD will end up with a reduction in the overall number of planned redundancies and detailed discussion focusing on the size of redundancy payouts and the level of support for employees to gain new jobs.

Closing: The closing phase gives the opportunity to capitalise on the work done during the previous stages. During the closing phase agreement is reached and the results are publicised and implemented.

I hope you have found the above useful, please do not hesitate to contact me if you require any additional information.

Case study style question 3

REPORT

To: CEO

From: Management accountant

Date: today

Report on the conflict within TUV

Introduction

In this report, the causes of the current conflict within TUV will be explained and recommendations will be made for how each type of conflict could be resolved. The report will also cover the factors which might influence the likelihood of a successful outcome for each type of conflict.

(a) **The causes of conflict**

The conflict in TUV encompasses both vertical and horizontal conflict.

Horizontal conflict

Horizontal conflict happens between groups of staff or between departments at the same level in the hierarchy. The conflict between the Weaving Department and the Cloth Inspection Department could be classified as horizontal conflict. The cause of the conflict is due to the fact that the tightening of standards in the inspection process has had the knock-on effect of machines standing idle. This has affected the productivity of weavers and reduced their bonus payments. At a more fundamental level, there is a conflict in the goals of the Departments, the weavers are focused on producing cloth to maximise output and hence receive bonuses. On the other hand, the key objective of the Cloth Inspection Department is the quality standard of the material. The two groups are rewarded in different ways.

Vertical conflict

Vertical conflict occurs between individuals or groups who are at different levels in the hierarchy, and often arises because of status and power differences amongst groups. In the case of T, conflict has arisen between mechanics and management over status and pay. Mechanics want the same percentage pay increase as weavers but management argues that weavers can justify the increase by increasing productivity, whereas the work carried out by mechanics has not changed. This has led to industrial unrest.

(b) **Managing conflict**

A useful framework for classifying different ways of handling conflict is known as the TKI. It is based on two conflict-management dimensions. These consist of the degree of assertiveness in pursuit of one's interests and the level of cooperation in attempting to satisfy others' interests. The relative strength of each of these produces five conflict-handling strategies.

It is difficult to determine the degree of assertiveness and the level of cooperation that exist in the case of TUV, so we cannot come to a conclusion here and now but the framework does provide a useful means of considering alternatives if we can gather the necessary information.

The five conflict-handling strategies are:

Avoidance – one or more parties in conflict may seek to avoid, to suppress or to ignore the conflict. This is not recommended as it does not resolve the conflict and may break out again when the parties meet in the future.

Accommodation – this involves one party putting the other's interests first and suppressing their own interest in order to preserve some form of stability and to suppress the conflict. Again, if the causes of conflict are endemic or lasting, the accommodation strategy may not resolve the differences. Also, the accommodating party may well lose out as a result.

Compromise – often seen as the optimum solution. Each party gives something up, and a deal somewhere between the two is accepted after negotiation and debate. However, in compromise, both parties lose something and there may be a better alternative. This approach could be used to resolve the conflict between mechanics and management.

Competition – this is a state where both or all parties do not cooperate, instead they seek to maximise their own interests and goals. It creates winners and losers. The resultant conflict can prove damaging to the organisation as well as to at least one of the parties. So it is not recommended.

Collaboration – from the perspective of all parties, this is likely to be the optimum solution. Differences are confronted and jointly resolved, novel solutions are sought, and a win/win outcome is achieved. This is the proposed strategy to deal with the conflict between weavers and the cloth inspection staff.

Managing horizontal conflict

The best approach to managing horizontal conflict in TUV would be collaboration where differences are confronted and jointly resolved. The desired outcome is a win:win for both groups. This could be achieved by holding meetings between the two Departments, including the managers, weavers and inspection staff. Solutions to how quality standards could be maintained while minimising the down time of machines could be discussed. Communications between the different Departments, sharing an understanding of each other's goals and objectives should assist the process. Perhaps, the organisation could look at some of the techniques associated with total quality management in resolving the problems.

Managing vertical conflict

The vertical conflict in TUV is an example of industrial relations conflict over pay claims. This type of conflict may be resolved through negotiation between management and representatives of the mechanics through collective bargaining. The representatives of the mechanics could present a proposal for consideration by management, followed by counter-proposals and concessions.

Conclusion

The outcome will depend on the relative power held by the mechanics (for example, withdraw labour, gain support from other workers and willingness to take industrial action) and the power of management (ability to replace mechanics, ability to switch production to other factories). A win/win situation is desirable but often industrial relations conflict is resolved through compromise.

Question 1

The complete sentences are:

The element in the communication process which makes it a cycle rather than a series of send-receive events is called **feedback**.

The process through which the message is symbolised is known as **encoding**.

Noise is anything which stops the message being received and understood as intended.

Question 2

A

Psychological distance refers to the situation where workers feel isolated from the organisation.

Goal incompatibility, task interdependence and functional specialisation are all examples of horizontal conflict.

Question 3

The correct matching is:

Stimulation and orchestration – This approach actively encourages conflict as a means of generating new ideas and stimulating change.

Resolution – The approach seeks to eliminate the root cause of the conflict by establishing consensus.

Reduction – The approach involved building of areas of agreement and on common objectives.

Suppression – The approach involves the use, or threatened use of authority or force.

Question 4

A

The channel is the medium through which the message is sent. It is important for the sender to select the correct channel to ensure the message gets through to the receiver as expected.

Question 5

The correct matching is:

Bargaining – Attempting to narrow the gap between the two initial positions

Preparing – Getting to know the background to the problem and the likely constraints

Closing – Reaching agreement which is mutually beneficial

Opening – Presenting starting positions and attempting to influence the other party

Question 6

The correct matching is:

Chairperson	Secretary
Ensuring all agenda items are discussed Summing up the issues discussed at the meeting	Preparing minutes of the meeting Preparing and issuing the agenda before the meeting

Question 7

A, C and F

The other principles of influence are:

- Social proof
- Liking
- Scarcity

Question 8

The correct definitions are:

Negotiation – The ability to discuss an issue with one or more other people to determine ways to reach agreement and mutual satisfaction.

Influence – The ability to change others' attitudes, opinions or behaviour and can be direct or indirect.

Persuasion – The ability to deliberately manipulate others to change an attitude, opinion, or behaviour.

Question 9

C

The approaches of competing, collaborating, compromising, accommodating and avoiding come from the Thomas-Kilmann conflict mode instrument. The collaborating approach attempts to find a win-win solution.

Question 10

The complete diagram is shown below:

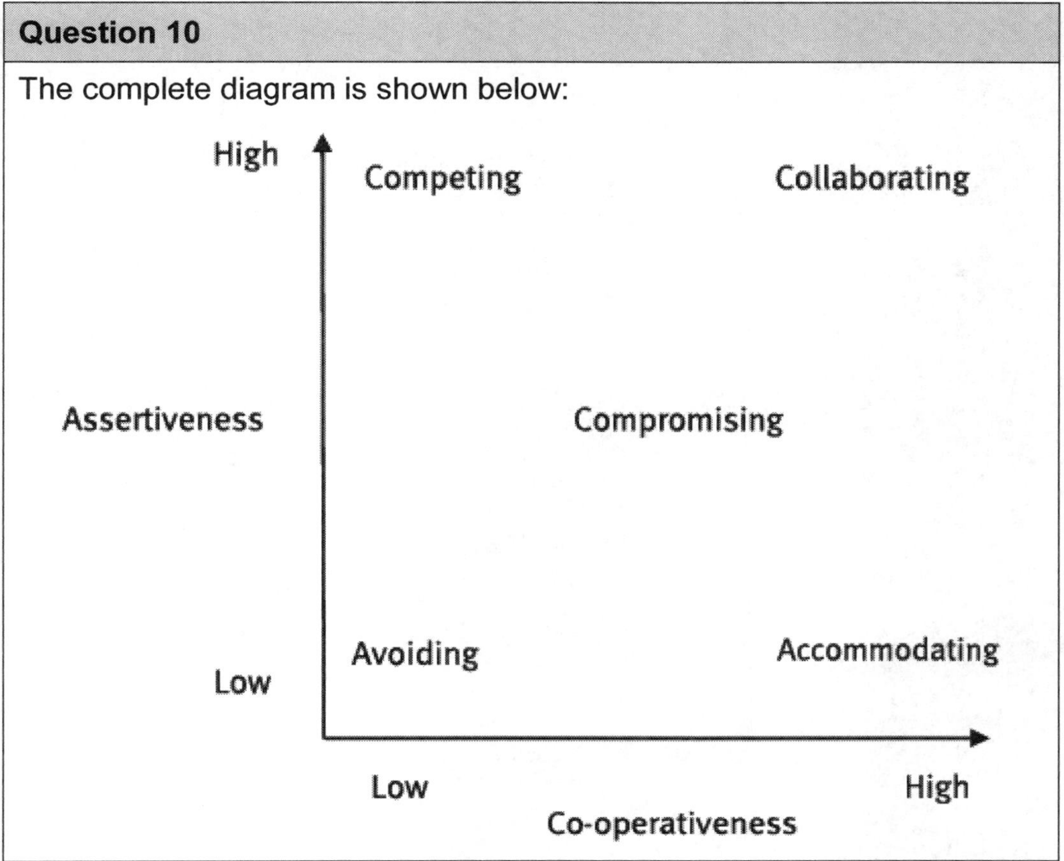

Chapter

9

The concept of project management

Chapter learning objectives

Lead	Component
C1: Describe the concepts and phases of projects	(a) Project objectives (b) Key stages of the project life cycle (c) Project control

Topics to be covered

- Overall project objectives
- Objectives relating to time, cost and quality
- Purpose and activities associated with key stages of the project life cycle.

1 Session content diagram

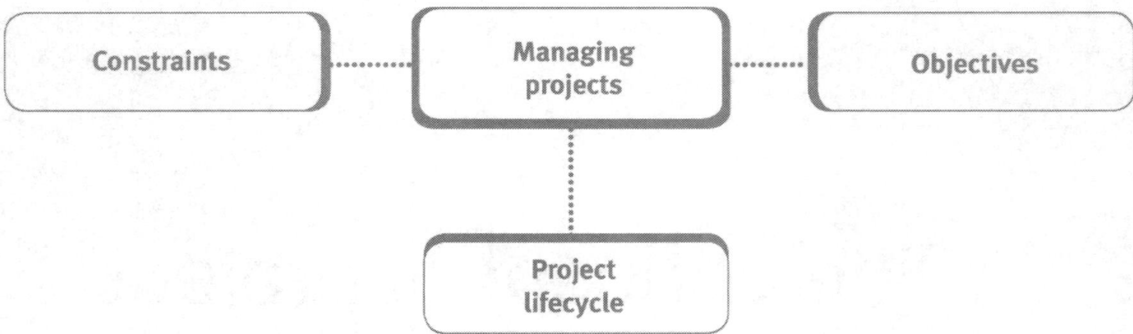

2 The importance of project management in delivering change

From the previous chapter it is clear that change is an inevitable part of today's organisations. Effectively managing this change is therefore critical to the ongoing success of the organisation and will be discussed as part of your Strategic Management (E3) studies.

Change will be delivered through projects, therefore understanding project management and being able to successfully complete projects is essential for organisations.

This and the following chapters cover the project management process in detail.

3 A project and project management

Project

A project has a number of key attributes which differentiates it from business as usual:

A project is a **unique** undertaking to achieve a specific **objective**.

A project has a **defined beginning and end**.

A project has **resources**, like staff and funding allocated specifically for the length of the project.

The project will also have **stakeholders**, i.e. all those who are interested in the progress and final outcome of the project.

A project will inevitably have some degree of **uncertainty** as the uniqueness of it will lead to some degree of risk in the deliverables and the activities to achieve the deliverables.

Once completed, it should then become integrated into the normal day-to-day activities of the business.

The Association of Project Managers defines a project as: **'A human activity that achieves a clear objective against a time scale.'**

Project management

Project management is the managing of the work of a team or teams to achieve specific goals and objectives. The teams will be put together for the sole purpose of achieving the project goals and objectives and will be disbanded after the completion of the project. The teams will be managed by the project manager who will make all of the day to day decisions in relation to the project and who is ultimately responsible for the successful completion of the project. The project manager will report to the project sponsor, who initiates the project, makes all of the high level decisions regarding the project and who provides the funding for the project.

The roles of these project stakeholders will be looked at in detail in the project leadership chapter.

Projects may run for anything from a few weeks to many years depending on their size and complexity. The process of project management however is very similar in all projects regardless of size or duration and it differs greatly from the process of business as usual management which generally consists of a long line of repetitive or similar functions stretching ahead indefinitely.

CIMA's ® *Official Terminology defines* project management as **'the integration of all aspects of a project, ensuring that the proper knowledge and resources are available when and where needed, and above all to ensure that the expected outcome is produced in a timely, cost-effective manner.'**

Project objectives

Project management objectives serve a very specific purpose. They break down the key steps to achieving overall project success. Project objectives also let project teams know what they should be focused on, what they should devote resources to, and how their activities serve wider business and organisational goals.

The main reason why effective objectives are important is that the clearer the objectives are, the more likely they are to be achieved. In addition, the project will be that much easier to manage.

Project objectives must be measurable and contain key performance indicators that will be used to assess a project's overall success. These indicators will often include criteria such as budget, quality, and time to completion.

Objectives are crucial as they provided a way to structure the project and validate its success. Therefore, the more effective the objectives, the more successful the project.

4 Project constraints

Every project has constraints. Constraints are anything which restricts, limits, prevents or regulates activities being carried out. When running a project it is critical that the constraints are known, so they can be taken account of throughout the project.

The primary constraints are **time, cost** and **quality**. These are often referred to as the 'project triangle'.

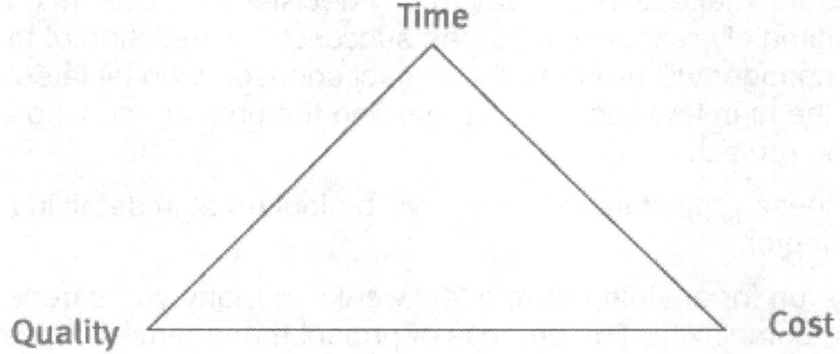

It is worth thinking about the conflicting nature of these constraints.

Time and cost tend to be positively correlated in projects (i.e. when time increases, so does cost), as taking longer to complete a project generally means that human resources are needed for longer. However, this is not always the case. If there is a degree of urgency in a project, it may be possible to reduce the timescale to completion by allocating additional resources, or by scheduling expensive overtime working. Both of these situations will increase cost while reducing time.

Project quality tends to be positively correlated with both cost and time, in that increasing the quality of the project will normally lead to an increase in both the cost of the project and its overall duration.

In additional to these three main constraints, there are a number of other constraints which will affect the project's delivery, such as legal, technological, political, environmental and ethical.

5 The project life cycle

Large-scale projects usually follow a life cycle made up of separate phases, which occur in sequence. There are a number of models which detail these phases. Regardless of which model is used, it is important to highlight the separate stages which the project goes through from beginning to end, and to understand what happens during each stage. A project life cycle is shown below:

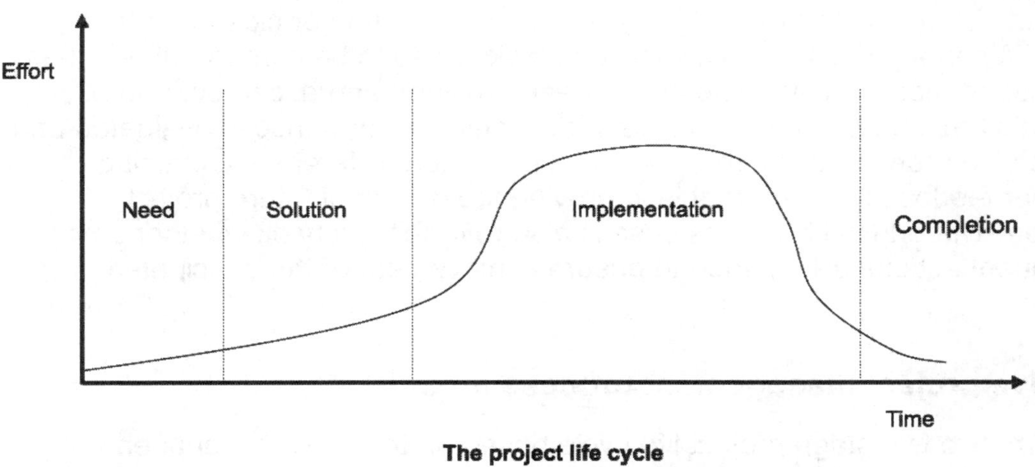

The project life cycle

Stages in the project life cycle

Gido and Clements identified four phases of large projects

Phase 1 – Identification of a need

The first phase of the project life cycle involves identification of a need, opportunity or problem. Initially, a feasibility study will be conducted to check the size of potential benefits and evaluate in broad outline potential alternative solutions and their lifetime costs. At the end of this phase, the company will decide whether to proceed with the project. If it does, then a project team is formed and a **project initiation document** (PID) is raised. This will include a vision and a business case for the project. The business case is an important guide to decision-making throughout the project, and the vision encourages motivation and congruent goals in the project team.

Phase 2 – Development of a proposed solution

The second stage of the project life cycle is the development of a proposed solution. All proposals for the solution will be submitted and evaluated and the most appropriate solution to satisfy the need will be selected.

Phase 3 – Implementation

The third stage of the project life cycle is the implementation of the proposed solution. This phase is the actual performance of the project and will involve doing the detailed planning, and then implementing that plan to accomplish the project objective.

The overall solution is subdivided into separate deliverables to be achieved at fixed points (milestones) throughout this stage of the project. Achievement of these deliverables may be linked to stage payments. The project's objectives of functionality, quality, cost and time are monitored regularly against each deliverable to ensure they are being met. Timely appropriate action can then be taken if any slippage has occurred.

Phase 4 – Completion

The fourth stage of the project life cycle is the completion or closure of the project. When a project closes, important tasks need to be carried out, such as confirmation that all deliverables have been provided and accepted, and all payments have been made and received. Project performance is evaluated and appraised in order to learn from the project for future reference. Obtaining customer feedback is important in improving the quality of future project provision. The original business case is also revisited to check whether any subsequent actions are needed to ensure achievement of the anticipated benefits.

6 Five project management process areas

An alternative five stage project life cycle based on the Project Management Institute's 5 Project Management Process Areas identifies the stages as:

- Initiating
- Planning
- Executing (implementing)
- Controlling
- Closing.

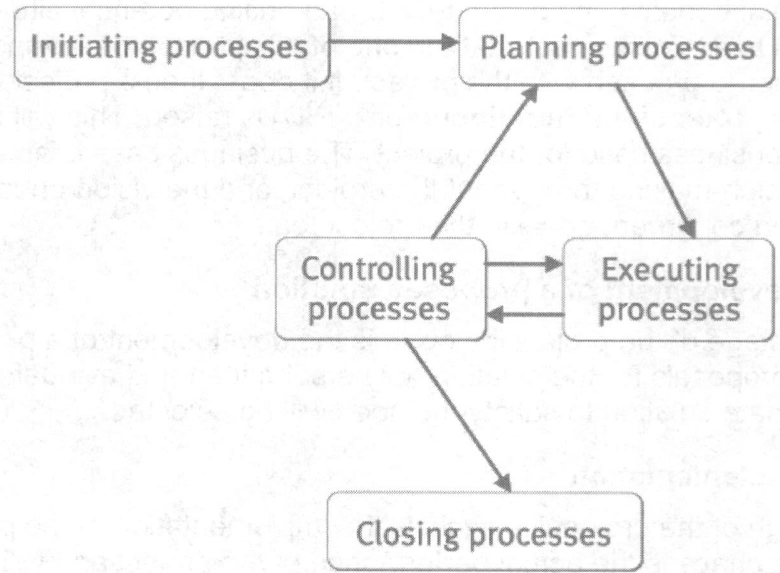

This model is very similar to the **Gido and Clements** project life cycle above. However, it places greater emphasis on the 'planning' and 'controlling' activities, as is to be expected from a professional project management institute.

It is important to understand the purpose of each stage of the project life cycle and the activities which are carried out at each stage. Each of the stages will now be looked at in detail.

7 Initiating

Projects are initiated when a need or objective is defined.

Objectives are those things that the organisation wants to achieve. Typically, top-level objectives are profit-oriented, or in not-for-profit organisations objectives will be to improve the standard of living or education, and so on of members. It is usually a function of the board of directors to determine the high-level organisational objectives.

There are a number of reasons why a project would be initiated:

- To help meet the company's long term goals and objectives.
- Process/service enhancement.
- Solve problems identified internally or externally.
- To take advantage of new opportunities.
- Statutory/legal requirement.

Companies may have a number of potential projects they would like, or need to undertake, but they may not have the resources to carry them all out. They often have to go through a selection process to establish the most worthwhile projects. The purpose of the initiation stage is to identify the most worthwhile projects to undertake. Only these projects will be taken forward to the planning stage.

One of the main ways companies select the most worthwhile projects is by considering the **feasibility** of the proposed projects and the **risk and uncertainty** relating to the project.

Feasibility

The development of any new project requires careful consideration and planning. It will consume large volumes of resources, both financial and non-financial, and is likely to have a major effect on the way in which the organisation will operate.

Feasibility studies may be carried out on a number of potential strategies and the aim of the study is to decide on which proposal to choose.

Sometimes the potential project manager is involved in the feasibility study stage of a project, but not always. However, it is important for project managers to understand the process of feasibility assessment.

Types of feasibility

There are a number of types of feasibility which could be considered, including the following:

- Technical feasibility
- Social (operational) feasibility
- Ecological (environmental) feasibility
- Economic (financial) feasibility.

Technical feasibility – can it be done?

There are a number of key aspects regarding technology which must be considered, for example:

- Is the technology available?
- Is the technology tried and tested?
- What performance do we require of the technology?
- Is the technology suitable to satisfy the objective of the project effectively?

Social (operational) feasibility – does it fit with current operations?

It is becoming increasingly necessary to assess operational/social factors affecting feasibility. These may include awareness of the social issues within a group or office (e.g. introducing a computerised system), or larger social awareness regarding the effect of projects or products on workers, employment or the environment. It is also important to ensure that the projects fits with business goals.

Social considerations include:

- Number of people required (during the project and after implementation).
- Skills required – identify recruitment, training, redundancy.

Some of these issues can be directly costed (such as training costs). Others have less tangible effects that must be documented in the feasibility report.

Ecological (environmental) feasibility – how does it affect the environment?

Ecological considerations may be driven by the understanding that customers would prefer to purchase alternative products or services as they are more ecologically sound and less harmful to the environment.

Ecological considerations include:

- Effects on local community and what that might do to company image.
- What pollution could be caused by the project?

Economic (financial) feasibility – is it worth it?

The project (proposed system) must provide a benefit to the organisation. Economic feasibility will be assessed through a cost-benefit analysis. Cost-benefit analysis helps to identify and evaluate the costs of the proposal over its anticipated life. The other side to cost-benefit is the identification and evaluation of the benefits of the project over its life.

Cost-benefit analysis

When considering economic feasibility, the benefits and the costs of the project must be considered in detail.

Financial costs and benefits can be evaluated using investment appraisal techniques such as payback and discounted cash flow approaches like NPV or IRR.

You would not rely on a single measure to determine the financial feasibility of a project.

The types of costs and benefits involved in a project will depend upon the precise nature and scope of that project and can vary greatly.

Benefits

- Tangible – those benefits that can be evaluated financially (reduction of staff costs when processes are automated).
- Intangible – those benefits that are not easy to evaluate financially (a new computer system may provide better information to managers for decision making and control).

Remember that any intangible benefits will have been excluded in the financial evaluation process.

Costs

- Capital Costs – costs incurred in the acquisition of assets plus any additional costs of installation and maintenance.
- Revenue Costs – any costs other than for the purchase of assets. These costs are incurred on a regular basis and include repairs and consumables.
- Finance Costs – finance costs are usually incurred as interest charges. Sources of finance include banks, shareholders, retained profit from the business and grants or subsidies from the government.

Illustration 1 – Feasibility

We will use the following example to explain the types of feasibility:

RST, a manufacturer of car components, operates from a large industrial site in V town where it is the largest local employer. RST is well respected in the town, and have always stated their commitment to the town and their employees. The current site is too small for the company's current needs and is in need of some upgrading. As such the board have been considering alternative courses of action to expand the current site.

Last week the board of RST was approached with an offer to buy their current site for a substantial sum of money from a neighbouring mining company who have plans to develop the site as an open cast mine. As part of the deal, the mining company have offered to build RST a new factory on land they own in H town, about 150 miles from RST's current site. The board of RST are considering all aspects of the offer including the project to build the new factory.

Technical feasibility – can it be done?

For RST, this may involve considerations such as the ability to set up a fully functioning factory in H town. Given the nature of RST's business, this may involve the moving and installation of large pieces of equipment. It will also have to be considered if all utilities required will be available at the new site, the ability to get planning permissions and so on. It seems likely that the project will be technically feasible.

Social (operational) feasibility – does it fit with current operations?

For RST, they may have difficulty with the social and operational feasibility of the project. It will mean moving from V town where they are a respected employer (and the largest local employer) and the move will result in many people losing their jobs. It is unclear how many jobs the mining operation would bring to the area, but it unlikely that the mining company would be able to take on all of those affected by the move. It would seem that the project would not be socially feasible.

Ecological (environmental) feasibility – how does it affect the environment?

For RST, there are some environmental implications of the proposal. Firstly, for V Town, they would be losing a factory but gaining an open cast mine. This could have large adverse implications for the local environment. On the other hand, the new factory operated by RST is likely to be more efficient and have less impact on the environment than the old factory, but the overall impact on the environment is likely to be adverse. How RST's board feel about this will depend on their view of social responsibility. They have always stated their commitment to V town, but if the plan goes ahead they will cause unemployment and environmental damage to the area.

Economic (financial) feasibility – is it worth it?

For SMK, the cost of the project will include the cost of planning and building the new factory. The costs will also include kitting out the new factory and they will have to consider the employment costs. A number of current employees will not be able to move to work at the new site, therefore SMK may face redundancy costs and they will also incur costs in hiring and training a new workforce for the new factory. The costs will be high but a substantial sum of money will be received from the sale of their existing site.

Benefits should derive from the business case that identified the need to expand the current factory in the first place (e.g. capital growth, increased equity, increased capacity and income, profits). It seems likely that the project would be economically feasible.

Project initiation document (PID)

The main output of the initiation stage of the project is the project initiation document (PID). There are two primary reasons for having a PID:

1. To secure authorisation of the project.
2. To act as a base document against which project progress and changes can be assessed.

The PID can be used to ensure that the project team and project stakeholders are in general agreement about the nature of the project and exactly what it is trying to achieve.

This document therefore:

- Defines the project and its scope.
- Justifies the project.
- Secures funding for the project, if necessary.
- Defines the roles and responsibilities of project participants.
- Gives people the information they need to be productive and effective right from the start.

Contents of a project initiation document (PID)

There is no set format required for a PID but it would generally contain the following sections:

- **Purpose statement** – explains why the project is being undertaken.
- **Scope statement** – puts boundaries to the project by outlining the major activities. This section is important in preventing 'scope creep', where additional activities are added making achievement of the cost and time objectives totally impossible.
- **Deliverables** – tend to be tangible elements of the project, such as reports, assets and other outputs.
- **Cost and time estimates** – it is a good idea to start with some feel for the organisation's expectations in terms of the project budget. These estimates will be modified later in the project, but are necessary to give a starting point for planning.
- **Objectives** – a clear statement of the mission, CSFs and key milestones of the project.
- **Stakeholders** – a list of the major stakeholders in the project and their interest in the project.
- **Chain of command** – a statement (and diagram) of the project organisation structure.

8 Planning

After the initiation stage comes the detailed planning stage.

The planning stage of a project is essential as it helps to:

- Communicate what has to be done, when and by whom.
- Encourage forward thinking.
- Provide the measures of success for the project.
- Make clear the commitment of time, resources (people and equipment), and money required for the project.
- Determine if targets are achievable.
- Identify the activities the resources need to undertake.

During the planning stage, a number of separate detailed plans will be drawn up. For example, separate plans for:

- **Time**. The time plan lists all the activities and how long each is planned to take. This includes the finish dates of each stage of the project life cycle, and the estimated completion date of the whole project.
- **Quality**. The quality plan includes identification of the project's customers, the key outcomes each expects and the acceptance criteria that have been agreed with them. This may include safety and security planning. It will also include an audit plan for the project management process.
- **Resources**. The resource plan checks peaks and troughs of workload to ensure the human resources plan is feasible. It also lists all purchases required for the project.
- **Contingency**. Contingency planning was mentioned earlier and includes deciding on what additional activities, costs and time need to be added to the plan to ensure a reliable budget and completion date. A risk register will identify contingency plans for each of the key risks and allocates responsibility for monitoring each.
- **Cost**. The cost plan uses a rate per hour for each activity in the time plan, plus cost of purchases from the resource plan, plus contingency costs to create a budget for the project. This will be phased over the project to provide a detailed cash flow forecast.
- **Communication**. The communication plan identifies the key people in the project, their likely concerns, messages needed, planned method of communication and who will be responsible.
- **Deliverables**. The deliverables plan will detail exactly what has been agreed as the deliverables of the project. This must be agreed by the users and sponsors at the outset of the project.

The project manager and planning

It is important to understand the responsibilities of the project manager within the planning stage. Their primary responsibility is to **define the project objective** clearly with the customer, then to **communicate** this objective to the rest of the project team, making it clear what constitutes a **successful project outcome**.

The project manager should involve the team members in the planning process, as this will encourage involvement, commitment and ownership of the project.

A project reporting information system should be set up to record and monitor the progress of the project against the plan. The comparisons between actual and plan should be communicated to team members on a regular basis. Responsibility structures may be used (i.e. ensuring that team members receive information on their own area of influence), but this must be carefully weighed against ensuring that project team members do not forget that their particular area of control is likely to affect other areas and will ultimately affect the overall achievement of the whole project objective.

Examples of project planning

A project is to be undertaken to upgrade the computer system of EFG, a company which deals with examination results. The deadline for completion is 30 September 20X7. Key personnel in the project are the project manager, H and J (EFG's IT manager). As the system will deal with examination results, security of the system will be critical.

The plan below would be issued to stakeholders such as corporate management, customers and the project team. There may be 'commercial-in-confidence' elements in it that would only be shown to the senior management. **There are no set layouts or contents of management plans.** Some illustrative examples have been used.

Section title	Contents
Overview or summary	Project objectives; organisation of the project team; schedule of work; resources required including the budget and an assessment of significant risks.
Project name	For example, project for the upgrade of a computer system for EFG.
Project players and responsibility	The project authorisation document will identify roles and responsibilities such as the project board, the project manager, and the project team. For example: H, Project Manager. Responsible for: initiating the project; selecting the project team; preparing and implementing plans; managing the successful delivery of the project to time, cost and quality applications.
Project objectives	For example, to design and implement an upgraded examination system for EFG, the customer, maintaining pre-existent standards but catering for an increase in candidate applications.
Project scope and contract	This is identified in the project authorisation document. Reasons for undertaking this project, what is to be achieved in terms of the deliverables (e.g. the completion of the contract with all user training by 30 September 20X7 at a cost of $x).
Methodology	The project team will use project management techniques consistent with accepted UK standards.
Assumptions	These may refer to site access, costs of supplies, the cost of borrowing money, inflation, the availability of particular staff and so on. A major assumption for the project is that the system is accessible in the quiet period between major application periods or examination dates.

Technical plan	The technical features of the project are identified. They will include requirements, specifications, system diagrams, site plans, tools, techniques, support functions, standards and any relevant document relating to the provision of the new exam administration system. In-house or subcontracted provision of modules will be specified.
Quality and management	The quality plan identifies our customer, EFG, the key outcomes it expects, acceptance criteria agreed, a test plan of how each outcome is to be tested, and responsibility for each test. Safety and security planning will be essential, as this system must be 100% secure. An audit plan will be included.
Communication plan	This will identify the key stakeholders in the project, what their interest in the project is and their concerns that will need to be addressed, what communication is planned and the responsible person. In our project, H will be responsible for communicating with J on a weekly basis to update her on the progress and to tackle any concerns she has. Monthly status projects, monthly resource reports (financial – critical to this project – and human resource reports) will be issued and any milestones will be reported on in writing. Should any critical status reports be needed, they will be made outside the weekly meeting.
Organisation and personnel	The organisation plan describes the structure of the project team and each person's responsibilities. Included will be any sub-contract staff and staff from EFG with any input to the project. Organisation charts will be drafted by position if staff need to be recruited. If so, recruitment methods, sources and training required will be identified with start times. In our project, we need to recruit one extra software engineer to bespoke the application.
Project schedule	This will describe the main phases of the project and highlight all key milestones. It is usually illustrated by a Gantt chart or with a network diagram. (these will be covered in the next chapter).

Resources and facilities including budget breakdown	This includes checks on peaks and troughs of workload to ensure the plan is feasible and to ensure procurement is achieved by the provision of lists. The cost plan will give a rate per hour for all work and the costs of purchases. Contingency costs are included to give the project budget. Time phasing will give a cash flow forecast. EFG has made it clear that no extra project money will be available, so H must ensure as much as possible that his costings and time/resources management are accurately assessed. The contracting company will be bearing the risk of overrun and any other contingencies.
Risk assessment and risk management	The risks are identified and contingency plans made, including extra activities and cost and time buffers to be added to ensure reliable budget and completion date. The risk register identifies each contingency plan for each key risk and allocates responsibility for monitoring. In the project, unauthorised access to candidate details or results is the greatest outcome risk. Security must be 100%. This may mean that the best encryption software will be needed for online applications. There will be cost implications which H has taken account of. He must also make contingency costing in line with his contingency plans.
Acceptance	The project manager will submit the final system for acceptance to the customer, in our example EFG. It may sign off the project or return it with a specific statement of requirements that will make it acceptable. Acceptance will be in writing. The managing director of EFG will sign off the project with J.
Change management	Details of how changes will be handled throughout the project will be specified, for example requests for change may be initiated by H or J. These will be reviewed and approved by the project board with decisions in writing.

Project constraints – time, cost and quality

Project constraints were discussed earlier in the chapter. It was highlighted that the successful accomplishment of the project objective is usually constrained by three main factors: time, cost and quality. Recognising these, and the other constraints the project faces, is critical at the detailed planning stage as these constraints, and their inter-relationships, will have to be taken into account within each part of the project plan.

Project time

The schedule is the timetable for activities involved in achieving the project objective. The project will have a finite date for completion, either set by the customer or negotiated and agreed upon with the customer. For example, planning a wedding will require organisation of all activities to occur at a specific time and on a specific date.

Project cost

The cost is the amount the customer agrees to pay for the final project or product. The project cost is based on the budget, which includes a cost estimate of the resources that will be used in the project. This will include salaries of the people working on the project, project materials, equipment purchase or hire, subcontractors' or consultants' costs and facilities costs.

Quality (customer satisfaction)

The objective of any project is to complete the project within the budget and by the agreed date to the customers' satisfaction and quality requirements. It is important to ensure that prior to the project planning the project team has a clear understanding of the customer specifications and requirements, that the customer is kept informed of project progress throughout the project life, and that the plan includes progressive testing to ensure that quality requirements are fully met. Quality in computer systems can be measured in the number and type of errors ('bugs') it still contains, response times, fitness for purpose (i.e. matches the business process it is intended to support) and so on.

Another important constraint is **scope/functionality**.

The scope of the project is all of the work that must be carried out to satisfy the project's objective. The customer will expect the work to be carried out to completion and that there is nothing expected which is missing. For example, when building a house the project scope will include clearing the land, building the house and landscaping, all within the agreed quality standards expected by the customer. Leaving windows or walls unfinished, a hole in the roof, or a garden full of rubble, will be unlikely to satisfy the customer! In computer systems, the scope is often defined by all the functions that the system is expected to fulfil.

Project scope tends to be positively correlated with both cost and time, in that increasing the number of tasks to be performed within the project will normally lead to an increase in both the cost of the project and its overall duration. Managing variations to scope is one of the most complex aspects of project management. The manager must ensure that every time the customer asks for a change or addition to the scope of the project, the customer is informed of (and 'signs off') the cost and time consequences of that change. Such changes should also be fully recorded and documented to avoid arguments about what changes were required and authorised.

9 Executing and controlling

Once the project plan has been developed and agreed by the customer and project team, the project can commence. At this stage, the project manager must provide leadership and co-ordination to the project team members and other stakeholders with the aim of successfully delivering the project objectives. This is the stage where stakeholders need to be focused upon the project tasks and the project team will perform the tasks they are responsible for, as and when scheduled in the plan.

This stage can be weeks, months or years long.

The executing stage is closely linked with the controlling stage.

Configuration management and change control

Change is an inevitable part of any project and it must be managed carefully during the execution stage.

Change control

Change may arise from internal or external factors, and can often change the outcome of the project. It is therefore important to have an agreed **change management process** in place so that everyone involved in the project is aware of how change will be managed.

Change can be required at all stages of the project, very often during the execution phase as new factors emerge. It is important that the initial project documents, such as the PID and the detailed project plan, remain as 'baselines' so that all changes can be carefully monitored and controlled.

A change control process is not to stop change happening, but to ensure that the changes, which will inevitably be required during the project, are agreed and communicated to all parties before they are implemented.

Problems if change is not managed:

- Team members may be working to the old plans which do not incorporate the changes. This can mean wasted time on aspects which may no longer be relevant.
- The project is unlikely to deliver the set objectives if change is not well managed.
- End users will be unhappy at the final product if their expectations have not been managed throughout the project and they have not been advised of changes.
- The project may end up costing more as costs may continue to be incurred on aspects of the project which are no longer required, but that team members were unaware of.
- It can cause confusion and conflict for the project stakeholders.

Change process

At the outset of the project a change management process must be agreed. It should include the following:

- **Method for prioritising changes requested**. Changes requested will range from:
  - **Must be done**. Without these changes the project cannot succeed, to
  - **Nice to have**. These are changes requests suggesting enhancements to the current project plan. Not all changes of this nature are able to be incorporated into the final project.
- **Authorisation for changes**. It must be agreed who has the authority to agree to changes. This may be set as a sliding scale whereby the project manager is able to authorise small, low cost changes, but larger changes must be authorised at the highest level, for example the project committee or the project sponsor.
- **Agreement of a change budget**. It is likely that changes will result in additional cost to the project. A change budget may be set up for this purpose to avoid the project sponsor having to authorise every dollar of additional spend.
- **Recording of changes**. A set procedure should be agreed for how all changes are to be recorded and who will manage this procedure.
- **Communication of changes**. The change management process must specify how changes to the project will be communicated to all interested parties.

Configuration management

Configuration management is an important element within projects. It involves tracking and controlling all aspects of the project and all documentation and deliverables from the project. The configuration management system for a project will specify how all aspects of the project are to be managed.

Included in configuration management will be:

- Version control for documentation
- Ownership and responsibility for documentation
- Authorisation and tracking procedures for any changes required to documentation
- Monitoring and control procedure to ensure only authorised documents and records are held
- Access control over project records.

The change control process discussed above will be part of the configuration management system.

Without configuration management, several versions of documents or product may be being used and no one will be aware of which is the correct version. It also helps to ensure that the project runs smoothly, even when key personnel are unavailable.

Throughout the execution stage of the project the project manager is responsible for monitoring and controlling its progress towards successful completion. The most important aspect of project control is ensuring that monitoring progress is carried out and reported on a regular basis.

Effective project control will involve a system to regularly gather data on actual project progress, costs and performance, and compare these against the project plan. If a deviation is discovered (such as overspending or taking longer than anticipated), and the project manager considers that corrective action needs to be taken, the project manager must:

- report the deviation
- obtain authorisation if necessary
- take corrective action to get the project back on track.

A regular project reporting period should be set up (e.g. daily, weekly or monthly), depending on the complexity or duration of the project. More complex projects are likely to require more frequent progress assessment and reporting.

What are the main purposes of a control system?

- Prevention of deviations.
- Correction of deviations.
- Prevention of any future deviations, by revising plans, target, measures etc.
- Implementation of recommendations from monitoring, reviewing and evaluating the project.

A project control system (Gido and Clements) is shown below:

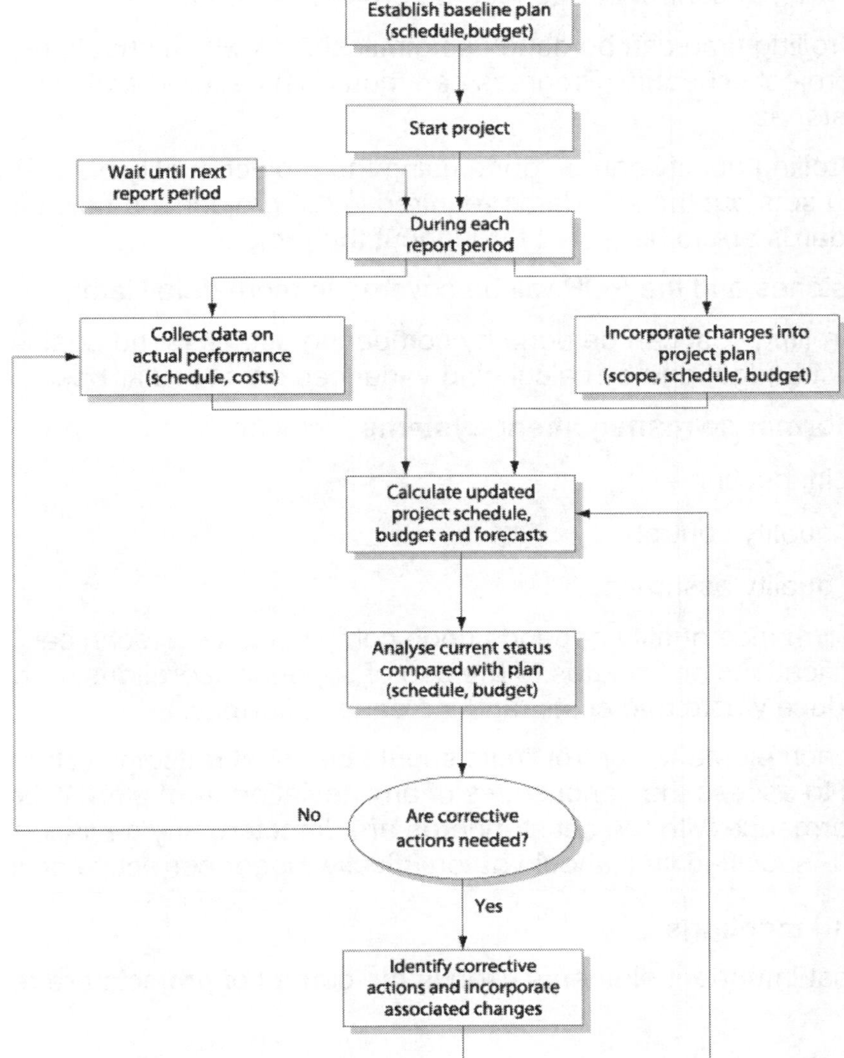

How elaborate a control system is depends on the size and scope of the task to be managed, as well as the size and distribution of the team working on it.

Performance and conformance management

Performance management

Performance management is required throughout the project in order to assess the progress of each aspect of the project.

Measurement to assess performance can include:

- Scope performance measures
- Functional quality measures
- Technical quality performance measures
- Client satisfaction measures.

The main project constraints of time, cost and quality are especially important to control throughout the project.

Controlling time can be done using milestones which should be built into the project schedule. Progress can then be measured against these milestones.

Controlling quality can be done using the project quality plan (PQP) which sets out the standards required in the project and how these standards are to be tested throughout the project.

Milestones and the PQP will be covered in more detail later.

Controlling cost can be done by comparing actual spend against the project budget and by calculating variances on a regular basis.

Conformance management systems focus on:

- inspection
- quality control
- quality assurance.

Conformance quality depends upon compliance with technical specifications and relates to the use of superior operations management to reduce waste and costs, and increase uniformity.

For each element, control limits should be set at outset which can be used to assess the seriousness of any deviation from plan. Where non-conformance with the set standards are detected, any deviation larger than a specified limit should automatically trigger corrective action.

Reports and meetings

The two most important elements used in the control of projects are reports and meetings.

Project reports

To enhance and facilitate the communication of control and progress throughout the life of the project, the following main reports are produced:

Exception reports

This is when everything is in accordance with the plan. Only exceptions are reported.

Progress reports

Both formal and regular, these note what has happened in the report period and the project status to date. It normally includes:

- Status against plan in terms of cost, timetable, and scope.
- Status and progress of resolving issues identified to date.
- New issues.

- Corrective action plan. (Corrective action requires consideration of alternatives before implementation. For instance, adding extra resources in order to get a project back on time will incur extra costs and may therefore overrun the project budget. The project manager needs to consider very carefully the implications of any corrective action upon the project scope, budget and schedule).
- Expected achievement of milestones before next report.
- Next report date.

Reports from the project manager to the project board should be made on a regular and frequent basis. In most projects, written reports are made monthly, with a major summary report quarterly (or on completion of a life cycle stage). These reports should have a standard format, both within and between projects, so the recipients become familiar with their content. Areas covered by the report would obviously focus on progress in terms of cost, scope, and time, with any anticipated variances from plan highlighted.

Project meetings

Regular meetings are an essential part of control within a project. As well as communicating the progress of the project, they can also enhance relationships with the project team and with other stakeholders.

The main meetings which should be held throughout the project are:

Team meetings

The project manager should hold regular meetings with the members of the project team. These may be formal or informal and may be held periodically or when a specific issue needs to be resolved.

Team meetings can foster good working relationships with the project manager and the members of the project team and also between the team members.

Regular team meetings ensure that all team members are aware of the progress of the project and any issues which have arisen.

Project progress review meetings

These are regular, formal meetings involving the project manager, team members, and the customer or steering committee.

In many projects, such a meeting might take place quarterly, and the project manager would present their summary report. This will allow those involved with the project to ask questions that are not covered by the written report. The purpose of the meeting is to provide an update on the project status, identify any issues and establish action plans from that point.

Other meetings

A number of other meetings may be held by the project manager throughout the project, such as:

Project problem solving meetings – these would be held on an ad hoc basis as required to deal with problems which have arisen.

Meetings with external parties – the project manager will also have to arrange meetings with external resource providers such as suppliers and sub-contractors.

Remember: meetings were covered in an earlier chapter. All of the material covered earlier is equally applicable to project meetings.

Case study style question 1

G is about to undertake his second project in the role of project manager. In his last project he was criticised by the project sponsor for the lack of reporting throughout the project. G has commented that he does not see the need for reporting as long as the project is delivered as it would just take his time away from managing the project.

Required:

The new project has the same sponsor and he has asked you to email G to explain to him the benefits of a well-defined project reporting system.

(10 minutes)

10 Closing

The final stage of the project life cycle is the closure of the project once the project work is finished. A number of activities must be undertaken at this stage:

- Project is delivered to users
- End of project meeting
- Formal sign off of project
- Project review meetings
- Final report issued
- Project team disbanded.

An end of project meeting confirms closure of the project by a formal sign-off. At this meeting or another shortly afterwards, a review evaluates how well the project was managed: if deadlines were met, quality standards maintained and budgets adhered to. Lessons learned from the review are used in future projects.

Project review meetings should be carried out both internally with project team members and externally with the customer.

End of project review meetings

The internal review (team)

This is:

- an opportunity to review the planning, management, reporting and control
- an opportunity to discuss the success and failures of the project process
- to establish what can be learned in future for the benefit of other projects
- an opportunity for the project manager to discuss with individual team members their role in the project and the means by which they could improve their own performance on future projects.

The external review (customer)

This is:

- a crucial aspect of project closure
- an important part of establishing whether the project has satisfied the customer's requirements
- to obtain feedback to help improve future projects
- when customers can voice any concerns regarding how the project was carried out.

The final report

The contents of the final project report will include:

- Brief overview of project.
- Customer original requirements and original project deliverables.
- List of deliverables which the customer received.
- Actual achievements re costs, schedules and scope.
- Degree to which the original objective was achieved.
- Future considerations.

To produce this report reference will be made to the following documentation:

- feasibility study and report
- PID
- project planning reports
- milestones and gates.

The purpose of the closing stage of the process is:

- To ensure that the project is finally completed and conforms to the latest definition of what was to be achieved.
- Formal comparison between PID and project outcomes.
- To evaluate performance of project against agreed levels of performance.
- Cost of the system in comparison with budgeted cost with an explanation of variances.
- Comparison of time taken with the budgeted time anticipated.
- Effectiveness of the management process.
- Significance of any problems encountered.
- To complete the project termination activities, such as:
  - Organising and filing all project documentation.
  - Receiving and making final payments to suppliers of resources.
  - Agreeing formally with the customer that all agreed deliverables have been provided successfully.
  - Meeting with project team and customers to report on project successes and failures.
  - Disbanding the project team.
- To provide continuous improvement and feedback. Any improvement, even a small one, is important.
- To learn from the experience.

Post Completion Audit (PCA)

A few months after the end of the project a meeting of managers, users and developers is held. This is designed to review the success of the project as a whole as well as to receive the users' feedback on it now that they have had time to judge it. It may also highlight specific issues with the project and the review meeting may organise a set of actions to deal with these issues. In addition it should also establish whether the project has helped the business to deliver the benefits defined in the original business case.

The primary benefit derived from the post-completion audit is to augment the organisation's experience and knowledge. This may be difficult to quantify, it may be necessary to justify the cost of the post-completion audit by carrying out a cost benefit analysis. In this case, the expected savings to future projects should be offset against the cost of the audit.

Other benefits of PCAs include more realistic forecasting of a project's costs and revenues, enhanced understanding of project failures, and improved future decision making and project management performance.

Post completion audit – key areas

Key areas to consider in the post completion audit:

- Technical performance review (was the scope of project achieved?).
- Extent to which the quality has been achieved.
- Whether benefits have been achieved.
- Cost/budget performance.
- Schedule performance.
- The effectiveness of project planning and control.
- Team relationships.
- Problem identification process.
- Customer relationships.
- Communication.
- Risk evaluation and assessment of risk management policies.
- Outstanding issues.
- Recommendations for future management of projects.

Continuous improvement

Many organisations view project management as a strategic competence, from which they can gain a competitive advantage. This is particularly true of organisations in project-based industries, such as engineering and consultancy.

Such organisations have begun to see that without continuing to improve their project management approach they will continue to make the same mistakes and poor practices will be carried forward. Excellence in project management requires the development of a strong approach (methodology), a culture that believes in the approach and an effort by all to continuously improve this approach.

Elements of continuous improvement can be seen in the activities carried out during the completion and post-completion stages of the project. As part of the internal review at the end of the project and the post completion audit, an aspect of learning takes place whereby the project team review how well the project was carried out and considers lessons learned which could be taken forward to benefit future projects.

Case study style question 2

T is about to complete his first project as project manager. Prior to this project he spent six months as a member of a project team working on the development of an educational visitors centre for the company.

Reflecting on his experiences whilst working on the previous project, he feels that the final stages of the project were not dealt with effectively, with the project members going back to their functional jobs without any discussion or feedback on the project performance and outcomes.

He is determined that he will improve the experience for his project team, however most of the project team in his current project were members of the team in the last project so T feels that he will have to convince them of the need to undertake certain activities as the project draws to a close.

Required:

T has asked you to write a report for him to circulate to the team members explaining the importance of the activities to be carried out at the closure and post-completion stages of the project.

(15 minutes)

11 Summary diagram

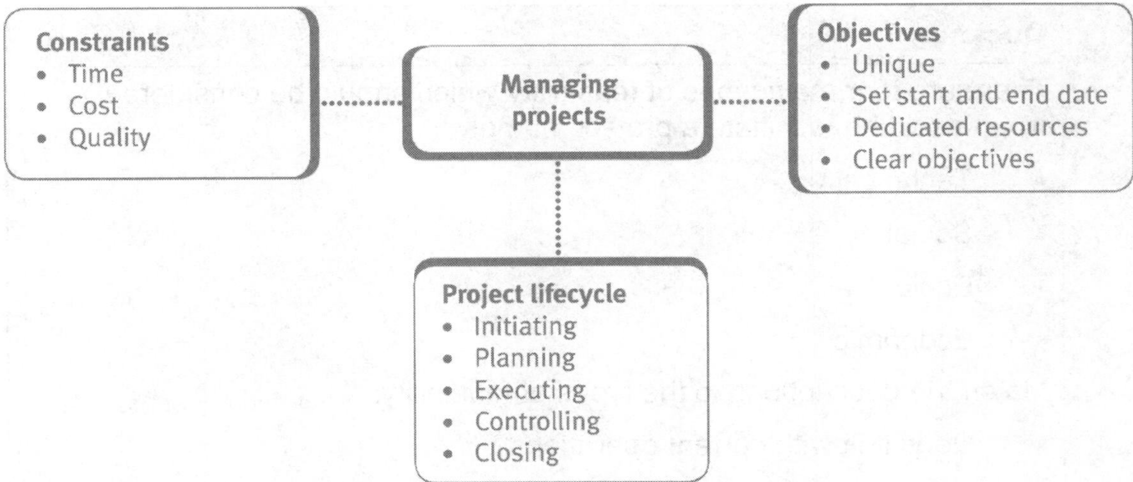
Constraints
• Time
• Cost
• Quality
Managing projects
Objectives
• Unique
• Set start and end date
• Dedicated resources
• Clear objectives
Project lifecycle
• Initiating
• Planning
• Executing
• Controlling
• Closing

End of chapter questions

Question 1

There are four main types of feasibility which should be considered when deciding to initiate a project, namely:

- Technical
- Social
- Ecological
- Economic

Match the descriptions to the types of feasibility.

- Does it fit with current operations?
- How will it affect the environment?
- Can it be done?
- Is it worth it?

Question 2

According to Gido and Clements, during which phase of the project lifecycle would ideas be submitted and evaluated?

A Identification of a need

B Development of a proposed solution

C Implementation

D Completion

Question 3

Which of the following are purposes of a project initiation document? Select all that apply.

A Acts as a base document against which progress can be assessed

B Assesses whether the project is technically feasible

C Justifies the project

D Defines the project and its scope

E Provides a method for prioritising change requests

F Considers alternative actions should uncertain events occur

Question 4

Complete the following sentences relating to project constraints, using the following words:

- reduce
- increase

Part way through a project to install a new IT system, one of the finance providers announced that it could no longer support the project. It is likely that the quality of the project will _____________ or the timescale of the project will ___________________.

It has now been made clear by the project customer that the system must be in place by the agreed date, or the company will lose a very valuable contract.

To get the project installed on time, it is likely that the quality of the project will ________________________.

Question 5

All projects have a number of constraints that which restrict their progress. The three main constraints are known as the project triangle. Which of the following constraints make up the project triangle?

A Legal

B Resources

C Quality

D Communication

E Time

F Cost

Question 6

Insert the correct word from the list to complete the sentences below:

- Completion
- Implementation
- Need
- Solution

The project stage where customer feedback would be obtained during an external review meeting is known as ____________________.

At the ________________ stage, a project initiation document would be completed.

The phase when the actual performance of the project is undertaken is known as ____________________.

At the ________________ stage, proposals are evaluated and the most appropriate is selected.

Question 7

Configuration management is designed to:

A track deviation from proposed deliverables

B track deviation from schedule

C track product changes and versions

D track co-ordination between different project teams

Question 8

Which of the following statements regarding project control are correct? Select all that apply.

A A project control system will ensure that the project meets its deadlines.

B Performance management is only required at the end of the project.

C Reports and meetings are important elements of control within projects.

D Project progress review meetings are regular, formal meetings involving the project manager, team members, and the customer or steering committee.

E The main purposes of a control system are to prevent and correct deviations.

Question 9

A number of activities are undertaken at the completion stage of a project. Further activities are undertaken a few months after the completion of the project, this is known as the post completion review. Match the statements below to whether they relate to the completion or the post completion stages.

Completion	Post completion

- The purpose of this stage is to establish whether the project helped the business to deliver the benefits defined in the original business case.
- The project team will be disbanded.
- The purpose of this stage is to ensure that the project conforms to the latest definition of what was to be achieved.
- At this stage the final report is produced.

Question 10

An important element in projects that is used to track and control all aspects of the project and includes version control and access over project records is known as:

A Change control

B Risk management

C Configuration management

D Project initiation document

Test your understanding answers

Case study style question 1

EMAIL

To: G

From: Management Accountant

Date: today

Subject: The benefits of a well-defined project reporting system

I have been asked by the sponsor of your latest project to write this email to explain to you the benefits of a well-defined project reporting system. I appreciate that your last project was a success and that you therefore see little point in spending time on reporting, but a well defined project reporting system will have the following benefits:

- It will enhance the communication throughout the project.
- It ensures that all team members are aware of the importance of regular monitoring and control. Everyone involved in the project will know that their progress will be monitored and reported on which will encourage hard work within the team.
- It ensures that all stakeholders can be kept informed of the progress of the project, which means that issues affecting the project are advised to the relevant parties on a timely basis.
- Corrective action can then be undertaken sooner to ensure that the project stays on track.
- It is necessary to compare with planned performance, although it must be done regularly to ensure progress is maintained. Reporting can be daily, weekly or monthly, depending on the complexity and timescales involved.
- Standard reports will make it easier for all parties to follow the progress of the project, and to compare the progress of projects against each other.

I hope that you have found the above useful and that you will see the benefit of implementing a project reporting system for this and all of your future projects. Please do not hesitate to get in touch if you want to discuss this further.

Case study style question 2

REPORT

To: Members of the project team

From: T

Date: Today

Subject: The importance of the activities at the closing and post-completion stages of the project

Introduction

In this report, the importance of the activities at the completion and post-completion stages of the project will be considered.

Project closing

Project closing is the final stage of the project life cycle and occurs once the project work has finished. The purpose is to ensure benefits are gained in the final stages. It is important that all members of the team maintain commitment until all the work is completed since people tend to be more motivated to move on to new projects rather than tying up the loose ends. It is also important to evaluate the conduct of the project in order to learn from experiences which will help the company improve on its performance in future projects. The questions that could be asked include:

- Was the project completed to quality, on time and within budget?
- Did the project deliver according to the objectives set?
- Are there lessons to be learnt?
- Are there any follow up action on this project needed?

Project closing activities would involve practical tasks such as organising and filing all project documentation and ensuring that members of the project team have jobs to return to. It should also involve formally agreeing with the 'client' that all the agreed deliverables have been achieved. The business case should be reviewed to check that intended benefits are likely to be realised. In other words, examining project performance by comparing achievement with the original project plan to show that the project has delivered the outputs.

Post completion review and audit

In addition, there should be a review of the project organisation and methods to recommend future improvements. This can be achieved through the post completion review and audit. The main purpose of the post completion review is to evaluate the overall project and to learn from the experiences gained before the project team is disbanded. This might involve debriefing meetings which enable all parties involved in the project to assess their own performance.

It provides a forum to discuss with individual team members their role in the project and how they could improve their own performance for the future. An evaluation from the client's perspective will establish if the project was successful in satisfying their requirements and has given them the opportunity to voice any concerns.

The review will provide an opportunity to discuss the successes and failures of the project process. The feedback should provide reinforcement of good skills and behaviours and the identification of areas for improvement or change in practice for the smooth running of future projects.

The post completion audit is the final stage and involves conducting a formal audit of the entire project against a checklist. This will include an assessment of:

- whether the required quality of the project has been achieved; the efficiency of the solution compared with the agreed performance standards
- the actual cost of the project compared with budgets and reasons for over/under expenditure
- the time taken to develop the solution compared with target dates and reasons for any variances
- the effectiveness of project management methodologies.

Together, the review and audit can provide a case history of the project, providing a repository for the knowledge captured. The project manager should issue a report summarising project performance and advising on how it could be improved in the future. The reason that post project activities are not always undertaken is that it is often difficult to quantify in a tangible way the benefits derived, given the associated costs of review and audit.

Conclusion

The activities carried out at the closing of the project are important as they help to ensure that the project is completed successfully, they help to review not only what was delivered by the project but how it was delivered. This allows all parties to the project learn lessons which will help them improve the management of future projects.

Question 1

The correct matching is:

Technical – Can it be done?

Social – Does it fit with current operations?

Ecological – How will it affect the environment?

Economic – Is it worth it?

Question 2

The second stage of the project lifecycle is the development of a proposed solution. All proposals for the solution will be submitted and evaluated and the most appropriate solution to satisfy the need will be selected.

Question 3

A, C and D

Assessing if the project is technically feasible would be done as part of the feasibility study.

A change process provides a method for prioritising change requests.

Contingency planning considers alternative actions should uncertain events occur.

Question 4

The complete sentences are:

Part way through a project to install a new IT system, one of the finance provides announced that it could no longer support the project. It is likely that the quality of the project will **reduce** or the timescale of the project will **increase**.

It has now been made clear by the project customer that the system must be in place by the agreed date, or the company will lose a very valuable contract.

To get the project installed on time, it is likely that the quality of the project will **reduce**.

Question 5

C, E and F

The 3 main constraints which make up the project triangle are:

- Quality
- Time
- Cost

Question 6

The complete sentences are:

The project stage where customer feedback would be obtained during an external review meeting is known as **completion**.

At the **need** stage, a project initiation document would be completed.

The phase when the actual performance of the project is undertaken is known as **implementation**.

At the **solution** stage, proposals are evaluated and the most appropriate is selected.

Question 7

C

Configuration management involves tracking and controlling all aspects of a project and all documentation and deliverables from the project.

It includes version control for documentation and all aspects of change management.

Question 8

C, D and E

A project control system will aim to reduce the risk within a project but cannot ensure that a project will meet its deadlines.

Performance management is required throughout a project to assess the progress of each aspect of the project.

Question 9

The correct matching is:

Completion	Post completion
The project team will be disbanded. The purpose of this stage is to ensure that the project conforms to the latest definition of what was to be achieved. At this stage the final report is produced.	The purpose of this stage is to establish whether the project helped the business to deliver the benefits defined in the original business case.

Question 10

C

Change control is used to ensure that all changes to the project are agreed and communicated before they are implemented.

Risk management considers how the risks associated with a proposed project can be managed.

A project initiation document is used to authorise the project and to act as a base document against which the project deliverables can be assessed.

Chapter

10

Project management – tools and techniques

Chapter learning objectives

Lead	Component
C2: Apply tools and techniques to manage projects	(a) Project management tools and techniques (b) Project risk management tools

Topics to be covered

- Workstreams
- Work breakdown schedule, Gantt charts, network analysis
- PERT charts
- Sources and types of project risks
- Scenario planning
- Managing project risks
- Project management software.

1 Session content diagram

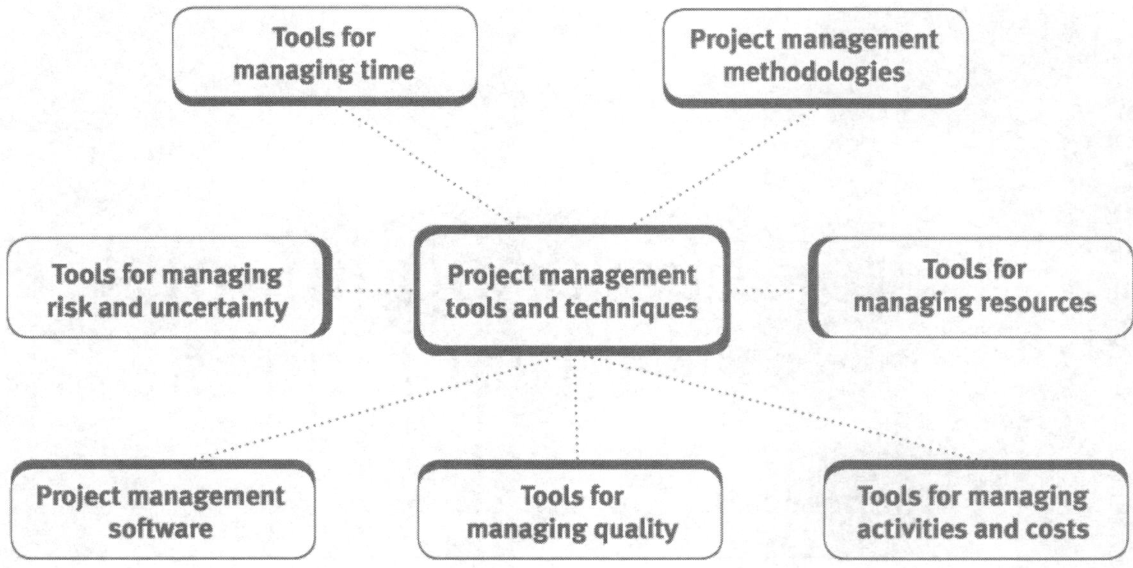
Tools for managing time
Project management methodologies
Tools for managing risk and uncertainty
Project management tools and techniques
Tools for managing resources
Project management software
Tools for managing quality
Tools for managing activities and costs

2 Tools and techniques

There are a number of tools, techniques and documents which are used throughout a project, particularly at the planning stage. These can be summarised as follows:

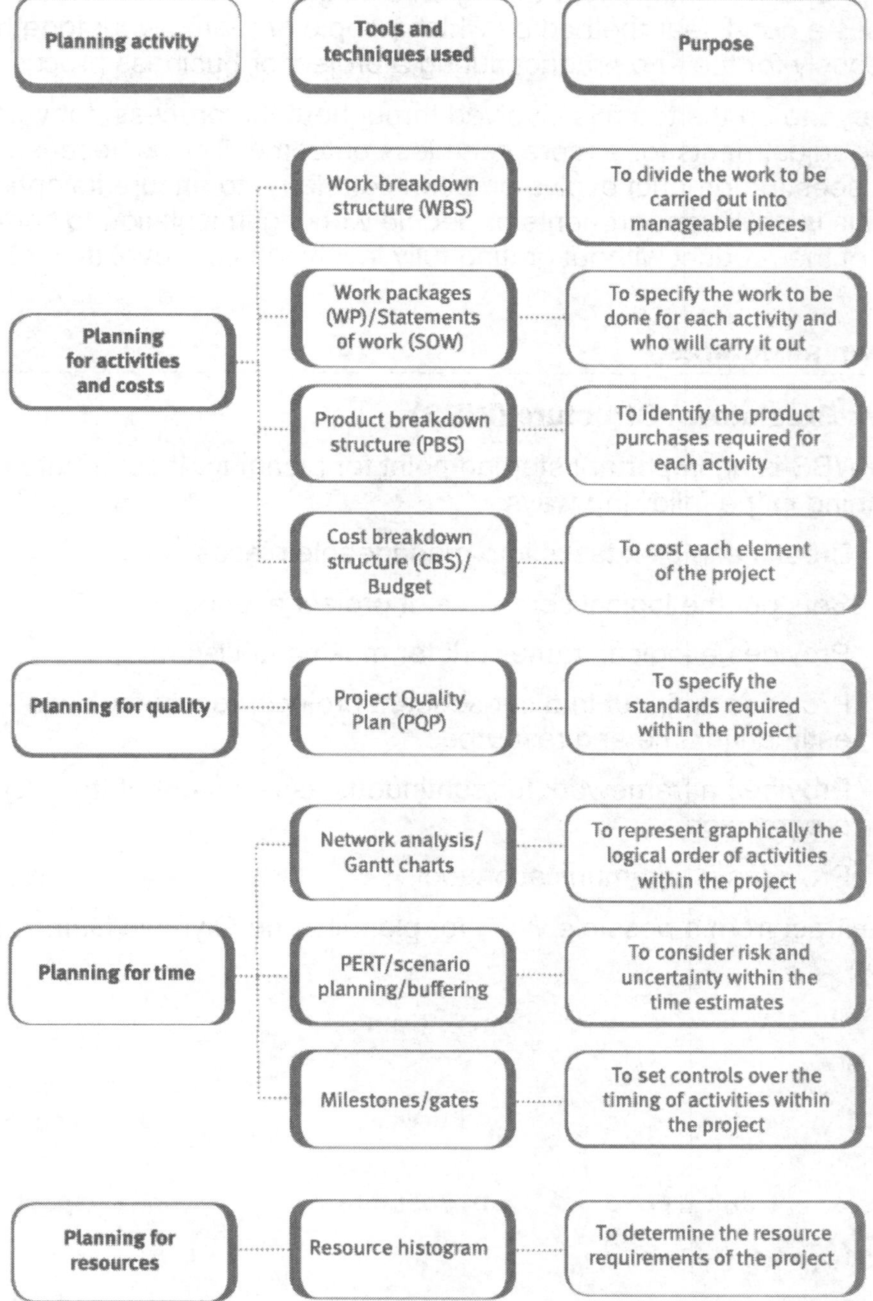

3 Planning for activities and costs

Workstreams:

A workstream is the progressive completion of various tasks that are done by different groups in a company, working on a single product. A work stream emphasises a non-linear method by which people or teams work together simultaneously for the end product during a project or business process.

Since everyone on the team is involved throughout the process, they can make necessary adjustments for a more seamless outcome. This is because everyone sees the product evolve and can contribute to ensure its optimum quality. This is unlike departments or people working in isolation to complete their part of the product without getting fully involved in the evolution of the product.

Breakdown structures:

1 **Work Breakdown Structure (WBS)**

The WBS is an important starting point for planning. It contributes to planning in the following ways:

- Breaks complex tasks into manageable pieces.
- Sets out the logical sequence of project events.
- Provides a logical framework for making decisions.
- Provides an input into subsequent project processes, such as estimating time and resources.
- Provides a framework for continuous assessment of the project progression.
- Provides a communication tool.

An extract from a possible WBS for planning the Olympic Games is shown below.

Olympic Games

1. Events		2. Facilities	3. Security
1.1	**Track & Field**	**2.1 Spectators**	**3.1 Spectators**
1.1.1	Long Jump		
1.1.2	Javelin		
1.1.3	Hurdles		
1.2	**Equestrian**	**2.2 Competitors**	**3.2 Competitors**

2 **Work Packages (WPs) and Statements of Work (SOWs)**

- The work package specifies the work to be done for each package described in the work breakdown structure.
- The statement of work describes the deliverables against which the project can be measured.
- Both types of document identify in detail work to be done and may state the standard to which the work is to be done.
- The statement of work also indicates who is responsible and when the work needs to be delivered.

3 **Product Breakdown Structure (PBS)**

- The products required for each activity would then be listed, for example the Long Jump would require:
  - Sand pit
  - White board
  - Measuring equipment.
- A description of the machinery and equipment required for the project would be made.
- This allows different suppliers to be compared.

4 **Cost Breakdown Structure (CBS)**

This will include information gathered from:

- The WBS, WP, SOW and PBS.
- Capital and revenue costs identified in the cost-benefit analysis and feasibility study documents.

It describes the categories that require costing to ensure nothing is left out of the budget process.

Numbers and costs would be allocated to each product.

This creates the detailed **financial plan (budget)** for the project.

The benefits of using breakdown structures include:

- Summarising all the activities comprising the project, including support and other tasks
- Displaying the interrelationships of the various jobs (work packages) to each other and the total project
- Establishing the authority and responsibility for each part of the project
- Estimating project cost
- Performing risk analysis
- Scheduling jobs (work in progress)
- Providing a basis for controlling the application of resources to the project.

4 Planning for quality

Project Quality Plan (PQP)

This major document details the **standards** that must be adhered to in order to ensure a successful development process. It will provide a clear indication of procedures and policies that must be followed to maintain quality within the work carried out. It generally includes:

- **Risk assessment** – of the possible internal and external risks that are likely to affect the project and the alternative actions which are required to reduce the risks.
- **Project overview** – outline of the main activities to be carried out.
- **Project requirements** – details a description of the work to be carried out, timescales and deliverables and is cross referenced to the requirements specification.
- **Project organisation** – stating management roles and responsibilities, this will help to determine the allocation of resources to each of the project activities.
- **Monitoring and reporting procedures** – cross referenced to the project standards, this section identifies how the project will be monitored and what to do if slippage occurs. It also states the frequency and content of reports as well as key control processes, such as end of stage meetings, for example, when the steering meetings will take place and procedures for evaluating the final installed system.
- **Key development stages and processes** – the activities that will need to be completed during the life cycle.
- **Key standards to be used in the project (quality assurance)** – this will help to ensure quality outputs, standards that need to be evaluated and will include hardware, software and development standards such as notation of modelling techniques.
- **Testing strategy** – this will identify the stages of development where testing is to be carried out, by whom and of what.
- **Procurement policy** – the procedures and standards for procurement will be stated and any variation from the normal procedure noted, with reasons.
- **Configuration management** – how this will be dealt with should be set out so that each version of the deliverables is identified.

5 Planning for time

Network analysis

Network analysis is a general term, referring to various techniques adopted to plan and control projects. It is used to analyse the inter-relationships between the tasks identified by the work breakdown structure and to define the dependencies of each task. Whilst laying out a network it is often possible to see that assumptions for the order of work are not logical or could be achieved more cost effectively by re-ordering them. This is particularly true whilst allocating resources; it may become self evident that two tasks cannot be completed at the same time by the same person due to lack of working hours or, conversely, that by adding an extra person to the project team, several tasks can be done in parallel thus shortening the length of the project.

Critical Path Analysis (CPA)

One of the component parts of network analysis is critical path analysis or CPA (this is often called network analysis). It is the most commonly used technique for managing projects.

The process of CPA.

1 **Analyse the project**. The project is broken down into its constituent tasks or activities. The way in which these activities relate to each other is examined, for example which activities cannot be undertaken until some previous activity or activities are complete?

2 **Draw the network**. The sequence of activities is shown in a diagrammatic form called the 'network diagram'.

3 **Estimate the time and costs of each activity**. The amount of time that each activity will take is estimated, and where appropriate the associated costs are estimated.

4 **Locate the critical path**. This is the chain of events that determines how long the overall project will take. Any delay to an activity on the critical path will delay the project as a whole; delays to other activities may not affect the overall timetable for completion. That is the distinction between critical and non-critical activities.

5 **Schedule the project**. Determine the chain of events that leads to the most efficient and cost effective schedule.

6 **Monitor and control the progress of the project**. This implies careful attention to the schedule and any other progress charts that have been drawn up, to monitor actual progress in the light of planned achievement.

7 **Revise the plan**. The plan may need to be modified to take account of problems that occur during the progress of the project.

The network diagram:

The diagram is made up of two parts: activity lines and nodes. The diagram is drawn and read from left to right.

A complete network diagram (CPA) would look like this:

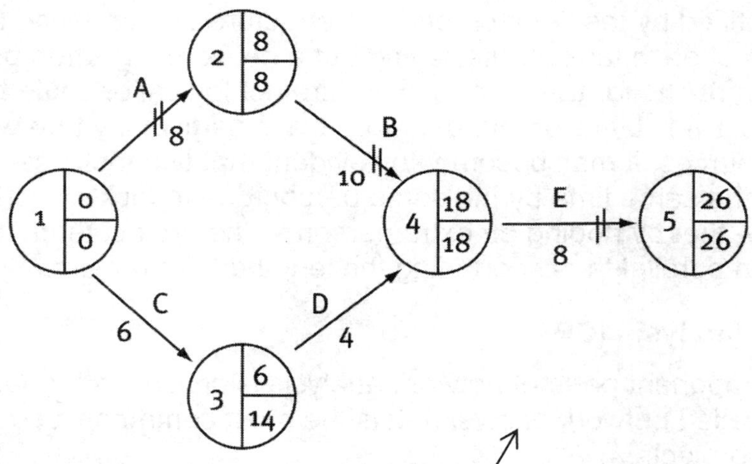

- Each activity is represented by an arrow
- The activity letter or description (or both) is written on the arrow.
- The activity duration is written below the arrow.
- The activities on the critical path are identified with //
- Activities start and finish in circles known as nodes (O).
- Nodes are numbered so that each node has a unique identifier.
- The nodes also contain information on two times:
  - The earliest event time (EET)
  - The latest event time (LET).

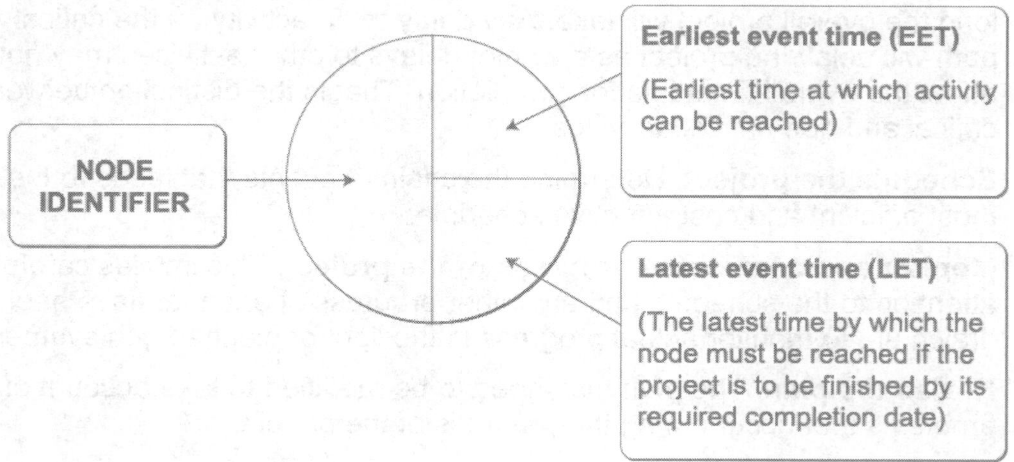

Drawing the diagram

- First draw a dot-to-dot diagram – this can be completed quickly and allows the logic of the diagram to be tested before you begin to draw the final version.
- Once the network has been drawn, calculate the EET and LET for each node.
- To calculate the EET, work left to right. Take the EET from the previous node and add this to the duration of the activity. **Where you have a choice of EETs, always select the highest.**
- To calculate the LET, work right to left. Take the LET from the previous node and deduct the duration of the activity. **Where you have a choice of LETs, always select the lowest.**

Reading the diagram

- The EET and LET of the final node will always be the same and this will equal the **overall duration** of the project.
- We can also identify the **critical path**, i.e. the activities where any delay will lead to a delay in the overall project. These are the activities for which EET = LET.
- Some activities could increase in duration and yet the project could still be completed by the required target date. Such activities are said to exhibit **'float'**. Float can generally be calculated as the difference between the LET and the EET.

Rules for drawing the diagram

- If two activities occur in parallel, **dummy activity lines** are inserted to allow only one activity arrow to join nodes together. Dummy activities do not consume any time or resources and are drawn in the diagram to make it clearer.

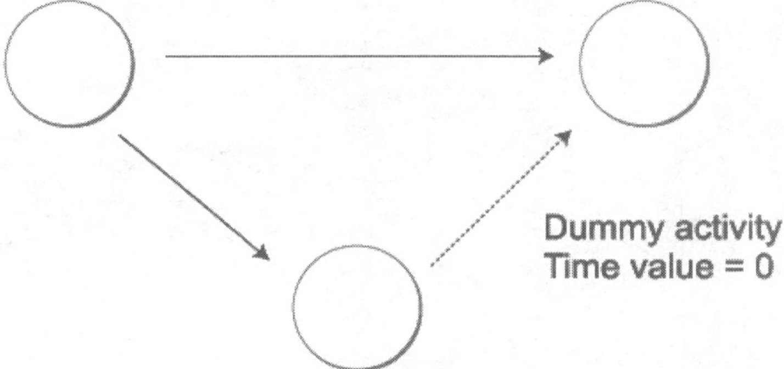

- Loops are not allowed because the network essentially shows a series of activities progressing through time. It focuses on the passage of time, not on the successful completion of activities. In other words, you cannot have a series of activities leading from one event that lead back to the same event. For example, the following diagram is not allowed.

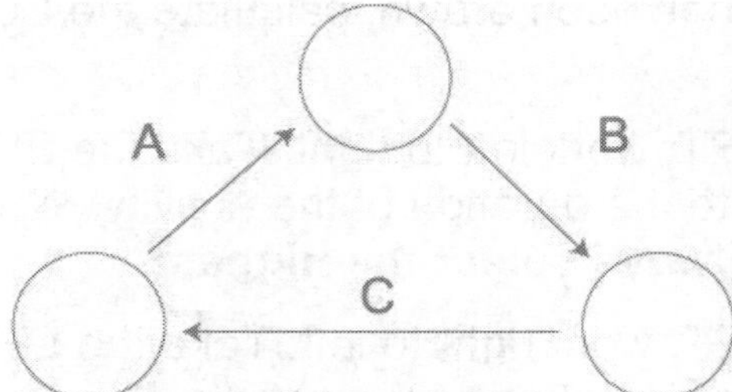

It would be redrawn including a new activity.

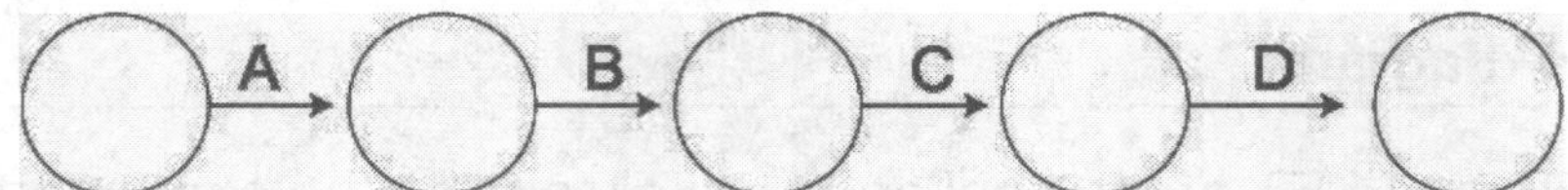

- An activity can only occur once, so there cannot be two lines with the same activity. For example, this diagram is not allowed:

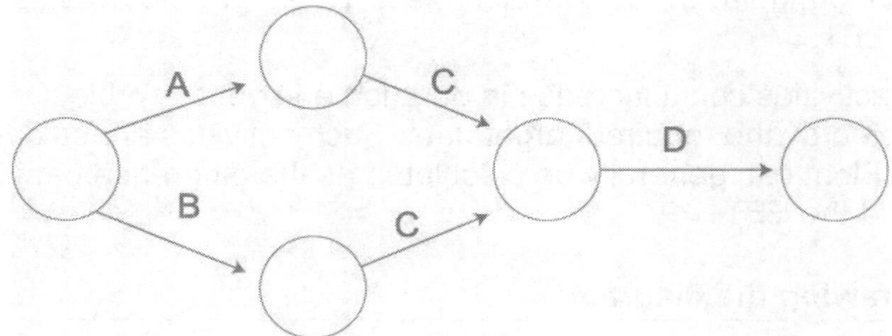

The diagram may need to be redrawn and/or a dummy activity used.

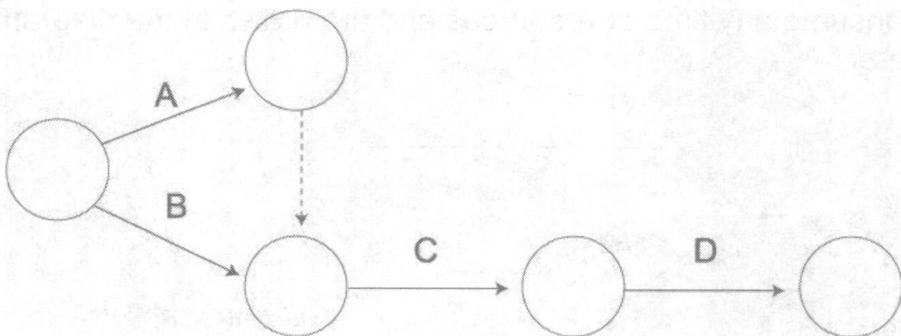

Illustration 1 – CPA worked example

Consider the follow details about a project. You are given the list of activities, their durations and the preceding activities. This last column tells you which order the activities must be drawn in.

Activity	Duration (weeks)	Preceding activity
A	8	–
B	10	A
C	6	–
D	4	C
E	8	B, D

Required:

Draw the network diagram, and identify the critical path, the estimated project duration and any float on any activity.

Solution:

Step 1: draw the basic network diagram, showing the order of the activities. Remember the rules above when you are drawing it. You are aiming to move across your page from left to right.

Each activity must start and end with a node, so the first thing to do is to identify the activities which can start straight away – these are the ones with no preceding activity. In this case A and C can start straight away.

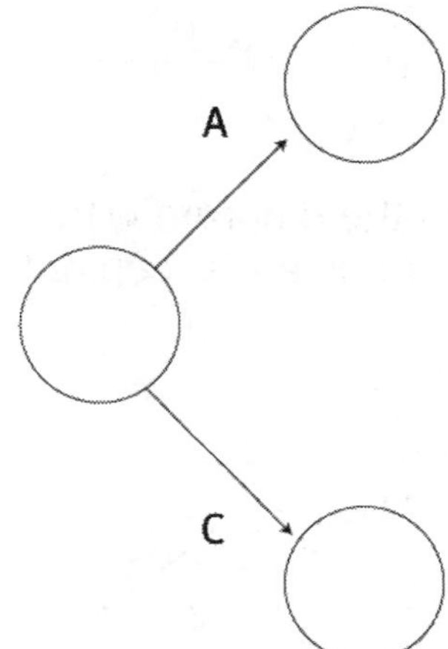

Now you can draw in the other activities. B follows A, and D follows C:

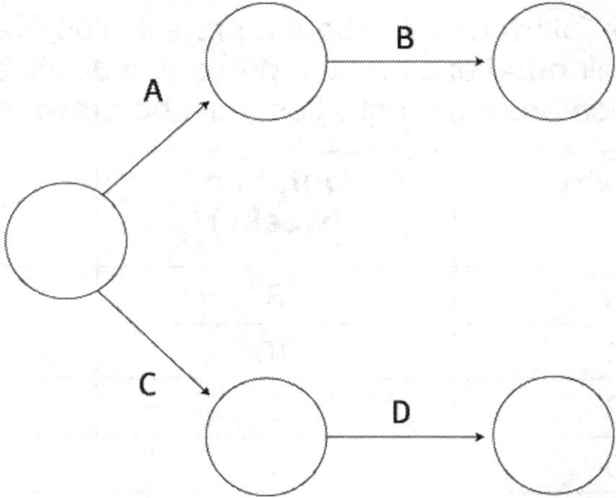

Activity E is a bit harder, because it follows B and D. This can be drawn using a dummy line. Connect the nodes at the end of B and D with a dummy line, and show E following that combined node:

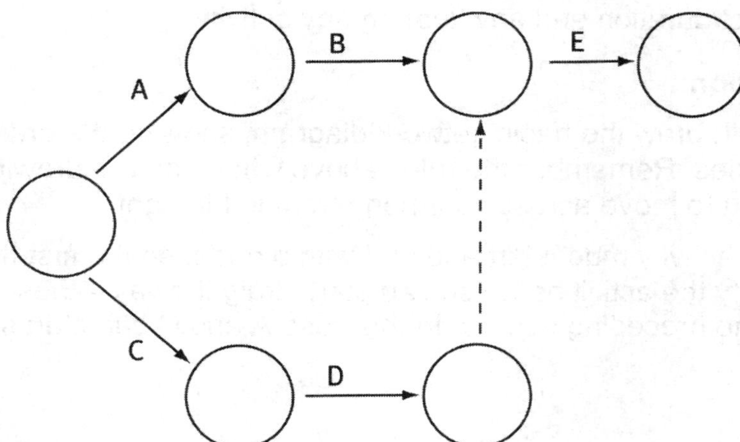

You could have drawn the diagram without the dummy line, as shown below. Both of the diagrams are acceptable and both show the correct flow of activities.

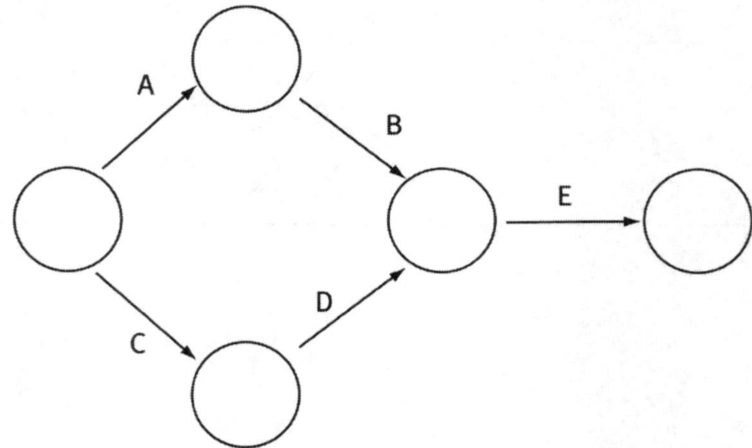

Step 2: Now the basic network diagram has been drawn, we can start to add in the details of the durations of each activity. These are shown on the activity lines. You can now draw in the node lines, ready for the calculations of EET and LET.

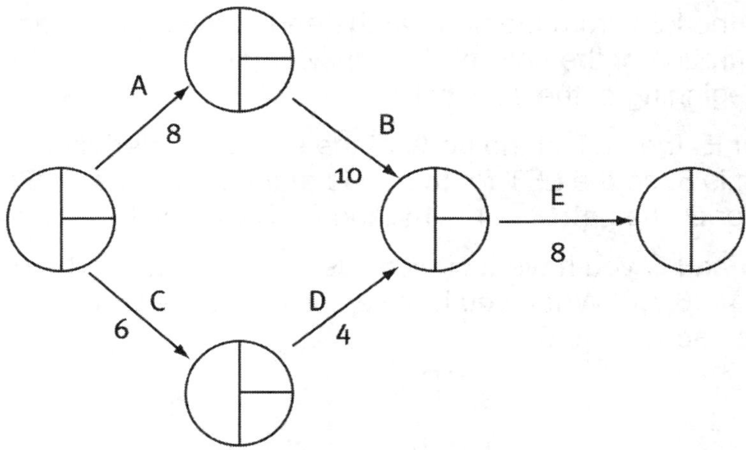

Step 3: Calculate the Earliest Event Time (EET) working left to right. Start at the first node: the EET of the first node must always be zero. You then look at each activity in turn.

Take the EET from the node at the beginning of the activity line, and add it to the duration of the activity, the answer gives you the EET for the node at the end of the activity line.

So for A, EET at the start is 0, add the duration of A, which is 8, so the EET for the node at the end of the activity line is 8. For C, we get 0 + 6 = 6.

You have to be careful when looking at B and D as they lead to the same node – this is a choice:

For B: 8 + 10 = 18, or for D: 6 + 4 = 10. Remember for the EET, when you have a choice, you select the highest, so we use 18.

E is straightforward: 18 + 8 = 26.

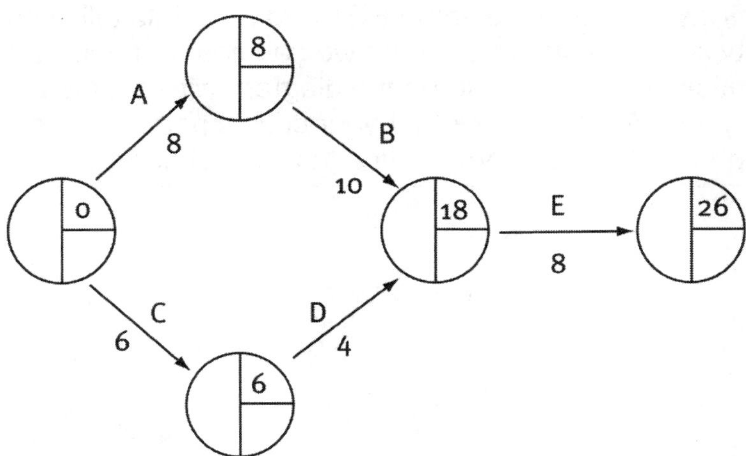

Step 4: Calculate the Latest Event Time (LET) working right to left. Start at the last node: the LET of the last node must equal the EET of the last node, so in this case the LET of the last node is 26. You then look at each activity in turn.

Take the LET from the node at the end of the activity line, and deduct the duration of the activity. The answer gives you the LET for the node at the beginning of the activity line.

So for E, the LET of the node at the end is 26, deduct the duration of E, which is 8, so the LET for the node at the beginning of E's activity line is 18. For D, we get 18 – 4 = 14, and for B we get 18 – 10 = 8.

For A and C you have a choice. Using A we get 8 – 8 = 0, or using C we get 14 – 6 = 8. When you have a choice for the LET, you always use the lowest, so we use 0.

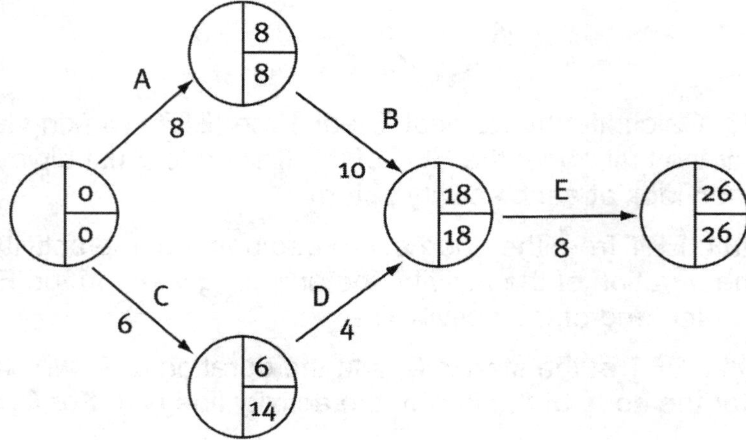

Our CPA is complete. We can now put in the reference numbers in each node (there are no rules here, just work left to right and number each node, it is just used for identification purposes).

We can now work out the critical path:

Look at your diagram. Where the nodes at the beginning and the end of an activity line have the same EET and LET, this tells you that the activity is critical. In our diagram we can see that activities A. B and E are critical. We note these on the diagram with double lines on the activity line. Always check that your critical path is a continuous path through the diagram from the first to the final node.

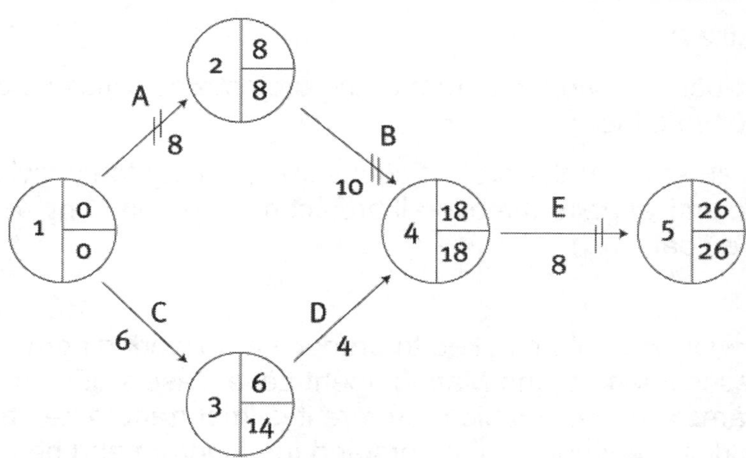

From our diagram, we can also see the overall duration of the project. This is the same as the EET and LET of the final node, so in this project, the overall duration is 26 weeks.

We can also work out of there is any slack/float on any activity. This can be seen from those activities which are not on the critical path. The amount of float can be calculated as the difference between the EET and the LET. In our diagram, activities C or D have a float of 8 weeks.

Case study style question 1

The details of activities and duration for Project YT you are managing are shown below.

Activity		Duration (weeks)	Preceding activity
A	Problem definition	2	–
B	Prepare feasibility report	3	A
C	Studying existing system	2	A
D	Logical and physical design	4	C
E	Software and hardware development	4	B
F	Systems development report	8	D, E
G	Testing	4	F
H	File conversion	3	D, E
I	Changeover	6	G, H

Required:

Construct a network diagram of the project's activities as detailed within the above table.

Write an email to the project sponsor explaining the activities which are on the critical path, the overall project duration and any activities that have a float.

(15 minutes)

Note: you will not be asked to produce a network diagram as part of the E2 assessment, or the Management Level case study but network diagrams are examinable therefore it is important to be able to draw the network so that you can understand the diagram and be able to answer questions about them.

Limitations of CPA

- It may be time consuming to produce and monitor for large projects.
- Difficult to use for less routine projects with lots of uncertainty.
- Overly complex for some smaller short-term projects.

Benefits of CPA

- Assists in identifying all activities required for completing the project.
- It will assist in identifying those activities that need to be completed before the next activity can start (dependent activities), and those that can happen at the same time (parallel activities).
- The network diagram will identify those activities that lie on the critical path. These activities cannot overrun, otherwise there would be delays in the overall project.
- The network diagram will identify those activities that are non-critical and exhibit float or buffer. This allows management to rank each activity in relation to how much flexibility is available.
- The network diagram will show the minimum completion time for the project, and will allow for sensitivity analysis to be introduced into the project.

6 Planning for resources

Resource histogram

This is a graphical aid for determining the total requirement for a specific resource during the project. The histogram identifies, in block graph form, the fluctuating need for finance, staff, technology resources or vendor services at any stage in the project. This can assist in planning. Reallocation of key tasks can reduce the excessive requirement at certain periods, providing a smooth flow of resources throughout the project.

This smooth flow is easier and cheaper to plan for. The histogram may also assist in control activities.

A resource histogram shows the amount and timing of the requirement for a resource or a range of resources using a stacked bar chart.

Illustration 2 – Resource histogram example

It is very common for a project budget to be constructed as shown below. Variance analysis and financial control are much easier when a spreadsheet package is used for project budgeting.

Month	1	2	3	4	5	6	7	8	9	10	11	Total
	$	$	$	$	$	$	$	$	$	$	$	$
Salaries	420	285	662	850	122	453	411	502	850	421	409	5385
Materials	0	125	0	0	1000	250	400	325	100	125	800	3125
Overheads	180	55	320	123	249	402	111	122	451	123	201	2337
Sub-con.	0	200	200	200	200	0	0	560	560	250	0	2170
Total	600	665	1182	1173	1571	1105	922	1509	1961	919	1410	13017

Such a budget can be shown as a histogram for immediate visual impact, as shown below:

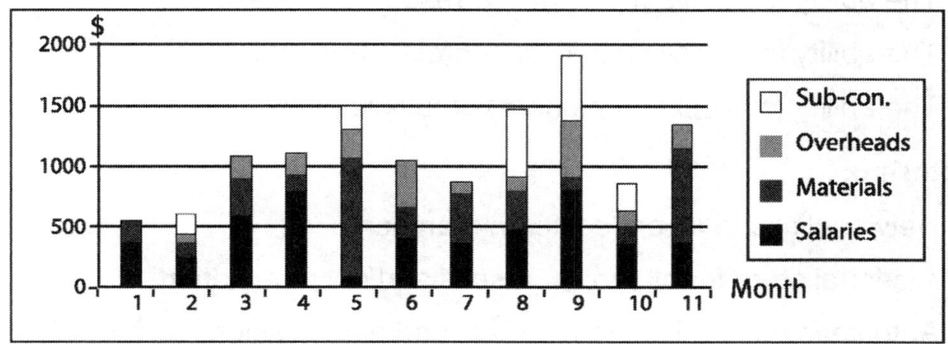

Resource histograms can be used for all resources, such as equipment or human resources.

Benefits of resource histograms:

- It helps with capacity planning, resource scheduling and management
- Resource availability and allocations can be shown on a histogram, to highlight overloads and under-utilisation
- Easy visualisation of resource requirements
- It is drawn in real time.

7 Project management software

Most project management today will involve the use of project management software.

Project management software can assist considerably at the planning stage of the project in the production of network diagrams, Gantt charts and resource histograms. It is also useful at the other stages of the project.

There are a number of different software packages available on the market. The type of output produced by the package will vary depending upon the package being used.

Project management software may be used in a variety of ways throughout the project and can provide the following:

Planning:

- The ability to create multiple network diagrams.
- The ability to create multiple Gantt charts.
- The ability to create Project Initiation Document (PID), Project Quality Plan (PQP) and Work Breakdown Structure (WBS).

Estimating:

- The ability to consider alternative resource allocation.
- The ability to create and allocate project budgets.
- The ability to allocate time across multiple tasks.

Monitoring:

- Network links to all project team members.
- A central store for all project results and documentation.
- Automatic comparison to the plan, and plan revision.

Reporting:

- Access to team members.
- Ability to create technical documents.
- Ability to create end of stage reports.

Advantages of using project management software

- **Improved planning and control**. Software includes various tools which can aid planning. All project data can be held centrally and this facilitates comparison between planned and actual data.
- **Improved communication**. The creation of technical documentation in addition to calendars, report generation and scheduling of activities can all aid communication during the project.
- **Improved quality of systems developed.**
- **Accuracy**. Particularly in large projects, manually drawing network diagrams can be prone to error.
- **Ability to handle complexity**. For large, complex projects, PM software is indispensable in managing and controlling large volumes of activities.
- **What if analysis**. The software allows the user to see the effect of different scenarios by altering elements of the project data. This enables the project manager to plan for contingencies and to assess consequences.
- **Timesheet recording**. In order to ease the project manager's burden of recording the actual effort and revised estimates to complete a task, a number of PM software packages allow this data to be captured from individual team member.

Project management software recognises that there is a sequence in which activities need to be performed. The use of software can help to ensure that all necessary tasks are carried out as required.

When choosing project management software, or indeed any software package, it is important to:

- determine requirements of organisation including its current and future needs.
- document requirements including the essential functions/important/wish list.
- review all available packages to identify three/four products which meet the essential functions and fall within budget.
- have a demonstration of the packages on a trial basis if possible.
- select a package including 'roll out' strategy with installation, training, etc.

Project management software functions

The following is a list of functions that would commonly be found within a standard project management software package, such as Microsoft Project:

- **Budgeting and cost control**. At any time during the project, actual costs can be compared with budgeted costs for individual resources or activities, or for the whole project.
- **Calendars**. Calendars can be used for reporting purposes and to define working periods.
- **Graphics**. The ability to create and modify graphics, such as Gantt charts, is a useful feature of PM software. It will allow the tasks in Gantt charts to be linked so that preceding activities can be shown.
- **Multiple project handling**. Large projects often have to be broken down into smaller projects to make them more manageable. Alternatively, project managers may be responsible for more than one project at a time. Most PM software packages will store numerous projects quite easily.
- **Planning**. All PM software allows the user to define the activities that need to be performed. It will maintain detailed task lists and create critical path analyses. It will allow the project manager to plan several thousand activities, by allocating resources, setting start and completion dates and calculating expected time to complete.
- **Scheduling**. Most systems will build Gantt charts and network diagrams based on the task and resource list and all of their associated information. Any changes to those lists will automatically create a new schedule for the project. It is also possible to schedule recurring tasks, to set priorities for tasks, to schedule tasks to start as late as possible, and to specify 'must end by' and 'no later than' dates.
- **Resource planning**. A critical issue in project planning is resource management, that is ensuring the project has the correct level of manpower, equipment and material at the right place at the right time and in right quantities.

- **Resource histograms**. These provide the project manager with a visual display showing the usage and availability of resources over the project's life. This allows the project manager to see quickly and easily where there are either too few resources or where there are surplus resources to carry out a particular activity. The project manager then has the ability to reallocate resources or to obtain additional resources to ensure that critical activities are achieved on time and therefore the critical path is achieved. An example of a resource histogram is shown on top of next page.
- **Reporting**. The project manager has to report on the progress of the project to the stakeholders. PM software provides the facility to generate standard reports, such as progress to date, budget reports, allocation of resources reports, individual task or WBS reports and financial reports.

Case study style question 2

You are a trainee management accountant working for management consultants XYZ who have been contracted to assist in the management and control of a large international sporting event due to take place in four years' time.

A significant part of the project will be the provision of new buildings and facilities. Major new works associated with the project include the construction of a 30,000-seat indoor athletics stadium and a world press and media centre. A further consideration is the upgrade of the current transport network, with major development work required on the local rail system between the main stadium and the city centre, and an airport bus link.

Success will be measured in terms of trouble-free performance of the events, level of customer enthusiasm and satisfaction, and sustained economic activity generated in the region. Completion of the project on time is critical, even if cost or quality are adversely affected.

The main software development aspect of the project is the development of the communications software in the form of an information database. This will require development of a dedicated website to give public access to event information. The database will contain information about competitors and their events, time and location and availability of tickets.

> The database will be designed to allow the general public to monitor the events, order tickets from the website for any event, and purchase merchandise. The website will also contain links to local hotels and restaurant facilities. The whole package of communications software and the telecommunications and IT hardware has been called the 'Communications Infrastructure'.
>
> A work breakdown structure has been produced and the project has been broken down into over 20 activities, all with varying durations. Each of the activities will be carried out by individual specialist project teams, and led by a project team manager. It is critical that these events are co-ordinated and planned effectively, as timing is critical to the success of this project.
>
> One of the key tasks to undertake immediately is the determination of the critical path.
>
> **Required:**
>
> You have been asked by your management to prepare a report which includes an explanation of the importance of undertaking critical path analysis for a project such as this and an explanation of how using project management software may assist during this project.
>
> **(20 minutes)**

8 Project management methodologies

A project management methodology is a set of guidelines which defines methods and processes to be followed which should help the project be delivered successfully. It can be seen as a systematic and disciplined approach to project management. The development of standard processes is obviously helpful as these, together with standard templates for the documents used, help many project issues to be anticipated and worked around.

Since every organisation is unique, and undertakes unique projects, there is no 'one-size fits all' answer to which project management methodology to use.

A popular choice – PRINCE2 or PMBOK

PMBOK provides a knowledge base and roadmap for effective project management while PRINCE2 provides a more pragmatic 'How To' approach. Both approaches are customisable which is beneficial as it allows for better integration into the level of project management maturity the organisation is currently at and aspires to be at in the future.

Benefits and limitations of a single methodology

Benefits of a single methodology:

- Provides a structured step-by-step approach to managing projects.
- Stages in the methodology become familiar which speed up the completion of the project.
- Helps to keep the project on track and to identify any deviations at an early stage.
- Users become familiar with the tools and reports used, so can compare different projects.
- Team members and project managers become familiar with the approach used and this improves the overall management of projects.
- The methodology can be developed over time and can result in a best practice approach.

Limitations of a single methodology:

- If the methodology selected is unsuitable , it may make managing projects more difficult.
- No one methodology can be suitable for all projects.
- All projects are different, so the methodology may need modifying for each project, but this may be difficult.
- Some methodologies will be too detailed for smaller projects.
- Strictly adopting a methodology may become too bureaucratic.
- All features of the methodology may not be required for all projects.

9 PRINCE2 methodology

PRINCE2 is a project management methodology, capable of supporting complex projects. The UK Government as an open standard method for managing Information Technology projects originally launched PRINCE in 1989. Since then it has been adopted by many organisations both within government and in outside industry for all types of projects.

PRINCE2 (PRojects IN Controlled Environments, version 2) is a process-based approach for project management providing an easily tailored and scaleable method for the management of all types of projects. Each process is defined with its key inputs and outputs in addition to the specific objectives to be achieved and activities to be undertaken.

The main purpose of PRINCE2 is to deliver a successful project, which is defined as:

- delivery of the agreed outcomes
- on time
- within budget
- conforming to the required quality standards.

To do this it contains a large number of control elements which can be applied to all sorts of projects, small and large.

The main control features are:

- It enforces a clear structure of authority and responsibility.
- It ensures the production of key products – PID, project budget, plan and progress reports.
- It gives a clear understanding of the tasks to be completed.
- It contains several quality controls, such as clearly defined procedures.

PRINCE2 structure

The major component parts of the PRINCE2 methodology address the issues of:

- **Organisation** – PRINCE2 suggests using an organisation chart for the project so that there is a clear structure of authority and responsibility. Everyone on the project should understand their role and responsibility for the delivery of objectives.

  Within PRINCE2, responsibilities are defined in terms of roles, rather than individuals. The basic PRINCE2 project organisational structure is illustrated below (arrows indicate accountability):

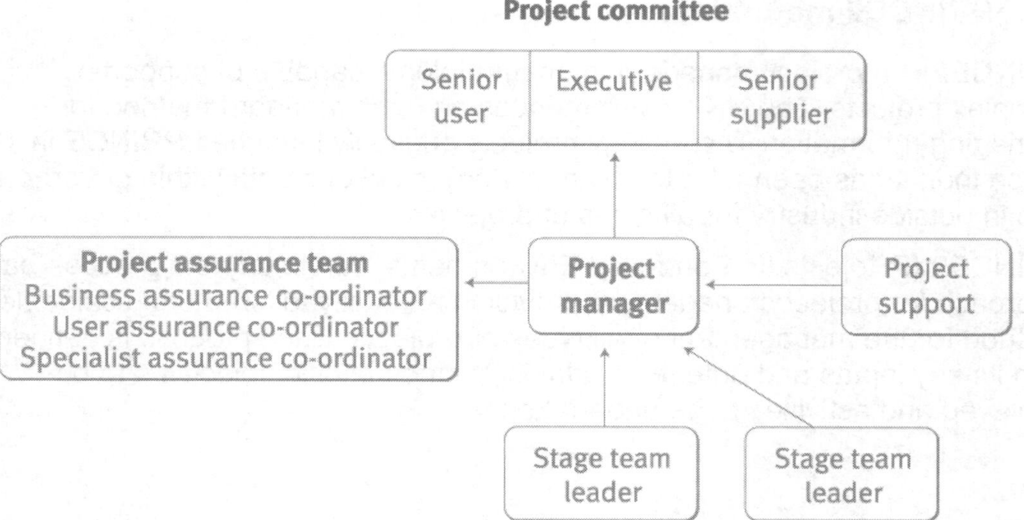

- **Plans** – successful control includes setting plans/standards for everything that needs to be delivered (time, quality, responsibility, communication).
- **Controls** – regular and formal monitoring of actual progress against plan is essential to ensure the timeliness, cost control and quality of the project.
- **Products** – includes a number of tools associated with the control of projects (initiation document, budget, progress reports).
- **Quality** – quality should be defined and controlled on the project. The aim should be zero defects. Quality plans (PQPs) should set the standards required.
- **Risk management** – identifying different types of risk will allow us to plan to reduce them or avoid them.
- **Control of change management** and configuration management – any change to the project should only be after the appropriate approval has been authorised. The management of these changes means knowing which versions are the current ones.

PRINCE2 process areas

- **Starting up a project** – a pre-project process, this stage involves designing and appointing the project management team, creating the initial stage plan and ensuring that information required by the project team is available.
- **Initiation** – similar to a feasibility study, this stage establishes whether or not there is the justification to proceed with the project. The Project Board take ownership of the project at this stage.
- **Managing stage boundaries** – the primary objective at this stage is to ensure that all planned deliverables are completed as required. The Project Board is provided with information to approve completion of the current stage and authorise the start of the next. Lessons learned in the earlier stages can be applied at later stages.
- **Controlling a stage** – monitoring and control activities are carried out by the project manager at each stage of the project. This process incorporates the day-to-day management of the project.
- **Managing product delivery** – this includes effective allocation of Work Packages and ensuring that the work is carried out to the required quality standard.
- **Project closure** – bringing the project to a formal and controlled close approved by the Project Board, it establishes the extent to which the objectives have been met, the extent of formal acceptance obtained of deliverables by the Project Customer, and identifies lessons learned for the future. An End Project Report is completed and the project team disbanded.

Whilst these could all be considered to be elements of any good project management, the difference with PRINCE2 is the level of structure and documentation that is required. This helps in providing controls on the planning and execution of projects and forces the identification of potential problems.

Note: students are advised to read the article on PRINCE2 from the AICPA® & CIMA website, www.aicpa-cima.com

10 The Project Management Body of Knowledge (PMBOK)

While not strictly a methodology, the US-based Project Management Institute (PMI) has defined best-practice project management principles and processes. The Project Management Body of Knowledge (PMBOK) describes nine key areas in terms of inputs, outputs, tools, techniques and how they fit together.

The PMBOK describes nine Project Management Knowledge Areas:

1 **Integration** Management – processes for ensuring that the various elements of the project are properly co-ordinated.

2 **Scope** Management – processes for ensuring that the project includes all the work required and only the work required to complete the project successfully.

3 **Time** Management – processes for ensuring timely completion of the project. All projects are finite, and time ranks as one of the main limits.

4 **Cost** Management – processes for ensuring that the project is completed within the approved budget. All projects must have a budget.

5 **Quality** Management – processes for ensuring that the project will satisfy the needs for which it was undertaken.

6 **Human Resource** Management – processes required to make the most effective use of the people involved in the project.

7 **Communications** Management – processes required to ensure timely and appropriate generation, collection, dissemination, storage, and ultimate distribution of project information.

8 **Risk** Management – processes concerned with identifying, analysing and responding to project risk.

9 **Procurement** Management – processes for acquiring goods and services from outside the performing organisation.

PMBOK is not intended as an alternative to the project life cycle, but rather as a view of the knowledge and skills required in order to carry out each of the stages of the life cycle. It can be viewed as a toolbox. So, for example, at the 'initiating' stage, the project manager would need to consider integration management activities, scope management activities, and so on.

Case study style question 3

RST, a manufacturer and retailer of fashion clothes, has invested in a new technology system to improve the logistics of the movement of clothes between its warehouses and chain of 250 retail outlets. Ensuring that the outlets have the right supply of clothes is a critical success factor for the company.

However, the warehousing stock control and logistics project set up to develop and deliver the new system has experienced numerous problems. The project ended up being well over budget and was also late in delivering the system. Now, only three months after the new system has been installed, it is apparent that the project has not delivered its objective. Instead, the company is facing a crisis with many store managers complaining that they are not receiving the correct stock. Even worse, some stores are out of stock of key ranges, whereas the warehouses are full of clothing.

RST's CEO (J) held a meeting with the project manager and some of the project team. It ended up with everyone blaming each other, saying it was not their responsibility. It is clear that they did not use a project management methodology and did not have adequate control systems in place so that the problems that have now transpired could have been identified and rectified earlier in the project life cycle.

Required:

You have been asked for help by J. Write an email to J recommending a project management methodology/approach, explaining how it could have helped to prevent the failures of the warehousing, stock control and logistics project.

(15 minutes)

Why do some projects fail?

Despite the use of a strong project methodology, extensive use of project management software and detailed project planning, projects can still go spectacularly wrong, over schedule and/or budget.

Here are some common reasons why projects can still fail:

- **Poor leadership**. One of the most important elements for a successful project is a good project manager. A project manager who does not demonstrate all of the required skills may not be able to effectively manage the project team and in turn may struggle to deliver the project successfully.
- **Emphasis on maintaining the plan rather than managing the project**. In a large project, maintaining the plan can be a full-time task. This can leave little time for dealing with important project issues. It is often better for project managers to delegate the input/maintenance responsibility to a project administrator and receive regular reports as a basis for managing the project.

- **Resources may not be managed realistically.** This especially applies when tasks are over-budget. Adding new people into a project at a late stage can make it later since the new team members will be slower at grasping what is required and actually divert the attention of other team members.
- **Poor estimates**. For planning purposes, the accuracy of estimates is vital to the identification of the critical path and the key milestones of the project. However, estimates are subjective and can vary wildly. Also, estimates have been made at a fixed point in time with a particular set of assumptions.
- **Inadequate skills**. Projects require project teams made up of individuals with the right skill sets. Project plan tend to talk about resources when actually they are referring to human beings with all the uncertainty that it brings. Where one individual may find a task within his/her skillset, another person may struggle. It matters which person does which task and this is not always well planned.
- **Work breakdown**. Some projects fail because the work breakdown into tasks does not match with how people work. Work breakdown assumes discrete units of work that someone will spend a fixed amount of time on a task before moving to the next task and not all projects will work in this way.

11 Planning for risk and uncertainty

Risk and uncertainty

Another important activity which is carried out at the initiation stage is to undertake a risk assessment to consider the risks associated with the proposed project and to consider how these risks can be managed.

Risk management process

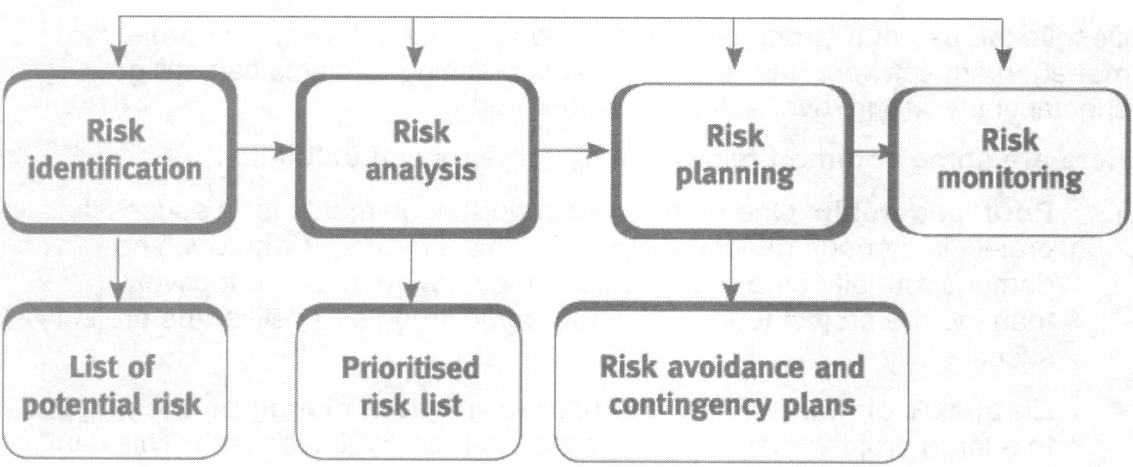

- Identify risk – produce a list of risk items.
- Analyse risk – assess the risk in terms of the probability of it materialising and its potential impact if it was to materialise.
- Prioritise – produce a ranked ordering of risk items.
- Management – plan how to address each risk item, perhaps by avoiding, transferring or reducing the risk. (see below)
- Resolution – produce a situation in which risk items are avoided or reduced.
- Monitoring – continually monitor the progress towards resolving risk, and identification of new risks.

Managing risk

Once the risks have been identified they can be analysed depending on their relative likelihood and impact. They can then be plotted on the following grid which helps determine the best way to manage each risk.

IMPACT \ LIKELIHOOD	Low	High
Low	**Accept**	**Reduce**
High	**Transfer**	**Avoid**

A useful way to remember the risk management approaches is **TARA (Transfer, Avoid, Reduce, Accept)**:

Transfer	Risks with low likelihood and high impact can be transferred, for example by subcontracting the risk to those more able to handle it, such as a specialist supplier or by insuring against the risk.
Accept	Low likelihood and low impact risks can be accepted. Some risks are an inevitable part of doing business. It is important to continue to monitor these risks to ensure that their potential impact or likelihood do not increase.

Reduce	Risks with high likelihood and low impact should be reduced. An alternative course of action with a lower risk exposure could be taken or investment could be made in additional capital equipment or security devices to reduce risk or limit its consequences. Another way of reducing risk is to implement more internal controls.
Avoid	If any risks are defined as high likelihood and high impact, the project should be abandoned as the risk is too great.

Uncertainty

Unlike risk, uncertainty is impossible to evaluate because it is impossible to assign probability to an uncertain event. If the event is uncertain we cannot put in place management control to reduce the probability of its occurrence, simply because we do not know that probability. Instead we must use contingency planning.

Contingency planning

Contingency planning involves considering alternative actions which could be taken if uncertain events occur.

Contingency plans may include:

- contacting lenders to discuss possible additional finance.
- re-planning the remaining project with a longer duration.
- identifying if required materials are available from other possible suppliers.

The purpose of contingency planning is to avoid unnecessary delays in the project. The contingency plans may never be used, but we can do our contingency planning when it suits us. If we wait for the uncertain event before doing any planning, this may further delay the project.

Case study style question 4

It is often claimed that all project management is risk management since risk is an inherent and inevitable characteristic of most projects. The aim of the project manager is to combat the various hazards to which a project may be exposed.

L is a new project manager and is about to undertake her first project. She is concerned about risk management as she knows it is an important part of her role as project manager. She has come to you for advice.

Required:

Write an email to L explaining the concept of risk and the ways in which risk can be managed in a project.

(15 minutes)

Dealing with risk and uncertainty when planning for time

Risk and uncertainty at the initiation stage of the project has been covered above. At the detailed planning stage, risk and uncertainty must be considered again when the project manager is planning the time aspect of the project. There are a number of techniques which can assist with this:

- Project evaluation and review technique (PERT)
- Scenario planning
- Buffering.

Project evaluation and review technique (PERT)

This can be used to overcome uncertainties over times taken for individual activities in a network diagram.

Each task is assigned a time.

- An optimistic (best) time (o)
- A probable time (m)
- A pessimistic (worst) time (p)

It then uses a formula to calculate an expected time, and by calculating variances for each activity, estimates the likelihood that a set of activities will be completed within a certain time.

The expected time for each activity is then calculated as:

$$= \frac{o + 4m + p}{6}$$

These estimates are used to determine the average completion time.

Advantages:

- It gives an expected completion time.
- It gives a probability of completion before the specified date.
- It gives a Critical Path.
- It gives slack through earliest and latest start times.
- It allows calculation of contingency to be added to the plan.

Limitations:

- The activity times are very subjective.
- Assumes probability distribution of project completion time as the critical path.

Scenario planning

Although the use of PERT is one way to cope with risk in time planning there are ways of planning in a contingency for risk that are less complex. Wherever risk is identified as taking the form of alternative outcomes, a series of contingency or scenario plans may be constructed for each alternative.

Scenario planning involves considering one or more sets of circumstances that might occur, other than the 'most likely' or 'expected' set of circumstances used to prepare the budget or plan for a project. Each set of assumptions is then tested to establish what the outcome would be if those circumstances were actually to occur.

This would allow the project manager to switch to the appropriate plan for whichever contingency arose.

Buffering

A more simplistic way to incorporate risk by adding artificial slack into risky activities. It adds padding to the original estimates and allows for the fact that it can be very difficult to ensure that all stages and activities are carried out exactly as planned. This is known as 'buffering', but should not be encouraged because it leads to a build-up of slack in the programme and may lead to complacency.

Gantt Chart

This is an alternative or complementary approach to network analysis. It also provides a graphical representation of project activities and can be used in both project planning and control.

A Gantt chart is a horizontal bar chart where the length of the bar represents the duration of the activity.

When a Gantt chart is used to help control a project it is usual to use two bars, one showing the planned duration and the second showing the actual duration.

To create a Gantt chart:

- Display a schedule of activities using bars.
- List the activities down the side of the page.
- Using a horizontal timescale, draw a bar for each activity to represent the period over which it is to be performed.
- Both budgeted and actual timescales can be shown on the same chart.

Illustration 3 – Gantt chart example

An example of a project undertaken to examine the current procedures in the accounts payable department.

The project manager's first step is to break down the project into phases:

		Estimated time to complete
Phase 1	Document current procedures	4 days
Phase 2	Produce flowcharts	3 days
Phase 3	Summarise paper flow and methods for receiving, processing and sending information	5 days
Phase 4	List problem areas and develop initial recommendations	6 days
Phase 5	Develop improved processing procedures	3 days
Phase 6	Track sample transactions for one week under existing procedures	5 days
Phase 7	Track sample transactions for two weeks under proposed new	10 days
Phase 8	Prepare and deliver a final report to the treasurer, including recommended changes in procedures and an estimate of savings	2 days

This could then be expressed in a Gantt chart using the most common method, the bar chart, the start of which is shown below. The budgets for the activities are shown, together with the actual durations underneath:

Days	**1**	**2**	**3**	**4**	**5**	**6**	**7**	**8**	**9**	**10**	**11**
Document current procedures											
Produce flowcharts											
Summarise paper flow and methods for receiving, processing and sending information											
List problem areas and develop initial recommendations											

Benefits of Gantt charts:

The Gantt chart shares some advantages with network analysis:

- Assists in identifying all activities required for completing the project
- It will assist in identifying those activities that need to be completed before the next activity can start (dependent activities), and those that can happen at the same time (parallel activities)
- The Gantt chart will show the minimum completion time for the project, and will allow for sensitivity analysis to be introduced into the project.

In addition, the Gantt chart has further advantages over network analysis:

- Easier visualisation of relationships
- Unlike CPA, activities are drawn to scale so the most significant activities can be highlighted
- It is drawn in real time
- Actual durations can be shown alongside budget
- Aids resource allocation.

Limitations of Gantt charts:

The Gantt chart is a useful tool for tracking your project and anticipating delay problems before the final deadline is compromised. However, it will be of limited use when you have to deal with a relatively large project team. The more complex the team structure the higher the likelihood of schedule delays.

Remember, charting phases and monitoring progress is only a tool, not the solution itself.

For the more complex projects the Gantt chart has the following limitations:

- It does not identify potential weak links between phases.
- The chart does not reveal team problems due to unexpected delays.
- The chart does not coordinate resources and networking requirements needed at critical phases of the schedule.
- It does not show the degrees of completion for each phase.

Case study style question 5

A new on-line order entry system is currently being developed in your organisation. As part of the implementation procedures, users of the new system will require a number of training activities.

K has just taken over as project manager from H who left the project due to ill health. K has found the following network diagram for the project but is not sure what it tells him.

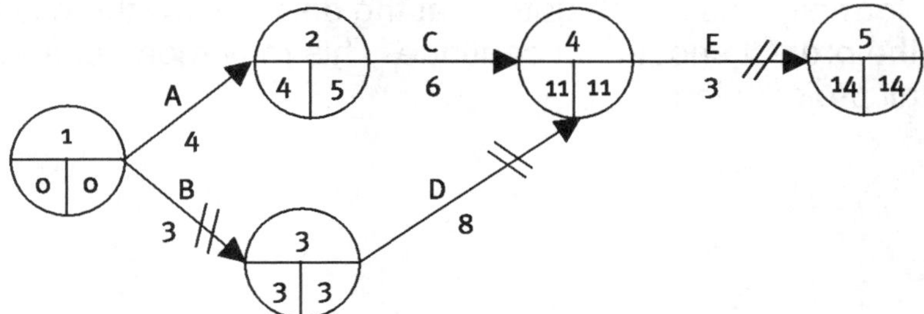

Required:

Write an email to K, explaining the information he should be able to establish from the network diagram. You should also explain how a Gantt chart might be of more use in this context.

(15 minutes)

Milestones and control gates

One of the main reasons for constructing a network diagram is to improve the control of the project duration.

In order to facilitate this, a number of milestones can be identified in the network. They are not specifically shown on the diagram (except of course for the end activities), but they are shown on a Gantt chart as a small triangle or other symbol.

A **milestone**, as the name implies, is an event that is clearly identifiable as a measure of how far the project has progressed, and how far it has to run. This involves partitioning the project into identifiable and manageable phases that are well defined key events and unambiguous targets of what needs to be done and by when, and should be established during the project planning phase.

Milestones are important in assessing the status of the project and quality of the work. Monitoring the milestones enables the project manager to keep control over the projects progress, and allows any delays to be identified immediately.

Some milestones are key points in the project life cycle which give the project sponsor or steering committee an opportunity to review project progress, and make a decision whether to proceed further or to terminate the project. These milestones are called **control gates** and represent the significant completion of milestones. A gate can only be 'passed' if the progress meets pre-defined performance standards. This could take the form of technical reviews or completion of documents.

Control gates should be identified in the project plan and a review will be required to formally pass each gate. If at the gate review the criteria have not been met, the project should not continue. This may mean changes are needed to the overall project plan.

12 Summary diagram

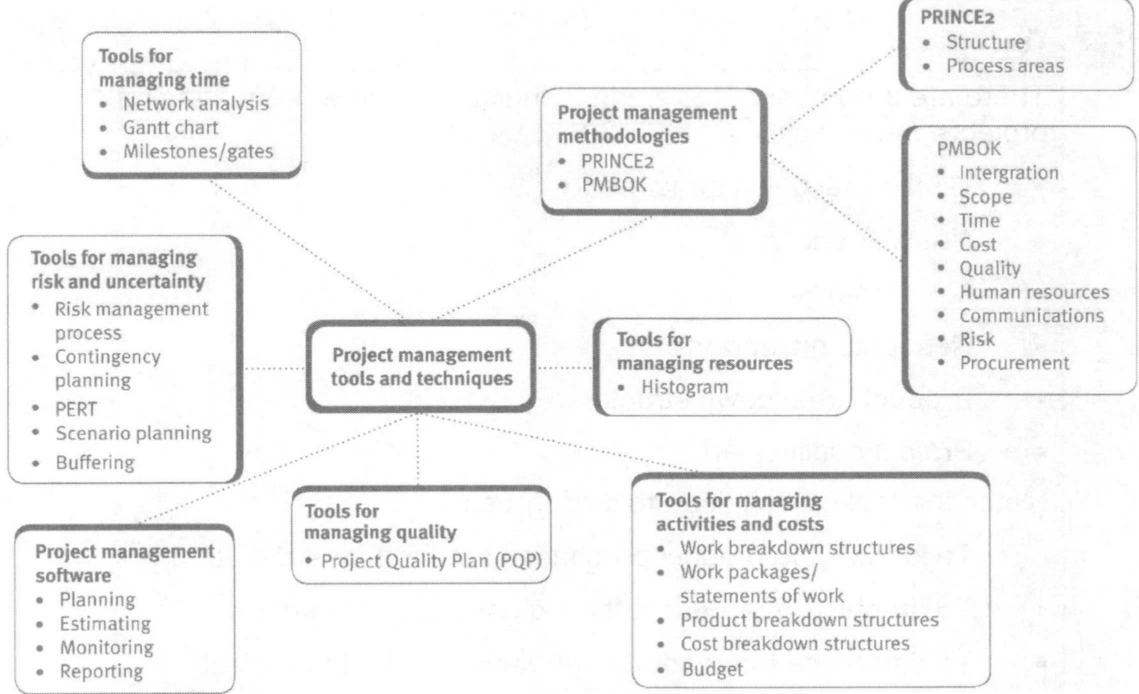
Tools for managing time
• Network analysis
• Gantt chart
• Milestones/gates
Project management methodologies
• PRINCE2
• PMBOK
PRINCE2
• Structure
• Process areas
PMBOK
• Intergration
• Scope
• Time
• Cost
• Quality
• Human resources
• Communications
• Risk
• Procurement
Tools for managing risk and uncertainty
• Risk management process
• Contingency planning
• PERT
• Scenario planning
• Buffering
Project management tools and techniques
Tools for managing resources
• Histogram
Tools for managing quality
• Project Quality Plan (PQP)
Tools for managing activities and costs
• Work breakdown structures
• Work packages/ statements of work
• Product breakdown structures
• Cost breakdown structures
• Budget
Project management software
• Planning
• Estimating
• Monitoring
• Reporting

End of chapter questions

Question 1

There are a number of tools and techniques used when managing projects, including:

- Work breakdown structures
- Network analysis
- Milestones
- Resource histograms
- Product breakdown structures
- Project quality plan

Match the tool or technique to its purpose.

- To identify the product purchases required for each activity
- To graphically represent the logical order of activities
- To determine the resource requirements for the project

Question 2

Which THREE of the following are PRINCE2 process areas?

A Controlling a stage

B Identification of a need

C Managing product delivery

D Planning

E Post completion audit

F Project closure

Question 3

The following shows a network diagram for a project. The durations are shown in weeks.

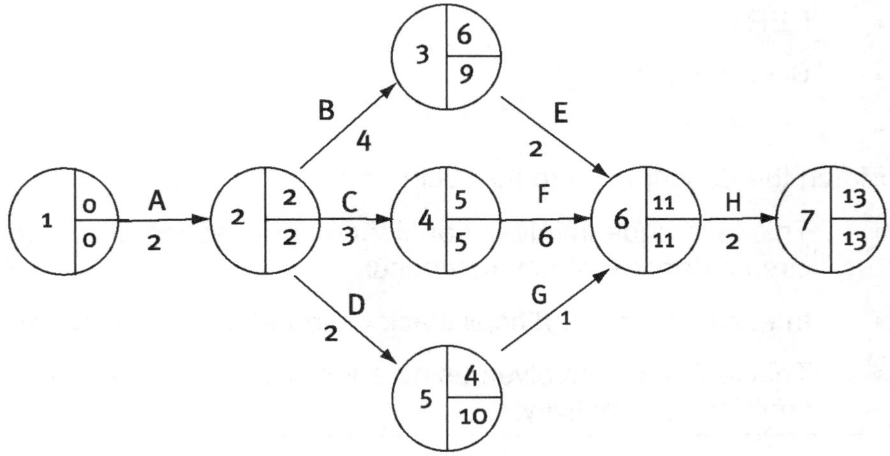

Using this diagram, which of the following statements are true? Select all that apply.

A The overall duration of the project is 13 weeks

B The critical path is ADGH

C Activities B and E have slack of 3 weeks

D Activities D and G have slack of 7 weeks

E Activity E is on the critical path

F The critical path is ACFH

Question 4

Which of the following statements regarding critical path analysis is FALSE?

A Each activity line must begin and end with a node

B Latest event times are calculated working left to right

C When there is a choice in calculating the earliest event time, select the highest

D Activities that are not on the critical path will have float

Question 5

When planning a project, there are a number of techniques that are used to take account of risk and uncertainty:

- PERT
- Scenario planning
- Buffering

Match the descriptions to the technique.

- This technique involves considering and testing one or more set of circumstances which may occur.
- In this technique artificial slack is added to risky activities.
- This technique involves using a formula to calculate an expected time for each activity.

Question 6

Which of the following are project management knowledge areas as defined by the Project Management Institute? Select all that apply.

A Communications

B Legal

C Leadership

D Procurement

E Integration

F Scope

Question 7

The following diagram shows a critical path diagram for a network. The durations are shown in weeks.

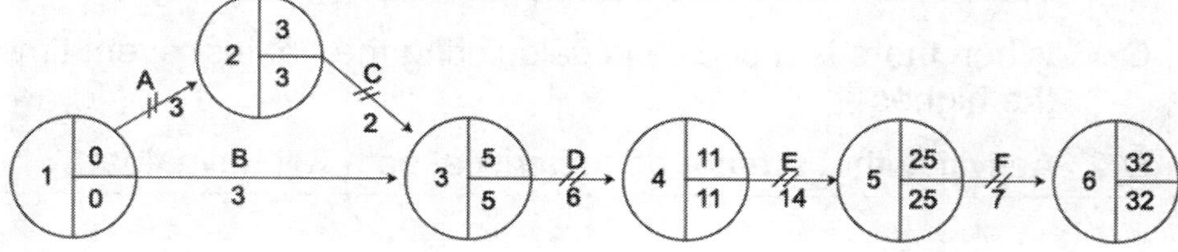

Which of the following statements regarding activity B is true?

A There is no slack in activity B.

B Activity B is on the critical path.

C Activity B can overrun by 2 weeks.

D Activity B can only start after the completion of activity A.

Question 8

Which of the following statements regarding project management software are true? Select all that apply.

A Software can only be used at the planning stage of the project

B Software improves the accuracy of drawing network diagrams

C Using project management software will ensure the success of the project

D Software can be used to undertake 'what if' analysis

E Using software can improve communication during a project

Question 9

Which of the following statements regarding milestones and gates is **incorrect**?

A A milestone is used to measure the progress of a project

B If a milestone is not met, the project should not continue

C Milestones can be shown on gantt charts

D A control gate can only be passed if progress meets pre-defined performance standards

Question 10

Which TWO of the following statements regarding the PRINCE2 structure are correct?

A In the PRINCE2 organisation chart, the project manager reports to the project sponsor.

B The project committee is made up of senior user, senior supplier and project support.

C The PRINCE2 structure includes organisation, plans, controls, products, quality, risk management and control of change management.

D Initiation documents, budgets and progress reports are part of the PRINCE2 products.

E The project assurance team is made up of business assurance co-ordinator, customer assurance co-ordinator and supplier assurance co-ordinator.

Test your understanding answers

Case study style question 1

EMAIL

To: Project sponsor

From: Project manager

Date: today

Subject: Project YT – Network diagram

I have completed the network diagram for project YT. This is shown below:

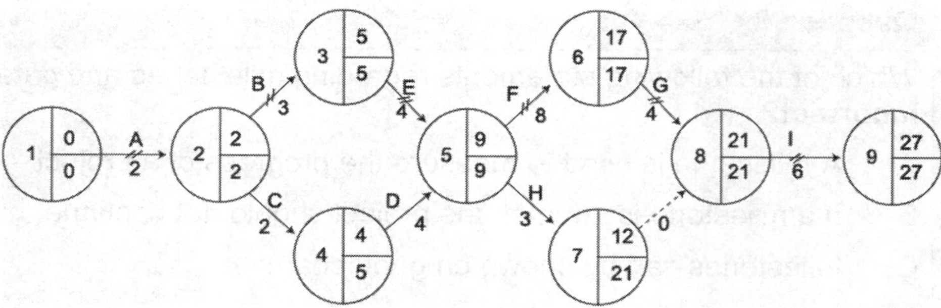

The diagram gives us a number of pieces of information which will be helpful to us in running the project.

From the diagram, the overall duration of the project is 27 weeks.

A number of the activities are deemed to be 'critical'. Critical activities are those activities which must be done on time, or the overall duration of the project will be extended to beyond 27 weeks. In project YT, the critical activities are A, B, E, F, G and I. Extra care must be taken to ensure that these activities run to plan.

The diagram also highlights those activities which have float, or slack. Activities with float or slack in this project are C and D which have one week of float, and H which has nine weeks.

I hope this information is useful to you. Please get in touch if you have any questions or want to discuss any aspects further.

Case study style question 2

REPORT

To: Management of XYZ

From: Management Accountant

Date: today

Subject: Critical path analysis and use of project management software

Introduction

In this report the importance of undertaking critical path analysis will be explained and the useful of using project management software will also be explained.

The importance of critical path analysis

Critical path analysis is an important technique to assist with project management, when a project has to be completed within a given amount of time, or before a final target date. A CPA chart shows all the activities that must be carried out in order to complete the project, the sequence in which they must take place, the budgeted time for each activity, the minimum overall completion time for the project and the earliest times that each activity can start and must be finished to make sure that the target project completion date is achieved. The analysis therefore enables management to:

- decide whether the target date for completion is achievable
- if the target date is achievable, what is the latest time the project can begin
- identify which activities are critical to completion on time and must be started at the earliest possible time
- identify those activities that are non-critical, and how much 'slack' they have, so that they can be started late or might take longer than planned without affecting the overall project completion time
- identify which activities cannot start until another activity (or other activities) have finished, and which activities can be undertaken in parallel with each other.

Regular monitoring of actual progress against the CPA chart will provide management with valuable information to assist with efforts to ensure completion of the project on time.

Project management software

Project management software can be used throughout the project in a number of ways. It is especially useful in planning, estimating, monitoring and reporting.

Planning

Project management software can be used to enter activities, estimates, precedents and resources to automatically produce a network diagram (showing the critical path) and a Gantt chart (showing resource use). These diagrams can be difficult to produce.

Estimating

Project management software allows the entry of actual data – the hours or days actually taken to complete a particular task. Many of these tasks are the same in systems development across different projects and so a considerable amount of information can be collected about the time taken to complete common tasks.

Monitoring

Project management software allows the entry of actual data, which can be used to monitor the progress of the project and to re-plan the rest of the work.

Reporting

Most project management software packages have comprehensive reporting requirements, which allow managers to print out the progress and status of the project. This means that standard progress reports can be produced automatically.

Conclusion

This report has looked at two important project management tools, namely critical path analysis and project management software. Both of these assist in the management of the project.

Case study style question 3

EMAIL

To: J

From: Management Accountant

Date: today

Subject: Project management methodology

A project management methodology that could have been used by RST is PRINCE2. This is an acronym for PRojects IN Controlled Environments and is a structured approach to project management, used by the UK government and private sector organisations. It includes bureaucratic controls on the planning and execution of projects, identifies some of the potential problems that may arise and early resolution. Whilst it could be argued that aspects of PRINCE2 could be considered to be just good project management, the difference is in the level of structure and documentation required.

The key processes of PRINCE2 methodology offer a number of features that would have benefited RST including:

- A defined management structure
- A system of plans
- A set of control procedures
- A focus on product based planning.

The main purpose is to deliver a successful project, which can be defined as:

- Delivery of agreed outcomes
- On time
- Within budget
- Conforming to the required quality standards.

PRINCE2 has a set of progressive documents for a project and control is achieved through the authorisation of work packages. These include controls on quality, time and costs and identify reports and handover requirements, all of which are problems that have led to the failure of the project in RST. The methodology includes a series of 'management products', for example project initiation documents, project budget, quality plan and various checkpoint and progress reports, which would have improved controls for RST's project.

The key processes and documentation of PRINCE2 would have enforced the project team in RST to have a clear structure of authority and responsibility between members in the project team, so that each party has clear objectives. As part of this, the control responsibilities of the various members of the project team would have been determined. This should mean that the different participants in the warehousing stock control and logistics project would have had a clearer understanding of the various tasks and the relationships between them and should have prevented the problems RST is now facing.

The exception plan concept in PRINCE2 would mean that if RST's project was going to exceed its tolerance, for example variances in time, cost or quality, this would have been reported to the project board. The implications on the whole project deliverables should have been discussed and plans amended to reflect any changes needed to ensure the project delivered its objectives.

I hope you have found the above useful, please get in touch if you need any more information about this.

Case study style question 4

EMAIL

To: L

From: Management Accountant

Date: today

Subject: Risk management

Risk can be defined as the probability of an adverse or undesirable event occurring. Undertaking any project carries an element of risk and project management will be concerned with understanding what is risky about a particular project or activity within the project. Essentially this will involve identifying the different risks within the project and then deciding how best to manage them.

Risk management can be seen as a process which follows a number of key stages.

The first stage is to identify the risks. A list of all risks within the project should be produced and a risk register produced.

Each risk should them be analysed with the intention of prioritising them so that your efforts are directed towards the most important risks first. Different levels of risk require different management strategies. This analysis will help you to decide on the best way to manage each risk.

Risks can be analysed by considering the probability of the risk occurring and the likely impact on the project should they occur. The likelihood and impact of each risk should be assessed as either high or low allowing the outcomes of the assessment to be plotted on a matrix as shown below.

IMPACT \ LIKELIHOOD	Low	High
Low	**Accept**	**Reduce**
High	**Transfer**	**Avoid**

The matrix is used to suggest the appropriate strategy to be used to manage each category of risk.

- Avoidance of risk. The only way to completely remove risk is to avoid the activity giving rise to it. If you analyse any risk to be high impact and high likelihood, the best course of action would be to abandon the project.
- Reduction of risk. Where the risk cannot be fully removed, its likelihood should be reduced. This can be done by improving internal controls or bringing in new processes.
- Transference of risk. The risk is unlikely but the impact would be significant. In this case it is best to try to pass the risk on to someone else, for example through insurance or sharing the risk with another party such as a supplier or sub-contractor.
- Acceptance of risk. This is when the potential risk is accepted in the hope or the expectation that the incidence and consequences can be coped with if necessary, perhaps having contingency plans should the risk occur. Risk exists in all business and a certain level of risk must be accepted.

It is important to remember that risk management is a continuous process throughout the life of the project. It is therefore important not to view risk management as a one off exercise carried out at the start of the project, rather an ongoing activity throughout the project. Regular review and monitoring must be carried out to ensure that the risks identified are being properly managed and that new risks have not appeared.

The above steps will enable you to monitor risk factors and take appropriate action throughout the project.

I hope you have found the above useful, please get in touch if you need any more information about this.

Case study style question 5

EMAIL

To: K

From: Management Accountant

Date: today

Subject: Network diagram

I have reviewed the network diagram for the on-line entry system project. The diagram gives us a number of pieces of information which will be helpful to you in running the project.

From the diagram, the overall duration of the project is 14 weeks.

A number of the activities are deemed to be 'critical'. Critical activities are those activities which must be done on time, or the overall duration of the project will be extended to beyond 14 weeks. In this project, the critical activities are B, D and E. Extra care must be taken to ensure that these activities run to plan.

The diagram also highlights those activities which have float, or slack. Activities with float or slack in this project are A and C which have one week of float.

The network diagram is useful in giving the above information, but it can be difficult to understand. Another tool which could be used to show much the same information is the Gantt chart. This is a straightforward method of scheduling tasks; it is essentially a chart on which bars represent each task or activity. The length of each bar represents the relative length of the task. Its advantages lie in its simplicity, the ready acceptance of it by users, and the fact that the bars are drawn to scale.

It also has the advantage over the network diagram in that the actual activities can be added alongside the scheduled activities which is useful in monitoring progress once the project is underway.

I hope this information is useful to you. Please get in touch if you have any questions or want to discuss any aspects further.

Question 1

The correct matching is:

Product breakdown structures – To identify the product purchases required for each activity.

Network analysis – To graphically represent the logical order of activities.

Resource histograms – To determine the resource requirements.

Work breakdown structures are used to break complex tasks into manageable pieces.

Milestones are used to assess the status of the project and how far the project has progressed.

Project quality plans are used to detail the standards required in the project.

Question 2

A, C and F

The other PRINCE2 process areas are:

- Starting up a project
- Initiation
- Managing stage boundaries

Question 3

A, C and F

The true statements are:

- The overall duration of the project is 13 weeks
- Activities B and E have slack of 3 weeks
- The critical path is ACFH

Question 4

B

This is false as latest event times are calculated working right to left.

Question 5

The correct matching is:

PERT – This technique involves using a formula to calculate an expected time for each activity.

Scenario planning – This technique involves considering and testing one or more set of circumstances which may occur.

Buffering – In this technique artificial slack is added to risky activities.

Question 6

A, D, E and F

The project management institute's nine process areas are communications, procurement, integration, scope and:

- time
- cost
- quality
- human resources
- risk

Question 7

C

Activity B has slack of 2 weeks. It is therefore able to overrun by 2 weeks without affecting the overall duration of the project.

Given that the activity has slack, it cannot be on the critical path as activities on the critical path must start and end as scheduled.

From the diagram it can be seen that activity B can start right at the beginning of the project and has no preceding activities.

Question 8

B, D and E

Project management software can be used throughout the project. Using software will contribute to the success of the project but cannot guarantee it.

Question 9

B

This is incorrect as a milestone is simply a measure of progress in the project. If a control gate is not met, the project should not continue.

Question 10

C and D

In the PRINCE2 organisation chart, the project manager reports to the project committee and the project assurance team.

The project committee is made up of senior user, senior supplier and executive.

The project assurance team is made up of business assurance co-ordinator, user assurance co-ordinator and specialist assurance co-ordinator.

Chapter

11

Project leadership

Chapter learning objectives

Lead	Component
C3: Explain the concepts of project leadership	(a) Project structure (b) Roles of key project personnel (c) How to manage project stakeholders

Topics to be covered

- Project structures and their impact on project performance
- Role of project manager
- Role of key members of project team
- Life cycle of project teams
- Managing key stakeholders of projects
- Leading and motivating project team.

1 Session content diagram

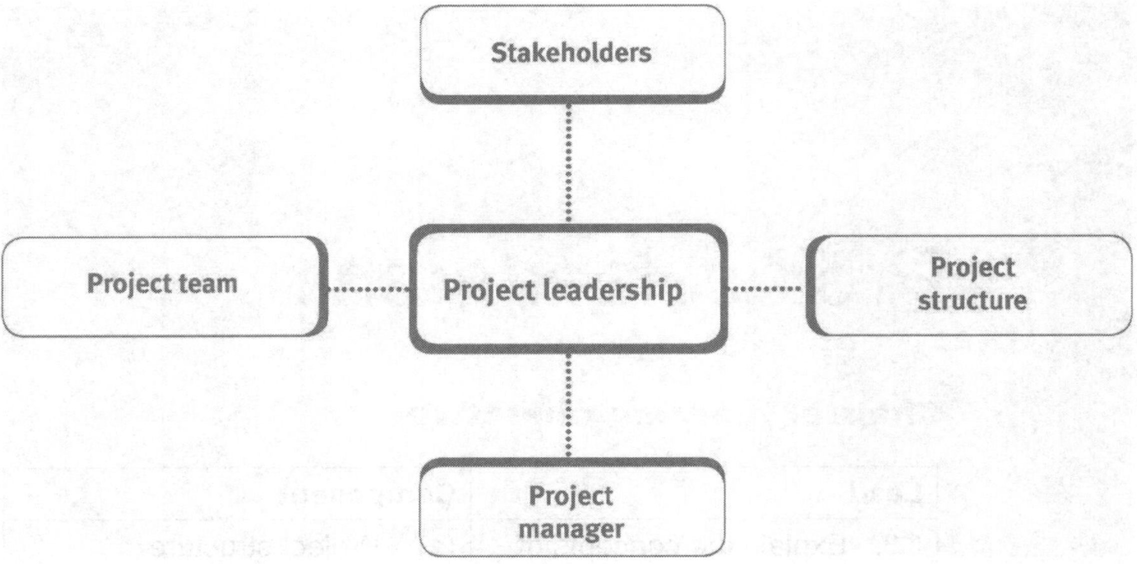

2 Who is involved in the project?

A lot of the material in this chapter will be familiar from the earlier chapters on relationship management. Much of the material in the relationship management part of the CIMA® syllabus will be equally applicable in the context of a project.

A key aspect in ensuring the success of a project is having the right people involved in the project. Decisions need to be made about the people involved in the project after the need for the project has been identified and the methodology has been selected.

Having the right people, with the right knowledge and skills, involved in the project will significantly enhance its chance of success.

There are various interested parties who are involved in or may be affected by the project activities. They are known as its '**stakeholders'**, as they have a 'stake' or interest in the effective completion of the project. Obviously, the number of people involved will depend on the size of the project.

A project is much like an organisation in that it has a hierarchical set of relationships. This hierarchy is put in place for two main reasons:

- to create a structure of authority so everyone knows who can make decisions, and
- to create a series of superior-subordinate relationships so each individual or group has only one 'boss'.

Project stakeholders should all be committed to achieving a common goal – the successful completion of the project.

Stakeholder hierarchy

Based on the principles of 'one person – one boss' and a decision-making authority, the hierarchy shown below is adapted from the one shown in *Successful Project Management*, **Gido and Clements** (1999).

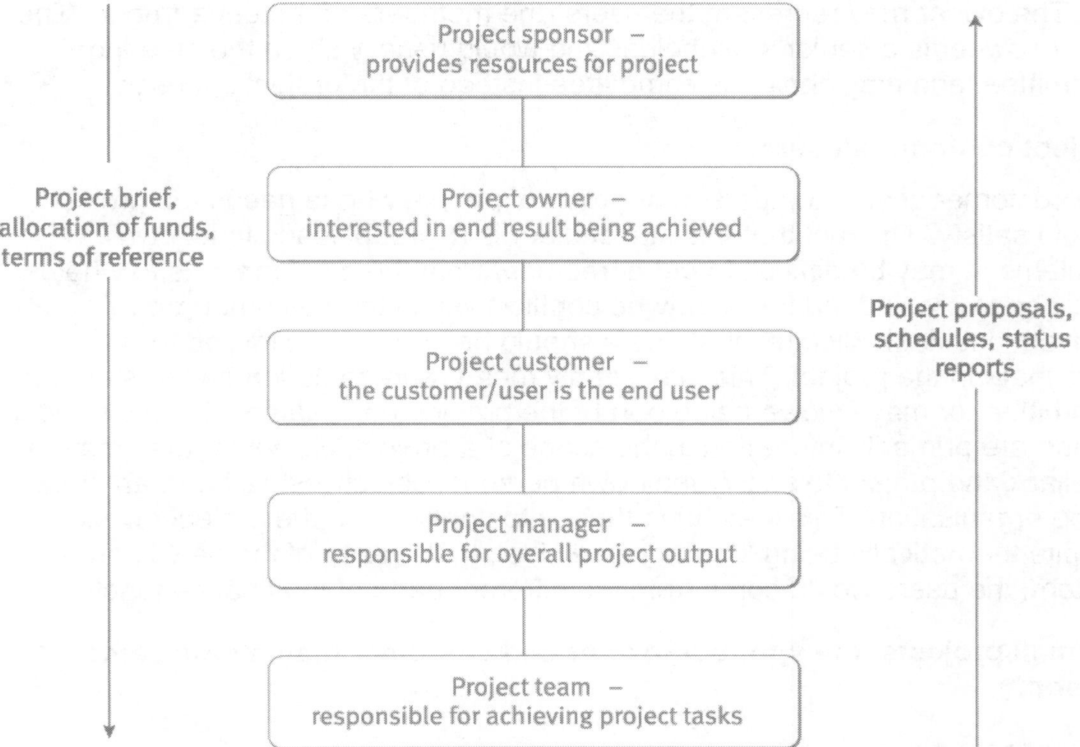

The roles of the various stakeholders:

Project sponsor:

The project sponsor makes yes/no decisions about the project.

The role of the sponsor:

- Initiates the project. They must be satisfied that a business case exists to justify the project.
- Appoints the project manager.
- Makes yes/no decision regarding the project. The sponsor is responsible for approving the project plan.
- Provides the resources for the project and are responsible for its budget.
- Monitors the progress of the project from the information provided by the project manager.
- Provides support and senior management commitment to the project.

Project owner:

The project owner is the person for whom the project is being carried out. They are interested in the end result being achieved and their needs being met. They are more concerned with scope and functionality than in budget. The project owner may be the head of the department for which the project is being carried out. The owner may represent the users (the members of the department). The project owner is a senior stakeholder and would usually sit on the steering committee, and may chair this committee instead of the project sponsor.

Project customers/users:

The customer/user is the person or group of people whose needs the project should satisfy. The fact that this stakeholder is a 'group' leads to its own problems. It may be difficult to get agreement from the customers as to what their needs are; indeed there may be conflicts within the customer group. Conventional logic dictates that users should be, if possible, invited to participate in the project. This may simply mean representation on the steering committee, or may involve being part of the project team. Users, like the project owner, are primarily interested in the scope of a project. However, they may try to 'hijack' the project to satisfy their own personal objectives, rather than those of the organisation. This may bring them into conflict with the project owner, despite theoretically being 'on the same side'. In the case of the new finance system, the users would come from the different parts of the finance function.

In small projects, the sponsor, owner and customer may be the same person.

Project manager:

The project manager is responsible for the successful delivery of project objectives to the satisfaction of the final customer. As projects are interdisciplinary and cross organisational reporting lines, the project manager has a complex task in managing, coordinating, controlling and communicating project tasks.

The role of project manager involves:

- Ensuring project objectives are achieved.
- Making decisions relating to system resources.
- Planning, monitoring and controlling the project.
- Selecting, building and motivating the project team.
- Serving as a point of contact with management hierarchy.
- Communicating with the chain of command.
- Selecting and managing subcontractors.
- Recommending termination where necessary.

In essence, the project manager takes responsibility for providing leadership to the project team who carry out the project tasks in order to achieve the project objectives. The project manager will lead and coordinate the activities of the project team to ensure that activities are performed on time, within cost and to the quality standards set by the customer. An important aspect of project management is to ensure that the team members are organised, coordinated and working together.

Project team:

The members of the project team will be given individual responsibility for parts of the project. As projects are often interdisciplinary and cross organisational reporting lines, the project team is likely to be made up of members drawn from a variety of different functions or divisions: each individual then has a dual role, as he or she maintains functional/divisional responsibilities as well as membership of the project team.

Project steering committee/project board

Overseeing the project and making all high level decision regarding the project will be a steering committee or project board. In smaller projects there will be either a steering committee or a project board, but larger scale projects will have both. Where a project has both, the project board sits above the steering committee in the hierarchy and is in charge of the overall management of the project. All high level decisions regarding the project will be made by the board.

While the steering committee may meet monthly, the board will meet less frequently, maybe only several times a year. They will require progress reports about the project, but these will be high level reports, focusing on the main aspects of the project. A strong project board can make the difference between success and failure of a large, complex project.

The steering committee/board will normally be chaired by the project sponsor and the members should represent all major areas of interest in the project, for example the project owner would sit on the committee/board. The representatives of each area should be at a sufficient level of seniority so that they have the authority to take decisions on behalf of their areas. The project manager will report all progress to the steering committee/project board.

Project Champion

Some high profile projects may have a project champion, or supporter. This is an informal role within the project, with no decision making or reporting responsibility. The role of the project champion is simply that, to campaign on behalf of the project at the highest levels of the organisation. They will show their support of the project by marketing it at every opportunity, even though they have no formal role in the project.

Other stakeholders

In addition to the above, suppliers, subcontractors and specialists are also important stakeholders. The project will often require input from other parties, such as material suppliers or possibly specialist labour, such as consultants. Each of them will have their own objectives, some of which conflict with those of the project. For example, suppliers will seek to maximise the price of the supply, and reduce its scope and quality, in order to reduce cost. This conflicts directly with the objectives of the sponsor and customers. In the case of the new finance system, suppliers may provide hardware and software, and specialists might include members of the organisation's IT, purchasing or internal audit departments.

The role of Certified Management Accountants (CMAs) in projects

Management accountants can undertake a variety of roles within projects, including:

Project manager – many accountants undertake the role of project manager. The range of skills possessed by the management accountant, such as leadership, communication and analytical skills are the skills required by the project manager.

Project sponsor – the project sponsor, who supplies the funding for the project is often a senior member of the finance function.

Project customer/user – all areas within organisations can be affected by projects and many projects will have an effect on the financial systems and procedures, therefore the management accountants will often be involved in terms of assessing the impact the changes will have on the accounting function.

Member of project team – management accountants are often required to be part of project teams. They bring financial knowledge and are able to analyse and advise on the financial impact of the project on the organisation.

Providing financial information for the project – the finance department is often involved in supplying financial information to the project manager. At the outset of the project when the economic feasibility is being considered, the management accountant would be involved in undertaking the cost-benefit analysis. Throughout the project, the project spend should be monitored and compared to the original budget and this information is usually produced by the management accountant.

3 Managing stakeholder relationships

At the beginning of a project potential stakeholders need to be identified and their interest and power in the project assessed. This is a vital project management activity to enable the relationships within the groups to be managed. A plan can be drawn up to secure and maintain their support and to foresee and react to any problems. The project manager can concentrate on the critical stakeholder relationships, assess the risks associated with certain groups, indicate where attention needs to be focused and thus reduce the vulnerability of the project.

The project manager has to balance a number of values, beliefs and assumptions in attempting to navigate a project to a successful conclusion. These values, beliefs and assumptions relate to the stakeholders in the project, who may be defined as any party with a vested interest. The ability to be able to discern stakeholder values, beliefs, assumptions and expectations is a positive tool in the project manager's 'competence toolbox', not least because they often conflict and may not always be benevolent to the project.

Once stakeholders are identified they can be mapped in relation to:

- The likelihood of each stakeholder group attempting to impress their expectations on others.
- The power and means available for them to do so.
- The impact of stakeholder expectations on the project.

Mendelow's matrix, which was covered in the concept of business ecosystems chapter and the alternative approaches to business models chapter, could be used to aid the project manager in managing the project stakeholders.

Stakeholder conflict

Most conflict within projects arises from the interaction of individuals, and a good project manager must have the interpersonal skills to be able to manage conflict.

Within a project, there will be a number of stakeholders and they may not share the same objectives, which may cause conflict. Among the most common reasons for conflict within projects are the following:

- Unclear objectives for the project.
- Role ambiguity within the project team.
- Unclear schedules and performance targets.
- A low level of authority given to the project manager.
- Remote functional groups within the project, working almost independently.
- Interference from local or functional management.
- Personality clashes, or differing styles of working.

The project manager should establish a framework to predict the potential for disputes.

This involves:

- risk management – since an unforeseen event (a risk) has the potential to create conflict; and
- dispute management – matching dispute procedures with minimum impact on costs, progress and goodwill.

The techniques used for dispute management are:

- **Negotiation** – involving the parties discussing the problem. This may or may not resolve the problem.
- **Mediation** or 'assisted negotiation' – involves a neutral third party (the mediator) intervening to reach a mutually agreeable solution. In practice, disputes are often resolved by accepting the view of the stakeholder that has financial responsibility for the project. In such a situation, mediation and negotiation may only deliver an outcome that is a reflection of the original power imbalance.
- **Partnering** – focuses on creating communication links between project participants with the intention of directing them towards a common goal – ahead of their own self-interest.
- **Compromise** – is the most obvious approach to conflict management, although it does imply that both parties in the conflict must sacrifice something.

Case study style question 1

A project is being undertaken by the ABC Regional Health Authority to connect all medical centres and hospitals within the region to a national information network, called the 'Healthweb'.

You are a senior management accountant working for one of the regional hospitals, and, as part of the project team, it is your responsibility to communicate with all the medical centres and hospitals on the progress of the project.

ABC is one of four regional government-controlled authorities, responsible to the central government. Each regional health authority manages and controls the provision of medical care to the public within its local area. ABC is responsible for fifty medical centres and ten hospitals within the region, all of which are publicly funded. The project has been initiated by the central government and T has been appointed as the project manager.

ABC has been set a target by the central government to have 80% of all medical centers and 90% of all hospitals within the region connected to the Healthweb by July 20X7. Prior to the project commencement, most information within the hospitals and medical centres was kept by a manual, paper-based system, and all data exchange was done by means of telephone or by post. The senior management team of ABC set up a project board to oversee the progress of the project and to specify the project objectives.

Required:

You have been asked by the executives of your own hospital to prepare a report to the other senior managers in the hospital which should discuss the relationship of T, the project manager to:

- the project sponsor (i.e., the central government)
- the project board
- the medical and administrative users (in medical centres and hospitals).

Your report should also Include a discussion of the potential conflicting project objectives of the above stakeholders.

(20 minutes)

4 Project manager

The skills required by a project manager

The skills that the project manager brings to the project are critical to its success. A project manager requires a number of varied skills:

Main project management skills

Leadership

Leadership is the ability to obtain results from others through personal direction and influence. Leadership in projects involves influencing others through the personality or actions of the project manager. The project manager cannot achieve the project objectives alone; results are achieved by the whole project team. The project manager must have the ability to motivate the project team in order to create a team objective that they want to be part of.

Communication

Project managers must be effective communicators. They must communicate regularly with a variety of people, including the customer, suppliers, subcontractors, project team and senior management. Communication is vital for the progression of the project, identification of potential problems, generation of solutions and keeping up to date with the customer's requirements and the perceptions of the team.

Project managers should communicate by using a variety of methods:

- regular team meetings
- regular meetings face-to-face with the customer
- informal meetings with individual team members
- written reports to senior management and the customer
- listening to all the stakeholders involved in the project.

Negotiation

Project managers will have to negotiate on a variety of project issues, such as availability and level of resources, schedules, priorities, standards, procedures, costs, quality and people issues. The project manager may have to negotiate with someone over whom he or she has no direct authority (e.g. consultants), or who has no direct authority over him or her (e.g. the customer).

Delegation

A further key skill required for a project manager is that of delegation. A project manager will communicate and clarify the overall project objective to the team members, and will then further clarify the individual team member's role in achieving that objective by a process of delegation. Delegation is about empowering the project team and each team member to accomplish the expected tasks for his or her area of responsibility. The project manager has neither the time nor the skills to carry out all the project tasks, so he or she must delegate responsibility to those who do have the skills.

Problem solving

Project managers will inevitably face numerous problems throughout the project's life. It is important that the project manager gathers information about the problem in order to understand the issues as clearly as possible. The project manager should encourage team members to identify problems within their own tasks and try to solve them on their own, initially. However, where tasks are large or critical to the overall achievement of the project, it is important that team members communicate with the project manager as soon as possible so that they can lead the problem-solving effort.

Change-management skills

One thing is certain in projects, and that is change. Changes may be:

- requested by the customer
- requested by the project team
- caused by unexpected events during the project performance
- required by the users of the final project outcome.

Therefore, it is important that the project manager has the skills to manage and control change. The impact that change has on accomplishing the project objective must be kept to a minimum and may be affected by the time in the project's life cycle when the change is identified. Generally, the later the change is identified in the project life cycle, the greater its likely impact on achieving the overall project objective successfully. Most likely to be affected by change is the project budget and its timescale.

The project manager and negotiation

A key skill required by the project manager is negotiation. While running a complex project, the project manager may get involved in a number of negotiations.

Project managers will have to negotiate on a variety of project issues, such as availability and level of resources, schedules, priorities, standards, procedures, costs, quality and people issues. The project manager may have to negotiate with someone over whom he or she has no direct authority (e.g. consultants), or who has no direct authority over him or her (e.g. the customer).

The following table gives examples of the types of issues for which the project manager may get involved in negotiation.

Negotiation point	Possible issues	Negotiate with
Resources	Funding	Senior management
	Staff	Line managers
	Equipment	Purchasing
	Time scale	Customer/senior management
Schedules	Order of activities	Customer/teams
	Duration of activities	Line managers/team members
	Timing of activities	Line managers/team members
	Deadlines	Customer/line managers
Priorities	Over other projects or work	Senior management
	Between cost, quality and time	Customer/team members
	Of team members' activities	Team members
Procedures	Methods	Team members
	Roles and responsibilities	Team members/customer
	Reporting	Senior management/customer
	Relationships	Team members
Quality	Assurance checks	Customer/teams
	Performance measures	Customer/teams
	Fitness for purpose	Customer/team members
Costs	Estimates	Accountants/team members
	Budgets	Customer/senior management
	Expenditure	Customer/accountants
People	Getting team to work together	Team members
	Getting required skills	Team members/line managers
	Work allocations	Team members/line managers
	Effort needed	Team members/line managers

5 Project team management

The basic project team consists of the project manager (and possible team leaders), and a group of specialists assigned or recruited for the project.

The project team should include everyone who will significantly contribute to the project, both managerial and non-managerial people, whether they are full-time or part-time.

The project team will obviously include all of the technical people responsible for the project's efforts toward research, design, development, procurement, production and testing. Team members are expected to attend all project meetings, and to participate in project decision-making. Therefore, care should be taken in making sure that the team does not have any non-performing members. The project team is likely to be made up of a range of staff with different skills and experience. Effective team working is essential for the success of a project and it is important to foster this through regular meetings to establish team cohesion, helping to develop a team which is integrated, has common objectives and positive group dynamics.

The ideal project team will achieve project completion on time, within budget and to the required specifications. They will do all this with the minimum amount of direct supervision from the project manager.

The project manager must get the individual team members to view the project from the 'big-picture' perspective, and to concentrate on overall project goals.

Lifecycle of project teams

Tuckman's model of team development can be used to show the lifecycle of the project team.

The stages are:

- **Forming** – a collection of individuals are brought together, often from different areas of the organisation. The project manager has an important role at this stage to provide clear direction to the team and ensuring they understand the project objectives.
- **Storming** – As the individuals start to operate as a team, most teams go through this conflict stage. Team members may try to test the project manager's authority and may challenge the role they have been given. The project manager must demonstrate strong conflict resolution leadership skills at this stage.
- **Norming** – The individuals settle in to their roles and the team starts to perform. The project manager will begin to pass control and decision-making authority to the team members.
- **Performing** – The team is capable of operating at full potential at this stage. The project manager will concentrate on the performance of the project.
- **Adjourning** (dorming) – Once the objectives of the project have been achieved, the team can be disbanded and the individuals can go back to their previous roles, or move on to work on a new project.

These stages can be considered alongside the project lifecycle as shown below:

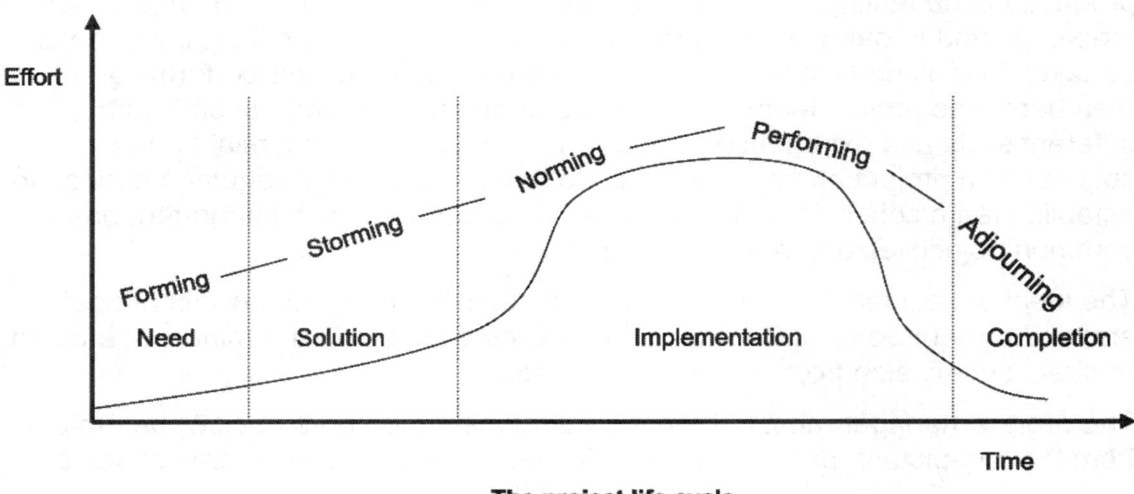

The project life cycle

Likewise the other models of team building, such as Belbin, can also be applied to project teams. These models should be reviewed at this stage and consideration given as to how they could be applied in a project scenario.

Managing project teams

In the management of project teams we must pay attention to two particular characteristics of each team:

- Each project is a complete entity, and unique in terms of experiences, problems, constraints and objectives.
- The members of the team concerned may well have not worked together as a group on any previous occasion.

The **style of management** for the team must be the relevant approach aimed at the creation of the appropriate internal team environment or, in other words, team climate. Some large organisations provide the team with initial status by providing it with all the necessary support and resources, such as office accommodation, a budget, support secretarial staff, and so on. Other organisations simply appoint a leader, authorised by the board to appoint team members and acquire resources at his or her own discretion.

The **planning and controlling of the team** activities are vital aspects of management in that a major project cost lies in the fact that team members are not undertaking their own tasks but have been taken from these temporarily. It is essential that there should be an unambiguous statement of:

- the project objective(s) – what is to be achieved?
- the project approach, methods – how is it to be achieved?
- the location of activities – where is it to be achieved?
- the allocation of responsibilities – what is to be done by whom?
- the project budget – at what cost?

Leading and motivating project teams

All aspects of leadership and motivation which were covered in the leadership and management chapter are equally applicable in the context of a project team as they are to business as usual. The models covered in the leadership and management chapter should be reviewed at this stage and consideration given as to how they could be applied in a project scenario.

The project manager does not and cannot complete a project on his or her own. It requires effective teamwork and team motivation. To foster a motivated project team environment, the project manager needs to understand his or her team members first in order to understand what motivates them. The project manager should attempt to create a project environment that is supportive and where team members feel enthusiastic and want to work towards the overall project goal.

The project manager can create such an environment by:

- Ensuring that the team is made up of the correct people. The project manager should be aware of Belbin's model and ensure that all required roles in the team are met. This will avoid conflict and foster good working relationships.
- Adequate knowledge and experience in team. The project manager must ensure that all team members are able to participate fully in their role and that they possess the required knowledge and skills.
- Adopting a participative style of management.
- By encouraging participation in project decision-making.
- By delegating decisions to the team members, thus encouraging involvement and ownership.
- Holding regular project meetings whereby team members can participate and air their views and put forward their opinions.
- Holding regular one-to one meetings with individual team members, encouraging them to put forward their own ideas and suggestions for project improvement.
- Ensuring that conflict is minimised by ensuring that all team members are clear about their role and what is required of them.

The project manager needs to demonstrate that he/she values the contribution made by team members and that their contribution is important to the overall project.

Case study style question 2

EFG is a large construction company that has just won a major contract for a road-widening scheme through an area of countryside that has been officially designated as an 'area of outstanding natural beauty'. The work will be carried out to some extent by direct employees of EFG, but most of the work will be undertaken by sub-contractors.

The scheme has already attracted a considerable amount of publicity and the Preserve the Countryside Movement, a large national pressure group, has already announced its intention to organise demonstrations and protests against the construction work. More extreme and radical protest groups have threatened disruptive action.

The project is being financed by the transport department of the central government, and the managers of EFG who are responsible for the project have already spoken to the police authorities about the preservation of public order. A security firm will be employed to provide physical protection to employees and assets.

A traffic survey conducted for the central government has suggested that, during the time that the road widening is taking place, there will be severe disruption to normal road traffic and severe delays for drivers on their journeys will be inevitable.

P has been appointed as project manager, but this is the largest and most complex project he has managed. He knows that in this project he must give strong leadership to get the best possible performance out of the project team, but he is concerned about how he is going to manage this aspect of the project.

Required:

Write an email to P suggesting what leadership style is most likely to be successful for a project such as this road-widening scheme. Give your reasons and make reference to any theories of leadership style with which you are familiar.

(15 minutes)

6 Project structure

Establishing an effective project management structure is crucial for its success. Every project has a need for direction, management, control and communication, using a structure that differs from line management. As a project is normally cross functional and involves partnership, its structure needs to be more flexible, and is likely to require a broad base of skills for a specific period of time. The project manager needs a clear structure, consisting of roles and responsibilities that bring together the various interests and skills involved in, and required by, the project.

In conventional (functional or divisional) structures, there is often a lack of clarity as to how authority is divided between line managers and project managers. If a project is relatively small or short term, for example an information system redevelopment, this may not be a major issue. However, if the project forms a major part of the business of the organisation, such as in a construction company, this may necessitate an organisation structure such as a matrix, where lines of authority are clearer.

Matrix and project structure

A matrix structure aims to combine the benefits of decentralisation (motivation of identifiable management teams, closeness to the market, speedy decision making) with those of co-ordination (achieving economies and synergies across all business units, territories and products).

The matrix structure seeks to add flexibility and lateral coordination. One way is to create project teams made up of members drawn from a variety of different functions or divisions. Each individual has a dual role as he/she maintains their functional/divisional responsibilities as well as membership of the project team.

Both vertical and horizontal relationships are emphasised, and employees have dual reporting to managers. The following diagram shows a mix of project and functional structures.

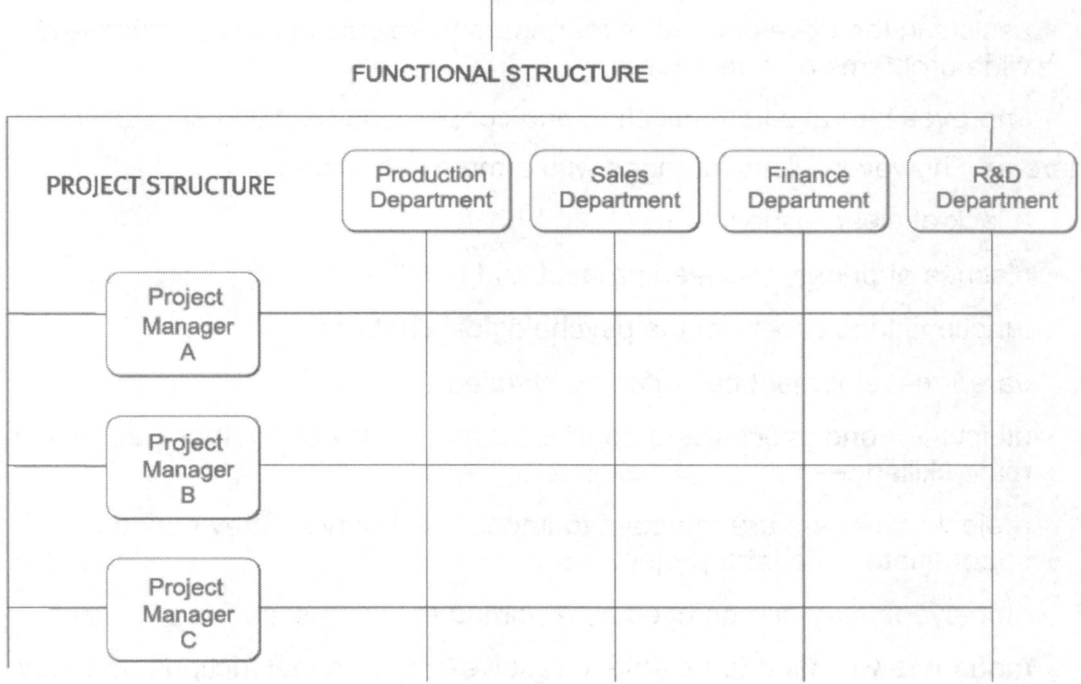

The matrix organisation structure has been widely criticised, but is still used by many project-based organisations in industries such as engineering, construction, consultancy, audit and even education.

The matrix structure is most suitable where:

- The business of the organisation consists of a series of projects, each requiring staff and resources from a number of technical functions.
- The projects have different start and end dates, so the organisation is continually reassigning resources from project to project.
- The projects are complex, so staff benefit from also being assigned to a technical function (such as finance of logistics) where they can share knowledge with colleagues.
- The projects are expensive, so having resources controlled by functional heads should lead to improved utilisation and reduced duplication across projects.
- The projects are customer-facing, so the customer requires a single point of contact (the project manager) to deal with their needs and problems.

Impact on project achievement

The matrix structure can impact on the achievement of the project as follows:

- improved decision-making by bringing a wide range of expertise to problems that cut across departmental or divisional boundaries
- replacement of formal control by direct contact
- assists in the development of managers by exposing them to company-wide problems and decisions
- improves lateral communication and cooperation between specialists.

There are, however, disadvantages with a matrix structure:

- a lack of clear responsibility
- clashes of priority between product and function
- functions lose control of the psychological contract
- career development can often be stymied
- difficult for one specialist to appraise performance of another discipline in multi-skilled teams
- project managers are reluctant to impose authority as they may be subordinates in a later project
- employees may be confused by reporting to two bosses
- managers will need to be able to resolve interpersonal frictions and may need training in human relations skills
- managers spend a great deal of time in meetings to prioritise tasks.

Case study style question 3

HIJ designs and manufactures sports equipment and is currently positioned as the market leader in the industry. However, whilst operating in a growth market, there are new competitors entering the market with innovative new product offerings. The marketing director is aware that to retain market leader position, the company must improve its practices involved with new product development (NPD), and the time taken to get from the product idea to launch needs to be much quicker.

The company has a functional structure with the marketing director heading up the marketing function, and the R&D director heading up the function responsible for research and product development; in addition, there are separate functions for production, human resources, finance, sales and IT.

The marketing director feels that the functional structure is impeding the NPD process. Having recently read an article on organising for NPD, he is proposing that the best way to manage the process would be through introducing a matrix structure and the use of cross functional teams. However, at a recent meeting of the functional heads, the R&D director said that, in his experience, the potential difficulties in using a matrix structure offset the benefits.

The managing director is unsure as to whether HIJ should adopt a matrix structure and has asked for your advice.

Required:

Write a report for the managing director describing the advantages and disadvantages of HIJ using a matrix structure in project management work for NPD.

(15 minutes)

7 Summary diagram

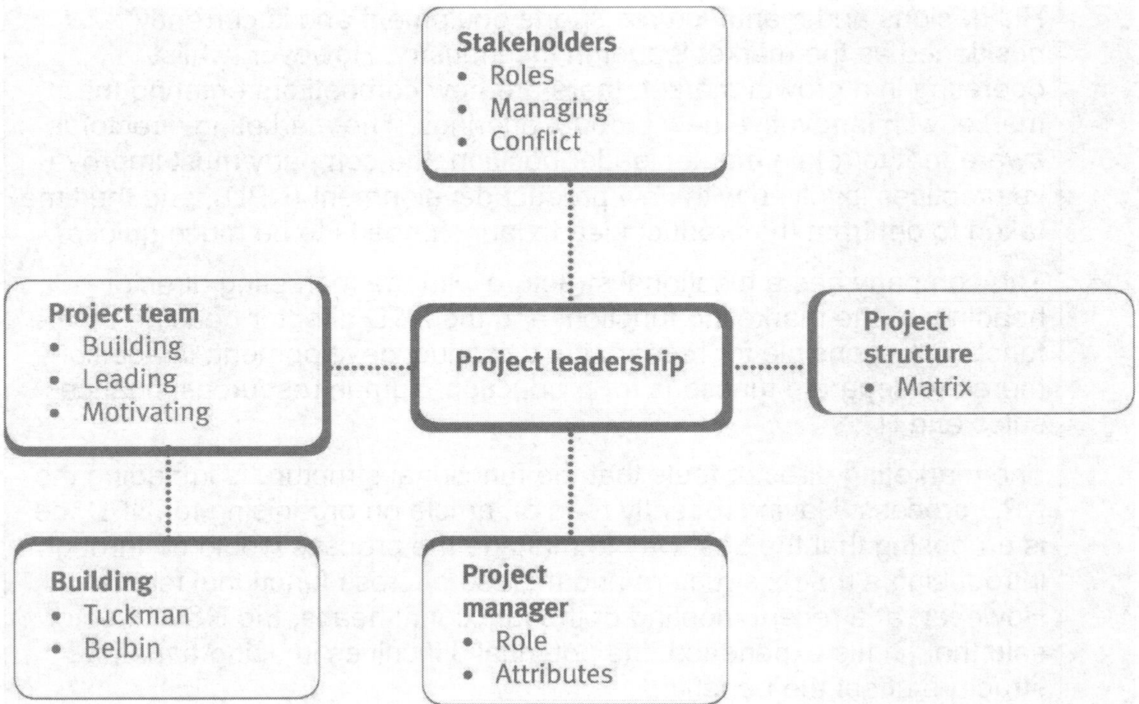

End of chapter questions

Question 1

There are a number of people involved in a project. Match the people to the correct description.

Project sponsor	Responsible for the successful delivery of the project
Project owner	The person for whom the project is being carried out
Project manager	Responsible for making all high level decisions about the project
Project board	Provides resources for the project

Question 2

The person responsible for approving the project plan is which of the following?

A Project manager

B Project owner

C Project sponsor

D Project user

Question 3

Organisations that run a number of projects often adopt the matrix structure. Which three of the following characteristics lead to the matrix structure being the most suitable?

A The projects have different start and end dates.

B The projects are all of short duration.

C The organisation runs projects occasionally.

D The projects are expensive.

E The organisation has a dedicated project team which works on all projects.

F The projects are customer facing.

Question 4

H is a project manager. He has just been appointed to manage a project on behalf of XYZ, a property development company, to build 300 low-cost family homes in R Town. XYZ has recently acquired an area of land on the outskirts of R Town and have just received planning permission from R Town Council for the building project.

R town council see this as a way of addressing the problem of lack of affordable housing in R Town.

R Town university however are opposing the development. They say that the building will spoil the view of the university. They claim that the picturesque setting of the university is one of the main attractions for students and staff and that this development will detract from their reputation.

As project manager, H must manage the project stakeholders. Using the Mendelow matrix, match the two stakeholders to the correct management strategy.

R Town Council	Key player
R Town University	Keep satisfied
	Keep informed
	Minimal effort

Question 5

Which three of the following statements are true regarding the matrix structure?

A Requires centralised decision making

B Employees have dual reporting to managers

C The structure seeks to add flexibility and coordination

D Reduces the time spent in meetings

E Clear lines of responsibility

F Replaces formal control with direct contact

Question 6

Which of the following would be the role of the project manager? Select all that apply.

A Selecting, building and motivating the project team

B Providing resources for the project

C Making all high level decision regarding the project

D Recommending termination of the project if necessary

E Main point of contact with the management hierarchy

F Communicating with the chain of command

Question 7

Project managers require a number of skills including:

- Delegation
- Negotiation
- Communication
- Problem solving
- Planning and control
- Leadership

Match the following activities to the required project manager skill.

- The project manager may have to deal with disputes between various stakeholders.
- The project manager must ensure that all stakeholders are kept up to date about the progress of the project.
- The project manager must clarify each team member's role and must empower them to achieve their objectives.
- The project manager must motivate the project team so that the team works hard to achieve the project objective.

Question 8

Which three of the following statements regarding the project manager are true?

A They must be effective communicators

B They must have all the technical skills required in the project

C They may have to negotiate on a variety of issues

D They must adopt the democratic style of leadership

E They are responsible for the project budget

F They must have change-management skills

Question 9

A key role of any project manager is to build and lead the project team. When putting together a project team, Belbin's model of team roles can be used.

Which of the following statements relating to Belbin's model of team roles is true? Select all that apply.

A The team worker is concerned about the relationships within the team.

B A successful team requires at least eight members.

C The plant promotes activity in others.

D All of Belbin's roles should be filled for an effective team.

E The implementer is practical and efficient.

F The completer/finisher is thoughtful and thought provoking.

Question 10

Tuckman's model of team development can be used throughout a project. Match the project stage to the most suitable stage in Tuckman's model.

Project stage	Tuckman stage
Need	Norming
Solution	Performing
Implementation	Adjourning
Completion	Storming
	Forming

Test your understanding answers

Case study style question 1

REPORT

To: Hospital senior managers

From: Management Accountant

Date: Today

Subject: Project relationships

Introduction

This report will consider the various relationships which exist within the Healthweb project. In any project the project manager will have relationships with the project sponsor, the project board and the project users. This report will cover each of these relationships and will also consider the potential conflicting project objectives of these stakeholders.

Project manager and project sponsor

T, as the project manager is responsible for delivering the project.

The project sponsor is usually the party responsible for payment of projects, but in this case the amount of funding from the central government is not clear, neither in the initial funding nor the on-going running costs. Therefore, the project manager will need to work with the sponsor to resolve potential conflict over project costs. The role of the central government in this project as a fund provider may cause conflict between central government and ABC.

The project manager may have little direct reporting/communication with the central government, as responsibility for the project progress is mainly to the project board.

However, central government, as the project sponsor, will be evaluating strategic level objectives and who will be concerned with ensuring that the whole project is not seen to waste public resources.

Project manager and the project board

The project manager is responsible for achieving the objectives set by the project board. The project board is responsible for the overall running of the project, and their objectives are to delegate the achievement of the sponsors' targets without disrupting the achievement of their own business objectives.

Direct communication between the project manager and the project board is necessary, with on-going regular reporting of project milestone review meetings.

The project board will be concerned with the achievement of management/business level objectives, in particular that the project improves business efficiency and effectiveness.

Project manager to medical and administrative users

The project manager is responsible for the overall delivery of the final working system to the end users. The objectives of the users are to care for their patients, while minimising their workload. The first role of the project manager is to 'sell' the benefits of the new system to the users, as without their backing the project is unlikely to succeed. Good communication between the project manager and the end users is essential to the implementation of a successful project. The project manager is responsible for reviewing the needs of each group of users to ensure that systems design meets the needs of the users as far as possible within the project constraints, and ensuring that training is effective. In addition, the project manager will need to manage both medical and administrative staff expectations of the system as the project progresses.

The administrative and medical staff will be evaluating the operational day-to-day objectives of the project.

Possibility of conflicting objectives

The sponsor's objectives are the achievement of improved service to patients. This may conflict with the objectives of the staff, who will seek to minimise their workload while providing good care for their patients. Staff are likely to have concerns about the implementation workload, the ongoing costs and workloads and the patient record security.

There is also likely to be conflict between the sponsor and the project board over funding.

In addition, the central government and project board may be concerned with funding and cost minimisation, whereas the end users may see this as cost-cutting, thus reducing the value of the end product.

As a public sector project, financial objectives should not be primary ones. Quality and customer perspective should be of more importance to all of the stakeholders. However, public funds must not be seen to be wasted.

Conclusion

There are many stakeholders in any project and they often have different objectives which can lead to conflict within the project. It is important to recognise potential conflict in a project to ensure that it is managed so that it does not affect the successful delivery of the project.

Case study style question 2

EMAIL

To: P

From: Management Accountant

Date: today

Subject: Project management leadership style

The most effective leadership style within an organisation will depend on the circumstances, and might well differ for different types of employee and different types of task.

According to Adair, the most appropriate leadership style depends on the relative significance of three factors – task needs, group needs and individual needs. Task needs refer to the tasks that the leader must carry out, such as setting objectives, planning tasks, allocating responsibilities, setting performance standards and giving instructions for work to be done. Group needs refer to the management responsibilities for communication, team-building, motivation and discipline. Individual needs relate to the manager's responsibilities for coaching, counselling and motivating individual employees. The relative significance of task needs, group needs and individual needs will vary from one situation to another, and the most appropriate leadership style will depend on the relative significance of each of these three factors in the given circumstances.

In managing a road widening project, it seems likely that the task needs will be the most significant and individual needs the least. If this is the case, a task-orientated leadership style – in other words an authoritarian style of leadership – might be most appropriate.

Fiedler, another contingency theorist, argued that the most appropriate leadership style in a given situation depended on the extent to which the task is highly structured, the leader's position power and the nature of the leader's existing relationship with the work group. If the task is highly structured and the leader's position power is high, and if the relationship between the leader and the work group is already good, Fiedler suggested that the most appropriate leadership style would be a task-orientated leader. These circumstances probably apply to the management of construction projects such as a road-widening scheme.

A similar conclusion might also be made if Hersey and Blanchard's situational theory is considered. They argued that the most appropriate leadership style in a given situation depends on the maturity of the individuals who are being led. The greater the maturity of the employees, the more a leader should rely on relationship behaviour rather than task behaviour. With construction work, the maturity of many employees might be considered fairly low, however, and a task-orientated leadership style would therefore be more appropriate.

I hope you have found the above useful, please get in touch if you need any more information about this.

Case study style question 3

REPORT

To: Managing Director

From: Management Accountant

Date: today

Subject: Structure

Introduction

The structure adopted by a company when undertaking projects can have an effect on the success of the project. There are a number of possible structures which could be adopted by HIJ. This report will consider the advantages and disadvantages of the matrix structure.

Matrix structure

As the marketing director in HIJ has noted, the ability to develop new products and get them to market quickly requires the cooperation of a range of individuals from various functions. HIJ could fundamentally reorganise to form a matrix structure. This type of structure is based on a dual chain of command and is often used as a structure in project management. In the case of HIJ it would involve establishing a cross functional team to design and develop new sports equipment products. Each individual would have a dual role in terms of their functional responsibility as well as membership of a project team. For instance, an individual could belong both to the marketing function and to the NPD project. Employees would report both to a functional manager and a project manager.

Benefits of a matrix structure

As the marketing director suggests, this structure does bring a number of benefits to NPD project work. The matrix structure is particularly suited to a rapidly changing environment, such as that facing HIJ, creating flexibility across the project, with the aim of speedy implementation. It can improve the decision-making process by bringing together a wide range of expertise to the new product development process, cutting across boundaries which can be stifled by normal hierarchical structures. Lateral communication and cooperation should be improved. From an employee's perspective it can facilitate the development of new skills and adaptation to unexpected problems, broadening a specialist's outlook.

Disadvantages of a matrix structure

Whilst there are benefits, the R&D director is also correct in his view that there are downsides to the matrix structure. One of the main problems is associated with the lack of clear responsibilities and potential clashes and tensions between the different priorities of the project tasks and the specialist function. Employees may end up being confused by having to report to two bosses and deciding whose work should take precedence. There is also the question of who should do the appraisal of their performance?

The complexity of the matrix structure can often make it difficult to implement. Inevitably, conflicts will arise due to the differences in the backgrounds and interests of staff from different functional areas.

Conclusion

The matrix structure is fairly complex and can cause issues with lack of clarity in reporting lines, however it also offers a number of benefits for project work.

HIJ will have to consider both the advantages and disadvantages carefully in deciding whether or not to implement the matrix structure.

Question 1

The correct matching is:

Project sponsor	Provides resources for the project
Project owner	The person for whom the project is being carried out
Project manager	Responsible for the successful delivery of the project
Project board	Responsible for making all high level decisions about the project

Question 2

C

The role of the project sponsor is to make all the yes/no decisions for the project, including approving the project plan. Note: in larger scale projects, there may be a project board. In addition the project sponsor also supplies the funds for the project.

Question 3

A, D and F

In addition, the matrix structure is most suitable when the organisation carries out a number of projects which all require teams made up of individuals from different technical backgrounds.

Question 4

The correct matching area is:

R Town Council – **Key player**

R Town University – **Keep informed**

The council have high power as they are able to give permission for the development. They also have high interest as they want the development to bring much needed housing to the area. This puts them in the category of key players.

The university have high interest as they do not want their view spoiled, but they have limited power to stop the development. This puts them in the keep informed category.

Question 5

B, C and F

A drawback of the matrix structure is that there can be an increase in time spent in meetings. In addition the lines of responsibility can be confusing as members of staff have two reporting lines. The matrix structure requires decentralised decision making.

Question 6

A, D, E and F

Providing resources for the project and making the high level decisions for the project will be the responsibility of the project sponsor.

Question 7

The correct matching is:

Negotiation – The project manager may have to deal with disputes between various stakeholders.

Communication – The project manager must ensure that all stakeholders are kept up to date about the progress of the project.

Delegation – The project manager must clarify each team member's role and must empower them to achieve their objectives.

Leadership – The project manager must motivate the project team so that the team works hard to achieve the project objective.

Question 8

A, C and F

Project managers do not require all the technical skills to run a project as long as someone in the project team has the required skills.

In terms of the leadership style they adopt, the democratic style has been shown to be effective. However the manager will have to make all the decisions regarding the project and they may not be able to allow team members to contribute to that decision making. They must adopt the most suitable leadership style depending on the situation.

The responsibility for the project budget rests with the project sponsor.

Question 9

A, D and E

According to Belbin, all of the team roles should be covered, but members can hold more than one role, therefore a team does not need to have exactly eight members.

The plant is the creative, ideas person in the team. The shaper promotes activity.

The completer/finisher is the person who chases the progress of the project, ensuring all documentation is complete and deadlines are met.

Question 10

The correct matching is:

Need – **Forming**

Solution – **Storming**

Implementation – **Norming/Performing**

Completion – **Adjourning**

O

P

R

S

T

V

W